Relentless

Tim Schum

RELENTLESS

The Story of American Soccer
and the Coaches
Who Grew the Game

Meyer & Meyer Sport

British Library of Cataloguing in Publication Data
A catalogue record for this book is available from the British Library

Relentless
Maidenhead: Meyer & Meyer Sport (UK) Ltd., 2023
ISBN: 978-1-78255-224-6

Aachen, Auckland, Beirut, Cairo, Cape Town, Dubai, Hägendorf, Hong Kong, Indianapolis, Maidenhead, Manila, New Delhi, Singapore, Sydney, Tehran, Vienna

Member of the World Sport Publishers' Association (WSPA), www.w-s-p-a.org

Printed by Integrated Books International
Printed in the United States of America

ISBN: 978-1-78255-224-6
Email: info@m-m-sports.com
www.thesportspublisher.com

CONTENTS

ACKNOWLEDGMENTS

Thank you to the following for their support of photographs that appear in the book:

Indiana University Archives; Ohio Wesleyan Athletics – Mark Beckenbach; United Soccer Coaches – Steve Veal/staff; Unites States Air Force Academy – Marcus Rodriguez; New York University Athletics – Jeff Bernstein; Slippery Rock University Athletics – Dajah Mincey; Hobart and William Smith Athletics – Mackenzie Larsen; New England Revolution Soccer – Adam Kilonsky; St. Louis Soccer Hall of Fame – Jim Leeker; St. Louis University Athletics – Brain Kunderman; University of Massachusetts Athletics – Riley Ubben; Grand Canyon University Athletics – Joe Hauser; SUNY Cortland University – Fran Elia; University of Redlands Athletics – Jon Sena/Lance Franey; The Pingry School – Stacy Schuessler; University of Rochester Athletics – Dennis O'Donnell; University of Akron Athletics – Sean Palchick; East Stroudsburg University Athletics – Ryan Long; Seton Hall Athletics – Nick Santoriello; Swarthmore College Athletics – Matt Judge; Clemson University Athletics – Jackson Sternberg; Southern Connecticut University – Mike Riccio; Duke University Athletics – Alex McKeon; Charlotte Independence SC – Tom Finlay; Penn State Athletics – Nicole Praga; University of Pennsylvania Athletics – Mike Mahoney; Hartwick College Athletics – Chris Gondek; U.S. Military Academy – Mandy Salvani; Los Angeles FC – Seth Burton; University of North Carolina Athletics – Jeff Camarati; University of Connecticut Athletics – Colin Stewart; U.S Soccer Media Relations.

Also several individuals answered the call when special photos were needed including Marcelo Curi, Karl Dewazien, Bob Dikranian, Jay Hoffman, Joe Machnik, Francisco Marcos, and Kevin Sims.

A good many photos were scanned from past issues of the United Soccer Coaches publication, "Soccer Journal." The organization has allowed for those photos to be produced in support of the book.

INTRODUCTION

Three of the most influential U.S. soccer coaches are shown with author Tim Schum (right).
From left are Walter Chyzowych, Joe Morrone and Steve Negoesco.

For some, a glance at the title of the book, *Relentless: The Story of American Soccer and the Coaches Who Grew the Game,* may beg the question: Why delve into the contributions of coaches of a sport that, until recently, has been relegated to second-class status in the hierarchy of U.S. athletics?

The answer to that inquiry is two-fold. The initial reason for the research has been to acknowledge the role of soccer coaches over the past 100 years in helping soccer steadily receive its due in this country. It is my contention that, absent an influential political organization that charted an effective approach to promoting the U.S. game, there is plenty of evidence that soccer coaches, as an entity, performed a great deal of the heavy lifting that has been responsible for soccer's U.S. progress.

The second motivation for publishing *Relentless* revolves around the fact that I believe that followers of American sports have, since early in the 20th century, been intrigued by sports coaches.

As long-time Ohio Wesleyan University coach Jay Martin noted in *Soccer Journal* (July-August, 1996), the role of the coach was expanded during the first part of the 20th century: "As the United States entered the 1920s (called the golden decade of sport by some), the marriage between sport and education was solidified. The coach became important.... [and] the position developed some very high expectations. And those expectations of a coach are unique to the United States.... A German soccer coach is responsible to teach/coach soccer. An American soccer coach must teach/coach soccer and must develop character, sportsmanship, honesty, fitness, psychological balance, etc."[1]

And so the second of the book's objectives includes an aspiration: to record the lives of those individuals who exhibited a persistence of purpose and who, at different times and against formidable odds (and not appreciated by many), have risen to the occasion and overcome soccer's obstacles. Whatever the impediments, the book's storyline will share examples of the commitment of those individuals in the U.S. soccer coaching community who promoted the play of the game and, in turn, celebrated its inherent beauty to others.

The book's organization was determined to some extent by chronology. That is, soccer's earliest history was orchestrated by a select group of individuals who were introduced to the game in other countries and helped establish it principally on the East Coast of the United States. Much of that information was gleaned from an earlier book written by Coach Joe Bean and me.[2]

In specific chapters I will share background information about coaches that will serve to enliven their careers beyond the typical wins and losses that underpin their legacies. For instance, many soccer coaches served the game on a part-time basis and were forced to find outside employment in order to make ends meet. The coach who served as an aide to a blind attorney while also contributing to the game for nearly a half-century is but one example.

Absent a well-organized and progressive national body to promote soccer, it is my contention that it remained for individual coaches in their locales and, in many cases, later in conjunction with NSCAA and U.S. Soccer, who have been responsible for overcoming the problem areas of the sport.

One issue was the need for the introduction of programs to improve and expand coaching education. I will seek to acknowledge the contributions of those individuals who have played vital roles in that mentoring process. From Glenn Warner's film work to the insertion of comprehensive curricula into the educational process, such individuals as Cramer, Chyzowych, Gooding, Lennox, and Tipping will emerge as personalities who have advanced coaching education during their careers.

And it was through their institutions that the coaches Brock, Parker, Holloway, and Martin provided guidance to students who have, in turn, become coaches and utilized their mentors' examples to instruct future generations of players. It was through creation of their "coaching trees" that these individuals and others have expanded and improved soccer play throughout the U.S.

Of nearly equal importance was oversight of laws governing soccer play. The book will cover how that task was assumed by a variety of coaches, with the names of Stewart, Waters, and McCrath among those who have addressed rules issues.

The name Guelker stands out when reviewing the explosion of U.S. youth soccer play, for it was his St. Louis model that was later replicated in countless communities in this country.

Coaches have been innovators when it came to offering other avenues for player improvement, with coach Yonker's introduction of the soccer camp concept a case in point. Others, including the Chyzowychs, Machnik, and McKeon, followed his lead.

Coaches have also played roles outside the normal Xs and Os; in many cases, they orchestrated the startups of league structures while also reaching across professional lines to coordinate with organizations such as the NCAA, NAIA, and NISOA to develop various facets of the game. Here the names of coaches Briggs, Morrone, and Squires will emerge.

All professions hold memberships to certain standards of conduct. So, as soccer play became more refined (and competitive!), the names Eiler, Baptista, and Bean emerged from the soccer coaching community to lead the way toward accepted ethical standards.

While individuals such as Bill Jeffrey sought by their efforts to promote the game, it was through the collective work of organizations, including the NSCAA, that a means was found to honor players, coaches, and teams for their contributions. That these acknowledgements annually take place at the largest gathering of soccer coaches in the world is a tribute to the cadre of coaches who founded the event and nurtured it to its present status.

Obviously, the fielding of competitive teams has generated publicity for the sport, and coaches Arena, Bahr, Dorrance, Guelker, Hyndman, Holleman, Miller,

Morrone, Negoesco, Yeagley, Bradley, and Cirovski have proved to be trend setters in developing teams whose players have, in turn, later contributed to soccer's progress in various capacities.

It was through the legislative process that women's soccer emerged in the 1970s, with Anson Dorrance's example helping others in terms of how to successfully address the coaching of female players. Individuals including Burreigh, Echtermeyer, Gallimore, Heinrichs, and Wilber have followed Dorrance in growing the women's game. The name DiCicco resonates alongside Dorrance for his role in elevating the USWNT to worldwide prominence.

As the U.S. began to establish a means to compete internationally, several coaches, including Arena, Bradley, Gansler, Schmid, and Sampson, offered their coaching expertise to our national teams, and it was Steinbrecher who solidified the administrative end of things for the teams. With the formation of the MLS, the U.S. soccer community has contributed the above-named coaches along with Sarachan, Liekoski, and Porter to lead various teams.

I have cited and aligned names associated with elevating various facets of U.S. soccer, but there are other coaches whose names resonate in their locales as movers and shakers of the game. By book's end, it is hoped that Avedikian, Schellscheidt, Bugliari, Robinson, Greening, and Dezawein, while not household names in the game's history, will also be appreciated for their contributions to our country's soccer ascendency.

To that end, soccer is indebted to one individual who has earlier collected all manner of soccer memorabilia and information. His first name is Mickey, and I challenge readers to dig into the book to identify his last name.

Finally, and I know it will be a legacy of the book that some readers will wonder: Why isn't so-and-so's career covered? Well, just as with a soccer game itself, you don't win them all, and you can't chart everyone. So I apologize for any oversights, but what remains is one person's approach to lauding the efforts of many, if not all, of the many soccer coaches who have helped lift the sport to its rightful place in our country's sporting hierarchy.

A note on the QR codes: Sometimes there is just so much information on a subject that it can't all fit within a printed book. Placed throughout this book are QR codes that, when scanned, will provide additional (and interesting, I think) information on the subject. To access the content, simply scan the QR code with your smartphone camera, or, if reading the eBook, simply tap the QR code with your finger.

CHAPTER I

EARLY HISTORY

Soccer's First Coaches Lay the Sport's Foundation

A study of who did what and when in terms of establishing a foundation for the sport of soccer in the United States is revealing in that it points out that while, organizationally, the United States Football Association was entrusted by FIFA with advancing the game in this country, it had neither the resources nor the administrative capability needed to achieve that objective.

Rather, history reveals that much of the credit for sustaining soccer in the early part of the 20th Century can be laid at the feet of a rather small cadre of dedicated coaches, some foreign-born. The latter's passion for the sport was fueled, in part, by soccer's prominent place in their former countries. When that energy was coupled with the enthusiasm of an emerging group of American coaches, such commitment cannot be ignored in terms of its impact on the sport's slow but steady progress through the 1920s and 1930s.

And, as will be described, the collective work of the pre-World War II soccer coaching community was limited principally to the East Coast of the United States.

The author will recount the importance of the publication *Soccer Guide* during this era, as it was an important conduit for annually promoting the sport as well as serving to connect its leadership. Edited by coach Douglas Stewart, the *Guide* offered a yearly summary of soccer activity at the intercollegiate and secondary school levels of play along with identifying each year's mythical national intercollegiate championship team(s). Also included in the periodical was a listing of that year's All-American team.

Also recorded will be the role coaches played spearheading the formation of leagues that enabled schools to partner with as they began to sponsor the sport. In terms of improvement of coaching education, the era under discussion offered little other than the staging of sporadic clinics whose impact was minimal in terms of their impact on improvement of individual and team play.

With a dearth of officials, it was left to coaches in their locales to identify and assist in referee development. In relation to the application of playing rules, coaches and school administrators began to adapt rules that were in sync with the educational objectives of U.S. colleges and secondary schools. It was here that modifications to restrictive FIFA substitution rules were first introduced.

It was during this era that conflicting viewpoints between individuals representing the educational institutions of the country and those whose attitudes were formed abroad were first emerged. While some coaches were associated with both groupings, in the long run, historic disagreements on a variety of soccer-related issues did not lead to the type of unified problem-solving needed to advance the sport.

With World War II approaching and while soccer progress had been steady, much still needed to be accomplished in the areas of coaching and referee development, along with identification of new ideas for the promotion and marketing of the game.

It would be up to the next generation of post-World War II coaches to address those challenges.

The Early Years of Soccer in the United States

Despite the fact that soccer historians can hark back to ancient times in terms of chronicling the start of the sport, when it comes time to chart the growth of the game in the United States, the term most associated with its progress is "spasmodic."

Though there are references to games that somewhat resembled soccer in ancient Greece and Rome, and there is mention of medieval towns in England kicking the head of any decapitated invader from one end of a village to the other as a soccer-like activity, it wasn't until the late 1880s that formalized soccer was taking hold in this country.

The action involved teams of Scottish, Irish, and English immigrants playing games largely among themselves and primarily in locales on the East Coast of the United States. Reportedly, in the late 1870s, more formal teams were organized in the West Hudson area of New Jersey; other similar leagues followed in New England led by Portuguese seamen in Fall River, Massachusetts. About the same time, Midwest centers of soccer interest popped up in St. Louis, Chicago, Detroit, Cincinnati, and Cleveland. In the Far West, Denver and San Francisco were reported centers of soccer interest.

Early Organization

The first attempt to organize the game took place in Newark, New Jersey in 1884-85 when a group formed the American Football Association (AFA). In 1885, a group of teams unrelated to the AFA played organized matches in New York City's Central Park. A year later, in New England, the Bristol County Soccer League was announced, centered in Fall River. In 1887, the New England Football League came into existence.

Various immigrant groups largely organized these aforementioned events. In St. Louis in 1890 a group of Americans were playing under the Kensington team banner. Interest was also reported in Western New York. In 1901, the formation of the Football Association of Eastern Pennsylvania was announced. Similar associations were formed in those Midwestern and Far Western cities previously referenced.

In 1904, the East Coast visit of the Pilgrims, a British amateur team, exposed various fledgling U.S. teams to a more sophisticated brand of soccer, with the invaders winning 21 of the 23 matches played. Later, similar visits by the Corinthian Football Club (1906 and 1911)) and the return visit of the Pilgrim SC in 1909 provided standards for various American teams to achieve, with the teams compiling a combined 47-6-5 record during their visits.

In 1905, a group of Eastern colleges that included Columbia, Cornell, Harvard, Haverford, and Pennsylvania were playing soccer and formed the Intercollegiate Association Football League (IAFL).

USFA

After a somewhat protracted internal political battle between the American Football Association and the American Amateur Football Association (AAFA) in 1913, the Federation Internationale de Football Association (FIFA), in 1914, recognized the United States Football Association (USFA) as the governing body for the sport in the United States. USFA shortly affiliated 24 subsidiary regional organizations under its umbrella.

Dr. G. Randolph Manning and Douglas Stewart were two prominent individuals associated with the formation of USFA. Manning was a leader of the amateur group (AFAA) and hailed from New York City, and Stewart was a force in Philadelphia. When negotiations for FIFA recognition between the two aforementioned groups ensued, it was reported that Stewart's throwing his organization's support to Manning's group resulted in the FIFA endorsement of the new organization.

Formed to oversee the sport in this country, USFA principally sponsored two national soccer competitions. The National Challenge Cup (open to both amateur and professional teams) was first contested in 1912-13, with teams competing for the Dewar Cup, a trophy valued at a reported $500! Later, in 1922-23, USFA introduced the National Amateur Challenge Cup.

In 1919, and following World War I, the IAFL became the Intercollegiate Football Association of America (IFAA) and was reorganized in order to accommodate the influx of new colleges that began soccer play. The principal roles assumed by the organization were rules codification and interpretation and referee training. The establishment of various leagues and promotion of the game were also items on the IFAA agenda.

ISFAA and the NSCAA

In 1925-26, and for the third time, the group changed its name to the Intercollegiate Soccer Football Association of America (ISFAA) and continued promotion of the game at the college level. Due to fiscal constraints, it merged its efforts with the National Soccer Coaches Association of America in 1996.

In the post-World War II period, as the game's ascendency continued at the nation's colleges, but more so at the secondary school level, the National Soccer Coaches Association of America (formed in 1941) began to play a role in the growth and promotion of the game.

Shown is the first meeting of the NSCAA held in New York City in January 1942.

The NSCAA's stated objectives in 1941 included the following.

- Encourage the development of the sport of soccer in secondary schools, colleges, and universities.
- Develop mechanisms to better publicize the sport.
- Organize clinics to better teach the sport.
- Evaluate current teaching methods and improve them to make for better teaching of the sport.
- Seek to enroll more soccer coaches in the NSCAA to better achieve the above goals.

President John Brock of Springfield College led the NSCAA's first slate of officers. Those included coaching legend Bill Jeffrey of Penn State, who was appointed chairman of its soccer clinics committee.

Early Cooperation

With two organizations now established with similar goals, cooperation, rather than conflict, was necessary in order for the game to progress.

To some degree, this took place as USSFA sought to select the player roster for the resumption of Olympic soccer competition at the 1948 London games.

Earlier, in 1946, and in an effort to showcase the playing ability of its collegiate players, the ISFAA organized an intercollegiate all-star game in New York City. The game matched a Middle Atlantic/Southern team versus one from New York/New England.

The following year, a joint USSFA/ISFAA committee was formed to evaluate a series of tryout matches to select the 1948 U.S. Olympic team. Perhaps the eventual makeup of the team's roster reflected the USSFA influence, because only one player of the 15-player team roster was a college player. Five starters hailed from Fall River, Massachusetts.

Soccer's Pioneer Coaches

As the game progressed in the first half of the 20th century, it was highly dependent on coaches to carry it forward in their respective regions. A few individuals, hired by various intercollegiate institutions, were noteworthy pioneers in accomplishing that objective.

Underpinning their commitment to popularizing the game, these men had a genuine fondness and concern for the game and a belief that, if they were dedicated enough, others would begin to develop a similar appreciation for it. Readers should recognize that, in reviewing their coaching accomplishments, they were achieved at a time when travel and communication were far more time-consuming.

Douglas Stewart
Soccer became a cult at Penn, and he was its high priest.

As noted, the name of Douglas Stewart can be reported as one of the founders of what became the USSFA and the ISFAA. He was also among a group of foreign-born coaches hired by Ivy League institutions when they formed collegiate soccer teams. Stewart played on some of the best English and Canadian soccer teams before landing in Philadelphia in the early 1900s, where he found work as a paralegal for a blind attorney.

Douglas Stewart's success can be attributed to his knowledge of the finer points of soccer, which were still foreign to many Americans. Stewart also was known as a militaristic despot who utilized fear as a principal teaching instrument. He was the commanding officer, and players were the enlisted men. Stewart called everyone by his last name. He was known to strike a player across the legs with his walking stick for assorted soccer offenses.

He soon helped in the 1904 formation of that area's first referees' association, coached in the Philadelphia Cricket League, and, most importantly, initiated the soccer program at the University of Pennsylvania. In 1905, Penn became a charter member of IASL. Between 1914 and 1925, Penn won six IASL championships.

Douglas Stewart cast a long shadow over soccer in the first part of the 20th century.

Stewart was aided by assistant coaches (one of whom was later Philadelphia coaching legend Jimmy Mills) and a battery of student managers. The managers were required to bring him a typed report of each day's practice by eight o'clock the same evening. Often, Stewart's practices began under the direction of an assistant. Soon, however, he would leave his office, walking stick in hand, and head to the soccer field. He was critical of his players. Yet, despite his tyrannical nature, Stewart's program gained the admiration of his players, friends, and the opposition in his 33 years at Penn.

One manner in which the ISFAA sought to promote the game was through the annual publication of what might be termed a soccer yearbook. Titled *Soccer Guide*, it was published by A.S. Barnes in New York City. Appointed by ISFAA, Douglas Stewart served as its editor for 27 years. In addition to listing the playing rules and a review of the previous season, the booklet contained a number of instructional articles for players, referees, and coaches. Referees' names were listed by geographical region. In time, interpretations (Stewart's!) were listed alongside the rule itself. It also included the names of those chosen for the previous year's all-intercollegiate team, which Steward chose from 1920 through 1925. The *Guide* was a publication eagerly awaited each year.

Adding to his stature, Stewart served as a member of the National Collegiate Athletic Association Rules Committee and was the final word on rules interpretations. In soccer's infancy, he annually encouraged teams to exhibit more refined technical play. He also constantly noted that the game needed better-qualified officials. Here he lamented that roughhouse tactics demanded an increase in courage by players and referees alike. He also tutored soccer enthusiasts around the country. Perhaps more than any single person, he helped advance soccer as an intercollegiate sport in America.

Zander Hollander noted Stewart's accomplishments in his book, *The American Encyclopedia Of Soccer* (p. 34). Mr. Hollander had adapted much of Stewart's biographical information that Dr. Robert C. Baptista (an NSCAA Honor Award recipient in 1975) had utilized in his 1962 doctoral dissertation "A History of Intercollegiate Soccer in the United States of America." Hollander noted, "Douglas Stewart was one of the early coaching legends of the kicking game."

Brock and Springfield

*… "Regretfully I must report that as a freshman we laughed and mimicked him behind his back … By the time we were seniors there wasn't one of us that wouldn't have killed for John Brock." –*Alden "Whitey" Burnham

Coach John Brock's leadership qualities were evident when, in 1908, he captained the first soccer team fielded by his *alma mater*, Springfield College. The Chiefs at the time (they're the Maroons today) split their two-match season.

Coaching at Springfield
Brock joined the physical education faculty at Springfield in 1920 and was appointed soccer coach in 1929. He remained as coach until his retirement in 1947. During those 15 seasons, the Chiefs enjoyed many great years. Included were seven New England

John Brock was the legendary coach at Springfield College.

collegiate titles and four (1931, 1937, 1946-47) mythical ISFAA national titles.

The most notable were his last three seasons. His charges compiled a 5-0-1 record in 1942 and, after a three-year hiatus during World War II, came back to win consecutive national championships in 1946–47. The team's combined record in those years was 17-0-0, with the Chiefs putting together a string of 23 straight unbeaten matches. In that era, that was quite an accomplishment.

Dr. Brock earned his Ph.D. at New York University in 1939 and, in addition to teaching in Springfield's physical education program, coached its tennis team.

Glenn Warner, later coach at the United States Naval Academy (he later became president of the Association in 1953), spoke of Brock in endearing terms. "Coach Brock was a very quiet man. You respected him. It was difficult to get any enthusiasm from John. He was not that type of person. But respect was his main forte. He knew the game of soccer."[3]

In addition to Warner, Brock coaching alumni includes noted coaches Huntley Parker, Alden "Whitey" Burnham, and his successor, Irv Schmid.

Schmid spoke of his mentor when coach Brock became a charter member of the NSCAA's initial Hall of Fame in 1991: "Known as 'Sleepy John' by his students and players, he was one of the most loved and respected professors on the faculty. He was a slow-moving, quiet, easygoing person, most knowledgeable in many, many areas. Although he appeared to be not listening, he was always wide-awake. He coached and played great tennis, but soccer was his game."[4]

Alden "Whitey" Burnham offered another glimpse into John Brock: "A gentle man? My college coach, John Brock. Regretfully I must report that as a freshman we laughed and mimicked him behind his back because he seemed so unreal, with a half smile on his face most of the time, he walked around as though in a reverie. By the time we were seniors there wasn't one of us that wouldn't have killed for John Brock."[5]

The First NSCAA President

As it turned out, John Brock gave early stability and organizational skills to the Association. He was an inspirational leader, making certain that the newly founded organization kept focused on its original purpose and pursued its common goals. He was a courageous and skillful leader who seized the opportunity to change things for the betterment of the soccer community. He was available and willing to serve. It is hard to imagine that there was a better man to fill the role of NSCAA's first president than John Brock.

Dr. Brock found time for outside pursuits such as oil painting, music, and French. In addition to his Hall of Fame honor, John Brock was the third recipient of the NSCAA Honor Award in 1944.

Thomas Taylor – U.S. Naval Academy

The value of this program on teaching and developing the fundamentals of soccer cannot be overestimated in terms of its eventual impact on the development of the sport in this country once these newly indoctrinated soldiers returned to their communities as new soccer advocates.

Tom Taylor was another foreign-born coach who left his mark on the growth of the game in this country. A native of Bury, Lancashire, England, Taylor was the longtime coach at Navy, having begun coaching the Midshipmen in 1919. He coached Navy for 27 years with his final 1943, 1944, and 1945 teams compiling a 19-1-1 record. The 1944 Navy team was recognized by the ISFAA as the nation's best.

When Tom came to the United States, he brought with him a consummate knowledge of the game of soccer, and he immediately put it to use as he served as the physical training director at the city mission in New Bedford, Mass. In the ensuing years, physical training had to give way to more profitable work. In 1911–12, he was in Mexico in the midst of the revolution. At one time he was actually taken prisoner, and it was here that he learned the Spanish that was to prove so helpful in later managing some of his great South American stars at Navy.

During the First World War, he served in the Canadian Army, where he trained the world-famous Black Watch Division. Located in Baltimore after the war, he continued teaching physical education and found time to help with social work in the city areas and parks. It was in Baltimore in 1919 that the Naval Academy Commander James Richardson approached the gifted Englishman and offered him the post at the Naval Academy that he was to hold for 32 years. That fall, he collected 25 men and put the Naval Academy soccer program into action.

Through 1946, when he retired as head soccer coach, Taylor compiled a remarkable record of 112 wins, 53 losses, and 20 ties. His last three teams produced a total of thirteen All-Americans. His enthusiasm concerning the Army-Navy clash is reflected in his persistent disappointment in losing his last game to Army after having beaten them on so many previous occasions.

While World War II curtailed intercollegiate soccer play, it did present an opportunity for coaches, particularly collegiate coaches, to introduce thousands of our armed forces to soccer's fundamentals.

The major contribution that coach Taylor made to the NSCAA was the concentrated soccer instruction provided to many men in our armed forces during World War II through the Naval Aviation Pre-Flight Training programs.

Coach Taylor made certain that several prominent college coaches were assigned to this fitness program that utilized soccer as a fundamental part of the regimen. Among them were Earle Waters (West Chester), Walter McCloud (Trinity), and John Squires (Connecticut).

In 1943, as a tribute for his role in promoting the sport, Taylor was the first soccer coach presented with the NSCAA Honor Award.

Thomas Dent

Along with Stewart and Taylor, Tom Dent at Dartmouth College was another Ivy League coach with a foreign pedigree. Enrolled at Birmingham University in England, he found the call of soccer so strong that he left his studies to play professional soccer with the great Aston Villa team in the English League.

In 1924, Tom was hired to teach French and coach soccer at Dartmouth. In 1927, he added lacrosse to his coaching resume and, although he had never played the game, he soon mastered its intricacies. Under his tutelage, Dartmouth soccer and lacrosse teams won many New England championships, and a number of individual Dartmouth players earned All-American berths.

In addition to his coaching duties, Tom served soccer in many capacities. He was one of the founders of the National Soccer Coaches Association and was a former president of the Intercollegiate Soccer Football Association of America. In 1951, he served as the only representative of the U.S. college soccer coaches on the Olympic Soccer Selection Committee.

He also helped establish a high school soccer league in northern Vermont, and he organized soccer clinics and furnished soccer officials for schools in and around Hanover, NH. One of the first to utilize soccer films for instructional purposes, he also was credited with having a major influence on the rules of the game.

As with many coaches of his era, Tom Dent was a well-rounded individual. He served for a number of years as chairman of New Hampshire's Fish and Game Committee. In 1946, he received the Francis J. Parker Trophy, awarded annually by the New England Outdoor Writers Association to the person who has done the most for conservation in New Hampshire.

An NSCAA Honor Award recipient in 1951, Dent was inducted into the organization's Hall of Fame in 1992.

Bob Dunn

In addition to this outstanding collegiate record, Bob Dunn coached soccer at several area high schools as well as for various other Philly amateur, professional, and industrial clubs. It is reported that the teams he guided achieved an amazing 106-5-1 composite record.

Turning once more to the *Soccer Guides*, a preview of things to come is found in an article by Doug Stewart in the 1921 issue referring to coach Bob Dunn's first Swarthmore College team: "The caliber of the Swarthmore team is high, the team was well-coached and worked together so well that the Lehigh team is the only one which made any real stand against them. For a newcomer into collegiate soccer, Swarthmore has made a very good showing, only being beaten by Syracuse and Princeton. It follows therefore, that if Swarthmore again wins the State Championship it will be considered to have developed sufficient strength to warrant a trial with some of the Intercollegiate League teams..."[6]

Bob Dunn (right) Swarthmore coach from 1920-60 is shown here with Willis Stetson (left), Swathmore's all-time leading scorer, and James White (center), his successor as coach.

Photo courtesy of Swarthmore College.

These words were indeed prophetic, for "Dunny," as some 500 Swarthmore soccer alumni fondly called him, coached 28 championship soccer teams at suburban Philadelphia schools, including Swarthmore's mythical national co-championship team in 1928. Ninety-one of his players received All-America honors, and seven of his protégés became college coaches.

Like with many of his colleagues, Dunn's activities and contributions to local and national athletic groups were noteworthy. He has served as secretary of the Middle Atlantic Conference Baseball League and as vice-president of the Middle Atlantic Intercollegiate Soccer League; he developed the present Philadelphia Public High School Soccer League; and he organized the Middle Atlantic Conference Soccer League and served as its chairman from its inception in 1934 until 1953. In that same year, he compiled an exhaustive statistical history of the league. In his spare time, he was also an approved soccer, basketball, and baseball official. He is one of the pioneers and founders of the National Soccer Coaches Association of America and the Philadelphia Soccer Coaches Association.

He also lent his administrative expertise to various committees of the Intercollegiate Soccer Football Association, the NSCAA (president in 1946), and the NCAA. With the latter group, he served as past chairman of its Soccer Rules Committee while helping organize its first soccer championships.

The Decline of the ISAA

By 1995, the Intercollegiate Soccer Association of America (ISAA), the formative body that was responsible for organizing intercollegiate soccer beginning in 1905, was disbanded and formerly absorbed into the NSCAA.

Leading up to World War II, and then known as the Intercollegiate Soccer Football Association of America (ISFAA), ISAA had performed much of the "heavy lifting" in terms of giving direction to the college game. But with the formation of the NSCAA in 1941, the soccer landscape began to change, especially at the secondary school level, and the NSCAA became better equipped to promote the game at that and *all* levels of play.

Loss of Identity

Up to the post-World War II period, ISFAA still was the body that determined the mythical national championship team. But with the staging of the NCAA and NAIA national championships in 1959, that ISFAA function was superseded.

Earlier, in 1950, another change occurred when the NSCAA Awards Committee usurped ISFAA's other important function, selection of the college All-America team. In particular, that process was made more objective through the introduction of coach Fred Holloway's mathematical scheme.

With the loss of the two programs came questions from its member dues-paying colleges as to the value of their ISFAA membership. Basically, what remained of value was that colleges annually received the ISFAA *Guide* that it published each fall. Eventually, that publication was published by the NCAA and *distributed* to member institutions by ISFAA.

Historically, many of the NSCAA officers would, at the end of their terms, move on to lead ISFAA affairs. It was left to ISFAA President John Eiler, in 1962, to defend the role of his faltering organization. "I am convinced," he stated, "that there is a need for both the ISFAA and the NSCAA to promote soccer in this country. Each has objectives that are not immediately related, but in the overall picture there is a cooperative effort to put soccer in its rightful place with other sports. The ISFAA approaches its promotional responsibility in one way and NSCAA in another. Both organizations are needed. One to provide administrators of colleges and universities an interest in the game, and one to keep coaches interested. I suggest that our job is to support any group willing to advance soccer and to be an effective part of a larger, united effort."[7]

The well-respected Eiler's declaration proved to bring about a mutual respect for each organization's role in the game. It was left to ISFAA for the next 30 years to identify and administer programs that met the criteria of both, appealing to its membership for budgetary purposes and serving to meet its stated objectives.

The Rating System Introduced

... In many cases regional chairs reported receiving calls from sports reporters seeking the rating of college teams in their circulation areas....

One role that ISFAA did continue to play in the post-war period was that its college coaches served on the NCAA Rules Committee that annually reviewed and issued via the *Guide* the playing rules each year. By the late 1950s, the members of the rules committee began planning, under the leadership of Connecticut coach John Squires, for the staging of the first NCAA tournament. The question of how to rate and select teams for that and succeeding tournaments was left to NCAA regional committees. And until those final selections were announced, there was little buildup to the tournament itself. College soccer was losing an opportunity to promote what would be its culminating event.

What was needed was a national rating system for teams, and that was what Pat Damore, men's soccer coach at the State University of New York at Fredonia, proposed at the ISFAA meeting on January 9, 1969. Although not a determinant in acceptance to the NCAA tournament, the season-long ISFAA rating system helped identify teams for consideration while keeping college soccer in the spotlight throughout the regular season.

Simple in concept, ISFAA formed rating committees in six regions of the country. Each regional chair established a rating board that rank ordered teams each week based on teams' results. Each regional chair then reported their top four ranked teams to the national chairperson. When all regional rankings were completed, the collective regional chairs rank ordered the 24 teams, and the chair would tabulate the votes and share the weekly national ratings via the wire services. Generally, by Monday morning, the regional ratings were released, followed by the national ratings that evening. In many cases, regional chairs reported receiving calls from sports reporters seeking the rating of college teams in their circulation areas.

Beginning the week of September 22, 1969, with Damore serving as the first national chair, the first rankings were released. Counted among the first regional chairpersons were New England, Cliff Stevenson (Brown); New York, Garth Stam (SUNY-Oneonta); Penn-NJ-Delaware, Will Myers (William Patterson); South, Tom Johnson (Emory); Midwest, Fred Taube (MacMurray); and Far West, Hank Eichin (Air Force).

Subsequently, Myers and Taube served as national chairs, as did coaches Tom Griffith (Wisconsin-Green Bay), Ibrahim (Clemson), Hank Steinbrecher (Appalachian State), and Owen Wright (Elizabethtown).

The introduction of the weekly ratings proved a boon to the struggling ISAA ("football" was dropped in 1974) and was a marketing coup for college soccer. The regional ratings were mailed weekly to each member college. Up until 1982, all colleges were eligible for rankings. As an example, one week in 1974, relative unknown Binghamton University was ranked number 15 nationally based on the season it was having! And so, until the NCAA created three divisions of soccer play in 1982, every school had a chance to earn a place in the weekly rankings each season.

ISAA, in addition to the implementation of the rating system, continued each year to distribute the annual NCAA rulebooks and also dispersed annual college soccer almanacs that contained team schedules and other valued information.

Frank Longo and the ISAA Programs

Alongside the introduction of the college rating system, in 1973, through a joint effort of ISAA and NSCAA, the first of the SportCraft coach of the year (COY) awards was underway. Reportedly the result of an informal conversation between John McKeon and Al Miller with SportCraft, Ltd's marketing manager, Judd Dunn, the company sponsored the awards through 1980. Chairing the COY committee was Frank Longo of Quincy College. St. Louis University's Bob Guelker was the first award recipient, and SLU, as part of the agreement, also received a $500 scholarship award.

A year later, the SportCraft COY program expanded to honor NJCAA and secondary school coaches.

Frank Longo.

By the 1980s, with soccer exploding at various levels of play, Metropolitan Life Insurance Company took over the sponsorship of the COY awards program. By the end of the decade, COY awards were being presented to men and women coaches of teams representing schools playing at the NCAA, NAIA, NJCAA, and NCCAA levels. Also, COY awards for secondary school and USYSA coaches would be instituted, with the scholastic coach awards further defined by awards to include awards for coaches of private/parochial school teams.

By the turn of the century, most every identifiable level of amateur coaching was being honored with a COY award. By 2019, rather than define a singular person as COY, the now United Soccer Coaches organization initiated coaching "staff" of the year awards for its now 22 coaching groupings! It is estimated that the United Soccer Coaches now annually presents over 11,000 awards to its member coaches.

Frank Longo, for his career achievements at the college level, was recipient of the ISAA Bill Jeffrey Award in 1977. Presently, it is one of four long-standing annual career awards, along with the United Soccer Coaches Honor Award, the Robert W. Robinson (High School) Award, and the Charlotte Moran (Youth) Award.

The Partners of the Americas Program

... It concentrated not only on sports exchanges but also developed programs that focused on health, agriculture, and other areas of mutual benefit....

For several years, beginning in 1976, the ISAA, under the leadership of Frank Longo, sponsored the Partners of the Americas coaching exchange program.

Long associated with Quincy College, and the "man behind the scenes" as the school began to accumulate a record 11 NAIA men's soccer championships, Longo was responsible for making arrangements for various Quincy teams to fine-tune their play through foreign trips to Israel, Holland, Mexico, and Scotland.

Quincy traveled to Sao Paulo, Brazil in 1973 and, as an outcome of that trip, Longo helped orchestrate Brazil's MacKenzie University soccer team's tour the following year for a series of matches versus U.S. colleges.

By 1976, Frank Longo had arranged for the ISAA and NSCAA to assume a role in the sports segment of a U.S. government-sanctioned exchange program with Brazil called the Partners of the Americas Program. It concentrated not only on sports exchanges but also developed programs that focused on health, agriculture, and other areas of mutual benefit.

In 1976, six U.S. coaches, including Quincy's Jack MacKenzie, Bob Guelker (SIU-Edwardsville), Jerry Yeagley (University of Indiana), Steve Janczak (Lewis College), Horst Richardson (Colorado College), and Harry Keough (St. Louis University), traveled to Brazil, where they spent two weeks immersed in its soccer culture. In turn, by that fall, a like number of Brazilian coaches toured the United States and were hosted by various college coaches, many of whom had been beneficiaries of the Partners program. When visiting, the Brazilians conducted soccer clinics and made appearances at various school and community functions.

While the program was short-lived, it was Longo who deserved full credit for orchestrating the Partners program that served to cement relations between the two countries. It was also Longo who later helped to arrange the appearance of Brazilian national team coach Claudio Coutinho at the 1988 Washington, D.C. convention. It started a trend of Brazilian coaches offering convention clinic sessions that has endured to the present.

Senior Bowl Sponsorship

... Seeking other means to maintain its place, in 1983, the ISAA began recognizing the best U.S. college soccer goalkeepers ...

In 1972, in an attempt to expose the best collegiate players to NASL teams, the ISAA staged the first of what would be the Senior Soccer Bowl Classics. These matches were staged in communities offering some form of fiscal support and matched all-star teams on an East-West format. Additionally, two coaches, based on their teams' seasonal records, were selected to manage the teams.

The event itself was the brainchild of then-ISAA president Wayne Sunderland of Pratt Institute. He was cited as engaging Frank Longo and John McKeon as administrators in the staging of the Senior Bowl events. In fact, ISAA was the beneficiary of Longo's management skills for, through the late 1970s and early 1980s, he served as the organization's executive secretary.

The Senior Bowl event was staged in the Orlando area for the first seven years before moving to Tampa in 1979 and Fort Lauderdale in 1980. The 1981-82 matches were played in Tulsa (OK). With the NASL closing shop in 1984, the final Senior Bowl Classic was held in Las Vegas (NV) in 1983.

Seeking other means to maintain its place, in 1983, the ISAA began recognizing the best U.S. college soccer goalkeepers by establishing and annually awarding the ISAA Goalkeeper of the Year Award for male and female keepers. Among the women recipients were Mary Harvey (Cal-Berkeley) in 1986 and Brianna Scurry (Massachusetts) in 1993. Each starred on U.S. women's World Cup championship teams. Male honorees included Kasey Keller (1991-Portland) and Brad Friedel (1992-UCLA), both of whom later starred on USMNT World Cup teams.

Along with the keeper awards, in 1984, ISAA began its Men's Player of the Year (POY) awards, with a similar award for women players beginning a year later. Among the male honorees were Bruce Murray (Clemson-1987) and Brian McBride

(St. Louis-1993), both of whom starred on USMNTs, while Mia Hamm was selected twice as ISAA POY, along with six others who starred on U.S. world championship teams.

By 1995, with its influence waning, the ISAA merged its efforts with NSCAA, and the aforementioned awards were discontinued.

As for Longo, the unsung hero of so many soccer ventures, he joined U.S. Soccer Secretary General Hank Steinbrecher as his chief of staff in 1991 and served in that capacity until 1995. Colleague (and race track buddy) John McKeon summarized Longo's legacy when he commented on the occasion of Frank's passing in 1999: "He really didn't want the limelight. He got a sense of accomplishment by arranging things, making them happen. We all know he contributed a great deal to the growth of soccer."

The Secondary Schools Rankings

Borrowing on the success of the ISAA team rankings system, in 1988, secondary schools' representative Gene Chyzowych convinced the NSCAA executive board to introduce a similar system for the nation's high schools.

Quaker Oats Company's marketing director, Hank Steinbrecher, had come forward with funding to help get the project started. Promoted as the NSCAA/ Gatorade National Top 20 Poll, it debuted in the fall of 1988 and only ranked boys teams and teams that played in the more-traditional fall season.

The following year, rankings included girls teams, and shortly thereafter, poll results were compiled for teams that played winter-spring seasons.

If NSCAA member Jerry Durovic's letter is any indication, the introduction of a ranking system for secondary school teams was an overwhelming success. In 1989, after noting that as his area high school began to be ranked in the top five teams nationally, there was greatly increased interest in the area media in reporting the team's results on an ongoing basis. He also shared the following with *Soccer Journal* readers: "The national poll increased interest in soccer across New York State. For example, when Shenendehowa HS boys traveled to play non-league games against other state powers, the size of the crowds increased significantly. Alumni, coaches and spectators with no previous interest in soccer came to watch 'nationally-ranked teams' play. . . ."If the purpose of the poll was to heighten interest in high school soccer, it was a resounding success in my opinion.[8]

Aiding Chyzowych in conducting the girls' poll were Jay Gavitt (NJ), T.J. Williams (MA), Paul Kruppa (NY), Bob Morris (NJ), Gary Shrader (TN), Vic Garcia (CO), and Rick Caldwell (CA).

By 1997, the rankings had continued to evolve, with 25 boys and girls teams now ranked in both the fall and winter/spring polls. Doug Eisenhauer (MD) now chaired the boys' committee, with John Blomstram (CT), Joe Borrosh (NY), Tim Storch (MI), Norm Hillner (IL), Vic Garcia (CO), Eric Lane (TX), and Bob Barry (HI) assisting.

As of 2020, the annual rankings of secondary school teams have remained one of the most valued benefits of United Soccer Coaches membership.

Soccer in the 1920s

The period following World War I was marked by some growth in soccer play and was led by two coaches, Bill Jeffrey and Earle Waters.

During the 1920s, USSFA's role in growing the game focused largely on sponsorship of its Open and Amateur Cups. It was the staging of those events that led to a confrontational relationship with the then-thriving American Soccer League and had long-term consequences as professional soccer sought to gain a foothold in the country.

For it was in the post-war period that the professional game was presented a chance to solidify itself, only to be thwarted by USSFA hardheadedness. Buoyed by an influx of talented European players who could earn greater wages in U.S. factories and on company-sponsored teams than they could earn in their homelands, the ASL thrived.

Playing principally weekend matches, the league found itself in conflict when asked to rearrange its league fixtures when such matches ran counter to the Federation's Cup matches. And, as many historians have pointed out, USSFA seemed unwilling to compromise in pursuit of organizational power to regulate soccer matters nationally. Its fiscal struggles (the USSFA treasury depended on player registrations and Cup fees) only made the problem worse. And then the world-wide recession hit.

Thus, absent any great explosion of schoolboy and collegiate play in the 1920s, there emerged the legend of Bill Jeffrey, long-time soccer coach at Penn State University.

Celebrating Bill Jeffrey

"I believe it is fair to say, historically speaking, Bill Jeffrey is to college soccer what Knute Rockne is to college football." –Mickey Cochrane, NSCAA Historian (1991)

The comparison offered by Mickey Cochrane is apt, as chronicling the career of Bill Jeffrey offers a perspective on why the man was held in such high regard by the players he coached and within the soccer community where he was so impactful.

Bill Jeffrey was celebrated for his many valued contributions to the sport.

From Valued Player to Formative Coach

Born in Edinburgh, Scotland, in 1892, Bill Jeffrey was reportedly urged by his mother to stop playing semi-professional soccer and get on with his life. Thus, in 1912, she encouraged his immigration to the United States, where he lived near his uncle in Altoona (PA). Perhaps, to some degree, his playing reputation preceded him, for the railroad shop's team in Altoona signed him to play, as did later teams in the Pennsylvania communities of Homestead, Braddock, and Bethlehem.

In 1925, player-manager Jeffrey took the Altoona team to State College for an exhibition match against the college team. Whatever the circumstances, following the contest, he was offered the coaching position at Penn State College.

It was a fortuitous hire for Penn State, for in the 27 years that the transplanted Scot served as its coach, the school emerged as the nation's preeminent intercollegiate soccer team.

The Remarkable Coaching Record

Assigned teaching duties in the Industrial Engineering Program, Jeffrey's primary focus was on teaching skillful and patient soccer to the Nittany Lion undergrads.

That he was statistically successful is without question, as Penn State teams accumulated a 153-24-29 (.813) record during his tenure. At one point, his teams went 65 matches without defeat, with the 1935 team unbeaten and *unscored upon*! Thirteen of his Penn State teams recorded unbeaten seasons.

Beginning in 1926 and on eight occasions thereafter (1929, 1933, 1936, 1937, 1938, 1939, 1940, and 1949), his Penn State teams were accorded national or co-national championship status by the ISFAA. The successes were fueled by the fact that 37 of Jeffrey's Penn State players were accorded All-America during his tenure.

Along the way, he found resources in 1935 (recall these were Depression years!) to take his team for a visit to his native Scotland. Later, in 1951, the U.S. State Department funded Penn State on a goodwill trip to Iran.

Quite a coaching record, but it doesn't reflect Jeffrey's total soccer involvement.

Soccer's Pied Piper

In addition to his coaching, Bill Jeffrey was also totally immersed in the marketing and promotion of the game.

Over time, he became involved with NSCAA and USSFA. In fact, NSCAA records note that he was a founding member of the organization and was appointed chairman of several committees, including its clinics committee.

It was when serving as NSCAA president in 1948, and indicative of his commitment to "grow the game," that Jeffrey reported that he had presented eight coaching clinics at various Eastern sites. The sessions generally consisted of a soccer film, a field session, and promotion of his soccer book, *"The Boys with the Educated Feet."*

He was also called on by USSFA to help in the selection of national team players for Olympic and World Cup rosters. In 1950, at age 58, Jeffrey was named coach of the U.S. team that participated in the World Cup held in Brazil. It was there that the Jeffry-inspired team pulled off the historic 1-0 victory over heavily favored England.

WALTER BAHR RECALLS BILL JEFFREY

Playing on the 1950 team was midfielder Walter Bahr, and he shared some thoughts on coach Bill Jeffrey:

"People should understand that Bill did not select the team. It was selected by an USSFA/NSCAA committee who determined that eight players were to come from the East and eight players from the Western part of the country.

"Further, he didn't have a lot of time to train the team. Obviously we traveled there by ship and so that cut into training time.

"But Bill did a couple of things that I thought were good coaching. He didn't 'over-coach.' He had good judgment of where to place players in terms of where they normally played on their club teams. This way the players rarely played in unfamiliar places on the field. In fact, I think only two players were asked to play 'out of position.' Further, if a player was on the quiet side, Bill might surround him with a teammate who was a little more assertive, etc.

"As far as the England match was concerned, I recall him saying that he wanted us to make a good showing and not embarrass ourselves."[9]

In retrospect, obviously, at least in the England match, the embarrassment was laid at the feet of the losing side.

Revered by His Colleagues

Following retirement from Penn State coaching in 1952, Bill Jeffrey continued his relationship with the game he loved.

That year, the affable Jeffrey conducted clinics for U.S. servicemen in Germany and Italy and in 1953 did a coaching stint at the University of Puerto Rico.

Bill Jeffrey was always an honored presence at the annual NSCAA meetings in New York City, and it was there, in January 1966, that, despite the efforts of two Naval Academy players to revive him, he collapsed and died amongst his admired coaching colleagues.

Attesting to the perceived dedicated importance to soccer, Bill Jeffrey was honored by his colleagues on several occasions. His yeoman service to NSCAA was acknowledged in 1949 when Jeffrey was presented its Honor Award. In 1951, USSFA honored his accomplishment with the 1950 World Cup team with induction into its Hall of Fame. Later, in 1972, the ISAA established the Bill Jeffrey Award, and it continues to be annually presented to an individual for long-term contributions to intercollegiate soccer. That same year, the Penn State soccer stadium was named Bill Jeffrey Field, and in 1991, Jeffrey was in the inaugural class inducted into the NSCAA Hall of Fame.

"An avid storyteller, he often kept his teams entertained as they traveled to and from games ... Occasionally he would spice his orations with a 'Scotch lassie joke and a 'wee-bit of poetry' for he was an ardent admirer of Robert Burns and could quote much of his poetry verbatim. We were enraptured and listened to his every word." –Clarence "Ray" Buss, Fleetwood (PA) High School

Bill Shellenberger, soccer coach at Lynchburg (VA) College, offered an interesting insight into Jeffrey's coaching style: "Practice was a pleasure. There were no prima donnas. Everyone was treated the same and no one violated his team rules. There was such respect for the man. He still played in practice scrimmages and could execute even in his later years."

Jeffrey always was on the outlook for prospective soccer talent. "Every spring he watched intramural soccer play," recalled Ron Coder. "As a sophomore, I had never played competitive soccer or even watched the college team play. But after watching me at a IM game he cornered me and told me he liked how I moved my feet and invited me to turn out for the team the next fall.

There he asked: 'Laddie, can you catch a ball?' Thus, Coder became a goalkeeper, sharing duties the first season and starting the second as Penn State was accorded national championship honors in 1949 and 1950.

He continued to play in the service and was one of four players to represent the armed services on the 1956 U.S. Olympic team that competed in the Australian Games of that year. "Obviously I owe all my soccer experiences to Bill Jeffrey," recounted Coder in a February 2015 interview.[10]

Jeffrey's Poetic Humor

Bill Jeffrey was a noted author.

"This Can Happen"
By Bill Jeffrey
He said he was a forward
    So we put him on the wing,
He could not raise a gallop
    And his shots – they had no sting.
We tried him at center
    But, alas, it was the same
He never could accept a pass
    In fact, he spoiled the others'
game.
At halfback then we played him
    Shoved him in among the rest
He tried to feed the forwards

But he fed the grandstand best.
At fullback then we played him
    But what a mess he made
He never stopped a single run
    He really seemed afraid.
At last at goal we played him
    But he was dogged by fate
Because he only saved a single shot
    And let in forty-eight.
We put him on the transfer list
    And I don't think we did wrong
Because he's starring now, they say
    Not at soccer, but PING PONG.[11]

Two Jeffrey Legacies

Bill Shellenberger played for Bill Jeffrey for three seasons in the 1940s. Assigned to a Marine training unit stationed at Penn State, he eventually was part of the World War II invasion of Iwo Jima. Following the end of the war, Shelly returned to State College to earn his undergrad and graduate degrees in Physical Education. He later led Lynchburg (VA) College soccer to 31 straight winning seasons. Bill received the Jeffrey Award in 1978 for his outstanding contributions to the collegiate game. He was later inducted into the NSCAA Hall of Fame in 1995.

Harry Little was a three-time All-America player (1948-50) for Jeffrey and enjoyed coaching success at Dover (PA) High School, where, among his players, was a later noted U.S. coach, Jay Miller.

Earle Waters

One of the old professor's guiding principles was that a coach should never yell at or reprimand a player in public. He was an advocate of dealing with players on an individual basis. He favored taking a player aside and sitting him on "the log" alongside his practice field and dealing with the problem "man to man." He rarely made more than a suggestion or two during or at halftime of a game. He felt that players' greatest learning took place during practice sessions and he let the game "be enjoyed." –Joe Bean

Earle "Muddy" Waters, in addition to serving as the lone three-time president of the NSCAA (1942-45), was probably one of the most-opinionated and successful of those early founders of the organization.

He joined the teaching staff at West Chester (PA) Teachers College in 1927, and that year he instituted Golden Ram soccer, which he then coached for the next 29 years. During that time,

Earle Waters addresses the Hall of Fame audience at his 1992 induction.

his teams compiled the phenomenal record of 174 wins, 28 losses, and 12 ties, which included seven undefeated teams, two of which (1936 and 1950) were declared national champions.

Muddy was credited with being a founding member of NSCAA and was subsequently involved in its committee structure, including the origins of its ethics committee.

Active in ISFAA, he chaired its Referees Ratings Committee for many years. Among his contributions was an annual rating of officials that appeared in the annual *Soccer Guide*. He also produced numerous ISFAA All-America players, including Dr. Tom Fleck, who would later make significant contributions to the sport.

As with many coaches of his generation, Earle was a featured clinician appearing at some as distant as Germany or as nearby as Troy, New York.

It was while serving as a Commander in the U.S. Navy during World War II that Waters collaborated with coach John Eiler in the preparation of the Naval Aviation Physical Training Manual titled *Soccer*. At the time, the book was rated the best American-produced publication in the field.

In 1958, after 31 years of service, West Chester granted "Muddy" his first and only sabbatical in order to travel to Germany along with Coach Tom Dent and referees Harry Rodgers and Jimmy Walder to present soccer clinics to the U.S. troops.

A highlight of the trip included meeting the now famous Dassler brothers, founders of adidas. Via the Dassler connections, the American contingent attended a match between Austria and Germany. Waters discovered with great delight that the teams were utilizing a three-back system—one that he was already teaching at West Chester but which was not favored by many of his U.S. coaching contemporaries.

No Shrinking Violet on Soccer Matters

According to author Joe Bean, Waters had strong opinions on various soccer matters.

When asked about whether the present game needed any rule changes to make it more interesting or acceptable to the American fan, coach Waters emphatically countered with, "Absolutely not! ... The world set up the rules. The world set up the size of the field, the markings, etc., all the rest of that is a bunch of crap!" Obviously, tampering with the rules was not part of his thinking.[12]

Waters also railed against the importing of soccer coaches from abroad. University of Pennsylvania's Douglas Stewart was one such individual. The fact that "The Ivys" kept West Chester and several other competitive soccer-playing schools off their schedules for a long time did not help endear Stewart to Waters.

One of Muddy's final "pearls of soccer wisdom" had to do with the psychology of coaching. He referred to a V-5 book he had helped produce and how he had devoted special sections that dealt with player management, including the application of proper psychology.

Soccer in the 1930s

By 1931, several colleges had begun to field soccer teams for the first time, including Temple, Brown, Hamilton, Illinois, Ohio State, MIT, Williams, Amherst, Wesleyan, and Western Maryland.

The impact of soccer coaches in the 1930s can be traced to a relative handful of individuals who had specific impact in terms of organizing those colleges into regional leagues, and these notable contributors not only played a role in the growth of the game, but also offered templates for others to emulate in future years.

Again, most of what is traceable occurred on the Eastern Seaboard; although, as one can see, more soccer activity continued to occur on the East Coast, the West Coast was beginning to make its presence known. In fact, in 1926, the California Intercollegiate Soccer Conference had been formed.

Specifically, the Metropolitan Intercollegiate Soccer League was formed in 1933, while in 1934 the New England Intercollegiate Soccer League and the Middle Atlantic Intercollegiate Athletic Conference debuted.

In many cases, these alliances are traceable to member coaches who led the way in such matters as scheduling, player eligibility, and annual championships.

Generally, for those schools sponsoring soccer play for the first time, affiliation with such conferences within their geographic regions enabled them to immediately begin fall competitions with institutions of similar athletic philosophies.

Meanwhile, in the city of Philadelphia, young Walter Bahr was beginning his love affair with soccer, and he recalled the state of the youth game during the 1930s.

Developing the Game in Connecticut

"I was nothing but trouble in high school, heading nowhere … Some years later, by the grace of God and the confidence of George Ritchie, I graduated with honors from his alma mater, Springfield College." –Alden "Whitey" Burnham

George Ritchie was another Springfield College (1927) graduate who made a significant contribution to soccer. He was a teacher by nature, a soccer official

42

with an impeccable reputation, and a respected school administrator. He spent his entire career coaching at Wethersfield (CT) High School, where he was also the school principal.

It was while at Wethersfield that he made his contributions to schoolboy soccer. While coaching soccer, basketball, and baseball, he accumulated a 440-278-40 record. Credited with the formation of the Central Valley League in Connecticut, his teams won seven soccer and six baseball league championships. He believed in athletics for all, and it is reported that 75 percent of the Wethersfield boys participated in intramural sports.

In addition to the Central Valley League, Ritchie is credited with launching the Connecticut Interscholastic Athletic Conference as well as the Central Connecticut Soccer Officials Association. A further tribute is the fact that he is one of the first Springfield graduates to referee soccer. He was most proud that three Wethersfield graduates, Alden "Whitey" Burnham, Tony DiCicco, and Irv Schmid, went on to significant soccer coaching careers.

Recalled Burnham: "Somewhere towards the end of my junior year, Coach Ritchie jerked me out of my tailspin. He kept a close eye on me my senior year. Finally he packed my mental and emotional suitcase with the 'right stuff,' pointed the direction and put me on the road, gave me a loving shove and off I went into the world."[13]

Ritchie was presented the NSCAA Honor Award in 1950 and, in 1991, was part of the first NSCAA Hall of Fame class.

Larry Briggs

Larry was also very good with people. "At one point I was having a problem with one of the players. He said to me, 'Let me talk to him.' When the player returned to the team, he never gave me a problem. Larry had sorted it out with him." –Peter Gooding

Larry Briggs' home base was the University of Massachusetts, where he initiated its soccer program in 1930 and was head coach for the next 37 seasons.

Briggs' contributions to the game were many and varied. He was among those early coaches who are credited with the formation of the New England Intercollegiate Soccer League (NEISL) in 1934.

He is cited as a founding member of the National Soccer Coaches Association of America in 1941 and was elected its President in 1947. He helped edit its first newsletter, which subsequently morphed into today's *Soccer Journal*. For many, his legacy is associated with his role in upgrading soccer officiating, and we will cover that accomplishment in another chapter. He was presented the NSCAA Honor Award in 1950 and in 1978 inducted into the USSF Soccer Hall of Fame as builder of the game. In 1991, he was welcomed to the NSCAA Hall of Fame as a member of its inaugural class.

Larry Briggs, a skilled administrator.

A Multi-Talented Administrator

Seemingly a man for all seasons, he was a professor of physical education at UMass, where he also coached many other sports with great success. He helped initiate the Western Massachusetts Soccer Tournament in 1946 and also served for many years as manager of the Western Massachusetts High School Basketball Tournament. An active archer, Briggs was President of the National Archery Association from 1940 to 1947 and twice hosted the National Archery Tournament at UMass. In his spare time, Briggs was a Council Commissioner of the Boy Scouts of America, President of the Massachusetts Society of Health, Physical Education and Recreation, and served as an officer in the United States Eastern Amateur Ski Association and the Intercollegiate Soccer Football Association of America.

Briggs and Peter Gooding

Recently, Peter Gooding, later the longtime coach at Amherst College, recalled his time with Coach Briggs. In 1966, Peter was attending the UMass graduate school and his fellowship included serving as Briggs' assistant soccer coach. "Basically he told me to coach the team. He quietly observed practices and games and never interfered with my coaching. He had a knack for picking out a coaching point or two and sharing them with me."[14] It should be noted that Michael Russo was captain of the UMass team that year. Russo would go on to produce excellent teams at Williams College in Massachusetts.

A Nod From Joe Morrone

On the occasion of his retirement dinner in 1968, UConn Coach Joe Morrone offered this tribute: "The thoroughness which you approached each new task, whether it was in soccer, archery, basketball, first aid, or the thousand-and-one other responsibilities; everything was done with unparalleled skill, always in an affirmative manner; always with perfection and understanding, always accomplishing more than five 'normal' men could possibly handle."[15]

T. Fred Holloway

"I didn't realize until I was almost out of college," he confided to a newspaper reporter several years after his retirement, "that I was better as an athlete than I thought. We just didn't have the coaching. I guess that's why I got so interested in coaching." –Fred Holloway.

By the time T. Fred "Prof" Holloway retired in 1973 after 35 years as a professor of physical education and legendary head coach of the State University of New York (SUNY) Cortland soccer team, he had established a legacy of excellence, inspiration, and tradition that today, two generations later, remains the standard by which Cortland athletes, past and present, continue to measure themselves and their accomplishments.

T. Fred Holloway.

Formative Years

Holloway was born in Glasgow, Scotland, in 1904, the son of a machinist. He immigrated with his family to the United

States in 1912, settling in Waterbury, Connecticut, where he developed an interest in athletics.

During his years at Waterbury's Crosby High School, "Prof" captained the school's track and cross-country teams and competed in soccer and swimming. After high school, he enrolled in Springfield College and there continued his athletic endeavors, playing soccer under John Brock, running cross country, and participating in gymnastics while earning bachelor's and master's degrees in physical education. He would later receive a Ph.D. from New York University.

Development of the Cortland Tradition

"Prof" entered coaching in 1929, beginning as a physical education instructor at the University of Pittsburgh.

Then, in 1936, he accepted a position as coach and instructor of physical education at the little-known Cortland Normal School (enrollment 850), where he began what was to become an unrivaled tradition of winning soccer teams. His Red Mules (later Red Dragons) posted a remarkable record of 191-94-23 during his 35-year tenure, including three teams that appeared in early NCAA tournaments. He and fellow SUNY coach Huntley Parker are credited with the formation of the State University of New York Athletic Conference in 1959. During his tenure, Cortland captured six SUNYAC championships. Today, the eastern division of the SUNYAC's most valuable player award is named in his honor.

A Notable Soccer Contributor

During his era, he was also a stalwart in national soccer coaching circles. As one of the country's preeminent coaches, "Prof" chaired the founding committee of the National Soccer Coaches Association, an organization over which he presided in 1952. He also devised a statistical system for the selection of NSCAA All America collegiate soccer players. His work later included a system for measuring teams' relative strength of schedule for NCAA tournament selection purposes. Eight of his former Cortland players were named to the All-America team at a time when there was no distinction between playing divisions. For many years, he chaired the New York Region NCAA Soccer Selection Committee.

His peers frequently singled out "Prof" for recognition. In 1958, he was selected by the NSCAA members to receive their coveted Honor Award. The citation accompanying the award characterized Cortland's soccer coach as "author and educator, leader of youth and leader of men, sportsman, athlete, coach, teacher, tireless worker and standard bearer for the sport of soccer." Named to the school's inaugural Hall of Fame class in 1973, SUNY Cortland formally honored its long-time and beloved coach by dedicating its soccer field to him in 1987.

GIVING BACK TO THE GAME THEY LOVE

Cortland has left a lifelong impression on a number of its former soccer players. Many of these individuals have represented or still represent the "Red Dragon Way" through their involvement in the game. Included in the list of over an estimated 100-plus coaches who played for Cortland coaches Fred Holloway or his successor, Fred Taube, are four coaches whose teams won New York State High School soccer titles, including Mike Campisi (Shenendehowa H.S.), John Eden (North Babylon H.S.), George Herrick (Vestal H.S.) and Gary Montalto (Arlington H.S).

While he never played soccer at Cortland, another noted alumnus was Joe Palone, long-time coach at West Point, who would be inducted into the United Soccer Coaches Hall of Fame in 2020.

As of 2020, the following is a partial list of SUNY Cortland soccer graduates who have given back to the game in various capacities:

Keith Agate – Cincinnatus H.S.

Ryan Argenziano – Deer Park H.S.

Steve Axtell - SUNY Cortland

Brady Battistoni – Arlington H.S.

Alan Benda – SUNY Canton

Mike Borra – Syosset H.S.

Kevin Bradley – Nassau C.C.

Mike Campisi – Shenendehowa H.S

Mike Carboine – Dryden H.S.

Alan Catu - Suffolk County C.C.

Joe Chiavaro – U.S. Military Academy

John Cossaboon – University of San Diego

Matt Daum – Wallkill H.S.

Hristos Dimitriou – Binghamton University

Josh Eaton - Mount Union College (Ohio)

Charlie Elkins – Misericordia (PA) College

Neil Edkins – President, N.Y.S. Referee Association

John Eden – North Babylon H.S.

Jamie Edson –Colonie H.S.

Jeff Ellis – Southhold H.S.

Paul Gannon – U.S. Military Academy

Jordan German – Franklinton H.S.

P.J. Gondek – SUNY Fredonia

Bob Gould – Mohawk Valley C.C.

Chris Gradwell – Sumter H.S. (South Carolina)

Lou Hanner – John Glenn H.S

Mike Heedles – Lake Luzerne H.S.

George Herrick – Vestal H.S.

Jim Hesch – Pro Player, Hershey Wildcats/Harrisburg Heat

Mike Hogan – Harborfields H.S.

Fred Hooper – Keene Central School

Mike Kelly – North Babylon H.S.

Bruce Kramer – Fowler H.S.

Bill Lehmann – MacArthur H.S

Craig Levernois – Guilderland H.S.

Anthony Marinello – SUNY Cortland

Scotty Martin – North Rose-Wolcott H.S.

Clarence Mepham – Brighton HS

Gary Montalto – Arlington H.S.

Tim Morgan – C.W. Baker H.S.

P.J. Motsiff – College of St. Rose

John Mullins – West Islip H.S.

Tim Mullins – West Islip H.S.

Perry Nizzi – Hamilton College

Kevin O'Connor – Marmion Academy (IL)

John Pagano – Huntington H.S

Joe Palone – U.S. Military Academy

Timothy Peabody – Pearl River H.S.

Matt Pedicini – East Meadow H.S

Chris Perkins –Wells College

Pat Pidgeon – SUNY Cortland

Kevin Quinn – Pittsford-Sutherland H.S.

E.J. Reutemann – SUNY Cortland

Don Riddall – Manlius-Pebble Hill

Tom Rogan, Sr. – Hudson Valley C.C.

Tom Rogan, Jr. – Fulton-Montgomery C.C.

Dan Rose – SUNY Potsdam

Paul Rose – Colgate University

C.J. Rozzi – Wando H.S. (SC)

Craig Sanborn – Arlington H.S.

Bert Severns – President, Patrick U.S.A.

Peter Schmitz – Brentwood H.S.

Keith Stanley – Massapequa H.S.

Chris Sweeney – Massapequa H.S.

Mike Trimarchi – Johnstown H.S.

Matt Vergamini – Greece Odyssey Academy

Chris Waterbury – SUNY
Plattsburgh

Dave Wilson – Binghamton
University

Phil Wingert – Wilkes
University (PA)

David Wright – Gettysburg
College (PA)

Ron Zorn – N.Y.S. Boys' H.S.
Coordinator

Carlton Reilly – A City Soccer Guy

"A serious student of the game, on four occasions Reilly traveled to England to hone his expertise under the guidance of famed Manchester United Coach Matt Busby."

Carlton Reilly's involvement in coaching included the inauguration of soccer at Brooklyn College in 1934. The 1988 Brooklyn College soccer team brochure reflected on the "Reilly Years" at the New York City institution: "Professor Carlton Reilly has done more for the game of soccer at Brooklyn College than any of the college's eight coaches."

Beginning in 1934, and with time out for military duty, Reilly guided the Kingsmen for 18 seasons, compiling a record of 87-34-8 that included six unbeaten seasons. Credited with helping in the formation of the Metropolitan Soccer League in 1933, Reilly teams would capture eight league championships during his tenure.

Of note was the emergence of the City College of New York team in the 1950s under the tutelage of Coach Harry Karlin. CCNY won six straight MSL titles (1953-58) and were declared mythical national champions following an unbeaten (10-0) 1957 season. The Beavers also participated in the first NCAA tournament in 1959. In addition to his CCNY teaching duties, Karlin was cited as serving as a choreographer at various burlesque houses in Queens during his spare time!

In 1978, Reilly was an inaugural inductee into the Brooklyn College Athletic Hall of Fame. Earlier, in 1957, Reilly received honors at the inaugural Adelphi College Soccer Clinic as the "Dean of Soccer in the Metropolitan Area" and as the one who had done most in the promotion of the sport over the years. That service included four years as president of the Metropolitan League (1934, 1935, 1949, and 1950).

In 1956, the United States Soccer Federation (USSF) appointed him representative to the Olympic Committee. That same year, Coach Reilly was also appointed by the General of the Army in Europe to conduct clinics for the men in the armed services. In 1958, he was nominated NCAA representative to the 1959 Pan American Games Committee and the 1960 Olympic Games Committee.

It was in 1960 that Reilly convinced USSF to sponsor a summer visit by Coach Matt Busby. Orchestrated by Naval Academy Coach Glenn Warner, the two organizations jointly funded an instructional coaching film that featured the ManU coach. The film would be added to the then-existent NSCAA Film Library.

Active in USSF and NSCAA politics, Reilly was named recipient of the 1961 NSCAA Honor Award, with the award committee citing his concerted efforts to encourage collaboration. "During the past year our Association has made a special effort to work more closely with the USSFA, and a concrete example of this effort is the 'Matt Busby' film. We believe that each group now has a better understanding of what the other is trying to accomplish and together we can make progress."

Dr. William "Pete" Leaness

"For his outstanding coaching record, Pete Leaness was named to the NSCAA Hall of Fame in 2005."

Dr. Peter Leaness (center) is shown with the 1952 Temple University soccer team members: (from left) Ed Tatoian, Jack Dunn, Lefty Didriksen, and Len Oliver.

Beginning in 1930, and for the next 40 seasons, Dr. William "Pete" Leaness coached Temple University in Philadelphia, achieving a 245-100-38 (.770) career record. During his long tenure he aided in the development of such players as Don Yonker, Walter Bahr, and the Chyzowych brothers, Gene and Walter, into influential careers in the game.

In 1951, and led by NSCAA All-America players Jack Dunn, Ralph Mange, and Len Oliver, Temple recorded an 8-0-1 record, and the Owls would go on to play the University of San Francisco in the Soccer Bowl, where a 2-0 win cemented the national championship. The match was played at Kezar Stadium before a crowd of 10,000 spectators. With Dunn and Oliver still on the roster, Temple was unbeaten (9-0) and repeated as national champions in 1953.

At Temple, John Rennie would come under the influence of Leaness. Pete was a part-time coach and a full-time chiropodist by professional training. "He was a calm guy, quiet and he relied on his captains to provide leadership for the team," John recalled, Rennie would later carve out his own Hall of Fame coaching career at Duke University.

While Leaness would produce three dozen All-America players during his tenure, John Rennie's promise (he scored six goals in his first varsity match) would not result in such honors, with a senior year knee injury ending his Temple soccer-playing career.

Augustine "Gus" Donoghue

"Donoghue was a great athlete, a great coach and a fine gentleman, exemplifying the highest qualities of human character. In 1975, USF created the Gus Donoghue Award. It represents the highest recognition USF can bestow upon a soccer player who wears the Green and Gold." –USF HOF Website

His friends called him "Gus," and it is Donoghue who is considered by many as the coach who first brought national attention to West Coast collegiate soccer.

Donoghue first learned the game of soccer at St. Aloysius Elementary School in Garnet Hill, Scotland. He came to San Francisco in 1925 and matriculated at St. Ignatius High School before enrolling at USF. As a player, Donoghue was the major factor in USF's first golden era in soccer, 1932-36. It was in this period when the three-

Gus Donoghue.

time All-America captained the Dons as they captured five Northern California Intercollegiate Soccer Conference championships. He was also a member of the U.S. Olympic team in 1936.

Donoghue served as the USF student body president and earned his degree in 1936. He obtained his master's degree from the University of California in 1937 and his Ph.D. from Stanford University in 1953. He took over the Hilltop coaching duties in 1941-42 and then left for military duty with the U.S. Navy. He returned to coaching at USF in 1946 and also served as an assistant professor of history.

Serving as head coach for15 years, Donoghue posted a record of 121-12-14, leading USF to 11 NCISC Championships. He received the Coach of the Year award in 1950, which was the same year in which USF played Temple in the first college Soccer Bowl game in the history of U.S. college soccer.

In 1952, Gus assumed the duties as USF director of admissions. He retired from coaching in 1960 and from USF in 1973.

For his contributions to the development of the game on the West Coast, he was inducted into the NSCAA Hall of Fame in 2001.

Walter Bahr and the Lighthouse Boys Club

Walter Bahr's love affair with soccer had its roots at the Lighthouse Boys Club (LBC) in the Kensington section of the city of Philadelphia. His recall of his time there provides historic background to the organization of youth soccer play in the 1930s.[16]

Kensington was a highly ethnic community populated by English, German, Irish, and Scottish immigrants who worked in the textile mills in the area.

In an effort to provide recreational opportunities for the children of the workers, Mrs. Robert P. Branford established the LBC in 1900. The club featured a gym, swimming pool, basketball court, and game rooms. By 1917, soccer became a major offering at the club as Mrs. Branford's brother, Dr. Howard Kelly, purchased 17 acres of land. On that tract, three baseball and soccer fields were laid out.

In 1920, Elmer Schroeder, a University of Pennsylvania law school graduate, became director of the club, and soccer began to flourish under his direction. It is estimated that during his tenure over 13,000 boys became club members. For his efforts at promoting soccer, including managing the 1928 and 1936 U.S. Olympic and 1934 U.S. World Cup teams, Schroeder was inducted into the National Soccer Hall of Fame in 1951.

In addition to Schroeder (and later Bahr), LBC has contributed six other former members to the NSHOF including Bob Gormley, Bart McGhee, Benny McLaughlin, Werner Meith, Francis "Hun" Ryan, and Dick Spaulding. Not only did LBC produce players, it also was credited with the startup of HOF careers of referees Jimmy Walder and Harry Rodgers.

It was in this very soccer-oriented culture that, in1937, Walter Bahr, age 10, joined the LBC. "What was of interest was the fact that once a boy was 12 he was expected to begin to coach teams in the younger age group," Bahr recalled. This "giving back to the game" mentality was thus imprinted early on by the leadership of the LBC.

Interviewed at the 2009 NSCAA Convention in St. Louis, the then 81-year-old Bahr reported he couldn't recall any formal coaching as he moved through the youth levels at LBC. "Kids are the best judge of talent," was his summary statement. "Players learned by playing. You began to know what you could or couldn't do on the field. The team members shaped the team. The best technical players were in midfield. The fastest were the wingers. The center forward was generally fast or could head a ball well. The back players tended to be a bit slow, but heavy-footed in terms of clearing a ball. It was generally left to the younger players to alternate in goal." (Bahr laughingly recalled: "Goalie or right field; no one wanted to play those positions!")

Among the LBC teams that played locally was one from the Nicetown BC. A member of that team was Eddie Stankey, who later became a National League baseball star.

Learning From the Professionals

While coaching was also minimal, it was obvious that Bahr's LBC involvement helped produce a young soccer phenom, as, in 1942, he signed an amateur contract at age 15 with the Philadelphia Nationals of the then American Soccer League.

Even at that young age, Bahr was a midfielder. What were the lessons he learned playing with older men? "First, you learn to hone your technical ability. If you were passed a ball and lost it, you generally knew; 'I better practice that technique!' If you couldn't make the right decision of where to go to receive a ball you probably wouldn't see many balls passed your way! So you watched how older skillful players handled themselves and copied their techniques and how they supported the ball with their movements. I guess we'd call it learning spatial awareness. If there was coaching it was generally done at practice or at halftime. I'd say if there was any coaching it was largely for the manager to sort out who was playing where. Otherwise – we played – and learned."

Following World War II, many teams in the ASL and the German-American League (centered in New York City) brought European professional players to our shores. "You have to remember that English professionals were limited to making 12 pounds a game, three pounds for a win and one pound for a tie," reminded the then still energetic, fun-loving Bahr in St. Louis. "Here in the States they could be hired by a company, say Bethlehem Steel, earn a good wage with the company and still be paid to play on the company-sponsored team. It was a good deal for them to come to the States."

As a result, play in both leagues became highly competitive, with the two leagues eventually combining players to form all-star teams that would annually battle such teams as Liverpool and Manchester United when they toured the United States.

The V-5 Soccer Training Program

While World War II curtailed intercollegiate soccer play, it did present an opportunity for Naval Academy coach Tommy Taylor to organize a cadre of soccer coaches, particularly collegiate coaches, to introduce the sport of soccer to thousands of our armed forces through the Naval Aviation Pre-Flight Training program.

The value of this program cannot be overestimated in terms of its eventual impact once these newly indoctrinated officers returned to their communities as new advocates for the sport.

The V-5 Program

Formally called the Naval Aviation Pre-Flight Training Program, it was commonly referred to as the V-5 Program due to the fact that a V-5 medal was awarded to those successfully completing the fitness component.

Navy coach Tommy Taylor was appointed by Commander Thomas Hamilton to develop a physical training program for naval aviators that showcased soccer as the featured fitness mechanism. A physical trainer by profession, the English-born Taylor was into his 21st season as head soccer coach at the U.S. Naval Academy when World War II broke out.

Hamilton explained the background of the Navy's thinking regarding soccer: "Soccer was included in the curriculum for the training of naval aviators because it teaches the cadets how to control their own weight and the ball at the

Commander Thomas Hamilton utilized soccer for training U.S. Navy aviators during World War II.

same time, and is a means of their gaining proficiency in coordination, agility and balance. Then too, the competitive angle brings out the 'will to win' that is so necessary if our boys are to do the job ahead of them and return home." For his soccer advocacy, Commander Hamilton was presented with the initial NSCAA Honor Award in 1942.[17]

Taylor enlisted other noted collegiate coaches such as John Eiler (Slippery Rock), Walter McCloud (Trinity), John Squires (Connecticut), and Earle Waters (West Chester) to provide the concentrated soccer instruction.

Earle Water's Review

In an interview conducted by Joe Bean, Earle Waters outlined the soccer instruction provided to the V-5 recruits as they participated in five 90-minute physical training sessions a week.

"Our work is very interesting. We teach soccer to about 240 cadets a day and have twelve soccer teams either practicing or playing each night. Each cadet going through here gets ten, 35-minute lessons in soccer. Needless to say this is high pressure teaching with little time spent on anything but the most fundamentals."[18]

Waters recalled that among the many servicemen introduced to soccer was Gerald Ford. He, of course, later became the nation's 38th President.

In one notable outcome from the program, Waters and John Eiler collaborated on the production of the book *Soccer*. It was published in 1945 and based on the coaching methodology utilized in the V-5 program. It later became a best seller with its strong emphasis on the fundamental techniques of the game, including appropriate lesson plans, further appealing to physical educators unfamiliar with the sport. Post-war editing by the authors enabled the book to stay attuned to ongoing trends in the sport. By 1950, the book was in its third printing.

It should be mentioned that, in addition to the Navy's program, the U.S. Army instituted a similar plan. Long-time Amherst College coach Eli Marsh coordinated one such course at Lexington, Virginia. He predicted that, long-term, the sport would benefit when many of his charges, most of whom were from the southern part of the country, returned home.

CHAPTER II

BUILDING ON THE PAST

In the post-World War II era, there were a number of coaches who emerged to take on the dual roles of elevating the teaching of the game and also working at its promotion.

The six coaches profiled fulfilled both functions admirably. All were trained as physical educators and, fortunately for the game of soccer, all focused significant energies to solidify the game in the areas of New England, the Middle Atlantic region, and New York State.

Also of importance was the fact that while having been mentored themselves by some of soccer's early leaders, they progressed beyond those experiences in terms of their methodologies. In terms of expanding soccer's influence, it was through both the excellence of their teams' play and their leadership roles in NSCAA and ISAA that that objective was addressed.

Perhaps most importantly, Walter Bahr, John Eiler, Huntley Parker, Irv Schmid, Glenn Warner, and Don Yonker epitomized the ideal of the model coach in terms of their deportment. While the facts of their short-term influences are evident, their long-term soccer impact was felt for years, as many of their players would follow their examples and make their own significant contributions to the sport.

Soccer in the Post-World War II Era

Following the end of World War II, the nation's colleges were overwhelmed with an influx of students, many aided by the GI Bill of Rights.

Perhaps the most widely-successful legislation ever adopted by the U.S. Congress, the GI Bill provided funding for many servicemen to fund their new dream of earning a college degree.

Also returning to the fold were a second-generation corps of coaches who had been mentored by several of those early pioneer instructors of the game and who not only introduced new methodology to soccer coaching but also become more pronounced advocates for it. Principally, this advocacy was channeled through the National Soccer Coaches Association of America.

Once more, in reviewing the roles played by several leading coaches, most of the contributions mentioned took place in the Eastern Seaboard region of the United States. It was a few years before other areas of the country saw such an explosion of soccer interest.

Walter Bahr – Great Player, Great Coach

Walter Bahr.

Walter Bahr is thought by many to have been one of our country's finest early players, and he also contributed mightily to the progress of the sport through a long and distinguished coaching career.

USMNT Play

In 1942, at age 15, Bahr was perhaps one of the country's youngest superstars and was playing professional soccer. He retired as a player in 1957, but not before playing for the USMNT on 19 occasions. He was a member of the 1948 Olympic team that played in England but most famously was a midfield starter on the 1950 World Cup team that played in Brazil.

In the most famous game in the early history of the sport in the United States, it was Bahr's shot to the far left post that glanced off Joe Gaetiens' head for the goal that proved decisive, as the Americans scored a monumental upset of England, 1-0.

Play for Man U?

Through his play at the 1948 Olympics, and subsequently in Brazil, Bahr had acquired an international playing reputation. A clipping forwarded to Walter from a Scottish friend quoted legendary Manchester United manager Matt Busby as stating: "If ever there was a 'natural,' the fair-haired graduate of physical education at Temple University is one … and [he] would be an asset to any one of our top-class league sides."[19]

In 1950, Busby discussed the possibility of Bahr joining the Man U side (there was never any formal offer). While enticing, Bahr elected to continue his soccer in the United States.

His Teaching/Coaching Career[20]

By 1949, he was teaching physical education at Jones Junior High School in Philadelphia and coaching the freshman team at Swarthmore, where former Lighthouse BC player Bob Dunn was the varsity coach.

In 1954, Walter returned "to his roots," taking over the reins at Frankford High School where his teams won "4-5 city titles." He remained teaching at Frankford but gave up coaching there in 1971 to succeed the deceased Pete Leaness at Temple.

Among the Temple players he coached who later entered coaching, Bahr cited John Boles (Temple), Lew Meehl (Drexel), Larry Sullivan (Villanova), Billy Snyder (Frankford HS), and Bob Peffle (LaSalle).

In the early 1960s, Bahr assumed union leadership of coaches in Philadelphia. He fought for additional pay for teachers who took on coaching assignments. Eventually, a strike of the coaches resulted in a settlement, whereby they were awarded additional salary for each sport they coached.

Onward to Penn State

In 1974, Bahr was offered the men's soccer position at Penn State. He remained in charge of the Nittany Lion eleven until 1988. During his tenure, his teams qualified 12 times for NCAA Tournament play.

When asked to talk about his coaching style, Bahr simply stated, "We tried to play 'thinking soccer' as opposed to 'brute soccer.' That's how I learned to play and that's how I tried to coach. But in saying that, I don't want to leave the impression that we didn't adjust. Sometimes the long ball, the more direct game is the way you have to play in order to be successful. So, as always, we adjusted, depending on the game. In the end, the game is the best coach. It tells you what is needed tactically."

He also tried to identify the best 11 players and let them sort it out on the field. "I always tried to finish the game with the 11 starters, as much as possible. I rarely substituted except when needed, say an injury or someone having a really bad day."

His successor at Penn State, Barry Gorman, assisted coach Bahr and recalls one occasion when Walt did substitute. The coach was intently watching the game and called out to the bench, "Jimmy, replace so-and-so." The "Jimmy" that Walt was referring to was NOT Jimmy Adams. And the "so-and-so" was NOT to have been one of the team's best players, Randy Garber. But before Walt could intercede, Adams was in, Garber was out.

You guessed it. "Didn't Jimmy Adams a minute or two after entering the field, score the winning goal," Gorman noted. "With that Walt turned to the bench and, in good humor, stated, 'Boys, that's what good coaching is all about!'"

Bahr's Coaching Principles

In terms of coaching principles he lived by, Bahr shared:

"I rarely recruited backs. I felt that it was always easier to move a player back than to move him forward." He cited one example: Fleetwood (PA)'s Troy Snyder was recruited as a wing but performed at midfield for Penn State and became an NSCAA All-America and USMNT player."

"I constantly reinforced the playing principle, if not sure, play the way you are facing!"

"I liked to imprint our style of play by having 11 players play what I termed 'dry run soccer.' We'd move the ball around the field without opposition and talk to the players about options they might have relative to other players around them or away from them. I guess they call it 'shadow play' nowadays. We did a lot of that, 10-15 minutes a day."

"I rarely talked to the team following a game. I would simply remind them of the next practice and let it go at that. Sometimes in the heat of the moment, you might say things to the team that were damaging. Better to 'sit on things' for a few hours, review them in your mind and then plan for how to address matters in later practices. We didn't do a lot of video-taping or filming of the games so I would try to review things based on my observations. In sharing your comments that you realize it *how* you state them that is most important."

"I occasionally phoned other coaches to get some information on a common opponent."

"I always hoped my teams were better at the end of the season than at the beginning."

"The perfect game was to win and play well. It didn't always happen!"

"I think that you, as a coach, have to recognize that sometimes 'less is more.' Players and teams need time to regenerate." Bahr was not in favor of all the concentrated play that dominates youth soccer today. "Players will sometimes benefit more from a day off and again, you as the coach, have to determine that."

He also shared that professional coaches in certain sports probably might evaluate if year-round practices are all that beneficial. "My son Chris was a scratch golfer and enjoyed his early off-seasons, first with Cincinnati and later with Oakland. He would play in celebrity tournaments with James Garner and come back to football with enthusiasm. Eventually, his pro football career became year-round. The teams would build weight-training and other off-season practices into their contracts. Again, I don't know how valuable all that is."

Finally, he noted that the pre-game training habits of some of his old teammates, while not traditional in any sense, worked for them. One teammate in particular would go "out on the town" every Saturday night and was no less for the wear come Sunday's kickoff. "I can't stay in on Saturday night and worry about the game. I've been doing this since I was a kid and it works for me," the late Vince Carney told Bahr. The coaching lesson: Allow for individual differences.

Player Recruitment

In terms of player recruitment, Bahr stated that he did it "99% by phone." Through his many years in the game he had developed a network of friends. "I guess I trusted my friends in the game and when I learned of a player from a certain region, I would call a friend in that area and ask a simple question: 'Can he play?' I guess my friends all understood what I meant! I think over my time at Penn State I only got 'burned' two or three times by my buddies recommending players."

He was also easy on Penn State's recruiting budget for soccer. "I think I only took three prospects out for a restaurant dinner. We didn't get any of them!" Bahr recalled.

His foreign contacts also came in handy. English friend Graham Ramsey was acquainted with eventual Penn State player Duncan MacEwan's father. The dad was a former Aston Villa professional and looking for the "right fit" for his son. When Ramsey mentioned that Walter Bahr was coaching at Penn State, the deal was finalized. Each pro knew of each other!

Related to his recruiting methodology, Bahr, like one of his predecessors, Bill Jeffrey, never left a stone unturned on his own campus. "We had a lot of foreign students at Penn State. Many would end up playing on a club team or in intramurals. I always took a look at that play as well. From time-to-time we'd come up with someone who 'could play.'"

When recounting his Penn State coaching career, Walt Bahr made it all seem so simple. And, in retrospect, for him it was. His genius, both as a player and coach, was that he simplified a game that others made more complex than necessary.

The Bahr Family

Walt and wife Davies Uhler Bahr met in Philadelphia. She would later graduate from Temple with a degree in physical education. She later joined the physical education department at Penn State, where she served as an administrator/teacher for 15 years.

Together, the Bahr family includes sons Casey, Matt, and Chris and daughter Davies Ann. All were standout athletes.

Casey was twice an NSCAA All-America player for coach Glenn Warner at Navy and was a member of the 1973 Philadelphia Atoms NASL championship team

Chris played for his father at Penn State, where he was a three-time (1972-74) NSCAA All-America choice. He also served as kicker for coach Joe Paterno and later earned two Super Bowl rings during a 14-year NFL career.

Son Matt played four years for his dad at Penn State and earned All-America honors as a football kicker in 1978. While he played in the NASL for both Colorado and Tulsa, he is best known as a NFL football kicker. During his 17-year career, Matt won two Super Bowl rings.

"Our boys always thought that Davies Ann was the family's best athlete," Walt proudly shared. She was a versatile athlete and earned All-America honors while staring in gymnastics at Penn State in 1978.

Don Yonker – A Most Influential Coach

Perhaps he was a bit biased, but it was left to Al Laverson to put Don Yonker's contributions in perspective when he stated, "Don should be credited with being the most influential coach of his time. He was the first American coach to stress work with the ball. He was a consummate gentleman, creative, innovative and articulate. He made a significant impression on soccer nationwide, but his crowning achievement was a national championship with Drexel."[22]

Perhaps no one coach contributed so extensively to the growth of the game in the period following World War II as did Don Yonker.

Drexel University's Only Championship

Born in Philadelphia, Yonker starred in athletics at the city's Frankford High School before enrolling at Temple University, where he became an All-America soccer player for legendary coach Peter Leaness.

After graduating with a degree in physical education, he was a coach and administrator in the city's public schools. In 1946, he was named the first men's head soccer coach at Drexel University, a position he held for 30 years. He compiled a 183-119-33 record during his tenure and in 1958 led the team to the mythical national championship. It is to this day Drexel's only national championship in any sport.

Don Yonker.

The 1958 team finished unbeaten (12-0) and featured players from England, Germany, Poland, Russia, Wales, and the Ukraine. Three players, Stan Dlugosz, Ozzie Jethon, and Robert Muschek, were among 15 Drexel players eventually accorded All-America honors.

Yonker's teams had winning records in 25 of his 30 seasons and, during a stretch that started in 1955, won eight or more games 10 times; in those 10 seasons, the Dragons were 100-21-5.

It was in that era that Yonker, in 1962, established Camp Munsee, which has been advertised as the first U.S. residential soccer camp, in Honesdale, Pennsylvania. There will be more on that later.

Editing *Soccer Journal*

Don Yonker's coaching achievements alone made him an early soccer notable, but it was also his 27 years as editor of the NSCAA's *Soccer Journal* that brought him to soccer prominence in the U.S. soccer coaching community.

It was in 1952 that NSCAA president Glenn Warner appointed the highly organized 42-year-old to take on the editorship of the then-NSCAA *Soccer Newsletter*. By 1957, the publication was retitled the *Soccer Journal (SJ)*.

Yonker had several topics of consistent and concentrated editorial interest, including such matters as sportsmanship, coaching ethics, and the need for fair play, along with sharing with coaches insights on developing one's coaching philosophy.

Able to translate in German, Italian, and Spanish, he kept members informed about international soccer developments and, at a time when colleges were tinkering with the rules (kick-ins from touch, play in quarters, a rounded penalty box, and elimination of the slide tackle!), was a consistent proponent of abiding by international rules. Oh, and by the way, he was a respected soccer official himself!

In an effort to cover U.S. news, he formed a network of individual coaches he termed "Keymen." They reported regional soccer news to him on a regular basis. When Yonker was later named editor of the annual *NCAA Guide,* these reports were fashioned into annual soccer summaries including news from the rapidly-expanding high school soccer programs.

It is obvious from researching those early issues of *SJ* that Yonker desired to do everything possible to make the magazine as interesting, provocative, and educational as possible. An example of his writing skill was his *SJ* tribute upon the passing of Bill Jeffrey.

Teacher, Author, Public Speaker

In addition to his editorship, Yonker was a well-respected clinician.

At one convention, he demonstrated various individual techniques exhibited by the world's star players of the time. Between observing every international match played in this country that he could purchase a ticket for and by also breaking down such movements as gleaned from the NSCAA film library, he had cataloged the special innovative skills of such greats as DiStefano (Argentina), Didi (Brazil), Gento (Spain), and Puskas (Hungary). Slowly, before an audience of fellow coaches, he broke down the ball skills of these great players.

Other Yonker literary accomplishments included authoring the book (with Alexander Weide) *Coaching to Win*, in 1976.

In addition to his writings, and as with many of his coaching contemporaries, the Drexel coach possessed well-honed public speaking skills. That expertise was utilized as he wrote and presented many NSCAA Honor Awards. He was the featured speaker at the luncheon commemorating the 75th anniversary of the first intercollegiate soccer match played between Haverford and Harvard in 1905.

His Legacy

The accolades Don Yonker received during his career included reception of the Philadelphia Old Timers Soccer Association Award in 1957; the NSCAA Honor Award in 1964; the Suburban Philadelphia Coaching Association Robert H. Dunn Award in 1975; the Bill Jeffrey Award in 1976; and the Drexel Institute of Technology Athletic Hall of Fame in 1977. Additionally, he was posthumously inducted into the NSCAA Hall of Fame in 1992.

Stan Dlugosz

It would be an oversight in summarizing Yonker's legacy not to acknowledge his former player, Stan Dlugosz.

A two-time first-team All-America player at Drexel, in 1963 Dlugosz joined the engineering faculty at what is today Mercer (NJ) Community College. He subsequently coached its soccer team from 1963-81, with Mercer capturing NJCAA national soccer championships in 1963 and 1968. Several Mercer players enjoyed significant soccer careers, including Glenn "Mooch" Myernick.

Coach Irv Schmid – A Composed Presence

As was stated previously, Springfield's outreach and influence on the growth of the U.S. sport of soccer has been substantial, and a great deal of the credit for that goes to the pioneering efforts of Irv Schmid.

Coach Irv Schmid spent 36 years directing Springfield College soccer.

In reflecting on the impact of Coach Irv Schmid, who spent 36 years directing the fortunes of Springfield College's men's team, former player Jeff Vennell likened his legacy to that of a large tree with lots of branches extending from its solid trunk.

In part, the analogy speaks to the fact that Springfield's influence on the growth of soccer has been expansive due in no small part to the professionalism of Schmid and his predecessor and mentor, John Brock.

Vennell characterized his former coach as "strict, formal, a man who knew who he was but underneath was a good guy. I guess you could say he was a bit Germanic in his approach, not overly communicative."

Page Cotton affirmed Vennell's recollection: "I think that Irv knew that his job was to help instruct Springfield undergrads to become effective physical educators. He was very clear on his expectations and as we all had the same mindset, there was little challenge to his methodology. With DePauw being a liberal arts college, I had to adjust to the fact that not all my players were cut from the same cloth.

They all had different goals for themselves. And they often wanted to understand the basis of why we were doing something."

To earn a starting spot, Springfield players needed to live up to the very exacting demands of Coach Schmid. Vennell recalls that he and others tried every day to please Schmid. "I would say that Irv was a man who you didn't fear; you respected him. I will never forget how excited, when in my junior year I learned on the trip to Colby that I was to start!"

Related to earning a starting spot, retired DePauw University coach Cotton learned he was close to starting when, in his sophomore year, he was issued uniform number 12. "Coach traditionally selected the starters by assigning uniform numbers 2-10 at the start of the season. When one of the backs was injured my number 12 elevated me to starting spot." By his last two seasons, he was a solid starter, wearing number 5.

Vennell also shared a 1965 anecdote that reflected on Schmid's firm ethical standards. "Perhaps our best player came to preseason training with a full head of hair. The team rules did not allow that and the player was told to cut his hair or leave the team. He left the team."

The Emphasis on Fundamentals

Vennell also noted that, as a physical educator, Schmid had acquired the ability to break down soccer techniques and refine them into soccer skill. Many of these almost exclusively American athletes helped Schmid-led teams to capture three New England titles, including a mythical national championship in 1957. Page Cotton underwent a metamorphosis during his Springfield career. "Coach Schmid constantly worked on the fundamentals with us. I have to say that I was a much improved player by my senior year. As a result over my time at DePauw we constantly devoted time improving those building blocks for the team."

Jeff and teammate Ray Cieplik remembered Schmid's training sessions as being fairly typical for the time. The coach had traveled to Germany and been exposed to the training methodology of that country's professional teams. Thus, Springfield practices began with 20 minutes of dynamic stretching followed by technical work with full-field scrimmage ending each session. The field also housed a goal-sized kick board that aided player's individual technical development.

Tactically, Schmid teams kept up with world-wide trends in the game. Members of the unbeaten 1968 (13-0-3) NCAA Atlantic Coast Tournament championship team noted that they played in a 4-2-4 formation first utilized and popularized by Brazil's 1958 World Cup champions.

The Springfield Connection

The coaching careers of many were greatly aided by Schmid and other Springfield faculty. Jackson attributed his first coaching position at Indiana to his soccer mentor. Cotton credited Maroon AD Ed Steitz for his first (and only) DePauw coaching post.

One has to examine the later contributions of members of the 1968 team to appreciate how the Schmid legacy contributed to the growth of the U.S. game.

Goalkeeper Tony DiCicco's name is enshrined as a result of his taking the U.S. Women's National Team to the 1996 Olympic and 1999 World Cup titles.

Captain Page Cotton enjoyed a 39-year coaching career at DePauw (IN) University, where his coaching record ranks ninth in NCAA Division III annals. Defender Alden Shattuck assisted at Hartwick College before head coaching stints at Syracuse and Maryland. Midfielder Bill Muse later assisted at Hartwick and become head coach at Princeton.

In addition to the 1968 team members who later contributed as coaches, the institution itself can rightly consider itself as producing a who's who of American soccer coaches.

Huntley Parker, Jr. at Brockport

How was it that by 1955, Brockport would be declared mythical national champions?

When later queried, the players gave full credit to the coach. In reference to the man, they used such terms as "gentleman," "never raised his voice," "great motivator," "a good teacher and winning coach," "he made sense," "honest and to the point," and "innovative." The latter comment referenced that the team played with three backs!

Huntley Parker's relationship to soccer was fairly typical for many who later became expert coaches of the sport.

Namely, they were also proficient in other sports. That was the case of Huntley Parker. Raised in Rochester, New York, where he became the first four-sport letterman in the history of John Marshall High School, Parker played soccer, basketball, baseball, and golf.

Nicknamed "Pud," he graduated from Springfield College in 1933, having lettered in baseball and soccer for three years. Playing fullback for coach John Brock, he was named an All-America fullback in 1931 and 1932. He completed his master's degree at Penn State in 1941. It was there that he came under the influence of coach Bill Jeffrey.

Parker's coaching successes at three Rochester (NY) area high schools (Nunda, Williamson, and Dansville)

Huntley Parker.

served to introduce his work to SUNY-Brockport AD Ernest Tuttle.

In 1946, Tuttle hired Huntley Parker to teach in the physical education majors program, supervise student teachers, and coach soccer. Eventually, Parker became the school's director of athletics.

The Parker Approach

David D. Doty's 2004 research paper focused on Brockport's soccer successes. It revealed that 60% of the 1946 Brockport team had no high school playing experience. Whether experienced or not, the players' reflective comments offered a glimpse of Coach Parker's coaching methodology:

Practices were every day, rain or shine. Players recalled them as "always fun," "organized, always a learning situation," "worked on individual skills," "runs before and at the end of practice," "small drills, set plays, small games," "scrimmages where we interchanged positions," and "volleyball soccer was a great diversion."

As to his style, he was reported by his players to be "calm, but firm," "knew the team and utilized the skills in it," "matter of fact and all business," "when we made a mistake he would call us over, discuss it calmly and send us back in the game [free substitution ruled the day!]."

Two key players in the early development of the program were goalkeeper Ted Bondi and forward Howie Whatford. Bondi earned All-America honors four times, Whatford on three occasions. From 1947-49 Brockport was undefeated, with 11 other players also earning All-America honors. Aiding in their development was that many Golden Eagle players honed their skills in the very competitive Rochester amateur league once their college seasons concluded.

The National Championship Team

Goalie Ron Broadbent summarized the then-advanced tactical approach employed by coach Parker: "The big innovation was moving to a formation that allowed us to play with three 'fullbacks,' three midfielders and four forwards. The skill, speed and conditioning were quite high. This was apparent throughout the season, but surely manifested itself when we played at West Point against the 'gray waves,' defeating them, 2-1." Of note was that West Point coach Joe Palone declared following the loss: "Your team was just in better condition than my Army team – and that rarely has happened."

Declared national co-champions with Penn State, the team won all 12 of its matches, outscoring the opposition 51-6.

Four of the players, captain Pete Hinchey (MF), Watson McCallister (F), Walter Schmid (F), and Bill Hughes (B), were among the 26 Brockport All-America selections. A majority of the roster went on to coach the game, including Hughes with the NASL Rochester Lancers (1974). Many developed close relationships with their former coach, including the team's captain, Peter Hinchey (see QR code, The Hinchey Influence). Hughes and Broadbent returned to their alma mater as coaches at different times.

A Record of Success

In his 23 seasons at Brockport, Huntley Parker had but two losing campaigns, as his 143-50-18 record attests. In four of these seasons his teams were undefeated, including the 1968 team that lost only to Army in four overtimes in the first round of the NCAA Tournament on total corner kicks. Yes, that was the tiebreaker at the time!

It should be mentioned that the Rochester area had a sizable soccer culture and Brockport's successes served to attract spectators to its matches. In 1961, the school focused its homecoming on soccer, and the game with Army attracted a reported 5,000 fans. Later games that season with CCNY, Cortland, and Rochester averaged 3,000 spectators.

A true leader and developer of young athletes, Parker was pleased with the fact that 17 of his former players were inducted into Brockport's Athletic Hall of Fame.

Honored Professional Service

Huntley Parker's career was also marked by his service to the game. He served as president of the National Soccer Coaches Association of America and the Intercollegiate Soccer Football Association, and he represented the latter organization on the U.S Olympic soccer selection committee.

For his outstanding service to the NSCAA, he was presented with its Honor Award in 1968, and in 1993 he was inducted into the organization's NSCAA Hall of Fame. In 1985, Parker was a charter member of Brockport's Hall of Fame. But in all likelihood, the 2005 naming of the SUNY-Brockport soccer field in his honor was his most favored acknowledgement.

Of note is the fact that three former Parker players, Mel Lorback (1974), Fred Taube (1976), and Ron Broadbent (1992), served terms as presidents of the National Soccer Coaches Association of America.

John Eiler's Total Impact

Ken Kutler still thinks about the life lessons that Eiler taught him. ... "It's been a long time since I was at East Stroudsburg, and that's quite a testament to the influence he had on my life and the respect I always had for him ..."[24]

Soccer was fortunate to have attracted the commitment of the late John Eiler to the sport. For it was he, along with a similar group of dedicated advocates, who were responsible for the accelerated development of the sport in that period following World War II.

No matter whether one is referencing his athletic career, his years as a professional physical educator and coach, or his time in athletics administration, all were marked by

John Eiler holds the 1962 NAIA championship trophy following presentation by then-U.S. Naval Academy AD Rip Miller.

a long list of significant accomplishments and all while serving as an inspiration to his players and professional colleagues alike.

Early East Stroudsburg Impact

Eiler entered East Stroudsburg State Teachers College in 1930 and was still a big Warriors fan at the time of his death in 2006 at age 93. He is memorialized by the fact that the Eiler-Martin Stadium on campus bears his name. He was inducted into the school's Athletic Hall of Fame in 1978.

Eiler's undergraduate athletic career at ESU was exemplary. Competing in football, gymnastics, and track, at graduation he was named the best all-around athlete in his class. He also was elected class president.

Prior to his World War II military service in 1942, he taught in the East Mauch Chunk (Pa.) public school system. It was there that he first began coaching soccer. While serving in the U.S. Navy, he was contacted by former U.S. Naval Academy coach Thomas Taylor and asked to co-author a soccer manual for Navy V5 officers. It was subsequently utilized as a physical training regime. It was one of the first U.S. books published on soccer coaching

After the war, he joined the faculty at Slippery Rock State College, where he taught in the professional physical education program, coached soccer, gymnastics, and track and field, and served as dean of men. He was inducted posthumously to the Slippery Rock Hall of Fame in 2017.

He returned to East Stroudsburg in 1956 and coached the Warrior soccer teams for 10 years. He led the squad to the NAIA national championship in 1962. His 1964 and 1965 teams reached the quarterfinals of the NCAA University Soccer Tournament before losing each time to eventual tournament two-time runner-up, Michigan State.

His overall coaching record was 150-41-6 over 20 seasons, including a 77-25-7 mark at East Stroudsburg State.

The Eiler Coaching Standard

"We all respected him," said former ESU soccer All-America Al Miller. "He didn't have a lot of rules, but those that he had were firm. He always meant what he said. "He had an enormous influence on my wanting to be a coach. I came into school as a baseball guy, but after meeting Coach Eiler I became a soccer guy," he said.[25]

Perhaps indicative of his excellent pedagogical skill, Eller received the Outstanding Teacher Award at Slippery Rock State College in 1956 and at ESSC in 1981.

Commitments to Soccer's Progress

Eiler was honored many times for his coaching achievements. In 1965, he received the Honor Award of the National Soccer Coaches Association of America, and in 1993, he was inducted into the National Soccer Hall of Fame in Oneonta, N.Y. He and Huntley Parker are believed to be the only individuals to have served as presidents of the NSCAA (1957) and the Intercollegiate Soccer Football Association (1962-65).

Both he and Parker were also noted as among the few soccer coaches to serve as athletic directors at their institutions. As Mickey Cochrane noted, "The soccer coaching community couldn't have been better represented at NCAA meetings than having those two gentleman as soccer's emissaries. For they represented our sport in outstanding fashion."

In 1952, he and a dozen close soccer-coaching colleagues gathered together in Florida to stage the first of a series of three Sarasota Soccer Forums. Basically, the coaches met to share ideas in terms of coaching and promoting the U.S. game. The events included collegiate all-star games.

When NSCAA president, he laid the groundwork for the organization's first marketing agreements. Appointed to the Wheaties Sports Foundation, by 1958 he had convinced that arm of the cereal company to enter an eight-year agreement to sponsor the NSCAA All-America team in exchange for an annual $1,000 rights fee.

It was also reported that earlier in the 1950s he had convinced the Soccer Sport Supply Company to expend $90 to advertise in the *NSCAA Soccer Journal*. At the time, the 24-page magazine was printed and mailed for $79!

Acknowledged by Many

A true physical education professional, John Eiler lent his leadership qualities not only to the sport of soccer but to a host of other sport-related organizations, including the NCAA and Eastern College Athletic Associations.

In acknowledgement of his regional contributions, Eiler received the Elmer R. Cottrell Award in 1969, the highest honor given by the Pennsylvania State

Association of Health, Physical Education and Recreation. In1983, he was recipient of the ECAC's coveted James Lynah Award in recognition of his service to that organization.

An Exemplary, Progressive Coach

Coach Jim Lennox' adjectives in describing Eiler's impact echoed those of others who came under the man's influence. "His deportment was exemplary. He was a model coach and without question, everyone respected him. He was also a good tactical coach and his training sessions were as modern as it got for that era."[26]

Eiler's coaching methodology was "unique compared to today's world," said former 24-year ESU soccer coach Jerry Sheska. "He was low-key, quiet and direct."

"I never saw him raise his voice," said Sheska. "He got across what he wanted by directly telling you what he expected; we all followed his direction because we respected him so much. I don't know many coaches who do that anymore."

Eiler described his approach during an interview in the 1970s: "I never believed in exploding and blowing up. I believed in frankness and in a person showing confidence and strength. I didn't think it made me stronger by insulting a player or being sarcastic. Strong people don't have to do that; weak people do."

Ken Kutler, a former athletic director at Hartwick and Ithaca colleges and the Warrior's soccer captain in the 1960s, still thinks about the life lessons that Eiler taught him.

"It's been a long time since I was at East Stroudsburg, and that's quite a testament to the influence he had on my life and the respect I always had for him," said Kutler.

"He was the consummate professional. He was interested in people, not necessarily to use them to win games, but because he believed that each player was important no matter what his role on the team."[27]

Glenn Warner and Navy

Glenn Warner was an early product of the NSCAA network system. He had great mentors. He played under James "Oppie" Springer and John Brock at Springfield College. Springer was the impressive freshman coach.

"I'll never forget him. He was the type of coach that spent a little time running right alongside of you in scrimmages, telling you when to move in and when to

Glenn Warner was inducted into the NSCAA HOF in 1992. He is shown receiving the honor at the then-Oneonta Hall as Mickey Cochrane looks on.

move back. He was young enough in those days, so that was the way to coach some of us inexperienced players."[28]

Glenn Warner coached at the United States Naval Academy from 1946 to 1975. In 31 years of coaching, he had but two losing seasons. His teams amassed a 251-65-33 record, including the unbeaten (15-0) 1964 team that won the NCAA National Championship. In a stretch from 1962-67, Warner's teams put together a string of 48 regular-season victories without a defeat and qualified for five-straight NCAA Tournaments.

At the time of his retirement from the Naval Academy, athletic director J. O. Coppedge said of coach Warner: "We are losing the services of a great coach and a great teacher. In his long tenure at the Naval Academy, he not only compiled a record unmatched in the history of intercollegiate soccer, but his tireless efforts and enthusiastic approach to the teaching of physical education is an example to everyone. He personified the word 'dedication.'"[29]

A Film Visionary

Glenn Warner's contributions to soccer were significant. He, along with John Eiler and others, nurtured the Florida Soccer Forum for several years in Sarasota and St. Petersburg. He also initiated action on what became the NSCAA film library. He was involved in producing some of the films and donating some in order to build an inventory. Warner was the first unofficial "chairman" of the Visual Aids Committee. The name was later changed to Film Library when films were the exclusive offerings available to the members for rental. Until its demise in the 1980s, the NSCAA Film Library served hundreds of coaches, players, and summer soccer camps. With the introduction of video and videotapes, film became obsolete. Many recall renting films that, upon their showing, had the scoring scenes obscured, as coaches had repeatedly rerun them for teaching purposes.

Exposing Navy Soccer

After guiding the University of Maryland's varsity team to an undefeated 8-0-2 record, Warner was hired at Navy in 1942 to serve as assistant to Tommy Taylor. He remained an assistant to coach Taylor until 1946.

His physical education schedule at Navy involved teaching swimming, which was his first love. His attendance at swimming clinics in Fort Lauderdale gave rise to the idea for the creation of the Florida Soccer Forums.

A favored clinician, he annually took his Navy team to New England, where they played preseason matches against colleges in the region. There, he and opposing coaches offered morning clinics followed by a match against teams such as Irv Schmid's Springfield team, Clarence Chaffee's Williams College's eleven and Joe Morrone's Middlebury team. "Chic" Jacobus at Kingswood School and Paul Sanderson, coach at Suffield Academy, helped organize the annual affairs.

On November 9, 2001, the United States Naval Academy dedicated the $4.5 million Glenn Warner Soccer Facility.

Warner is a member of the NSCAA Soccer Hall of Fame (1992) and was the recipient of the NSCAA Honor Award (1953).

CHAPTER III

U.S. COACHING EDUCATION TAKES HUGE STEPS FORWARD

With the hire of Germany's Dettmar Cramer by the United States Soccer Federation (USSF), U.S. soccer coaching methodology was dramatically improved beginning in the 1970s.

With the staging of its first coaching schools, USSF not only furthered instruction of the sport but, led by Cramer's successor, Walter Chyzowych, unearthed an entire new generation of coaches who would, in turn, upgrade teaching of the sport on a national and regional basis.

The Chyzowych dismissal and later questions about the USSF course environments led the NSCAA in the early 1980s to initiate its Academy instructional program that was founded on a different philosophical basis.

But while the soccer instructional component was progressing, soccer's rapid and substantial growth in the 1970s uncovered a number of issues that the collective soccer coaching community needed to address. More on that in the next chapter.

Dettmar Cramer Revolutionizes U.S. Coaching

"So long as better is possible ... good is not enough." –Dettmar Cramer[30]

Perhaps no single individual revolutionized American soccer coaching as did Germany's Dettmar Cramer.

And perhaps the United States Soccer Federation, alongside the NSCAA and ISAA, made its best investment in the future of the game by hiring him to direct its first coaching school at the Moses Brown School in Providence, Rhode Island, in 1970.

A Man Well-Traveled

Franz Beckenbauer called him "The Professor of Football"

Cramer was born in in the German state of Bavaria, played some professional soccer, and eventually came to the attention of famed German coaching legend Sepp Herberger.

In 1959, when it came time to name Herberger's replacement as director of coaching, the German Football Association (DFB) bypassed Cramer and appointed Helmut Schoen to the position. Reportedly, the fact that Schoen's professional playing career was more noteworthy than Cramer's was decisive in the DFB's decision.

Instead, Herberger recommended that the Association hire Cramer as its coach for the western region of the country, there to identify and train its best youth players. It was a position he held until 1963.

Briefly a sports journalist, Cramer was sent to Japan by the DFB to upgrade that country's national team in preparation for the 1964 Olympic soccer competition.

A stickler for detail, the night before he was to have his first meal with the team, he utilized two pencils to improve his chopstick skills. The diminutive (5'3") Cramer subsequently led the Japanese team to an upset victory of Argentina at the '64 Olympics.

In 1964, he was called back to assist Schoen in preparing the West German team for 1966 World Cup play. There, the team lost a controversial final to host England.

He returned to Japan and led its national team to a bronze medal at the '68 Olympics in Mexico. He also established the first coaching education curriculum in Japan.

Cramer admitted that his militaristic approach to teaching changed as a result of his immersion in the Japanese culture: "First thing I noticed was their gaiety – I'd been told never to smile. I had a foul temper, but they taught me patience. I don't know who learned more, the Japanese from me or I from the Japanese."

Thought of as "the Father of Japanese Football," Cramer was inducted into the Japanese Football Hall of Fame of 2005, and Emperor Hirohito personally awarded him the highest Japanese Order of Culture.

Dettmar Cramer.

Cramer's Influence on U.S. Coaching

Labeling Cramer as a "master teacher," Bob Gansler recalls turning up for every session, pen and paper in hand, mouth open.[31]

Soccer America's Mike Woitalla perhaps best captured the impact Dettmar Cramer had in interviews he conducted with various U.S. coaches.[32]

Al Miller attended that first coaching school in Providence and shared his perspective: "A lot of college coaches were physical education teachers trained by coaches who had never seen a game. Cramer modernized American soccer coaching."

Miller remembers Cramer's approach to fitness being greeted as "revolutionary. He believed in fitness but the fitness was with the ball," Miller said. "He called it specific fitness – getting fit for the game that you played by playing the game and using the ball to do the running and exercising and so forth."

Miller went on to explain: "He thought training without the ball was wasting time. Cramer stated, 'You run laps, you create lap runners!' Everybody bought into it, because we didn't have that much time with our players and he was teaching us how we could get more out of them."

In all likelihood, the curriculum Cramer shared with U.S. coaches was based on that developed for Japanese consumption. It emphasized use of the ball to teach the technical aspects of the game (passing, dribbling, shooting, heading, tackling), whereas small-sided games (1 v 1 through 3 v 3) taught the basic tactical approach to attacking and defending play. Eventually, of course, all the breakdown of the game's elements manifested itself in the 11-aside game.

Cramer also credited Herberger with development of another aspect of his coaching philosophy that he shared with his aspiring U.S. coaches, noting: "Herberger had a genius for resolving apparently complicated issues with simple practical examples." This was a method Cramer adopted himself, encouraging players to think "outside the box" – as described nowadays – to improve aspects of their games.

Manny Schellscheidt, who was awarded the first USSF coaching license by Cramer, stated in the Woitalla interview, "Of course, let's take into account that the game evolves. But what Dettmar put on paper is as good today as it was in those days."

Miller also stated that the curriculum that Cramer brought not only changed the American approach to coaching soccer, but it also created a tremendous camaraderie between the college, the high school, the adult club, and the youth coaches. "Early in my days we had a little problem because if you were a club coach, you thought college coaches were stupid," says Miller. "And if you were a college coach, you thought club coaches were stupid. I was kind of caught in the middle because I was coaching in college but playing at the club level."

"I thought that Dettmar's original schools crushed that and brought everybody together. That was one of the best things that came out of it, other than learning good fundamentals for coaching and getting educational coaching background."

Labeling Cramer as a "master teacher," Bob Gansler recalls turning up for every session, pen and paper in hand, mouth open. "He was unbelievable in terms of his presence, his manner. He was so articulate and knowledgeable. His demonstrations were so precise, always emphasizing the right points. And we had a wide variety

Dettmar Cramer at the first USSF coaching course attended by (bottom row from left to right) Trevor Pugh, Joe Machnik, Gene Chyzowych, James Bradley, Manny Schellscheidt; (top row from left to right) Bob Ritcey, Layton Schoemacher, (unknown), Lenny Lucenko, Tom Nevers, Dettmar Cramer, Bob McNulty, Hubert Vogelsinger, Joe Morrone, (unknown), Will Myers.

of coaches at the school. And he seemed to be able to know what buttons to push in order to meet all of the candidates' needs."[33]

Coaching Disciples

Part of Cramer's impact was the legacy he left in terms of identification of several American coaches to continue his work at development of coaching education in the United States.

Based on his showing at the first coaching school in 1970, Al Miller helped in conducting the next few schools. In 1974, Walter Chyzowych was appointed the first USSF Director of Coaching and continued utilizing the Cramer approach.

Of note also was Cramer's early appreciation of the goalkeeping expertise of Joe Machnik. It was Machnik who took on goalkeeping instruction at subsequent coaching schools in the 1970s and 1980s.

Post-U.S. Career

Cramer left his USSF coaching position to return to Germany to coach the Beckenbauer-led Bayern Munich club to European Championships in 1975 and 1976. Beginning in the late 1970s, Cramer spent time as a coaching missionary for FIFA, working his coaching magic in a reported 90 countries around the world.

Before his death in 2015, Dettmar Cramer was honored as the first coach to receive an honorary lifetime achievement award from the DFB.

The Third Generation of American Soccer Coaches

At the time, with soccer play exploding at the intercollegiate and secondary levels in the post-World War II period, the demand for experienced, well-versed soccer coaches far exceeded the supply.

Underlying the establishment of the USSF coaching schools was the premise that by furthering the coaching expertise of a widespread corps of instructors, those graduates could, in turn, utilize their newfound proficiency to elevate soccer coaching in their respective regions of the country.

In fact, it was at his first coaching schools that Cramer identified several men to carry on and expand his approach to soccer coaching instruction. Walter Chyzowych headed the selections. He and others might be classified as America's third generation of soccer coaches.

Walter Chyzowych.

The Cramer Impact

... in the post-World War II period, the demand for experienced, well-versed soccer coaches far exceeded the supply.

There is little question that Dettmar Cramer's appointment to oversee the country's first coaching schools was a seminal moment for the soccer coaching process in this country.

Supported by donations from the NSCAA and the ISFAA, USSF's establishment of the formalized coaching schools under the German's supervision exposed a segment of the U.S. soccer coaching community to how to more effectively organize on-field instruction of the sport.

Up to Cramer's selection, accepted coaching methods had been the purview of a small but dedicated group of physical educators who happened to have a passion for the game. Prior to Cramer, accepted soccer coaching practices were largely passed down from the Stewarts, Brocks, Jeffreys, and Waters to the Schmids, Parkers, Eilers, Bahrs, and Warners. And until 1970, that was how coaching expertise had been imparted as the sport entered the 1960s.

Walter Chyzowych – The Chosen One

Perhaps Walter Chyzowych's role in the elevation of U.S. coaching was best summarized by one of his former USSF coaching staff members, Bob Gansler, when he stated, "... his contribution [to American soccer] has been of such consequence, yet so diverse and substantial, that the total quantification is elusive."[36]

After the World Cup in 1970, Walt's coaching destiny became intertwined with Dettmar Cramer.

In the summer of 1970, it was Cramer who conducted the first three USSF Coaching Schools at the Moses Brown School in Providence, Rhode Island. Those one-week courses marked the beginning of professional coaching education in the United States.

Walt attended the second week of the course, and Cramer, recognizing Walt's playing skills, his pedagogical capabilities, and his magnetic personality, invited Chyzowych to assist his establishment of subsequent USSF's Coaching Schools.

Walter Chyzowych while coach at Wake Forest.

He worked alongside Cramer through 1974, and when Dettmar returned to Germany, Chyzowych became USSF Director of Coaching. For the next six years, he conducted the nationwide residential coaching courses.

Walt built on the Cramer curricula. This included conducting annual coaching school seminars where such esteemed coaches as West Germany's Helmut Schoen, Poland's Jacek Gmoch, Yugoslavia's Ivan Toplak, and Heerenveen's Hans Ooft shared their innovative coaching approaches with the USSF staff.

In addition to the issuance of National Coaching School licenses, and in collaboration with the United States Youth Soccer Association, Chyzowych designed non-residential coaching courses to meet the needs of that largely inexperienced coaching community. Labeled D, E, and F, these progressive courses aided countless youth coaches to meet the needs of a rapidly increasing population of youth players.

When you speak with these builders, you hear them echo what Dettmar said to Ursula Melendi, the invaluable manager of the coaching schools. When they were entering the candidates' names and assessments following the conclusion of the 1970 sessions, Dettmar stopped when they came to Walter Chyzowych's name. "Him," he said. "He's the one to lead."[37]

The Impact of Walter Chyzowych

His peers in the USSF named him the most dominant figure in American soccer in 1992.

His brother, Gene, recalls that in 1945, while both he and Walt were living in a displaced persons camp in Munich, Germany, the two of them traded their family's ration of butter for a basketball. The ball served as a soccer ball for them, and they organized games in their compound.

Some place between the butter and the 1992 accolade, Walt Chyzowych "paid his dues" and without doubt has left his mark on the American soccer scene.

Born in 1937 in Sambir, a small town in the Western Ukraine, Walter and Gene immediately found themselves in a soccer environment. His father, Vladimir, owned and managed the Dinister SC. The three brothers (Ihor being the third) all began their love affairs with soccer as they served as ball boys and performed other tasks associated with being the owner's sons.

Surviving World War II

As World War II ran its course and the Russians began to push the German army westward, first Vladimir and then mother Helen and the sons fled the Ukraine. The family unit was united in 1945 in Munich at a British/U.S. displaced persons encampment.

The promise of a cabinet-making job for Vladimir secured by relatives in Philadelphia allowed him to be the first to embark for the United States. The rest of the family followed later.

Gene recalls the language barrier was overcome as teammates of Gene's at North Catholic HS and at Walt's club team helped improve their English proficiency.

Walt followed Gene to Temple University, where both starred for coach Peter Leanness and Walt twice earned All-America honors, including one season where he scored 25 goals in nine matches. Their collegiate summers were spent in Toronto, where they played for the Ukrainians in a very competitive senior league. They delivered milk and eggs by day and practiced and played at night, earning "big money" according to Gene.

Coaching Textile

In addition to his playing career, Walt was named coach at Philadelphia Textile following his graduation from Temple in 1961. His Textile coaching tenure and his playing career both coincidentally lasted until 1975. Whatever the team, the crafty Chyzowych was usually a league's high scorer and, on several occasions, its MVP.

During this period, he began graduate studies at then-Trenton State University and was awarded his master's degree in 1966. That same year he, Gene, and Temple teammate Len Lucenko founded the All-America Soccer Camp, and it remained one of the largest until its closing in 1998.

At Textile, Walt would compile a 122-37-14 record and be named NSCAA regional COY in 1975. Upon succeeding Cramer, he would build a dedicated staff, and the number of schools flourished under his direction.

He also was named U.S. national team coach in 1975, and five years later felt he had a competitive team readied for the 1980 Olympics. Unfortunately, the Moscow Games found the United States boycotting the event.

Departure from USSF

By 1981, Walt and USSF had parted ways, with the Federation hiring Karl Heinz Heddergott as coaching director. Walt had served as a consultant when Major Indoor Soccer League was formed in 1977 and, following his departure from USSF, joined the league as its supervisor of its officials. For many, the latter post seemed a plausible assignment, as Walt was never reticent about offering officials advice when he was coaching!

He also continued teaching including serving as director of the NSCAA/Army clinics program. He would return to USSF in 1984 as director of coaching but resign two years later and return to collegiate coaching at Wake Forest University. During his eight-year tenure at the North Carolina institution, he led the Demon Deacons to four NCAA Tournament appearances and an ACC playoff title in 1989.

Walter Chyzowych's coaching career ended with his passing on September 2, 1994. It was fitting to some degree that Walt's death took place that year as the United States hosted the 1994 World Cup. The fact that the eyes of the soccer world were focused on this country was due in large part to his historic contributions to the growth of the game in his adopted country.

But the man's legacy lives on in anecdotes that survive to the present.

Many were worried the year previous when Walt underwent a hip replacement, but all seemed well until September 2, 1994, when he collapsed while playing tennis with Herb Magee.

This writer was pleased to be mentioned in the booklet at Walt's Pittsburgh roast as one of his soccer friends. I didn't realize that I had achieved that status— but, in retrospect, if you had an abiding interest and passion for soccer, you were Walt's friend.

As Bill Killen noted in a letter to brother Gene upon learning of Walt's passing, "There's an old Irish saying that goes something like this: 'You never really leave a place you love, part of it you take with you, leaving part of yourself behind.'"

The Chyzowych Awards

The "larger than life" legacy of Walter Chyzowych is memorialized each January at the annual United Soccer Coaches Conventions when a group of his former colleagues, headed by Joe Machnik, conduct a ceremony in his honor.

The recipients of the Chyzowych scholarships that enable worthy young coaches to attend either coaching schools and/or the convention itself are acknowledged. So too are two awardees from the soccer coaching community honored for their career accomplishments.

Fittingly, it seems the annual ceremony embodies Chyzowych's place in U.S. soccer; gone but fortunately not forgotten.

The Emergence of Bob Gansler

By 1973, Bob Gansler had already been coaching state high school championship teams at Marquette University High School when then Milwaukee-Wisconsin coach Timo Liekowski encouraged his attendance at the USSF Coaching School overseen by Dettmar Cramer.

Held at the St. Andrews School in Delaware, it was a career-enriching experience.

In Bob's overview of his immersion with coach Cramer, he noted that the man's more formal and expert manner meant that all concerned, even the great Beckenbauer, called him "Professor."

Bob Gansler and Walt Chyzowych celebrate in 1981 as the U.S. clinches a berth in the FIFA U-20 World Cup with a PK win over Honduras at RFK Stadium in Washington, DC.

Bob earned his B coaching license that year, and in 1974 and under director Walter Chyzowych was awarded the A license.

Impressed with Gansler's work at the '74 training sessions, in 1975, Chyzowych appointed him to the coaching school staff. Until Walter's death in 1994, the Chyzowych-Gansler relationship flourished. As Bob remarked in 1992, it was a tandem based on mutual respect.

It was the U.S. U-20 team's fourth-place finish at the 1989 World Youth Championships that led to Bob's appointment to coach the USMNT at the following year's World Cup in Italy. Post-World Cup, Gansler served at USSF Director of Coaching and focused his attention on furthering coaching education methodology.

In that role he also utilized the coaching expertise of famed Dutch coach Rinus Michaels.

Now, having been mentored by two of the world's coaching legends, what has been the legacy of those experiences?

In Gansler's own words, "What I appreciated with Cramer and Rinus was that they looked at our country and asked, 'What are the needs of U.S. in terms of coaching education and how can we help?' I never heard them utter 'we never do that in my country.'"[39]

As with Cramer, Gansler labeled Michaels a master teacher, reminding everyone that once his Ajax playing career concluded, the man honed his coaching craft by teaching soccer to young, hearing-impaired players.

Further, Bob admired Michael's flexible analytic approach to soccer problem solving. "He was very open to everything often stating – 'let's try this or that.'"

Following his stint as USSF Director of Coaching, the Gansler name was attached to State Director of Coaching positions in Idaho and Wisconsin . He returned to coaching in 2001, leading the MLS Kansas City Wizard franchise to the MLS Cup, while in 2004 the team captured the U.S. Open Cup.

Joe Machnik – Goalkeeping Guru

Perhaps the Machnik legacy in terms of coaching was the formalization of goalkeeper training. For many fledgling coaches in the post-World War II era, the training of the goalkeeper was a bit of a mystery in terms of its approach.

Dettmar Cramer can be credited with furthering Machnik's development as a goalkeeping specialist when Cramer asked him to instruct candidates at the first USSF coaching school. It was an assignment that endured through the 1980s.

By 1977, Machnik had established the first No. 1 Goalkeeper Camps. From 39 initial campers, interest exploded to 240 campers the following year. Over 43 years, the camps have expanded nationwide, and Machnik's clinics at a number of NSCAA conventions played no small part in helping market his business.

In addition to the hands-on approach at the camps, the Machnik methodology included two instructional books, *"So You Want to be a Goalkeeper"* and *"So Now You Are a Goalkeeper."* Videos also captured his goalkeeping instruction methodology.

Numbered among the Machnik graduates are Dave Vanole and Tim Harris and later MLS keepers Joe Cannon, Kevin Hartman, Nick Rimando, Jon Busch, and Matt Reis.

One of Joe's initial staff instructors, Greg Andrulis is among those No. 1 apostles who have continued to influence goalkeeper instruction throughout the United States. Today he is in charge of the overall management of the more comprehensive No. 1 Soccer Camps.

Nick Zlatar – NYC Workhorse

In staging one of the non-residential courses, Nick recalls initiating the course by holding a ball and stating, "This is a soccer ball." From the back of the room came a rejoinder, "Not so fast Nick!"[40]

His Serbian heritage exposed him to soccer, and his education equipped him with the pedagogical and leadership skills that enabled Nick Zlatar to become an effective teacher of the game.

In 1974, Zlatar received his USSF A coaching license, and that, in turn, opened the door for several significant assignments with that and other soccer organizations.

The first appointment came in 1970 and was a result of George Donnelly's role as the coordinator of the first Cramer courses. George was a former president of the Southern New York Senior Soccer Association (SNYSSA) and was so impressed with the Cramer experience that, upon his return, he requested that Nick, along with colleagues Ray Klivecka and Lenny Lucenko, establish a state-coaching course. In addition, the trio was asked to launch state youth and senior teams for the New York City metropolitan area. Eventually, SNYSSA evolved into the ENYSSA (Eastern New York Senior Soccer Association).

Subsequently, the D coaching course was designed. It, to some degree, mirrored the National A, B, and C residential courses. Later, the D was directed to the needs of those coaches with some physical education/teaching background. The latter courses were invaluable to the former players who wanted to acquire the fundamentals of teaching.

Time Liekoski – A Lot of Coaching Successes

Timo Liekoski was long associated with the USSF coaching schools and is another coach who can trace his background back to his undergraduate days at the small but influential Upstate New York school, Hartwick College.

Meeting Al Miller

*"Further, as time went on, I noted that he [Liekoski] was quietly passionate about being successful." –*Al Miller[41]

As with others, it was a fortuitous meeting with then-SUNY New Paltz coach Al Miller that changed the life of the young Finnish-born athlete.

The coach-player relationship took place in the summer of 1966. Miller was playing for the Kingston (NY) SC Kickers, and Timo, newly discharged from two years' service with the U.S. Army and living in the area, was recruited to play goalkeeper for the club.

Queried to the bonding that took place between the young, ambitious Miller and the somewhat reserved but talented Liekoski, Timo offered that he was "forever grateful" to the coach for his early mentoring and noted that "something clicked."[42]

Looking back at the relationship, Miller recalls that in the summer of 1966, in preparation for his playing goalkeeper at New Paltz, he put the athletic Liekoski through grueling goalkeeper sessions. It was those workouts that cemented a lifelong relationship between the two soccer fanatics. "He was an incredible talent, had great reflexes, and a real nose for the game," Miller recollected. "Further, as time went on, I noted that he was quietly passionate about being successful."

Following one year's play at New Paltz, Timo followed Miller when he became coach at Hartwick in 1967. Unfortunately, a broken wrist derailed plans for him to play in the goal his first season, and he never did return to goal during his 'Wick career. Instead, Miller installed him at right back, whereby his senior year he became a NSCAA All-America choice.

During their three years together, the Miller-Liekoski duo achieved a 30-6-1 record and reached the NCAA quarterfinal round in 1968 and 1969.

Initial Coaching Positions

... *"to say he was a "Student Of The Game" is an understatement. ..."* –Jeff Tipping

It was another Hartwick connection that landed Timo his first coaching position. Former Hartwick President Dr. Fred Binder, then President of Whittier (CA) College, offered him a chance in 1970 to coach and earn his master's degree.

In 1972, in what was the first of much subsequent relocation during his career, Timo became the first combined men's soccer and ice hockey coach at Wisconsin-Milwaukee.

It should be noted that, now bent on a career in soccer coaching, it was during this point in his career that in 1972 he enrolled in the Dettmar Cramer-led USSF coaching school. Noting that his Cramer instruction was "top quality," he is proud to hold USSF A License #13.

When Al Miller resigned as Hartwick coach in 1973 to enter the professional coaching ranks with the Philadelphia Atoms, Liekoski returned to his alma mater as coach. There he led the team to three NCAA Tournament during his three-year tenure, including a third-place finish in 1974.

Timo Liekoski (center) and Francisco Marcos visit the statue of Ferenc Puskas in Budapest in 2017.

Al Miller asserts that Liekoski's coaching success at Hartwick was no surprise based on the fact that he, in his mentor's mind, "is a real intellectual." Player Jeff Tipping weighed in with another impression of the coach: "We visited Timo's house for team dinners and social occasions and he really enjoyed having players over. I was impressed with the library of soccer books that Timo had. To say he was a "Student Of The Game" is an understatement. His knowledge of the game was "encyclopedic."

Jeff also credited the coach with having a tremendous work ethic that included a meticulous attention to detail. "While Francisco Marcos had convinced me to attend Hartwick, Timo flew to Liverpool and met with my parents and assured them that their son would be in good hands."[43]

Most important, by the time he resigned in 1975, Timo had combined with the aforementioned lifelong friend, Francisco Marcos, to assemble a roster that his successor, Jim Lennox, led to the 1977 NCAA title.

On to the Pros

By 1996, the 33-year-old Finn had determined that he was ready to step up and coach at the professional level of play.

Well aware of his protégé's coaching strengths and assured of his loyalty, in 1976, now-Dallas Tornado coach Al Miller hired him as his assistant coach. In short order, the Liekoski methodology was imprinted when he departed Dallas and become head coach of outdoor and indoor teams in Houston (1978) and Edmonton (1980) and indoor teams in New Jersey (1981), Cleveland (1982), and Canton (OH) (1989).

Looking Back

Recounting his first years as a professional coach, Timo cited that a large part of the coaching at that level is devoted to man management as well managing the media. "If you made a mistake of some sort at the college level basically it became something for you to sort out. Unfortunately at the professional level, the media nails you for your mistakes. Looking back, I could have used some more preparation to develop an expertise in dealing with the media."[44]

To some degree, that issue was mitigated when, in 1982, he was hired to coach the MISL Cleveland Force, who had employed media savvy Al Miller as general manager. One legacy of that move was that the Liekoski family (wife Katie and son Eric) established roots in Cleveland.

With the demise of the NASL in 1984, it was the U.S. indoor game that sought to keep professional soccer alive. The Force averaged more than 12,000 fans and reached the MISL playoffs each season. But by 1988, ownership folded the team.

Jumping off to coach the Canton (OH) Invaders of the new American Indoor Soccer Association in 1988, the Finn was twice named AISL COY while leading the team to successive titles.

U.S. Soccer and the 1994 World Cup

"He [Milutinovic] had the press in the palm of his hand!" –Liekoski

By 1991, and with U.S. Soccer focusing on preparing the national team for play at the 1994 World Cup, the well-seasoned Liekoski was exposed to coaching at the international level when he was hired as one of Bora Milutinovic's assistant coaches.

The assignment proved to be a valuable experience for Liekoski. "He was a master at player management," recalled Timo. It was among the many strengths that the Serbian coach shared with Timo and the coaching staff. "He also had but one fitness session where the ball was not involved; 90% of the training involved intrasquad play followed by meetings where that session was very thoroughly analyzed."

Citing the coaching experience that led the U.S. Team to qualify for the second round of World Cup play as "unique," Timo was particularly impressed with one facet of Milutinovic's expertise, noting that "He had the press in the palm of his hand!"

Following the World Cup, U.S. Soccer hired Timo to oversee preparation of its U-23 team for play leading up to the 1996 Atlanta Olympic soccer competition. While details are a bit sketchy, some are of the opinion that U.S. Soccer had in mind the hire of the University of Virginia's Bruce Arena, who was coming off winning his fourth successive NCAA Division I title. That conjecture became reality and in 1995, Arena was hired and Liekoski was replaced as U-23 coach. That, in turn, led to a return to his native Finland in 1997.

Back to the Homeland

Lost in the history of U.S. soccer coaching is the fact that Timo Liekoski, in returning to Finland, became the first American educated coach to be hired to coach a European professional team. Upon his return to Finland, Pertti Alaja, who had been his goalkeeper in Edmonton for two years, had become the General Secretary of the Finnish Federation. It was he who hired Timo in 1998 to coach the professional MyPa (Myllykosken Pallo) team that competed in the country's first division. Liekoski resigned MyPa in 1999 and joined the Finnish FA, where he coached for nine years.

Terming his time with the Finnish FA "his best job," Timo served the Federation as assistant coach of the national team with an emphasis on preparing its U-15 through U-19 youth teams for UEFA competitions.

Current Austin FC player Alexander Ring is a player developed during the Liekoski tenure and, in addition to MLS play, was also a mainstay on the Finland's national team for many years.

Returning to the States in 2010, Timo has made appearances at U.S. Soccer and United Soccer Coaches coaching schools and is quietly applying his passion to the game of golf, where he regularly walks 18 holes whenever weather permits, which is every day than ends in "Y."

Jim Lennox Lessens Walt's Workload

It was when coaching at Mitchell (CT) Junior College that Jim Lennox enrolled and earned his USSF A coaching license under Walt Chyzowych. In 1975, he was appointed to the USSF staff, a position he held for 20 years.

By 1979, the bit-overwhelmed Chyzowych had lessened his load and, recognizing his administrative capability, appointed Lennox coordinator of the USSF Coaching Schools.

In this role, he would assign to coaching courses from an impressive and diverse group of USSF staff coaches.

The NSCAA Academy Program – An Educational Alternative

One issue that was addressed in the leadup to January 1984 was that the new program would roll out as the "NSCAA Academy Program" to signify that its objective was focused on coaching education.

Perhaps at long last a seminal moment arrived for the NSCAA in 1981 at a midyear meeting of the group's Executive Board in Ojai, California, when the organization moved to formalize its educational component into what became its Coaching Academy Program.

Peter Gooding recalled the instance when the concept took hold: "A number of us were talking informally about coaching education that existed through the USSF Coaching Schools. As some had experienced the USSF schools, there was sentiment that their educational culture was wrong. Joe Morrone was particularly critical, citing the emphasis on candidate's playing ability while others remarked about a dismissive attitude by some staff towards candidates."[45a]

"You Guys Are Making a Big Mistake!"

Out of that informal meeting emerged the idea for NSCAA to develop its own coaching education initiative, with chairman Gooding appointed to investigate the concept.

In the spring of 1983, in Chicago, the chair convened a Blue Ribbon Committee to address the various issues surrounding the startup of a new coaching scheme. On hand were Bob Gansler, Jim Lennox, and Jerry Yeagley. "Bob and Jim were USSF staff members and there had been some sort of 'dust up' within the staff as the result of Walt [Chyzowych] leaving the Federation," explained Gooding.

Peter asked and Jim Lennox agreed to draft a course curriculum so that by the fall it could be presented first to the Executive Board for adaption and then shared with those attending the organization's annual January business meeting in Chicago.

Sigi Schmid was a Coaching Schools instructor.

Timo Liekoski was a valued Coaching Schools instructor.

Bob Gansler eventually ascended to head the Coaching Schools.

Graham Ramsey was an early Cramer/Chyzowych disciple.

Jay Hoffman was proud to wear the USSF badge at the Coaching Schools.

One issue that was addressed in the leadup to January 1984 was that the new program would roll out as the "NSCAA Academy Program" to signify that its objective was focused on coaching education. Further, candidates, upon successful completion of their course work, would be issued "coaching diplomas" rather than be licensed per the USSF model.

Gooding presented the Academy proposal at the annual meeting. He remembers there was some ambivalence among the membership, particularly those whose coaching allegiance was tied to USSF. "We recessed and in the restroom I remember Boosh Miller telling me, 'You guys are making a big mistake.'" After some discussion centered on the program's philosophy and the details of its launch, the Academy was ready for implementation.

Philosophically, the new initiative featured a more collaborative approach between the candidates and the coaching staff. This approach sought to turn out candidates who, by week's end, were better equipped to impart soccer knowledge to their players and who also had an appreciation of the role coaches play in the lives of those individuals.

Gooding – The Academy Advocate

"Peter has been an advocate of friendly cooperation between Academy candidates and the teaching staff " –Jeff Tipping

Peter Gooding was the ideal American coach to have been entrusted to orchestrate and bring the Academy Program to fruition.

He was well organized and well spoken. Further, having been born and raised in Islington, England, he was a product of that country's soccer culture. In turn, by the 1980s, he also was well versed in how U.S. soccer was evolving and what was needed to continue its future progress.

Jeff Tipping's comments reflect the important Academy role played by coach Gooding: "The coaches association has been fortunate to have Peter Gooding as an ally during some turbulent periods." He added, "he and the Academy also provided an opportunity for other coaching education programs, like The English FA, to emulate the collegiality shared between teaching staff and candidate." [45b]

Peter Gooding addressing an Academy course.

"None of the success of the Academy could have been done without Peter Gooding's vision *and* his understanding that people learn much better when they are treated as friends and colleagues. Peter, more than anyone else, illustrated the difference, at that time, between the NSCAA and the USSF's approach to coaching education. Although his work was done quietly, nothing would have happened without Peter's involvement. His talent for organization, administration and, especially, diplomacy are especially noteworthy."

The First Academies

Historically, the importance of the Academy Program was that it allowed NSCAA for the first time to establish a formal program of coaching education. One of the original goals of organization's formation, in 1941, was for its leadership to improve the standard of U.S. coaching education.

Over time, meeting that objective evolved, but in a less than systematic manner. The staging of clinics was largely left to the good intentions of individual members.

With the launch of the Academy Program, NSCAA was able to offer its membership a benefit that focused on coaching education on a residential and non-residential basis.

Jim Lennox was appointed the Academy's first director of coaching, and the Academy debuted at Duke University in the summer of 1984. Lennox's staff included Bob Gansler, Doug May, and Jay Miller. A second Academy was held at Quincy (IL) College later that summer. In all, a combined 53 coaches enrolled in the two courses.

In 1989, the first special topic course was staged in Rochester (NY). Anson Dorrance, Doug May, and Jeff Tipping dissected midfield play over the course of a weekend. Later, special topic courses focused on goalkeeping and play in various thirds of the field.

As agreed, the Academy director position had a term limit, and, in 1989, Notre Dame coach Mike Berticelli was named director. Upon his untimely passing in 1990, his assistant, Mike Parsons, was elevated to the post. In 1996, Jeff Tipping became the part-time director, and six years later he became the Academy program's first full-time director.

Until his retirement in 2019, Peter Gooding, as a senior staff member, served as the Academy's site coordinator at a majority of the residential courses. In that role he sought, at each course and in a light-hearted manner, to decrease candidate anxiety and also keep the courses on schedule. Generally he served to "mother hen them" each week—a role he assumed in unique fashion. It also fell to Peter to handle most of the classroom lectures.

Jim Lennox and the Soccer Academy

As noted, it was Jim Lennox who, in 1982, drafted the coaching curriculum for the new NSCAA Coaching Academy Program. Later, one of his former Hartwick assistants, Jape Shattuck, was also instrumental in fine-tuning other aspects of the NSCAA Academy curriculum.

"We knew that the USSF Schools' playing requirement was a problem and I think that basically the NSCAA curriculum was designed to allow a coach to become the best coach he could be irrespective of playing ability," said Lennox in offering a comparison.

Jim Lennox (right) and Jape Shattuck both coached at Hartwick College and combined efforts with the NSCAA Academy Program.

The first two Academy residential courses designed by coach Lennox were the National Diploma Course and the Advanced National Diploma Course. In participating in the residential courses, the candidates were reminded that valuations were based on coaching effectiveness.

Jeff Tipping – The Humorist

Much like Walt Chyzowych, Jeff Tipping struck a chord with the many Academy coaches he dealt with.

In 1983, Jeff Tipping was tabbed by Lennox, his former coach at Hartwick College to join the Academy coaching staff. In 1996, the Muhlenberg (PA) College coach earned his U.S. Soccer A coaching license and began part-time service as the NSCAA Director of Coaching. With his coaching reputation well established, he also served as a technical advisor to the 1998 U.S. Women's National Team. In 2002, he left Muhlenberg and become the first full-time NSCAA Director of Coaching. He served in that role position until January 2011.

Much like Walt Chyzowych, Jeff Tipping struck a chord with the many Academy coaches he dealt with. They respected the dedication and creativity he brought

Jeff Tipping would help launch the Academy program and later would become its first full-time director.

to the Academy program. And he accomplished his work with an added sense of humor.

One recalls watching the opening of one of his pre-residential course staff videos, where he spliced in a BBC interview with English coach Harry Redknapp. Seems the always-twitchy Redknapp was trying to respond to the interviewer's questions while his players were humorously kicking soccer balls at him. As the interview unraveled, so did Harry, uttering an expletive that had the Academy staff howling!

The Expansive Academy Program

An excellent clinician, Tipping, as the Academy's full-time director, proved to be creative in terms of the implementing an expanded NSCAA coaching curriculum.

In staging the variety of courses, they all met the stated fundamental objectives of the NSCAA Coaching Academy Program:

- To introduce the coach to the NSCAA's "Network of Support." Hopefully coaches will see the NSCAA as a family and utilize the organization's resources to grow personally and professionally.
- To recognize that soccer is a player's game and should be played with minimal coaching interference.

- To help the American coach develop the skills necessary to address the specific needs of the American player.
- To develop awareness in American coaches of the need for continued growth and study in the coaching profession; to become a skillful coach.
- To reinforce the concept that if the American game is to prosper that its coaches must have instructional, managerial, and promotional skills superior to those of coaches from other countries.

Soon after introducing the two residential courses, three new non-residential courses were offered, including
- the Parent-Coach Diploma, for coaches of players 5-8 years old,
- the State Diploma, for coaches of players 5-10 years of age, and
- the Regional Diploma, for coaches of youth/high school players 11-18 years of age.

During his directorship, Jeff Tipping was noted for bringing a variety of courses to fruition, all of which were designed to meet the varied needs of the NSCAA membership.

Seeking Improved NSCAA – USSF Relations

It was following his appointment as the first fulltime NSCAA Director of Coaching that Jeff Tipping sought to develop improved communication between the USSF Coaching Schools and the NSCAA Academy Program. Over time, the split between the Association and the USSF became less contentious. In fact, several coaches instructed in both programs.

That included Jeff Tipping. "When I became NSCAA Director of Coaching, I was invited in as a guest instructor by U.S. Soccer ... thanks to a very friendly Bobby Howe. We invited Bobby to do a session at the National Convention and the relationship between the two organizations became less tenuous. I found the Federation coaches to be welcoming and very competent. I had heard some disparaging things about the way the USSF treated their candidates with rigor. ... but I saw none of that at the USSF coaching schools. I did, actually, take the USSF B and A licenses myself when I was still playing pro. I did an awful lot of the demonstrations at the coaching schools."

He also feels that there might have been a slight change in the USSF methodology based on the Academy instructional approach. "I think the USSF staff found that it was unrealistic to have American coaches in their late forties and fifties run around like 20-year-olds and my observation was that the NSCAA approach had, somewhat, leaked over to the Federation and the wind, somewhat wisely, changed direction for each group."[47]

Seeking Staff Diversification

One major objective achieved in the Tipping administration was to increase the diversity of the Academy coaching staff. In time, a number of women, Hispanic, and black coaches were identified and appointed.

One of the major annual organizational honors is the presentation of the Mike Berticelli Award. It is presented to someone who has demonstrated excellence in coaching. On four occasions, its recipient has been a woman Academy staff member, including Nancy Feldman (2010), Laura Kerrigan (2012), Kim Sutton (2013), and Cyndi Goodwin (2017).

A second major issue facing all of U.S. soccer is how to effectively communicate information, coaching or otherwise, to its various communities.

To effectuate expansion of the Academy program, Tipping identified 13 regional technical directors to serve as advocates for the various courses, particularly non-residential courses. In turn, the regional appointees, in an attempt to break down the country into manageable sub-regions, helped form state coaching staffs. In addition to arranging to teach more localized offerings, the regional directors served as conduits for NSCAA members wishing to arrange courses. In many cases, such individuals were identified through attainment of excellent performances at Academy residential courses. Later, most were assigned to teach in the residential courses.

Seeking International Collaboration

Seeking to expand the influence of the NSCAA Academy, another Tipping public relations achievement was the development of domestic and international partnership initiatives.

In one instance, Jeff's wife, Christine, through her earlier service as the public relations officer for the Liverpool Football Club, introduced her husband to various members of the club's coaching staff who, in turn, proved to be valued contacts when the Academy later arranged tours for U.S. coaches to Great Britain and other European countries.

These initiatives included strengthening relationships with U.S. and international coaching associations. In particular, Tipping credits Scotland's Andy Roxburgh, former technical director for Scotland and UEFA, and his Scottish successor, Craig Brown, with having impacted his oversight of Academy affairs.

With Roxburgh, the Association developed an arrangement whereby any "American" coach with a distinguished pass grade in the Premier Diploma could take a UEFA B License.

"At that time there was definite interest amongst the Europeans to developments in the U.S. This was a high water mark for the exchange of ideas as numerous European coach educators became fascinated in not only the development of American soccer, but also the organizational philosophy and management of American [NFL] football."[48]

One outcome of the Academy outreach was that international coaches annually presented at NSCAA Conventions after having appeared as guest instructors at winter Academy programs in Florida. Included were coaches from Brazil, Mexico, the United Kingdom, and Europe. Meanwhile, Tipping (and the NSCAA logo) also appeared at numerous forums in the United States, Europe, and Latin America.

CHAPTER IV

COACHES' ROLES IN SOCCER'S PROGRESS

With major steps having been taken relative to improvement of soccer coaching education, as the sport entered the 1970s there remained other matters of concern that required resolution by the coaching community.

Two topics, while not new, continued to need resolution. The first was the necessity for adjustment of playing rules to meet new competitive challenges in the U.S. game. Allied with it was an ongoing concern for referee identification and development. Progress was reported on both fronts and in many cases was achieved through the collaborative efforts of coaches and referees.

Developed in response to emerging activities on the field and sidelines, codes of ethics were established to guide coaches as to what constituted acceptable behavior. Communication and enforcement of such guidelines lingered through the 1970s and remains a concern today especially in the greatly expanded youth segment of the game.

Meanwhile, the creative development of the soccer camp initiative, driven by coaches, has proven to be another means to improve player development while contributing to the establishment of a vast new U.S. business.

As coaches sought to identify new avenues to promote the game, the expansion of its nationwide awards program and a huge streamlining of its annual convention have proved to be effective creativities in bringing greater U.S. exposure for soccer.

What remains is to chronicle the exemplary efforts of specific coaches to develop the game in various geographic areas of this country.

Coaches and the Soccer Rules

One of the issues that has been divisive among the game's U.S. aficionados has been the divergence between the playing rules governing interscholastic and intercollegiate levels of play in this country versus the FIFA edicts that regulate worldwide play, including, of course, competitions of its U.S. Soccer affiliate.

There have been reasons for this departure, and they can be laid at the feet of various soccer coaches who, among other challenges, took it upon themselves to give oversight to soccer rules implementation and their execution.

Encouragingly, as the game has become more sophisticated within U.S. schools and colleges, a perusal of their rulebooks indicates a trend in those ruling bodies towards greater adherence to the FIFA standards.

Doug Stewart and Early Rules Oversight

... he [Stewart] cautioned that certain psychological factors were required in order for neophyte officials to become successful – including courage of one's convictions.

As the long-standing editor of *Soccer Guide* and a member of the USSFA rules committee, Doug Stewart was very influential in serving as soccer's high priest" when it came to knowledge and interpretation of soccer's playing rules. The initial *Guides* were published by the A.G. Spaulding Company and, beginning in 1914, featured annual updates of competitions sponsored by the United States Soccer Football Association (USSFA). Most importantly, the *Guides* annually published any updates to FIFA's 17 laws of the game that initially ruled intercollegiate play.

Beginning in 1921, the annual publication was retitled, "Spaulding's Official College Soccer Football Guide," with Stewart cited as its editor. The periodical was published by the National Collegiate Athletic Association (NCAA), and that body also assumed oversight of rules controlling intercollegiate play. Publicizing the laws became the responsibility of the Intercollegiate Soccer Football Association of America (ISFAA).

Thereafter, and until after World War II, Stewart published the game's rules with accompanying instructions to players and referees as to their interpretation. The *Guides* also listed the NCAA Soccer Committee members. Initially, those individuals were college athletic directors. Gradually, in the 1920s and 1930s, the names of noted coaches began to appear as NCAA Soccer Committee members. The list included coaches Robert Dunn (Swarthmore), Tom Dent (Dartmouth), Allison Marsh (Amherst), Nicholas Bawlfe (Cornell), and Walter McCloud (Trinity). Dent and Marsh, along with Stewart, were cited as serving on the group's referee subcommittee.

As part of his earliest seasonal reviews, Stewart bemoaned the poor state of officiating, frequently urging readers to encourage former players to become officials, though he cautioned that certain psychological factors were required in order for neophyte officials to become successful, including courage of one's convictions. Later, *Guides* listed the statewide names and affiliations of soccer referees.

By the early 1930s, and as more colleges sponsored soccer teams, there began deviations from FIFA rules. First, matches began to be played in 22-minute quarters. Further, three substitutions were allowed, with one of those allowed to be resubstituted. By 1933, the rulebook included what later became *approved rulings* that served to *amplify* the rule. These amplifications were located in the margins alongside the rule itself.

In 1941, the substitution rule was amended to allow for five players coming off the bench, with three of those permitted to reenter the game. The 1943 rulebook mentioned that there was concern among coaches related to interpretation of the throw-in rule. Later, in1945, the rulebook sought to bring clarity to the offside rule by publishing 21 illustrations dedicated to that perplexing subject.

Post-World War II Rules/Officiating

Meanwhile, with mayhem rampant, other relatively less important facets of soccer were given far more attention by neophyte officials.

As soccer play expanded following World War II, several intertwined issues emerged.

In many cases, there weren't enough experienced soccer coaches to fill the positions nor was there the needed supply of qualified referees to control games played by older men who were more prone to physical mayhem than exhibitions of skillful soccer.

In order to staff the increasing number of matches, the rules advocated that a single referee be assisted by two linespersons, whose primary function was to wave a flag/towel to indicate balls played out of touch or over the goal line. The NSCAA encouraged referees to join membership and, in particular, two officials, Jimmy Walder and Harry Rodgers, represented their segment of the soccer community in the organization.

FIFA had long endorsed the three-person system of officiating, but by 1947, Walder and Rodgers, aided by coaches Dent and Larry Briggs, offered an alternative, having designed a two-person or dual system of officiating. It borrowed from the mechanics utilized in basketball officiating. By the 1950s, the two-person system was endorsed for use in college and high school soccer. It is worth noting that in 1947 the rulebook stated that officials needed to emphasize that the charging of the goalkeeper rule did not include what appeared to be football-type blocks that were increasingly sending many net minders to the sidelines.

Earle Waters, veteran coach at West Chester State (PA), had strong opinions on various soccer matters, including any wide deviations from FIFA rule standards. When asked whether the present game needed any rule changes to make it more interesting or compatible to the American fan, coach Waters emphatically countered with, "Absolutely not! ... The world set up the rules. The world set up the size of the field, the markings, etc., all the rest of that is a bunch of crap!" Obviously, tampering with the rules was not part of his thinking.[49]

Changing the Face of the U.S. Game

The implementation of such stark departures from FIFA rules (along with other antagonisms) prompted the USSFA in 1962 to suspend the voting rights of the NCAA and the ISFAA for two years!

But it turned out that Waters' stance was not that of the NCAA Soccer Committee of 1950. Alfred A. Smith, longtime coach at Philadelphia's Germantown Friends

Academy, had succeeded Doug Stewart as *Guide* editor. Bill Jeffrey of Penn State was chairman of the NCAA Soccer Committee when it began in 1950 to invoke a series of rule changes that, in retrospect, had soccer purists shaking their heads. The modifications were offered in part to curb play in post-war games that were increasingly marked by rough play and inconsistent application of the rules by referees, many of whom came into the ranks from the gridiron game where physical contact was the norm. Meanwhile, with mayhem rampant, other relatively less important facets of soccer were given far more attention by neophyte officials.

A case in point was attention given by referees to the throw-in. By 1950, and in order to combat the number of whistles dedicated to enforcing proper technique of throwing the ball in from touch, the rules makers replaced the throw-in with an indirect kick from touch. Whatever its merits, the free kick now effectively lessened the value of the corner kick and further endangered the goalkeeper position due to the number of balls that were flighted into the goal area. A second new rule emphasis was that of fouling of the goalkeeper in the goal area, particularly when he was taking his four steps and in possession of the ball. If whistled, the infraction was an indirect kick offense. It should be noted that prior to inserting the four-step rule, a goalkeeper could dribble (per the basketball technique) the ball without restriction, leaving it to the officials' judgment whether he was wasting time or not.

Another rule that was frequently misapplied was that pertaining to what constituted a handball. The 1950 rules committee adopted the FIFA statute that stipulated only an *intentional* handball should be penalized. FIFA also stipulated a "play on" when a ball hit an official during play; it became a dead ball under NCAA rules. Later, the FIFA rule was adopted.

In 1958, under chairman James Reed of Princeton, another major change took place when a semicircular area with a 36-yard radius replaced the rectangular penalty area. The committee felt that some officials were reluctant to whistle penalty kicks when the infraction occurred on the outer edges of the rectangular area. With the circular area, that factor was eliminated! Because of its injury component, and also because of its uneven enforcement, the committee also eliminated the slide tackle from the game. The Committee allowed for shoes sporting nylon studs with steel tips, and time-wasting was minimized as the clock was stopped on all dead balls in the game's last 10 minutes. Further, as a means for greater spectator appreciation of the game, officials were instructed to use approved signals to indicate what type of foul was committed.

The implementation of such stark departures from FIFA rules (along with other antagonisms) prompted the USSFA in 1962 to suspend the voting rights of the NCAA and the ISFAA for two years!

Largely due to the work of rules committee member Larry Briggs, the New England Soccer League Officials group was organized. That was a precursor of coaches' seeking to become involved in raising officiating standards.

As equipment changed, so did the rules. Molded, soled shoes with plastic studs were approved in 1959, and officials were again advised to recognize and penalize rough play, including penalizing illegal charges on the goalkeeper with a direct kick. It seemed that officials could never win. At times they were criticized for too many whistles. By 1960, they were being encouraged to withhold whistles on "play on" situations.

As mentioned, the NCAA rules committee had for many years formed an officials subcommittee dedicated to upgrading the level of officiating. Until 1955, Earle Waters served as a one-man committee, annually rating officials in the *Guides* "acceptable" for college assignments or "others."

By 1961, the ISFAA formed a committee headed by Drexel assistant coach Al Laverson that listed approved officials within each state. The ISFAA also urged officials to form local soccer officials' organizations, with the thought that creation of such groupings allowed for improved communication between rules governing bodies, which, in turn, resulted in greater uniformity of rules enforcement.

The Substitution Rule

Perhaps no NCAA or National Federation of State High School Associations (NFHS) rules that have long been contentious between so-called soccer purists and those instituting rules for play in educational settings are statutes related to player substitution.

To some degree, the USSFA stance on substitution was related to a sense that players from educational institutions were compromised when competing for spots on its national teams because their development was thwarted by having played under less restricted substitution rulings. However, it appears that in 1947,

USSFA, under its president Jimmie McGuire, and in an effort to help Americanize the sport, agreed to set aside the FIFA standard and allow 15-man playing rosters, including allowance for player resubstitution. The change prompted a pro and con written debate between McGuire and traditionalist Jimmy Walder in that year's *Soccer Journal*. Shortly thereafter, USSFA returned to honor FIFA's rule edicts.

In relation to FIFA rule adjustments, the posture of the coaching community was twofold. On the one hand, they collectively were dedicated to utilizing soccer as part of the overall educational experience for their student-athletes. Thus, the greater number of players exposed to competitively playing the game, the better. Secondarily, by exposing as many young athletes to the game as possible, they were also trying to promote it within the U.S. sporting audience. As an aside, some purists charged coaches with trying, through the free substitution rule, to exert undue influence on the play of a game that they felt was "a players' game."

Whatever was one's stance, by 1958 the NCAA rulebook was modified to indicate that only 16 players could participate in a game, and those players could be resubstituted without limitation. However, the rule also indicated that the matter was left to schools to adjudicate when cementing game contracts with other schools.

The NCAA Versus FIFA Rules Debate

The debate between those who hold that only FIFA Laws should govern the entirety of soccer competition in this country versus those who support the actuality of various modifications to those international rules that regulate play for school/ college levels of U.S. soccer is complicated, but explainable, according to Cliff McCrath, former long-time secretary-rules editor for the NCAA Rules Committee.

Cliff notes that he and others on the rules body had long been advocates for greater adherence to FIFA-like rules adoption, especially for Division I and II levels of scholarship-supported play. By way of explanation as to what many termed "the status quo," he noted, "Two factors that continue to influence (reinforce?) the current formula - and, therefore, assurances that things are NOT going to change are: 1. We were informed in the mid-80s meetings that if we adopted FIFA Laws there would no longer be any need for an NCAA rules committee. It was their position that if we adopted the FIFA laws of the game, the 'control' of the game –

for collegiate purposes – would no longer allow the collegiate bodies to shape the game in keeping with the educational purposes the NCAA is sworn to uphold. 2. Perhaps, more significant, is the fact that NCAA would then not allow federated rules [playing rules for different levels of play] which, in addition to the chaos created when a DII school plays a DIII . . . is the fact that DIII by constitution is a non-scholarship (participation) membership which, for example, will never tolerate limited substitutions."[50]

The former Seattle Pacific coach finished his historical account of rules development with a note that every soccer coach who has chaired the NCAA Rules Committee during his tenure has desired to change/vary the substitution rule, but the NCAA Executive Committee through its PROP (playing rules oversight panel) always retreated to the safety (and sanctity?) of the NCAA's lifelong adherence to not surrender control and denied implementation of any FIFA-like change to the rules governing soccer play.

The Birth of NISOA and 1960s Rule Changes

"I tried to convince him that we should toss a coin..." –Joe Machnik

Shown here are many members of NISOA celebrating the induction of veteran Harry Rodgers (center, first row) into the organization's Hall of Fame.

With the NFHS adopting somewhat modified NCAA rules for secondary school play, the NCAA rules committee in 1963 added James Neely of Lancaster (PA) High School as a secondary schools representative.

Also that year, three soccer coaches were very influential in the formation of the National Intercollegiate Soccer Officials Association (NISOA). Prompted by New England soccer stalwart Larry Briggs, Princeton's Jimmy Reed and then-Middlebury College coach Joe Morrone joined forces with referees Paul Bourdeau, John Kalloch, Albie Loeffler, Harry Rodgers, Bill Rosenthal, and Jimmy Walder to form NISOA. Morrone composed the organization's initial constitution and by-laws and served as the organization's president in 1971. Many credit coach Briggs for significant work on rules refinement and improvement of soccer officiating standards during the post-World War II period.

LARRY BRIGGS

Larry Briggs' home base was at the University of Massachusetts where, beginning in 1930, he served as soccer coach for the next 37 seasons. But outside of coaching, it was in soccer officiating that perhaps he had his greatest impact on the game.

That included founding the Pioneer Valley Soccer Officials Association (PVSOA) in 1942. It is in his honor that the PVSOA annually presents the Briggs Award to that individual who has contributed to the game in its locale.

Three years later, in 1945, Briggs coordinated with respected officials Walder and Rodgers in the development of the dual system of officiating. In 1955, Larry began coordination of the annual New England regional clinics for coaches and referees. Two years later, in 1957, he helped form the New England Intercollegiate Soccer Officials Organization and shortly thereafter was coordinator of its referee evaluation system. Nationally, from 1960-64, and as a member of its rules committee, he was busy revising the format of the NCAA rulebook.

Perhaps his foremost accomplishments occurred in 1963 when he and a group of fellow coaches and referees formed the National Intercollegiate Soccer Officials Association. Considered by many the "Father of NISOA," Briggs established the first referee assignment committee for soccer officials and developed its first soccer officiating mechanics film in 1964. For his efforts at upgrading intercollegiate soccer officiating, he received the NISOA Honor Award in 1967 and was inducted into the NISOA Hall of Fame in 2001.

A founding member of the National Soccer Coaches Association of America in 1941, he served as its president in 1947. He earlier had helped edit its first newsletter that subsequently morphed into today's *Soccer Journal*. He was presented the NSCAA Honor Award in 1950, and in 1978 he was inducted into the National Soccer Hall of Fame as builder of the game. Later, in 1991, Briggs was a charter member of the NSCAA Hall of Fame.

The 1960s also witnessed further refinement with adoption of rules dealing with such matters as game delay by goalkeepers, the number and make of balls utilized in games, and clock stoppages (after goals, injuries, etc.).

In 1963, rules makers returned to the rectangular penalty area and the throw-in from touch and restricted substitution to when the ball was out of play over the goal line. That was followed by an attempt to institute a means of fairly deciding tied matches. In 1965, it was ruled that if matches were tied after four overtime periods, the team having earned the greater number of corner kicks was declared the winner.

Joe Machnik recalls coaching a Long Island University team versus Michigan State in the 1966 NCAA semifinal that finished 2-2 in regulation. LIU advanced on corner kicks, 7-6. He also noted that the 1970 NAIA Tournament game between New Haven and Davis & Elkins finished 0-0, with D&E advancing with a goal in the eighth overtime. "One of the referees was the legendary Pat Smith. I tried to convince him that we should toss a coin, which was a more humane tie-breaker than multiple overtimes!"

Remember Harry Rodgers? In 1967, he was named the national rules interpreter. That same year, the clock was stopped in the last three minutes of the fourth quarter when the ball was out of play. A year later, officials were expected to report on those players scoring goals and assists while also making certain that coaching took place from restricted areas only. They were also allowed to caution non-participants. The slide tackle? It was now back in play, with the defender having to contact the ball first; otherwise, it became a direct kick offense.

In 1969, with Bob Baptista of Wheaton as rules chair, the committee ruled that on an injury, one player from each team could be subbed, and the subtlety of what constituted a legal and an illegal charge was given added emphasis.

Rule Modifications in the 1970s

The red and yellow cards had been introduced at the 1970 World Cup in Mexico and they became part of the NCAA rules in 1974.

Several refinements crept into the NCAA playing rules in the 1970s.

Led by its executive director, Dr. Ray Bernabei, by 1972 NISOA had formally established officials' chapters throughout most of the country. Bernabei also designed hand signals that were adopted principally to inform spectators of the nature of various infractions.

Under chair Julie Menendez, coach at San Jose State, several changes to the rules occurred in the mid-1970s, including in 1973 when FIFA's 17 Laws were combined into seven sections. Included in the appointments to the rules body was the 1975 naming of Seattle Pacific coach Cliff McCrath to the committee as its recording secretary, a role he assumed for the next 39 years.

The big change was that, in 1973, the rules body aligned itself with FIFA in that if a game was tied following regulation in-season play, there was to be no overtime play. However, there was an overtime formula for advancing during postseason play.

The following year, the substitution rule stated that only 16 players could be utilized and they could be resubstituted without restriction (the number was upped to 18 two years later). Again, by mutual agreement, schools could set aside the 16-player limitation. Substitutes had to have been reported to the scorer's table prior to entry, and numbers were required on uniform shorts for the first time. The rules body retracted its "no overtime rules" of the previous year and inserted that two 10-minute overtime periods were to be played when matches were tied following regulation play.

The red and yellow cards had been introduced at the 1970 World Cup in Mexico, and they became part of the NCAA rules in 1974.

There was obvious disagreement within the NCAA Rules Committee regarding a disqualified player. In 1976, a red-carded player could be replaced, but the next year it was ruled that the player could *not* be replaced! In 1976, the committee established the dual system of officiating as mandatory, but by 1979, *either* the dual or diagonal officiating was approved for play. Years later, the committee inserted the word "recommended," as in, "It is recommended that the diagonal system of officiating shall be used."

By 1981, a red card was to be issued for violent play and, without warning, the offending player was required to leave the premises, which left his team left with no substitution option. Ungentlemanly conduct, on the other hand, *could* be carded, but with a yellow card. Also, by then the home team was required to wear light-colored jerseys and stockings, and the visiting team would wear dark jerseys and stockings. Also, by 1981, with overtime play back and NCAA berths at stake, an overtime loss in the tiebreaker reverted to a tie for tournament selection purposes.

Heading into the 1980s found the NCAA Committee allowing synthetic soccer balls for play though it specified that three balls of the same type were to be utilized during a match. With play becoming a bit more refined, it was recommended that colleges/schools upgrade and install electronic scoreboards for time-keeping purposes.

By 1981, the rulebook included sample situations that clarified the application of a given rule in typical game circumstances. In trying to create a more soccer-like environment for matches, the recommended referee uniforms were moving away from the earlier typical football style wear (striped shirt, white knickers) to black shorts and various contrasting colored jerseys depending on the uniforms worn by the competing teams.

One rule that was introduced in the 1981 rulebook but never implemented harked back to the earliest days of high school play when a goal counted as two points and a penalty kick one point. Whatever the reasoning, the rule never made it from the book onto the field.

"Dr. Joe" Machnik

"Some things you don't forget!" –Joe Machnik

Since 2013, it has been through the medium of televised soccer that the name of Dr. Joe Machnik has become synonymous with soccer rules and their interpretation. Whatever the level of play, and on various networks, "Doctor Joe," as he has become known, has been called on to share his expertise with viewers following referee calls as they emerge during matches.

It should be noted that he accumulated a fine coaching record, including leading Long Island University to three consecutive NCAA Tournaments from 1965-67, including a loss in

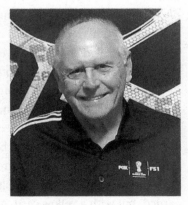

Joe Machnik has worn many "soccer hats," including serving as a rule interpreter on FOX soccer telecasts.

the 1966 final. His New Haven University men reached the NCAA DII final round in 1976-77.

His initial interest in officiating came as a result of refereeing numerous intramural sports at Long Island University. Later, at New Haven University, and not wanting to waste his Sundays, he began officiating USSF matches in the highly competitive leagues along the New England coastline.

When his collegiate coaching subsided, his assignments expanded when he became an NISOA collegiate official in June 1984. He vividly recalls the year he received membership: "Both Ray and Walt [Klivecka and Chyzowych] were helping administer the NSCAA All-Star match at West Point and wanted me to officiate the game. However, late in the going I was told that I needed to be a NISOA member to do so. So I journeyed up to Springfield (MA) the week of the game and took the rules test. Some things you don't forget!"[51]

For the next few years, Joe worked collegiate games, including the 1988 NCAA Division I final between Howard and Indiana universities. He noted that he is the only person to have played (1965-LIU), coached (1966-LIU and 1976-New Haven), and officiated in NCAA Division I final matches.

It was in 1978 that Joe also began to work part-time with Major League Indoor Soccer (MISL) as head of its referees and director of operations. He continued refereeing at various levels until his retirement in 1999.

Beginning in1996, he was hired by Major League Soccer as its VP of Game Operations and Director of the Office of Officiating Services. Since he retired in 2012, a host of changes have been instituted that have brought greater accountability and continued refinement of the performance of the league's game officials.

Dr. Joe's Recalls on Rules and Rulings[52]

- The early game allowed for the goalkeeper to be fairly charged while in possession of the ball and inside the goal area. You saw goalkeepers turn their body in anticipation of this charge as on-field players attempted to knock them and the ball into the goal. I believe that was the purpose of the Goal Area.

- This aspect of the game has been slowly weeded out to the point that goalkeepers now are almost "untouchables" and that they often take advantage of this status and use it to their advantage.

- Referee approved signals appeared in the NCAA rulebooks and were amended over time.
- The use of the whistle in the dual system was most annoying for players and spectators, as the whistle had to be sounded on every out of bounds. Too many whistles take away from the whistles that are important.
- Many colleges agreed to use more than the allotted substitutions, especially in NCAA Division III. I remember teams having 30-plus players on the bench and massive substitutions, which could turn the game if playing against a team with fewer players or if a coach had a different philosophy regarding the issue.
- In time, many college coaches had outside ball playing experience and saw the benefits of bringing the game closer to the international game, including going to a diagonal system of control.
- There was resistance by many college officials against the diagonal system ... some believed that two whistles were better than one and others, especially athletic directors, did not want to pay for a third official. New Haven (CT) University led the push in Northeast to go with the diagonal as one of the first schools to use it in regular season games.
- The introduction of synthetic balls, or a leather ball with rubber ribbings, was another cost saving device. The new balls would last longer and keep their shape better than the traditional leather balls. This was due to the fact that they were laminated with a synthetic surface to prevent the absorption of water.

The 1990s and Beyond

Presently, there is little question that the soccer coaching community has been highly influential in providing their best collective efforts at addressing its rules.

By the 1993 season, colleges introduced the FIFA rule back pass that restricted a goalkeeper from accepting teammates' passes other than by their feet. Colleges were also encouraged to experiment in spring matches with a 35-yard offside line as introduced by the NASL in the 1970s and to take another look at the kick-in from touch. Neither alternative gained traction.

By the 1990s, the NCAA committee had recommended that the diagonal (three-man) system be preferred for college matches. The substitution rule, which allows no re-substitution during the first half of matches and one player re-substitution during the second half, had also passed muster. It also permitted referees to intervene when time-wasting was evident.

Handling of recurring unsportsmanlike play on the part of players, coaches, bench personnel, and spectators, as indicated by accumulation of collected red cards, has been left to schools and their conference affiliates to adjudicate. Resultant game suspensions have had some impact on curbing such behavior, as has the introduction of awards to those teams who exemplify good sportsmanship.

The NFHS has tried to bring rules uniformity to schoolboy play by adopting a good percentage of the college rules, though there are numerous modifications based on the needs of its younger players.

Meanwhile, as youth soccer play has supplanted school-sponsored play, its organizing bodies have been unable to rein in poor conduct on the part of coaches and, particularly, overzealous parents towards referees.

In a sense, soccer history is repeating itself. In its earliest days in this country, the sport suffered from not attracting enough qualified officials to oversee play. Today, if unbecoming conduct towards officials is not curbed, soccer's non-professional future is threatened by persons unwilling to either endure or enter officiating's unhealthy atmosphere.

Presently, there is little question that the soccer coaching community has been highly influential in providing their best collective efforts at addressing its rules in hopes of having games played fairly and entertainingly by mitigating instances of unfair implementation of the game's laws.

Tackling Ethics in Coaching

"We all know ... that a soccer coach should be a good boy scout and be noble, kind, considerate, fair, etc. But what we should know is how much competitiveness is too much, what is considered allowable and what is not, when one becomes a stinker by taking advantage of the rules, etc." –Richard Schmelzer

An examination of the first 1941 NSCAA Constitution reveals the intention of the new organization to establish 12 standing committees. Of note, the formation of an ethics committee was not among the listings.

During World War II, many of the leaders of the NSCAA and the ISFAA served in the armed forces, where their behavior was governed by military codes of conduct. In all likelihood, as these men resumed their postwar coaching careers, they observed a host of new colleagues assuming soccer coaching positions. Many such individuals were inexperienced in soccer, including what might stand for proper comportment of themselves or their players. To compound matters, ISFAA concerned itself with issues dealing with collegiate soccer, while NSCAA's membership was open to soccer coaches at all levels of play, though coaches of soccer at the secondary level predominated.

When soccer play expanded in the 1950s, ethical issues arose primarily because some coaches and referees were ill-prepared to fulfill their roles. Particularly at the college level, such concerns as player eligibility and rough play were problems that needed adjudication. Complicating the problem was placement of blame for such behavior on the shoulders on neophyte coaches. Did they condone such unruliness out of ignorance of what were accepted standards of play? Or, did they deliberately encourage behaviors in order to accomplish winning at all costs?

As the game became better organized and more competitive, issues of player eligibility began to emerge, particularly in major cities where ethnic soccer leagues had a foothold and where some of the players manning college rosters had affiliations with their local clubs. Long left undetected, such individuals were finding means to continue to illegally "double dip" (generally also receiving "travel monies") during their college season, generally under assumed names.

Earle Waters on Coach Conduct

Earle Waters, coach at West Chester (PA) State, shared some of his coaching philosophy, which included ethical considerations, when, in 1955, he published an article in *Soccer Journal* bemoaning an issue that had long perplexed him and other professionals: coaching from the sidelines.

Earle Waters (left) poses with the late Tom Fleck. Tom was an All-America selection while playing for Waters at West Chest (PA) State University.

He advised that such behavior should never be condoned in soccer. He stated: "It is extremely questionable whether admonitions given while play is in progress can possibly be of help due to the highly individual nature of our game. For the most part, actions construed as sideline coaching are nothing more than highly partisan enthusiasm running away with an emotionally unstable coach. Though there may be some excuse for his emotional state, there is none for his instability, and he is as much to be criticized for such an ethical lapse. When his actions contribute to violent playing conditions on the field, then he has surely 'coached' or conjured up the mess, and the full weight of the law as outlined under Law V (k) should be brought to bear upon him and his charges. There is no excuse for a coach to 'go into his act' before players and spectators. The coach owes to his team and his institution a degree of dignity which can not be challenged by anyone who might observe him."[53]

Don Yonker – Placing Responsibility

"Avoid scheduling them – like we'd avoid the Plague." –Don Yonker

Waters was not alone in voicing his worry about what seemed to be a lesser assumption of responsibility by a new corps of coaches towards providing proper oversight of player conduct on and off the field.

Newly appointed *Soccer Journal* editor Don Yonker had also become concerned. In a 1954 column, he supported the need for the formation of an NSCAA Ethics Committee as a body that could seek to curb coach and player behavior. Yonker pointed out that while referees had, as their primary duty, to protect the players from serious injury, it was the coach who shouldered ultimate responsibility in the matter of rough, unsportsmanlike play.

"No," wrote Yonker. "If we look into the heart of the matter, we are forced into the realization that the coach – and it is he who is the example for his team, mind you – that sets the scene. Certainly we cannot blame the players who have been taught (or not taught, as the case may be) by their coach along what to them may seem to be approved lines of conduct. Without much doubt their tactics are fostered in the partisan encouragement, the sneering comment, the profane remark, the get-your-opponent-at-all-costs admonition, the caviling and carping attitude with opponents and officials. Thus develops the 'dangerous' side."

He concluded with a call for Ethics Committee attention to the problem. "If one could be sure that such tactics grew out of ignorance, precept and example of fair play set by each opponent would be sufficient to end the massacres. If, however the violent style is deliberately planned, only vocal and written objection to proper authorities will prove effective curbs. Teams, which are so inclined, are no credit to the fair-minded among neither us nor to the institutions they represent. And here, it would seem, is something for our newly-formed ethics committee to ponder."

Alongside publicly identifying teams that did not play according to the spirit of the game, Yonker noted that coaches could also enact another approach: "Avoid scheduling them – like we'd avoid the Plague."[54]

First Ethics Committee

Complicating the address of emerging issues in the game, the 1950s saw the NSCAA in a jurisdictional battle with the ISFAA over the matter of ethics in coaching.

The NSCAA perception was that ISFAA was slow in reacting to emerging problems in the areas of collegiate player eligibility and professionalism.

The NSCAA saw itself as an association of *all* coaches, whereas the ISFA represented strictly collegiate institutions playing the sport. Led by President John Eiler, in 1957 the NSCAA had formed its own Ethics Committee to oversee this area of concern. It was chaired by Don Minnegan of Towson (MD) State.

By 1959, Minnegan's committee issued a report that included several directives to ISFAA on these matters. The first order advised establishment of an educational program focused on ethics in coaching. To that end, the Ethics Committee included in its report a very detailed outline of a soccer code of ethics based on an already existent lacrosse coach's code of ethics that Minnegan had procured as a result of his residing in the lacrosse hotbed of Baltimore.

By 1962, John Eiler had begun a three-year term as ISFAA president (1962-65). During his tenure, he mitigated jurisdictional matters related to ethics. By the 1980s, the two groups established a joint Ethics Committee that concerned itself with acceptable coaching conduct.

John Eiler – A Model Coach

East Stroudsburg (PA) State's John Eiler was an example of a coach who believed in modeling proper coaching conduct.

One of the things player Al Miller took away from his time with the Stroudsburg mentor was that once a rule was established, you had to stick with it, no matter what the circumstances. "There were a lot of older guys, some returning from military service and so having a beer or smoking were part of their routine. But they never wanted to get caught doing so by Coach Eiler."

The Eiler mandates included bed checks for his players.

With the Stroudsburg team readying to play a Saturday away game at archrival West Chester in 1958, Eiler informed the team he wanted them in bed by 10 p.m. And, particularly, he wanted none of them to attend the Friday night home football game. "Well," Miller recalled, "Karl Mahle's girlfriend was cheerleading at the football game. It happened that I was Karl's roommate. So when John did the bed check and Karl was missing, Coach told me that Karl was off the team."

"We remembered Karl coming to the bus and pleading his case. But there was no going back by Eiler. Karl never saw action for Stroudsburg after that."[55]

Implementing Change

Editor Yonker (he also was the longtime coach at Drexel University) found Minnegan's Ethics Committee Report cumbersome (three pages of suggestions for coach, referee, linesman, and managers). He suggested that the report be pared down to something that fit on a placard and could be posted in every team's locker room.

Additionally, he wanted a second copy to be signed by each coach and sent to the chairman of the Ethics Committee as a pledge of the coach's support for the measures suggested by the committee. To him, this gesture by coaches affirmed their support for the aims and objectives of NSCAA.

In 1962, he called on the NSCAA Ethics Committee to act. "We submit it's time that coaches rated the play of each other for sportsmanship, and let the results be published and inspected each year at the annual meeting."[56]

Unfortunately, it soon became obvious that such aggressive tactics on enforcement of ethical conduct ran counter to another, more important document. Namely, the United States Constitution.

The Censure Issue

In 1973, NSCAA President John McKeon appointed one of his former Bridgeport players, Bill Brew, as chairman of a joint NSCAA-ISFAA Ethics Committee. By 1975, it appears that his counterpart representing the collegiate community was the new Navy coach Greg Myers.

The committee was moving forward in terms of enforcement by censure of coaches whose conduct had been brought to their attention.

In his annual summary, NSCAA President Sam Porch announced that the organization had retained an attorney, stating, " ... this is a highly sensitive area wherein 'due process' must be protected." In making the statement, the Glassboro State coach noted that a former University of North Carolina soccer player (under Marvin Allen), attorney Fred Parker III, had offered to serve *pro bono*.

"Putting teeth" into enforcement of the joint NSCAA/ISAA ethics code remained a lingering issue. As the committee grappled with enforcement, a letter from former retired NSCAA stalwart Richard Schmelzer framed the issue: "We all know," he stated, "that a soccer coach should be a good boy scout and be noble, kind, considerate, fair, etc. But what we should know is how much competitiveness is too much, what is considered allowable and what is not, when one becomes a stinker by taking advantage of the rules, etc." Further, he urged the committee to give guidance to young coaches whose jobs depended on wins and losses. "It isn't enough for the ethics committee statement to what one must be fair and high-minded about. It should give specific examples as to what is fair and what is not."[57]

The 1982 Ethics Code

Schmelzer's letter referenced a newly written code of ethics that was the work of Greg Myers and former 1978 NSCAA President Joe Bean.

Completed in the spring of 1982, it was a generic document, seeking to provide guidance for coaches of the game at all levels, though it couldn't escape having a focus for coaches in educational settings.

Its stated purpose was to "clarify and distinguish ethical and approved behavior from those practices that are detrimental." It focused on eight coaching responsibilities and offered 49 reminders to coaches that were also applicable to players and their institutions. The code contained suggestions related to the rules of the game; relations with game officials along with ideal behavior related to coaching responsibilities such as public relations; scouting; recruitment; and game day operations

The issue still before the coaches was how in the 1980s to integrate the code into the behavior of what was fast becoming a larger, more diverse, and much more competitive coaching community.

Honoring Model Behavior

Not the least of retired Wheaton (IL) College coach Joe Bean's accomplishments has been in the area of promoting ethical conduct in coaching.

Coach Joe Bean has long championed the issue of ethics in coaching.

He credits the late Springfield College coach Irv Schmid with awakening the issue of proper behavior. "When I was at Bridgeport one year we played Irv and being a young coach I was trying to establish myself. I thought being a 'yeller' and 'screamer' on the sidelines was acceptable behavior. During the game I observed Irv's behavior. He was calm and collected; he had done his coaching in practice. I tried thereafter to follow his model."[58]

Attacking the issue of how to better promote ethical behavior, in 1982, Bean took the lead, in coordination with the National Intercollegiate Soccer Officials Association, to annually grant NSCAA/NISOA Merit Awards to intercollegiate and high school coaches "who represent the highest ideals of behavior and sportsmanship toward players, coaches and officials both on and off the field." The first intercollegiate coach award was presented to Bean with the secondary school coach honored was Tony Schinto of New Trier (Ill.) High School. It was presented through the early 1990s, when the NISOA's relationship with NSCAA had declined.

In part due to his time on the NCAA soccer rules and tournament committees and his ongoing work on ethics, the Bean imprint is still evident today. One innovation was the establishment of coaching areas/boxes on the sidelines to help limit coaching movement. In addition, his annual tabulation of red and yellow cards eventually led to the NCAA rule suspending players and/or coaches for unsportsmanlike behavior.

Bean also utilized members of the NSCAA Ethics Committee to publish articles in *Soccer Journal* that promoted ideas and ideals related to ethics in coaching.

By 1993, the annual United Soccer Coaches' list of awards included the Team Ethics and Sportsmanship Awards. Credit for its design rests with coach Marvin Zuidema. It recognizes secondary school and intercollegiate teams who exhibit fair play, good sporting behavior, and adherence to the laws of the game. The criteria include that a team must not have received any red cards at any time during the regular or post season and that their yellow card percentage cannot exceed 50 percent based on the number of matches played during a season.

Although more punitive actions first espoused by various coaches have not seen their way onto any of the nation's court dockets, progress of a positive sort has enabled new light to be shed on standards of ethical behavior by coaches.

The Academy Initiative on Ethics

In 1999, Dr. Lauie Whitsel became the first woman president of NSCAA, and it was during her term that the organization refocused on the issue of coaching ethics.

In particular, the organization's educational component, the Academy program, inserted an ethics component into its curriculum.

The design of the curriculum was the focus of a 1999 summer meeting that then educational vice-president Mike Berticelli convened in Baltimore. Playing major roles in the design of the syllabus were coaches George Purgavie of Bowdoin (ME) College and Doug Williamson of Nebraska Wesleyan College.

Those in attendance agreed that delivery of a scripted lecture format on ethics was not an effective means of conveyance. Coach Purgavie was familiar with the work of fellow Maine author Rushford Kidder. It was Kidder's contention that case studies that demanded ethical decision-making on the part of an audience was the best method of imparting what stands for correct behavior in various situations.

Thus, beginning in the new millennium, the case study method was utilized in Academy courses. Specifically, three soccer case studies were designed and discussed, with the intended effect to expose a generally younger group of coaches to the type of short- and long-term decision-making that is an important part of their coaching education.

An added outcome of the Baltimore meeting was that Williamson reedited the then-existing NSCAA Code of Ethics from its 49 recommended behaviors to its present 12 core principles.

He comments that the 20-year-old code is due for a reedit due to the fact that other issues have emerged and need to be addressed.[59]

Still left unresolved is the matter of a governing body being legally able to tackle behavioral issues of coaches and players that bring disrepute to the game.

THE NSCAA CODE OF ETHICS[60]

- Soccer is the players' game. The paramount concern of coaches is the holistic development, welfare, enjoyment and safety of their players.
- Coaches bear the responsibility for teaching players to strive for success while playing fairly, observing the laws of the game and the highest level of sportsmanship.
- Coaches shall treat officials with respect and dignity, and shall teach players to do the same.
- Our opponents are worthy of being treated with respect. Coaches will model such respect for opponents and expect their players to do likewise.
- In both victory and defeat, the behavior of the coach shall model grace, dignity and composure.
- Coaches shall adhere to the highest standards and regulations of the institutions they represent: clubs, schools, sponsoring organizations and sports governing bodies.
- Coaches have a responsibility to promote the interests of soccer, including treating the media with courtesy, honesty and respect.
- Coaches shall model inclusive behavior, actively supporting cultural diversity while opposing all types of discrimination, including but not limited to, racism and sexism, at all levels of the game.
- Coaches are responsible for taking active roles in education about, and prevention and treatment of drug, alcohol and tobacco abuse, both in their lives and the lives of their players.
- Coaches shall refrain from all manner of personal abuse and harassment of others, whether verbal, physical, emotional or sexual, and shall oppose such abuse and harassment at all levels of the game.
- Coaches shall respect the declared affiliations of all players, and shall adhere to all guidelines and regulations on recruiting established by the governing bodies having oversight of their teams and leagues.
- Coaches shall seek to honor those who uphold the highest standards and principles of soccer and shall use appropriate protocol to oppose and eliminate all behavior that brings disrepute to the sport – violence, abuse, dishonesty, disrespect and violations of the laws of the game and rules governing competition.

The Youth Soccer Explosion

Informal youth sports in the United States began to organize more formerly after World War II. Prior to that time, it was principally in school settings that physical education teachers exposed students to a wide variety of developmental activities that included instruction in individual and team sports. Those students, principally boys, who were found to excel at a sport found their way onto their schools' teams; others may have competed at an intramural level of play.

That arrangement began to change when Carl Stotz took the concept of a youth baseball league, first formed in 1939 in Williamsport (PA), onto the national stage. Most recently, Little League Baseball, Incorporated reportedly organizes an estimated 180,000 teams *worldwide* that, in turn, attract over 2.6 million players.

Today, the Stotz organizational structure has been put in place for most every youth sport in the country, and the individual most often referenced for organizing youth soccer is Californian Donald Greer.

In retrospect, the insertion of Don Greer into the mainstream of U.S. soccer in the 1970s has been a mixed blessing.

By 1975, Walter Chyzowych was wrestling with a two-headed monster. On the one hand, he was serving as USSF's director of coaching education; at the same time he was coach of the national team program. In essence, he was trying to overcome a problem that had perplexed USSF since its formation—namely, how to organize an identification process that would unearth the country's best playing talent while also trying to put in place a coaching scheme that would insure that the instruction of its youth players was uniform and comprehensive.

Steinbrecher Looks Back

In hindsight, retired U.S. Soccer CEO-Secretary General Hank Steinbrecher offered what should have taken place at that juncture of the country's soccer history. "There is no doubt in my mind that Walter [Chyzowych] was the right man for the job that needed to be done. What needed to happen was that in coordination with Don Greer, USSF should have dictated that its director of coaching appoint each state association's director of coaching. That would have insured that everyone's coaching education and ODP programs were in sync with USSF's stated objectives. Further, in addition to assuring that the coaching education scheme was in good hands, such appointments would have been made with the confidence that state associations employed individuals had the competency to identify playing talent and communicate that to the national team coaching staff."

Hank Steinbrecher (right) gives a hug to Pingry coach, Miller Bugliari.

Steinbrecher went on to say, "But, and it is a big 'but,' at the time, Don Greer possessed enormous influence because his organization was responsible for putting USSF finances in the black for probably the first time in its history." Presently, each USYSA youth player is charged an annual two dollar and twenty-five cent registration fee, with one dollar of it paid to U.S. Soccer. That proportion in effect in the 1970s remains the same today.[61]

Also, in retrospect, Greer's organizational concept focused not necessarily on the quality of its participants but rather on the number of youth players. And, to his credit, he saw that youth numbers attracted corporate interest. Soon Coca-Cola signed on with USSF, with monies earmarked for investment with its USYSA affiliate. It was reported that Greer wanted every youth playing pass to have the Coke logo imprinted on it! Also, every youth cup competition site was to have Coke signage erected at its fields.

By the time Greer vacated his vice-presidency, youth enrollment had ballooned. The burgeoning impact of youth soccer was indicated when Hank Steinbrecher assumed the reins of U.S. Soccer in 1990; at that time, youth contributions to the organization's coffers represented 85% of its revenues!

The end result was that the needed synergy between the newly formed youth state associations and the national coaching scheme, as personified in Walter Chyzowych, did not take place on a coordinated basis. There were some DOC appointments in state associations that met with Chyzowych's approval, but there was no synchronized effort between Greer and the two objectives of quality coaching and player development that could be met at the same time.

Resultant USYSA Activity

In a short time, with volunteers filling the ranks of the 52 USYSA state associations, each developed into economic and political entities largely outside of USSF jurisdiction. In some cases, each state association entered into sponsorship agreements with companies that were competitors of those aligned with the national body! Also, other organizations, such as AYSO, organized youth play in regions underserved by the USSF.

With parents assuming major political roles in the state associations came conflicts of interest in terms of player selection processes. In time, with little guidance from the national body, parental interference and parental conduct at youth competitions have also had a ripple effect in terms of what constitutes ethical conduct.

Terry Fisher offers a perspective (see QR code).

So it was that the various USYSA state associations, not in consultation with Walt Chyzowych but beholden to Don Greer, appointed their DOCs. Subsequently, it was left to Chyzowych to identify and utilize his USSF coaching school staff to develop youth coaching courses for the state associations to offer its clients and, at the same time, make certain that his staff were chosen so that, geographically, the country was covered for player identification purposes.

It wasn't a perfect system that Chyzowych designed, but it could have been if the USSF had any ideas of bringing symmetry to its 1970s operations.

Dr. Thomas Fleck – Offering a Youth Soccer Perspective

The Fleck publications (books, articles, and detailed coaching curricula) all included a consistent message. Namely, first and foremost, they focused on the young player, a stance that defied the status quo by daring to suggest that teaching and learning and building from a properly understood foundation was much more important than winning.... Sadly, that message did not always resonate with youth coaches...

Dr. Tom Fleck had a long association with the United States Soccer Federation from his earliest playing days and through service in its coaching education programs and, briefly, as a coordinator for its youth programs. He, as with many of his generation, wore a number of "soccer hats" during a long and distinguished career in the game, including his leadership role in youth soccer education.

And that immersion in soccer all began in his native Philadelphia

Dr. Tom Fleck.

Role With USYSA

In 1978, USSF reached an agreement with the Coca-Cola Company to sponsor programming associated with its USYSA affiliate. Tom was appointed the first full-time director/coordinator of all of USYSA's programs that included showcasing the Coke sponsorship.

In effect, Fleck's job was to manage the programing designed by Don Greer. That included administrating four regional tournaments where state club teams of various age groups came together to determine regional champions. It also included insuring that Coke was featured in the ODP competitions organized by each state association.

In the coordinator's role, Fleck traveled extensively and soon, tiring of the grind, resigned in 1979. Today, the demands of that role require the attention of nearly two dozen individuals at the USYSA office.

Later, in 1979, he became GM of the NASL Philadelphia Fury. Following three years with the Fury team, he became DOC for the Florida YSA, a position he held until he became executive director and DOC for the Idaho Youth Soccer Association in 1996.

The Fleck Philosophy

Through his Lehigh and youth soccer coaching experiences, Tom Fleck formed the basis for what would be his approach to the education of youth soccer coaches. Namely that at the youth level of play their collective efforts should focus on the educational needs of their players rather than on winning games. Over time, Dr. Fleck achieved recognition as the leading authority on youth soccer development and education. He was the primary author of both the National Youth License and the USYSA Youth Soccer Assistant Coach Series. The Official USYSA Coaching Manual and Parent Coach Primer are still utilized by coaches across the nation and specifically in the state association coaching courses.

The Fleck publications (books, articles, and detailed coaching curricula) all included a consistent message. Namely, first and foremost, they focused on the young player, a stance that defied the status quo by daring to suggest that teaching and learning and building from a properly understood foundation was much more important than winning. Sadly, that message did not always resonate with youth coaches, many of whom were not schooled in the totality of youth development but instead were focused on becoming the Bill Belichicks of their youth soccer leagues.

Upon Fleck's passing, Sam Snow, former coaching director of USYSA, lauded his soccer influence: "Dr. Fleck's impact on our sport was profound. Tom educated and influenced generations of American soccer coaches and was a pioneer in the growth of our sport during the 'soccer boom' of the 70s and 80s. I was exceptionally fortunate to have had Tom as a mentor and he was a close friend as well. His passing is a loss to soccer in the USA."[64]

The NSCAA

..."To say that I am a proud member of this group would be an understatement...."
–Tom Fleck

In 1977, Tom Fleck agreed to serve as an officer of the NSCAA, rising to become its president in 1984-85.

In part, his appointment served many purposes, not the least of which was the goal that, due to his long association with USSF, he could serve to smooth relations between the two organizations. Also, his familiarity and contacts within USYSA were thought to be helpful as NSCAA sought to increase enrollment of youth member coaches (youth membership did triple!). Not the least of the skills was his knowledge of soccer marketing.

During his service on the NSCAA board of directors, Fleck was supportive of the establishment of the NSCAA Academy, the association's soccer coaching education division. He also helped execute marketing agreements with Adidas, Metropolitan Life, Gatorade, McDonald's, Challenge Soccer Balls, and the U.S. Army.

The U.S. Army agreement featured a weekend clinics program, which was orchestrated by Walt Chyzowych and staged principally on military bases.

It attracted an estimated 3,000 coaches and players. Also instituted was an Army Senior MVP Awards program that presented awards at 2,000 high schools throughout the country.

Some thought that his association with USSF might compromise or even shorten his NSCAA term of office, but his comment at the end of his tenure reflected what had been his commitment: "To say that I am a proud member of this group would be an understatement. How it goes about its business is a lesson that all organizations might learn from."[65]

Honors

Among his honors, Dr. Fleck, along with colleague Dr. Ronald Quinn, was the first American to present at the 20th Annual Union of European Football (Soccer) Trainers Symposium in Wembley, England, in 1999.

Earlier, in 1996, he was inducted into the Eastern Pennsylvania Soccer Hall of Fame.

Dr. Fleck was presented the 2004 NSCAA Honor Award for a lifetime of service to the organization. Also in 2004, Fleck received the Walt Chyzowych Award for Lifetime Achievement in Coaching Education. A year later, he was inducted into the West Chester State HOF and was the inaugural recipient of the USYSA Excellence in Youth Coaching Education Award. Subsequently, that award has been renamed in his honor.

Karl Dewazien – Putting the Fun in Youth Soccer

"We played some tough teams and so I was looking for the team to win some small victories," Karl recalled. *"So I informed the cheerleaders to scream as loud as they could – whenever we crossed the half way line with the ball!"*[66]

It is said that "age doesn't matter" and, further, "if you fail, try, try again."

Taking the second adage first, it took 18 tries before Karl Dewazien's family was granted Lithuanian visas to emigrate from post-World War II Germany to the United States.

The family settled near Fresno, California, where Karl eventually enrolled, in 1967, at a small Mennonite school, Fresno Pacific University.

Karl Dewazien, shown here coaching a youth soccer team, has always emphasized the "fun" aspect of youth soccer.

As for the age reference? "In my junior year just before the start of the season our AD met with the team and informed us that our coach had left to move to Montana to join the rodeo. Further, if we wanted a season, one of us would have to coach the team. He suggested that perhaps the oldest player should consider coaching. Well, that person was recently engaged and begged off. Guess who was second oldest?"[67]

Karl got up to soccer coaching speed by reviewing a World War II U.S. Navy soccer-coaching manual written by coaches John Eiler and Earle Waters. "We played some tough teams and so I was looking for the team to win some small victories," Karl recalled. "So I informed the cheerleaders to scream as loud as they could – whenever we crossed the half way line with the ball!"

Seeking to upgrade his soccer coaching expertise, in 1972 Dewazien enrolled at a USSF Coaching School conducted at Stanford University. With his German fluency, Karl, at times, was able to help famed coach Dettmar Cramer understand the English slang used by the candidates.

It wasn't long after that Dewazien developed a youth coaching curricula that was derailed by a certain Brazilian.

Chosen to Head CYSA

In 1978, the California Youth Soccer Association (CYSA), led by Peter Jebens, started a search to hire its first full-time director of coaching. The original job description was very vague, with little to no requirements given, but covered coaching education, recreation, camps, annual meetings, Olympic Development Programs, the TOPSoccer program for special needs children, and anything else where a coach might be involved.

It took four interviews before the CYSA agreed to hire Dewazien. "They were centered on development of a program concentrated on competitive soccer for youth. I told them I wanted a program that addressed the needs of everyone entering the program, as well as those leaving the program. They eventually agreed with my philosophy."

It was during this time that Dewazien established the Golden West Soccer Camps. The Golden West organization template caught the attention of those directing the Chyzowych All-America Soccer Camp on the East Coast. There were preliminary discussions of combining forces nationally, but the concept never materialized. Of interest was that, among the young instructors at the Golden West Camps, was one Sigi Schmid.

Offering CYSA Coaching Courses

"...Graham, no matter the hour, would offer to help us candidates...." –Karl Dewazien

Over a period of 34 years, CYSA offered three local coaching courses to its membership that were progressive in terms of their curricula. In the Dwaine-developed syllabus were residential State and National D courses that included testing of the candidates. The National D was an additional coaching course offered by CYSA. Upon successful completion, a coach could attend a USSF Coaching School and seek a "C" coaching license.

Speaking of the USSF schools, Dewazien at one time sought to overcome one candidate's complaint when he and Tom Lilledal proposed that the Golden West camps *and* the schools combine at various sites. The thought was that the older campers would serve as players for the candidates when they performed their assigned coaching topics. The idea never gained a foothold.

Asked to cite others who opened his eyes as to what good soccer coaching modeling was about, the introspective Dewazien noted Dettmar Cramer's impact but also mentioned Graham Ramsey. "While other USSF coaches left the premises in the evening, Graham, no matter the hour, would offer to help us candidates by meeting with us to relieve our anxieties. He showed a real interest in us as people."

Taking Pen to Paper

Added to Dewazien's promotional efforts were a series of FUNdamental Soccer publications he produced.

The succession of books sought to cover soccer basics, including practice organization, technique, tactics, goalkeeping, and the role of parents, as well as one addressing the needs of TOPSoccer children.

Related to book content, Karl stated, "In all the books I've tried to emphasize my belief that kids need to be taught to play soccer on their own. Youth coaches need to recognize that kids need to be involved in the learning process so that when they are by themselves they have an idea of how to start play."

Asked to whether the books have been reedited based on newer soccer trends, he replied there was little need to do so. "There was no need to change the texts; kids don't change in terms of their needs."

In 1980, Karl authored, copyrighted, and included in each of his future books the "Modified Laws of the Game" for U-6, U-8, U-10, and U-12 age groups, which, with some editing, were mandated as a national program by U.S. Soccer in 2017.

The Dewazien Philosophy

Asked to define what unleashed his soccer passion, Dewazien harked back to his post-World War II experience. "I think I always wanted kids to have a childhood I never had through the enjoyment soccer offers."

To that end, Karl holds to a long-range belief—namely, that "the outcome of our children unfortunately is more important than any game they will ever play."

In 2012, amid discussions with a newly installed Cal-North administration that related to educational philosophy (that were not unlike those held when he was first hired in 1978!), Karl Dewazien retired.

Not to be derailed as a force in soccer's progress, Dewazien's ideas have subsequently found a home on various Internet sites. It's hard to keep a man of his conviction and knowledge down!

The Summer Soccer Camp Phenomena

Beginning after World War II, and in an attempt initially prompted by the collective soccer coaching community to spread expert instruction in the game, was the introduction of what would become a part of the summer calendar for many—namely, the summer soccer camp.

Heretofore, the American camp experience had been reserved for families that could afford the sleep-away experience for their youngsters. Families turned the child-raising over to well-established encampments, in some cases for an entire summer. In some localities, social agencies, YMCAs, and the like staged summer day camps offering youngsters exposure to a variety of activities.

All research points to Drexel University coach Don Yonker for taking the soccer camp concept from vision to reality. These ventures were initially propelled by his and fellow coaches' desire to improve the overall quality of instruction. But in short order, soccer camps became huge businesses before the turn of the century. It is estimated that in their heyday, over 1,000 soccer camps operated, with those that were national in scope annually enrolling 3,000 or more campers. The numbers point to soccer camp businesses collectively generating millions of dollars.

Fine-Tuning Camp Munsee

...*"I know there were broken lamps, ash trays and the like ... so that each instructor would be ready come the following summer...."* –Whitey Burnham

As soccer play increased following World War II, especially in the secondary schools, a cadre of experienced coaches grappled with the question: What are the best methods of lending our expertise to those coaches and players seeking improvement? For many, conducting clinics in their geographic regions was one answer. But the affairs, while well-meaning, were a stopgap in terms of having a lasting impact.

It was in 1962 when, thinking he had an answer to the issue of enhanced player development, coach Don Yonker established what was advertised as the first U.S.

residential soccer camp at Camp Munsee in Honesdale, Pennsylvania. Billed the International Soccer Camp (ISC), its staff included Yonker's long-time Drexel (PA) University assistant Al Laverson along with later NSCAA presidents Whitey Burnham (Delaware) and Frank Nelson (Nyack HS).

A stickler for detail in the education process, Yonker's desire in founding the camp was to share his formula for imparting soccer technique to enrollees. And to clarify that his instructors were well-versed in how that process would unfold at ISC, Whitey Burnham recalls that Yonker would include introducing him and other staff members to the new

Coach Don Yonker established the first residential soccer camp in 1962.

exercises and circuits at the annual NSCAA January conventions. "He'd get his staff together in his hotel room, spread out the furniture and we'd get in our shorts and he would take us through the next curriculum. I know there were broken lamps, ash trays and the like, but Don would march the staff through everything old and new so that each instructor would be ready come the following summer. . . . He was the consummate teacher."[68]

Seemingly hired in 1974 to oversee Drexel's intramural sports program but hoping to also become part of Yonker's Drexel soccer coaching staff, Johnson Bowie was hired by ISC. Thus he had a birds-eye view of what took place at ISC. "I don't think Don had any idea of my soccer background [he'd played at Western Maryland] and so in essence, that summer he gave me a 'tryout' at the camp. It was like being in a graduate school for soccer. In addition to NSCAA people, I had a chance to interact with guys like Anson Dorrance, Peter Mehlert, Stan Startzell, Walt Ersing, and Dick Broad. I guess I made a positive impression when I returned to campus in the fall, in addition to my intramural duties, I was assigned to assist Drexel soccer."[69]

Identifying Emerging Coaching Talent

"While today every kid has a ball (or more), coach Yonker always stressed 'one player, one ball.' If a camper didn't have a soccer ball, he bought one at the camp." –Anson Dorrance

Veteran coaches like Yonker were always looking to add young, energetic, and emerging coaches to their camp staffs. This was the case when Anson Dorrance joined ISC. For the fiscal health of the camps themselves, it was also important that the staff attract players from their locales. "I liked the philosophy of the camp and every summer I brought a group of North Carolina kids north to experience the Yonker curriculum – and have fun," recalled Dorrance. "While today every kid has a ball (or more), coach Yonker always stressed 'one player, one ball.' If a camper didn't have a soccer ball, he bought one at the camp."[70]

Further, Anson noted that if the camp experience had the right balance between instruction and play, it would find kids and staff eager to return another year. Eventually, as the number of Carolina enrollees grew, the Tar Heel coach started his own camp, modeling its program after ISC's. Of course, Dorrance's stellar coaching accomplishments have proven an attraction for his University of North Carolina camps, which are one of the best-attended in the country.

In short order, other residential camps soon followed Yonker's lead. In the 1960s, Walt and Gene Chyzowych, Lenny Lucendo, and Wayne Sunderland opened the All-America Camp at the Ukrainian Workers Association in Glen Spey, New York. Coach Cliff Stevenson is credited with opening one of the nation's first camps at Brown University, and Wayne Sunderland joined John McKeon to open a live-in camp in Connecticut. McKeon also double-dipped by starting the Pocono (PA) Sports Camps. Brother coaches Irv and Mel Schmid's camp operated at Granite Lake (NH). Another early camp saw SUNY-Brockport coaches John Skehan and Huntley Parker operate Camp Skwim, a combined soccer-swim camp in southwestern New York. Bob Dirkranian worked his former coach John McKeon's camps and later struck out on his own, starting the Victory Soccer Schools in New England.

There were a number of outcomes that evolved from the startup of these soccer camp operations, not the least of which was that soccer coaching incomes were increased!

The Day Camp

"...the key to dribbling proficiency was simple: "At all times keep the ball so close to you that you can p---- on it...."

Many secondary school coaches, once they realized they had captive audiences for their product, started their own live-in or, more often, day camps in their communities. Among the benefits for coaches was the opportunity to expand pre-season training for their teams.

In some instances, and to vary the presentations, coaches would add guest coaches who might oversee the training of the campers for a day. Depending on the ages of the group, that person would often introduce and teach a special topic. Some coaches, such as England's Graham Ramsey, often indulged campers for a day or two before moving on to another venue nearby.

Joe Palone might have been in that situation when he appeared for a few days at an upstate New York camp. His straightforward coaching style might have been typified as "old school." Seems one day Joe was assigned to teach a group of eight-year-olds the art of dribbling. With his West Point baseball hat turned backwards and a ball at his feet, he informed the youngsters that the key to dribbling proficiency was simple: "At all times keep the ball so close to you that you can p---- on it." Whether the impressionable campers ever shared that explicit lesson with their parents was not reported![71]

Specialized Soccer Camps

While he has worn many hats, Joe Machnik's coaching legacy was the formalization of goalkeeper training. For many fledgling coaches in the post-World War II era, the training of the goalkeeper was a bit of a mystery.

Dettmar Cramer can be credited with furthering Machnik's development as a goalkeeping specialist when the German asked him to take on the instruction of candidates at the first USSF coaching school in 1970.

By 1977, the No. 1 Goalkeeper Camps were underway, with wife Barbara in charge of all off-field details and Joe focusing on the fieldwork. From 39 campers attending the initial camp, interest exploded to 240 campers the following year.

Over its 43 years, the camps have expanded nationwide, with Machnik's clinics at a number of NSCAA conventions playing a role in helping market the business.

In addition to the hands-on approach at the camps, the Machnik methodology included two instructional books, *So You Want to Be a Goalkeeper* and *So Now You Are a Goalkeeper*. Videos also captured his goalkeeping instruction methodology. Additionally, keepers could avail themselves of the latest in goalie equipment via the camp stores.

One of Joe's initial staff instructors, Greg Andrulis, was among those No.1 apostles who have continued to influence goalkeeper instruction throughout the United States. Today he is in charge of overall management of the more comprehensive No. 1 Soccer Camps.

Growth of National Camps

The No. 1 Goalkeeper Camps expansion to sites throughout the United States was replicated by former Austrian professional and Yale coach Hubert Vogelsinger and the goalkeeping duo of Dan Gaspar and Tony DiCicco. The Vogelsinger Soccer Academies were held at sites from coast to coast, as were the SoccerPlus offerings of Gaspar-DiCicco.

In some cases, different soccer manufacturers seeking nationwide exposure for their products affiliated their logos with the expansive camps. For instance, Puma allied with the Vogelsinger camps, and Diadora, an Italian company, threw in with Soccer Plus. But the logistics of these operations was not easy to control. At one point, Karl Dewazien attempted to combine the Golden West Camps with the All-America Camps on the east coast, but the merger never materialized.

Hubert Vogelsinger staged an annual nationwide series of Soccer Academies each summer.

As soccer camp orchestration became more refined, especially at large universities and colleges, premier soccer companies Adidas, Nike, Umbro, and others began to attach their logos and products (uniforms, balls, shoes) with camps that typically offered multiple weeks of camp exposure. Thus, camps operated by coaches Jerry Yeagley (Indiana), John Rennie (Duke), Ibrahim (Clemson), and Anson Dorrance (North Carolina) would display company logos throughout their summer sites.

The timing of these soccer affiliations in some cases predated the huge exclusivity contracts with athletic conferences that mark the intercollegiate landscape today.

Most recently, competition in the soccer camp business has taken another turn as national camps operated utilizing coaches from abroad have made their presence known.

The Annual Coaching Awards Program

It was the NSCAA member coaches who volunteered their efforts to produce the various All-America teams, with over six dozen coaches coordinating efforts that honored around 400 All-America players annually.

The All-America Selections

One of the most obvious means to promote soccer was to honor its best players each year. Until the 1950s, and at the intercollegiate level, the Intercollegiate Soccer Football Association of America (ISFAA) member teams and their coaches assumed that role.

From 1920-25, Douglas Stewart, the coach at Penn named the first All-America teams. Beginning in 1926, as editor of *The Official Soccer Guide*, he coordinated with other ISFAA coaches to identify and publicize the All-America choices in the booklet.

In the 1930s, as more schools sponsored soccer, three Eastern soccer leagues were organized for scheduling and other purposes, including honoring teams and individual players for their seasonal accomplishments. Among the leagues formed were the New England Intercollegiate Soccer League, the Middle Atlantic Intercollegiate Soccer League, and the Middle Atlantic States College Athletic Conference.

By 1936, the selection process was expanded, with coaches naming All-America players from the Middle Atlantic and New England areas. By 1939, a third district, the Southern District, chose its All-America players.

An examination of those chosen for All-America status is revealing from a number of standpoints. Many player names later surfaced as significant coaches of the game. In 1932, Huntley Parker (Springfield) was named to the team, and, in 1935, Charlie Scott (Penn) was chosen. Each carved out noteworthy coaching careers at SUNY-Brockport and Penn, respectively. Albie Loeffler (Connecticut) was chosen to the 1936 team, while Bruce Munro (Springfield) got the nod a year later. Loeffler coached at the secondary level in Connecticut and Munro at Harvard.

In 1940, the process was amended once more, as players were honored by positions played based on the then-traditional W-M system of play. Thus, the best three "insides" or "center forwards" or "center backs" were chosen and, when combined, constituted the All-America team. This change greatly expanded the number of All-America honorees.

Earlier, in the 1930s, those not making the "final cut" were listed as "outstanding players" and many, such as Temple's Don Yonker, were later cited worthy of All-America status!

With soccer play curtailed through World War II, it was left to veteran coaches Bill Jeffrey and Dick Schmelzer to finalize the All-America selections. Among the names surfacing as All-America choices during those years was Irv Schmid (Springfield), in 1941. Later basketball notables Bud Palmer and Butch van Breda Kolff of Princeton were chosen, in 1942 and 1945, respectively. Walter Bahr (Temple) was named in 1944 while Charlie Matlack (from Haverford *and* Penn) was a choice from 1943-45.

Refinement of the All-America Process

By 1946, the NSCAA had supplanted ISFAA as the organization overseeing the All-America selection process.

In 1948, coach C. Fred Holloway (SUNY-Cortland) introduced a new statistical formula system for choosing the All-America team. More objective, the process involved opposing coaches filling out information cards following a match. These cards were then forwarded to regional All-America chairpersons for final tabulation and submission to national chairpersons.

Alongside the introduction of a new formula for selection of All-America teams came an expansion of post-war collegiate play, and All-America choices began to emerge from newer regions of the country. Frank Nelson (North Carolina), in 1947 (there were 61 All-America players chosen that year!), and Steve Negoesco (San Francisco), in 1949, represented selections from the South and West Coast regions of the country, respectively.

Through the period from 1950-80, various coaches emerged to oversee the All-America selection process, with Huntley Parker named chairman of the NSCAA

All-America Committee beginning in 1955. Alden "Whitey" Burnham succeeded him in 1970.

Parker and Burnham were Springfield products, as was Terry Jackson, who succeeded Burnham in 1982 and was, in turn, succeeded by Ray Cieplik in 1988 as men's college All-America chair. In 1994, Ray was followed by Dr. Owen Wright.

An Expanded All-America Process

The explosion of soccer interest in the late 1970s saw the NSCAA All-America process meet the demand for selection of All-America teams at the secondary school and youth levels of play and further delineation of various levels of intercollegiate play.

By 1991, All-America teams were being announced for senior and junior college men and women (including teams at various levels of play [i.e., NCAA Divisions I, II, and III]), secondary school boys and girls, and youth boys and girls.

In every expansion of the All-America program, coaches were identified to oversee what has become a more streamlined process.

The All-America Selection Process

Shown in the photos are a few of the individuals who have had significant roles in determining each year's All-America teams. Burnham, Cieplik, Farnsworth, Gordon, and Rayfield all became NSCAA presidents.

Ray Cieplik.

Roy Gordon.

Steve Veal.

Janet Rayfield.

Jeff Farnsworth.

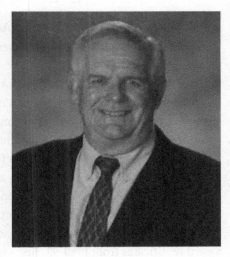

John Mayer.

Alden "Whitey" Burnham.

Marketing/Administration

...it is estimated the United Soccer Coaches annually issues over 11,000 awards.

Perhaps the most viable of the NSCAA programs in terms of annual outreach, the All-America team, beginning in 1958, has attracted corporate sponsorships. That year, then-President John Eiler convinced the Wheaties Sports Foundation to sponsor the All-America team. The eight-year deal was worth $1,000 annually.

Corporate monies invested in soccer began to flow in concert with the impact of the NASL in the 1970s. A marketing agreement between the NSCAA and NASL Marketing in 1978 resulted in Dr. Pepper becoming a short-lived sponsor of the All-America team in 1980, while McDonald's also had a fling in 1982. New Balance came aboard in 1985 as the title sponsor, and MetLife's logo graced All-America award certificates from 1989-92. Beginning in 1993 and extending through 2000, Umbro had the longest reign as sponsor of the awards program.

Most recently, John Mayer, as awards committee chair, and Steve Veal, as awards manager, have served to keep committees making annual awards selections on task. It has become a monumental job because, since 2020, it is estimated that the United Soccer Coaches issues over 11,000 awards each year.

Coaching Honors

...counting recipients of regional COY awards, it is estimated that 200 coaching staffs are acknowledged annually.

While the All-America player process is over 100 years old, in 1973, the NSCAA and the ISAA joined forces with the General Sportcraft Company to annually honor the country's coaches for their teams' outstanding play.

That year, coach Bob Guelker, then coaching at Southern Illinois at Edwardsville, was chosen for the inaugural award. A year later, the COY award program, now overseen by NSCAA, was expanded to honor the boys junior college COY in the person of David Ross of Suffolk (NY) County Community College.

Mirroring the expansion of the All-America program, by the early 1980s, the COY process was extended to acknowledge coaching accomplishment for men's and women's teams at the NCAA, NJCAA, NAIA, NCCAA, secondary school, and USYSA youth levels of play.

Until recently, the COY awards annually honored a school's head coach, but in 2019, the awards were renamed to honor the coaching *staff* of the particular school.

MetLife succeeded General Sportcraft as sponsor of the COY program in the early 1980s and was, in turn, supplanted by Umbro in the 1990s. By the turn of the century, adidas emerged to take on sponsorship of the program.

Most recently, and counting recipients of regional COY awards, it is estimated that 200 coaching staffs are acknowledged annually, with the identification process involving more than 40 committee and regional chairpersons.

The United Soccer Coaches Awards Committee, headed by John Mayer (he's been involved for more than 35 years!), in addition to giving oversight to the All-America and COY programs, coordinates with committees that annually decide recipients of such prizes as the Honor Award, the Bill Jeffrey, the Robert W. Robinson, and the Charlotte Moran Awards, with others selected by various coaching alliances (i.e., Latino coaches).

As noted, annually honoring player, coaches, and others for their contributions to soccer is just one area where coaches have designed and carried out programs that seek to acknowledge their colleagues as soccer's influence continues to expand in this country.

The National Soccer Coaches Convention

It is billed as the largest gathering of soccer coaches in the world, and its growth is the result of the collective energies of the NSCAA, now United Soccer Coaches, over a period of eight decades.

Of course, that reference is to the annual January gathering of the U.S. soccer community most commonly referred to as "The Convention."

The First Gatherings

The concept of a coaches' organization grew out of an informal meeting of the established Intercollegiate Soccer Football Association of America (ISFAA). That group, formed in 1926, annually met in New York City, and it was on December 11, 1941, following its meeting at the Harvard Club, that the concept of a coaches association was born.

At the time, there was also existent an Eastern Intercollegiate Coaches Association (EICA), an inclusive body of coaches of *all* sports. The EICA affairs were overseen by Ivy League graduate managers. They, soccer coaches felt, did not have promotion of soccer as one of their priorities.

While accounts of the creation of the NSCAA differ, a group of member coaches of the ISFAA and EICA met informally and agreed to start an organization dedicated to the advancement of soccer.

Throughout the remainder of 1941, and led by President John Brock, the group created several committees, including an annual meeting committee led by coach Howard DeNike of East Stroudsburg (PA) College. It was agreed to hold a meeting and a luncheon as part of ISFAA's annual meeting at the Hotel Pennsylvania in New York City. A historical photo exists of the NSCAA luncheon held on January 10, 1942.

Post-World War II Meetings

Those [meetings] were largely technical in nature and are recalled as being staged in hotel ballrooms with chandeliers sometimes placed at risk by the demonstrators. ...

Following World War II, and due to a number of factors, annual meetings (they became "conventions" starting in 1956) were convened in New York City, with the twin agendas of the ISFAA and the NSCAA the primary focuses of the gatherings.

In addition to the annual meeting committee, other NSCAA committees established included a research committee and others dedicated to publicity, rules, visual aids, newsletters, clinics, teaching methods, and officials. Also, the constitution, newsletter, and nominating committees sought to solidify the ongoing administrative workings of the NSCAA. Coinciding with NSCAA confabs were committee gatherings of the ISFAA coaches whose committee structure principally focused on advancement of the intercollegiate game.

Twin highlights of the early conventions were the business meetings of the NSCAA and ISFAA groups. At each committee, chairs reported out with summary information, while fiscal and other administrative matters were disclosed by the leadership of each group. By noon on Saturday, a culminating luncheon was held with the announcement of the NSCAA Oscar Award (renamed the Honor Award in 1949) its highlight. Following that, those in attendance were on the road back to their relatively nearby homes.

The described format held steady through the 1950s and 1960s, though chalkboard and panel types of talks were gradually replaced by active clinics. Those were largely technical in nature and are recalled as being staged in hotel ballrooms with chandeliers sometimes placed at risk by the demonstrators. In the early 1960s, those selected to the college or junior college All-America teams were invited to New York to be acknowledged at the Saturday luncheon (at the honorees' expense).

It was reported that Max Doss of Soccer Sport Supply presented the All-America players with a NSCAA patch in 1960 and Ralph Hyde presented each player in attendance with a pair of his newly fashioned soccer shoes in 1962. In 1963, it was Doss who is credited with displaying the first exhibit of soccer equipment on a hallway table, later joined by George St. Armond. The latter's fulltime job was operating a tugboat in the New York City harbor.

The Changing Face of the Convention

In 1972, and due in part to the combined interests of coach Bob Guelker of St. Louis University and a more adventurous NSCAA administration, for the first time the national convention was held outside New York City. In order to ease cost of the trip to St. Louis, a chartered airplane was arranged by coaches John McKeon and Al Miller to aid Easterners traveling to the Mound City. The story of coach McKeon temporarily misplacing the airfare receipts resides in the NSCAA archives!

1973 would be the last convention held in New York City, and the following year the site of the meeting was initially announced as the Playboy Club in New Jersey. Cooler, more conservative heads prevailed, and the convention unfolded in Boston. In 1975, the meeting was held in Chicago, though its staging at the Sheraton-O'Hare Hotel meant that attendees were an expensive cab ride away from the nightlife of inner-city Chicago.

Nye's Innovative Move

... the Nye origination can't be discounted in terms of its historical impact on coaching association revenues. ...

It is based on his service with the Golf Coaches Association of America (GCAA) that NSCAA president Bob Nye (1980-81) is credited with the introduction of a formalized trade show in conjunction with the soccer convention. With national brands such as Titlist and others renting spaces, the concept had generated a new revenue stream for the GCAA.

Bob Nye acknowledged Soccer Sport Supply's Max Doss for his company's role as the first exhibitor at the NSCAA conventions.

In 1979, and in what was a landmark change for the organization, Bob Nye convinced the NSCAA Board of Directors to stage a similar exhibit area at the Atlanta convention. There was one issue. Having already contracted for all the spaces at the hotel, there was a problem as to where the soccer merchandisers would show their wares. Creativity was called for, and Nye's solution was to cover the hotel's garage floor with green carpet and stage what would become the first NSCAA exhibitor show. The annual convention display of soccer merchandise has become a natural attraction for coaches and companies alike, adding significant revenues for the organization. Expanding from Max Doss's lone table in 1963, by 2020 in Baltimore, 263 exhibitors were displaying in the convention exhibit hall. With the convention accounting for an estimated 55 percent of the United Soccer Coaches annual budget, the Nye origination can't be discounted in terms of its historical impact on coaching association revenues.

Introduction of Convention Subcommittees

With the influence of treasurer Bob Robinson, the city of Philadelphia was chosen for the 1980 convention, and it was a resounding success, attracting its largest number of attendees. Operating under a new constitution and by-laws, that year saw the convention come under the purview of the first vice-president. So it was Tim Schum who would oversee the next three annual conventions, which were held in Philadelphia, Houston, and Chicago.

It was in Philadelphia that he formed the first convention subcommittee, consisting of coaches Johnson Bowie (Drexel), Ron Broadbent (Spencerport [NY] HS), Dr. Fred Taube (SUNY Cortland), and Robinson (Lower Merion [PA] HS). They would oversee the program, clinics, banquet, and exhibitor functions of the convention, respectively. By 1981, new executive director John McKeon was in charge of convention registration.

Following the historically smallest turnout ever at the Houston convention, which nearly bankrupted the organization, an analysis of convention budgets revealed that the annual membership dues that had underwritten their staging could no longer finance the conduct of future conventions.

Upon Schum's advice, for the first time a registration fee was charged for the subsequent Chicago meeting. That payment, when combined with increased attendances and added monies from the exhibit areas, meant that, from the Chicago onward, annual conventions were on solid fiscal footing.

With increased attendances came the need to carefully select future convention sites.

A Change in Convention Oversight

During his tenure, he has doubled the gross receipts generated by the meeting and quadrupled its profit margin. ...

Since his appointment as NSCAA treasurer in 1970, Bob Robinson has played various roles at the convention. From oversight of monies generated by the meetings beginning that year to organization of the exhibits later that decade to eventual formation and oversight of a convention committee beginning in the 1990s, Robby can be credited with managing its administrative aspects.

In 2011, under CEO Joe Cummings, management of the convention became the primary focus of Geoff VanDuesen. Appointed as the full-time director of operations and events, Geoff's soccer resume included playing for coach John MacKenzie at Western Illinois University.

Geoff's appointment that year followed several years of service on the Robinson convention committee.

Since assuming oversight of the convention, Geoff has managed a staff of two-dozen office staff members of the United Soccer Coaches in bringing

Geoff VanDuesen's role in directing the annual coaches convention aided in his elevation to the organization's CEO in 2021.

the event to fruition each January. During his tenure, he has doubled the gross receipts generated by the convention and quadrupled its profit margin. The scope of the January event is indicated by such facts that its meetings have attracted as many as 14,000 attendees. Meanwhile, on average, 225 education sessions are conducted; 500-plus meetings are held; 30-plus meal/social functions are staged;

300 exhibits are managed; 11,000 hotel rooms are booked; 125 members serve on the convention committee; and 300 volunteers assist in various capacities.

There is little doubt that from its initial meeting in 1942, the NSCAA convention, now the United Soccer Coaches convention, has been transformed into a major soccer happening that is on every soccer followers' bucket list come January.

CHAPTER V

BUILDING ON THE PAST IN NEW ENGLAND, NEW YORK, AND MIDDLE ATLANTIC REGIONS

Introduction

With much of the early foundation of soccer laid along the East Coast of the United States, it remained for a new group of coaches to build on that footing. Thus, beginning in the late 1950s, several individuals emerged who not only continued to field competitive teams but shaped successors who, in time, replicated, even improved, on their mentors' endeavors.

In New England, Springfield College leadership continued to churn out coaches. Many would fill positions as regional colleges and secondary schools introduced soccer. Also in the region, Connecticut coach Joe Morrone successfully addressed one lingering issue for the game—namely, how to creatively market soccer. It would be just one of his many contributions to the game.

The metropolitan area of New York/New Jersey continued its legacy in the sport with coaches Bugliari and Haas combining with others with foreign pedigrees (Schellscheidt, Chyzowych) to solidify that region's prominent place in the U.S. game.

Pennsylvania soccer unearthed several exemplary coaches who expanded on Philadelphia's earlier soccer prominence. The Keystone State produced legendary coaches whose efforts made an impact locally and nationally.

And so it has been in terms of New York State's contributions to the sport. Perhaps next to Springfield College, abundant graduates of the soccer programs at the State University of New York's colleges at Brockport and Cortland have made valued contributions to the sport. Another Upstate institution, tiny Hartwick College, beginning with exemplary coach Al Miller, has produced more prominent soccer personalities per capita than any other U.S. institution.

This chapter will offer a template for narratives that will chronicle the lives of coaches from other regions whose careers have elevated soccer to its present status in this country.

John Squires chaired the first NCAA Soccer Tournament Committee.

Tony DiCicco created his coaching legacy while leading the USWNT in the 1990s.

Coach Cliff Stevenson built nationally competitive teams at Brown University.

Among his accomplishments at Connecticut, coach Joe Morrone raised monies for a full scholarship for his team. He is shown with his family, having endowed another scholarship.

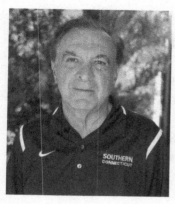

Bob Dikranian founded a model NCAA Division II program at Southern Connecticut.

Peter Gooding (center) receives the NISOA Merit Award with Al Colone (left) and Bill Fortin making the presentation.

Albie Loeffler was a coaching legend at Staples High School.

Boston University's Nancy Feldman is one of the longest serving women's soccer coaches.

New England Soccer Coaching Community

In the period following World War II, soccer activity in the New England region was on the rise. An examination of the careers of selected coaches reveals their varied contributions to the growth of the game.

We've reviewed the lengthy career of coach Irv Schmid at Springfield College, and he was followed by a number of other remarkable coaches who helped grow the game not only regionally but also nationally.

Dr. John Squires – The Father of NCAA Championship Soccer

While Dr. John Squires' tenure as soccer coach at the University of Connecticut certainly had its share of successes, his legacy in the game is principally tied to the beginnings of the NCAA men's soccer tournament.

For it was in 1959 that the quietly effective UConn coach was appointed to oversee the first staging of NCAA post-season play on his Storrs campus fields.

John's first year of service on the NCAA Rules Committee was 1958, and the following year, he and other regional chairs selected the field of eight teams that culminated with upstart St. Louis University defeating Bridgeport 5-2 in the finale.

Labeled by many as the "Father of NCAA Championship Soccer," Squires' 1960 UConn team earned a spot in the tournament, bowing out to a Maryland team that lost to St. Louis 3-2 in the final played at Brooklyn College.

Both Soccer and Swimming Excellence

Soccer was a principal focus for the Norwalk (CT) native when he entered Springfield College in 1930, with swimming a close second. In fact, in his senior year, John was the New England backstroke champion.

Following the 1941 season, he joined the U.S. Navy and Lieutenant Commander Squires and was credited with instructing thousands of sailors in aquatic survival training during World War II.

An Assisted Final Sail

Returning to UConn, the highlights of his coaching career included fielding an unbeaten (11-0) 1948 team that, in addition to earning the NEISL title, was accorded the mythical national title.

Squires was a charter member of the NSCAA and, in addition to his NCAA activity in 1960, he was serving as president of the coaches association that same year. He also served as the NCAA representative to committees that chose players for participation in both the Pan American and the Olympic soccer competitions of the 1940s and 1950s.

During his UConn coaching tenure, the respected Squires was noted for conducting annual soccer clinics at Storrs for the Connecticut Interscholastic Athletic Conference.

Summers found him offering Connecticut undergrads popular courses in safe boating and seamanship. Following his retirement from soccer coaching, he continued as Huskies men's swim coach until 1976.

He was always most comfortable on the water and in the days before his death in 2006 in Miami was able, at age 94, to take a final assisted sail.

Honors

Squires earned many awards and distinctions over the course of his career. For his valued contributions to their organizations, he was presented with the Honor Awards of the New England Intercollegiate Soccer League (1959) and the NSCAA (1973).

He was later inducted into the National Soccer Coaches Hall of Fame in 1993, the Springfield College Hall of Fame in 1996, and the Connecticut Soccer Hall of Fame in 2001.

Dr. John L. McKeon – Building Bridgeport Soccer

If there were a soccer organization that was involved in promoting soccer beginning in the 1950s, there was a good chance that Dr. John McKeon was among those leading its efforts.

Whether it was the United States Soccer Federation (USSF), the Intercollegiate Soccer Association of America (ISAA), or the National Soccer Coaches Association of America (NSCAA), McKeon was involved in their political affairs.

A Champion Track Athlete

Born in New York City in 1923, the lanky youngster played baseball with the New York Giants organization before entering World War II service. Earlier, he had twice been a member of his NYC championship high school mile relay team.

Utilizing the GI Bill, he enrolled at Drake (IA) University, where he competed in track and field and cross-country. He was a member of the school's NCAA championship cross-country team in 1946 and was Mid-Atlantic AAU champion in the half-mile.

He received a Bachelor of Science degree from Drake University in 1948, and both his master of education degree, in 1950, and his doctorate of physical education degree, in 1965, from Springfield (MA) College.

He began teaching physical education at the University of Bridgeport from 1953-65 before moving west to East Stroudsburg (PA) State University from 1966 until his retirement in 1988.

Elevating Bridgeport Soccer

John was one of the nation's most highly respected, most honored, and most successful soccer coaches and administrators over a 40-year period. His 1959 Bridgeport team qualified for the first NCAA Soccer Tournament, losing in the final to St. Louis University, 5-2 following a historic 11 overtime 2-1 win over West Chester (PA) State.

McKeon coached Bridgeport for 12 years, from 1953 to 1964, with his teams posting a record of 97-25-6. Bridgeport also reached the NCAA semifinals in 1961 and the quarterfinals in 1963 and 1964.

By 1966, Coach McKeon had departed New England to take the coaching reins at East Stroudsburg (PA) University where he continued his wide-ranging involvement in soccer.

Tony DiCicco – Goalkeeper, Coach, and More

As with many others, Tony DiCicco's contribution to soccer were multifaceted, ranging from his time as an All-America goalkeeper for coach Irv Schmid at Springfield College to, shortly before his passing in 2017, serving as a color commentator for ESPN and Fox Sports.

Following Springfield, he refined his goalkeeping skills while playing for the Connecticut Wildcats and Rhode Island Oceaneers in the American Soccer League (1971-75). His play earned him a cap with the U.S. National Team in 1973. His teaching of the position was enhanced when he and Dan Gaspar founded the Soccer Plus Goalkeeper Schools in 1981.

His coaching reputation was enhanced in the 1980s as he appeared as a clinician at several NSCAA conventions, and his articles on coaching goalkeeping also appeared in *Soccer Journal*.

Coaching the U.S. Women's National Team

DiCicco's coaching ascendency continued when he served as Anson Dorrance's assistant with the U.S. Women's team that won the first FIFA Women's World Cup in 1991.

When it came time to prepare the U.S. Women's National Team for the 1996 Olympics, U.S. Soccer (and coach Anson Dorrance) tabbed the experienced DiCicco to lead the way. His status as an important international coach was solidified when the U.S. women captured both the Olympic Games gold medal in 1996 and the FIFA Women's World Championship in 1999. His coaching record in FIFA-sponsored tournaments was further enhanced when he led the U.S. U-20 Women's team to the title in the 2008 FIFA U-20 World Cup, held in Chile. Overall, DiCicco's resume shows a combined 103-8-8 (.899) record while coaching U.S. women's national teams.

Of importance to the U.S. coaching community was DiCicco's sharing his experiences coaching women. The book, *Catch Them Being Good: Everything You Need to Know to Successfully Coach Girls,* was published in 2003 and co-authored with Colleen Hacker and Charles Salzberg.

Aiding the Women's Professional Game

With his reputation as a coach of women solidly established, Tony DiCicco lent his energies to helping establish the women's professional game, serving both as the founding commissioner of the Women's Professional Soccer Association, from 2000-03, and commissioner of its successor, the Women's United Soccer Association, from 2009-11.

DiCicco worked as a commentator and analyst for ESPN and FOX Sport's broadcasts of women's soccer, including the 2011 and the 2015 Women's World Cups.

Alongside those efforts he continued to operate his camp business while also serving as head goalkeeper instructor for the NSCAA Academy, a position he held at the time of his passing in 2017.

In honor of his noteworthy contributions to the game, he was inducted into both the U.S. Soccer Hall of Fame (2012) and the NSCAA Hall of Fame (2016).

Tipping on Tony

"Tony was, of course, much more than a coach of goalkeepers." –Jeff Tipping

Former United Soccer Coaches Director of Coaching Jeff Tipping recalls Tony's coaching contributions:

"Tony and I became friends through the NSCAA and, during my tenure as NSCAA Director of Coaching Education when he was appointed Director of Goalkeeping and wrote the goalkeeping curriculum for the NSCAA Academy. Consequently, Tony helped in the goalkeeping education of thousands of American coaches.

"Tony's Soccer Plus goalkeeping camp was a quality enterprise and he and Dan Gaspar (along with Joe Machnik) should get credit for the upsurge in American goalkeeping in the late 1990s.

"Tony was, of course, much more than a coach of goalkeepers and goalkeeping coaches. He was the essence of an outstanding all-round soccer coach and manager. In 1998, he asked me to come out to the U.S. Women's training camp in Chula Vista, California, and do some work with his back line players. I spent two weeks with the team, observing his management style in dealing with the best female players on the planet.

"With Mia Hamm, Kristine Lilly, Brianna Scurry, Brandi Chastain, Carla Overbeck, Joy Fawcett and Michelle Ackers on the squad, he was shrewd enough to recognize these women as real leaders and, sure enough, he let them lead."

"These high-level players did not like being beaten at ANYTHING ... their competitive level was through the roof ... and the demands they put on each other in practice made me think – 'This team's going to win the 1999 World Cup' – and they did.

"The competitive atmosphere Tony enhanced was balanced by excellent team meetings and events which developed team camaraderie. He was a genius at player management and, also, put together a strong USWNT coaching staff that included April Heinrichs among others.

"Tony stands as the ultimate example for all coaches to emulate. If you looked for the word 'gentleman' in the dictionary there would be a picture of Tony DiCicco. Although he, certainly, was no pushover, his dealings with people were of the highest order.

"To me Tony DiCicco falls into the 'Churchill Class' of human beings – UNFORGETTABLE!"[72]

Joe Morrone – An Organizational Guru

The name of Joe Morrone is still synonymous not only with the New England region where his multifaceted legacy has had a huge impact on all levels of soccer but throughout the U.S. soccer community as well.

At the time of his demise in 2015, his successor, coach Ray Reid, remarked, "Coach Morrone laid the blueprint not only for soccer at UConn but more importantly for college soccer in the entire country as well."

The Wrong Sports at UMass

Born in Worcester, Massachusetts, in 1935, the ambitious Morrone graduated from the University of Massachusetts, Amherst, in 1958, where he was named the school's outstanding senior athlete after starring in three sports: soccer, hockey, and lacrosse.

It was while at UMass that Morrone's lifetime commitment to soccer was shaped. For when as an undergraduate he protested to AD Warren McGuirk that he felt soccer (and other so-called minor sports) deserved greater scholarship support. McGuirk responded that Joe was unrealistic to expect more monies to be expended on minor sports, closing by stating, "you simply are playing the wrong sports!"

If there was one event that may have been responsible for Joe's subsequent untiring efforts to elevate soccer's status, then the director's comment most likely helped supply the needed impetus.

Middlebury (VT) College

Before arriving in Storrs, Morrone spent 11 years (1958-68) at Middlebury, where he was the nation's youngest head soccer (and lacrosse) coach.

While at Middlebury, his soccer teams never had a losing season. The 1965 team went undefeated (8-0-1), and his overall record of 64-21-11 included a NEISL title and two NCAA Tournament appearances.

In an effort to upgrade the officiating of soccer, in 1963 Joe, along with UMass coach Larry Briggs, were among the founding members of the National Intercollegiate Referees Association. He wrote the NISOA's initial constitution and by-laws and was NISOA President in 1971. The organization presented him its Honor Award in 1976 and inducted him into its Hall of Fame in 1977.

Establishing UConn Soccer

"Coaching was my life ..." –Joe Morrone

In 1969, he began a legendary 28-year coaching and administrative career at the University of Connecticut.

Underpinning the resultant success was Morrone's basic philosophy: "You must know your strengths and weaknesses and try to maximize the first while minimizing the second. In developing your approach, you should base it on your athletic career while also mirroring the positive actions of other successful coaches and individuals."

As he stated in a video prior to his passing, his goals were simple: "Coaching was my life and I was determined to work hard in order for the group to be successful. I hope that people will remember me as one who got the most out of his players."[73]

His overall coaching record was 442-199-44, and his contributions to the college game were recognized in 1991 when he was presented the Bill Jeffrey Award.

Taking over a struggling UConn program, Morrone's unrelenting recruitment process resulted in Husky teams qualifying for 16 Division I Tournaments during his tenure, including in 1981 when Connecticut captured the DI title with a 2-1 victory over Alabama A&M at Stanford University.

Establishing the UConn Brand

Due to Morrone's unrelenting efforts, the Connecticut program was a pacesetter in a number of areas of the game, including:

- Constructing what was to become Joe Morrone Stadium ("built literally by his own hands" according to current coach Ray Reid). It inspired construction on a number of other dedicated soccer facilities on other college campuses.
- Forming the Friends of Connecticut Soccer support group.
- Scheduling intersectional soccer play. Alabama A&M, St. Louis, SIU-Edwardsville, Indiana, and San Francisco were frequent guests while the Huskies took tours to Florida, Texas, and California in different years. Home matches concluded with post-game meals between the two sides.
- Scheduling home matches on Sundays so as not to compete with football.
- Designing a well-fined approach to media relations.
- Arranging for broadcasts of UConn soccer on a state-wide basis.
- Organizing private fundraising initiatives that resulted in UConn becoming a full-scholarship Division I program.
- Founding the Connecticut Soccer School at Mt. Holyoke College, where UConn coaching methodology was featured for 25 years.
- Annually hosting winter indoor soccer tournaments that attracted college teams throughout the Northeast.

Those enterprises resulted in what today might be labeled the "UConn Brand." While they brought UConn soccer to national prominence, the coach was also focused on youth player development. Statewide, he, along with Al Bell, co-founded the Connecticut Junior Soccer Association, while in his local community he spearheaded the formation of the Mansfield Youth Soccer Association.

The latter group spawned the successful playing careers of the three Morrone children. Sons Joe, Jr. and Bill played for their father and Joe, Jr. was named the Hermann Trophy recipient in 1980. Both boys were NSCAA All-America players, as was sister Melissa.

173

His NSCAA Presidency

"Get your ducks in order!" –Joe Morrone

Morrone served as President of the National Soccer Coaches Association of America from 1986-87.

While president, and dressed in his familiar white shirt, tie, and suspenders, he arrived to meetings with a crate of folders organized in order of deliberation. All knew that the meetings were going to be extended, detailed, and that, no matter how long it took, business concluded only when every folder was addressed.

Prior to presiding over NSCAA affairs, Morrone, due to the fact that he had spearheaded the formation of NISOA, was asked in 1977 to rewrite the NSCAA constitution and by-laws. Coordinating with NISOA's Ray Bernabei, they worked together to formulate a new organizational structure.

As past president, Morrone served on the NSCAA's legislative committee, where he lent his expertise to later administrations as they sought counsel on matters constitutional or otherwise.

But while serving as president, the precise Morrone was sometime a bit tedious when referencing the organization charts that detailed the organizational approach to NSCAA business. His New England-accented "chant(s)" will ring forever. However, the NSCAA *did* become a better-organized group under his tutelage.

In addition to legalistic matters, one of his constant reminders to everyone was to, "Get your ducks in order!" and, "Have backup! If you for some reason can't do it, have someone in line who can!"

Dedication, passion, commitment to the task and finishing the job—those were Morrone axioms.

Well Acknowledged by All

It took just three years for Morrone to put Connecticut into the national limelight.

Beginning in1973, the team had averaged over 15 wins a season and, as noted, won the coveted NCAA Division I National Championship in 1981. His Connecticut teams qualified for the NCAA Tournament 16 times in his 20 years at the helm. At his passing, his 340-plus Division I career victories placed him fourth among active collegiate coaches.

He has received numerous awards and accolades from his peers. The list includes six Coach-of-the-Year Awards as well as the University of Connecticut's Alumni Association Albert N. Jorgensen Award in 1983; the Honor Award from the New England Intercollegiate Soccer League in 1985; and The Bill Jeffrey Award in 1991 for his contributions to college soccer. He was presented the NSCAA's Honor Award in 1995 and inducted into its Hall of Fame in 2002.

His passing in 2015 evoked a lot of memories from his coaching friends.

Joe Morrone was indeed an organizational guru. His methods and proven administrative principles are, if not emulated, certainly the envy of every coach running a collegiate soccer program. In conclusion, Joe Morrone was a hero to hundreds of soccer aficionados in this country. And he has a special place in the hearts of countless friends in the soccer coaching fraternity. Without question, his legacy is intact.

Cliff Stevenson – A Program Builder

Cliff Stevenson was born and raised in New England and while he made his first coaching impression in the Midwest, he was among that group of coaches in various geographic regions of the country who took soccer in a direction that its pioneer coaches could not have imagined.

There are a number of adjectives that can be ascribed to the man who was a winner at every stop in his 46-year coaching career. His Brown University profile includes such words as pioneer, teacher, disciplinarian, legislator, evangelist, groundskeeper, and con man—not necessarily in that order.

His Springfield Soccer Education

Raised in Pawtucket, Rhode Island, Stevenson's high school did not sponsor soccer. His latent desire to play soccer was fulfilled when he matriculated at Springfield College in 1948, where he refined his skills under coach Irv Schmid. He earned All-NEISL honors in the fall sport while also lettering in a new sport, lacrosse.

The Record Oberlin Win Streak

Upon graduation from Springfield in 1952, he became varsity soccer and lacrosse coach and director of physical education at Oberlin College. Prior to the Stevenson appointment, under coach Ben Collins, Oberlin was the standout team in the Buckeye State.

Beginning in 1952, Stevenson continued the school's soccer success, recording three straight unbeaten seasons before a loss to Kenyon ended the school's 42-match unbeaten streak. The coach's enthusiasm for the game was reflected in the fact that a reported 78 undergrads turned out for places on the 1955 team. All-America midfielder Joe Molder later surfaced as coach at Columbia University from 1958-70.

One undergrad attracted to Oberlin because of its soccer prowess was Stu Parry. He later established one of the Midwest's first soccer dynasties at Akron University.

In eight years at Oberlin, Stevenson's teams were 48-16-7 and captured four Midwest Conference championships. In lacrosse, the beat was the same: a 56-12-4 record with three undefeated seasons and four Ohio Collegiate Association titles.

Brown – Nationally Competitive

Beginning with Joe Morrone's appointment as Connecticut coach in 1969, he and Stevenson were two of the country's most dogged pursuers of soccer talent.

In 1960, Cliff Stevenson arrived in Providence following a stellar coaching career at Oberlin (OH) College. Thus began a remarkable 30-season coaching tenure at Brown University.

After his appointment as Brown's first full-time soccer coach in 1960, Stevenson experienced his only losing season, winning but one of 10 games. Beginning in 1961 and continuing through 1978, Brown was one of the country's most competitive teams.

During that period, Stevenson's teams achieved a 183-71-18 record that included 13 NCAA post-season bids (due to Ivy League rules the team was precluded from NCAA play from 1966-67), reaching the semi-final round of NCAA play in 1968, 1973, 1975, and 1977. The Bears also captured 10 Ivy League titles and were declared New England Intercollegiate Soccer League (NEISL) titlists on seven occasions. Overall, during his 38-year Oberlin/Brown coaching career, Stevenson compiled a 299-176-12 record. Sixteen different Brown players were accorded NSCAA All-America selection from 1963-78.

Brown soccer waned from 1978 onward. Some attribute the decline to the fact that when several veteran New England and Ivy League coaches retired, they were supplanted by new younger, more ambitious coaches who were as relentless at the recruiting game as was Stevenson. From 1979 to his 1990 retirement, Bear soccer would not win an Ivy League title, have one of its players earn All-America honors, or see the team be selected to the NCAA Tournament.

He left coaching having established himself as one of those strong advocates of the game.

Peter Gooding at Amherst – A Dream Job

"I was actually being paid to coach a college team! I had died and gone to heaven."
–Peter Gooding

Peter Gooding was educated at England's Loughborough University and, in addition to obtaining a degree in physical education, he honed his soccer play under the guidance of English coaching legend Alan Wade. Among his teammates were Jack Detchon and Tony Waiters, who both later become featured NSCAA Academy staff members.

When he first alighted on the West Coast, Peter taught for a bit and played semiprofessionally for two seasons in Victoria, British Columbia. He then moved East to Amherst, Massachusetts, where, in addition to play with various New England semiprofessional teams, he earned his master's degree while assisting NSCAA pioneer Larry Briggs with the UMass men's soccer team.

After his degree at UMass, he served on the staff at Cape Cod's Barnstable (MA) High School. A chance meeting between Barnstable's AD and the president of Amherst College occurred at a time when the then-Lord Jeffs were looking for a new soccer coach; eventually, this led to his Amherst hire in 1968. In 1977, Gooding added to his coaching responsibilities when he was named Amherst's Director of Athletics.

Later, and upon reflection, he shook his head. "I was actually being paid to coach a college team! I had died and gone to heaven." In 21 seasons, the Gooding coaching record was 232-134-43, with the team reaching the NCAA Division III Regional Finals in 1998 and 2002. Win Smith '71 played on Gooding's first Amherst squad. He noted, "He had a unique ability to bring out the best in people."[77]

The hard-working former left back's legacy is allied with his role in establishing the NSCAA Coaching Academy, and that is discussed in another section of the book. He also served NSCAA as president in 1990-91. He was recipient of its Honor Award in 2001 and named to its Hall of Fame in 2015.

Honor Award Committee Chairman C. Clifford McCrath of Seattle Pacific University, in introducing Gooding as the award recipient, captured the essence of the man when he stated, "He is more than just brilliance and ironclad work ethic. He is propriety in leather boots—with a whistle and wit instead of a whip."[78]

He is also possibly the only American to have displaced the Portuguese legend Eusebio as a player!

Armand Bob Dikranian – A McKeon Prodigy

Bob Dikranian was born and raised in the borough of Queens in New York City. In 1958, he chose to attend the University of Bridgeport (CT), approximately an hour and a half from his Astoria home,

It has turned out to be a fortuitous decision for the former high school soccer star, because from his enrollment to the present, he has carved out a soccer coaching career that places him at the very top rung among NCAA Division II coaches.

Upon graduation from Bridgeport, the proud Armenian initiated the men's soccer program at Southern Connecticut State University and, in the process, set a new standard for other NCAA Division II institutions to attain.

Spotted by Renzulli

Encouraged by their father, Fred, who recognized the inherent values athletics helped instill in young people, Armand and brother Haig both played at Bayside High School, where they credit coach Allen Thail with accelerating their soccer development.

Playing as a forward, Bob attracted the notice of U.S. Soccer Hall of Famer Peter Renzulli, and it was he who chose him to play in the 1958 annual fall match between the New York City and Philadelphia schoolboys.

Alongside their school play, the eager youngsters played in the youth program sponsored by the German-American League clubs. They accompanied their father when he watched his favored talented Armenian Soccer Club. Bob recalled that his education in the game was also honed watching the play of various senior teams. "Most of the time we'd not only watch the Armenian team play but stick around Sundays and watch another match or two at places like the Van Cortlandt Park and others."[81]

Bridgeport and McKeon

College soccer during the 1950s was expanding in terms of the number of institutions sponsoring the sport, but also the quality of the play was improving as part of that growth.

Dikranian, in turning out for the Bridgeport team, was somewhat surprised by the overall excellence of the 1959 team that coach Dr. John McKeon had put together. He recalled, "They were loaded with solid players at every position."

1959 marked the staging of the first NCAA National Soccer Tournament at Storrs, Connecticut. Representing NEISL, unbeaten (9-0) Bridgeport defeated Colgate 3-2 on a Dikranian overtime goal before tackling West Chester in the semifinals. Tied 1-1 in regulation, the game had to be extended to a second day before Bridgeport won in the tenth overtime. As the saying goes, Bridgeport "won the battle, but lost the war," as it was a weary team that succumbed to St. Louis 5-2 in the final.

By his senior year, Dikranian had earned All-America honors and had developed a close relationship with coach McKeon. "Fortunately for me and a lot of others, John was both well-known and respected within the college soccer community. While there is no comparison today to the 1960s, but when you had someone like John McKeon in your corner and he recommended you for a job it was pretty much yours." And so it was that Dikranian moved 22 miles east to New Haven to take the Southern Connecticut job in 1963.

Incidentally, in addition to Bob Dikranian, two other 1959 UB team members later became involved in college soccer coaching. Bill Brew coached at Quinnipiac from 1965-77, while Jim Kuhlmann, a three-time All-NEISL selection, initiated the men's program at Fairfield University in 1962 and remained as Stags' coach until 1986.

Establishing Owl Soccer

It took three seasons before the first Southern Connecticut State men's soccer team took the field in 1966. In the following 21 seasons, the Owls amassed a

227-94-21 overall record in establishing what many consider the benchmark Division II program in the nation. Dikranian teams appeared in 14 NCAA Division II tournaments, including six straight trips to the semifinals (1978-83). After finishing as the bridesmaid for so many years, Southern rang the bell for its first-ever NCAA championship in 1987. The Owls coach was accorded NSCAA National Division II COY honors for 1982-1983, the first years the award was presented.

Pivotal to Southern's success was identification and enrollment of talented players.

Giving Back to the Game

When he handed over the Southern coaching reins to Ray Reid in 1990, Dikranian's energies have continued to apply to various components of the game.

That included his continued role as USSF Director of Coaching for Region I as well as utilizing his A License as a member of the organization's national coaching staff.

Always conscious of giving back to his community, at various times Bob coached the local Vasco DaGama Soccer Club, the New Haven Soccer Club, and the South Central Soccer Club. He also was a frequent host for coaching clinics in the New Haven area. These were in addition to national clinics and lectures for USSF and NSCAA.

Now in his ninth decade, Bob has continued to serve as assistant coach for both the SCSU men's and women's teams and, for a period of time, served in a similar role, as well as the Director of Operations for the Yale women's soccer team.

An accomplished soccer official himself (he worked the 1992 NCAA Division III final matches), the retired coach served for a period as the Coordinator of Soccer Officiating for the ECAC.

Scores of his former players have followed the Dikranian example and continued to play roles in the development of the game. Brian Bliss, in his role as Player Personnel Director at Sporting KC, is one example of the efforts of former SCSU players, while another is the recently retired Neil Roberts, who ended a 35-year career as head coach of the Boston University men.

Respected and Honored

Highly respected for both the number and quality of his contributions to the game, Dikranian has been honored many times for his coaching achievements. Perhaps the most notable were his inductions into the National Soccer Coaches Association Hall of Fame in 2013 and the Connecticut Soccer Hall of Fame in 1999. Bob was inducted into the Southern Connecticut State University Alumni Sports Hall of Fame, the University of Bridgeport Hall of Fame, the Connecticut Soccer Hall of Fame, and the New England Hall of Fame. In all, he has been honored over 35 times by various soccer organizations.

Secondary School Coaching Leaders

The nation's secondary school community includes a number of individuals whose extraordinary coaching and organizational skills have contributed to growth of soccer in their regions of the country.

In many cases, they owed their indoctrination to the sport to a mentor who had earlier made significant contributions to the game.

While certainly not exclusive, here are the resumes of some of those New England coaches who stood out for their varied contributions to the game.

Albie Loeffler – A Staples Legend

Perhaps the accolade he most cherished was the 1998 naming of the Staples field as Albie Loeffler Field.

Albie Loeffler began his playing career in the mid-1930s under UConn's first full-time coach, Jack Dennerly. Named to the All-New England All-America team in 1936, he later regretted not finishing his career under Dennerly's successor, John Squires.

He began coaching at Ellsworth High School (1942-52) in Windsor (CT), where his teams won two state titles in basketball and one in soccer. Moving on to Staples (Westport, CT) High School in 1952, he coached basketball, baseball, and track before initiating its soccer program in 1957. Over the next 20 years, he led Staples to several national records, including seven state championships, 25 consecutive shutouts, and a 43-straight-game win streak. Also noteworthy was that Staples teams lost just two home games between 1965 and 1975.

At the time of his 1978 retirement, his 314 wins were a national record. Albie was a two-time National Coach of the Year, with more than 175 players who went on to play college soccer, including 11 players who earned All-America honors. Staples grads who entered coaching include former coaches Steve Baumann (Penn), Larry McFaddin (North County [NY] Community College), and Jim Kaufman (Curry [MA] College). Other Staples grads currently coaching include Clemson coach Mike Noonan and Matt Lamb, Rhodes (TN) College.

Current Staples coach Dan Woog is another Loeffler product and estimates that there are 8-10 other Staples grads coaching soccer at the secondary school level.

In addition to coaching, Albie was instrumental in the formation of the National Intercollegiate Soccer Officials Association (NISOA) and helped develop the two-man system of officiating. Added to his resume is the fact that he officiated the first NCAA championship match, between St. Louis and Bridgeport at Storrs (CT), in 1959.

A member of the NISOA Soccer Hall of Fame (2000), Loeffler was inducted into the United Soccer Coaches Hall of Fame in 2019. Perhaps the accolade he most cherished was the 1998 naming of the Staples field as Albie Loeffler Field.

Despite his many other accomplishments, his 20 years as Staples soccer coach defined him for the rest of his life. His quiet demeanor—he indicated anger by slowly picking up grass and throwing it into the wind—and dry sense of humor were hallmarks of his soccer coaching career, though his basketball and baseball players remember a more vocal side!

"The Staples soccer community — all of Staples, in fact — has lost a legend," Woog said at the time of his passing. "None of us who love Staples soccer would be here today without his quiet leadership and determined vision.

"He created something that has positively impacted thousands of lives directly, and tens of thousands more indirectly. I would not be who I am had I not known Albie Loeffler—and I know countless others would say exactly the same thing." 82

Two other New England secondary school coaches achieved noteworthy careers matching Loeffler's, including one who suited up for Manchester United during his playing days!

Four New Jersey Soccer Coaching Icons

There are a number of standout New Jersey coaches who helped elevate soccer following World War II and beyond. Otto Haas helped pave the way; later, coaches such as Miller Bugliari, Gene Chyzowych, and Manny Schellscheidt took up the cause and left their imprint on the game in the Garden State.

Otto Haas – An Early Coaching Legend

In 1992, and perhaps indicative of his stature among the country's soccer coaches, former Chatham (NJ) High School coach Otto Haas became the first secondary school coach inducted into the United Soccer Coaches Hall of Fame.

The induction was in tribute to Haas's legendary 33-year career at Chatham, where his teams captured 16 New Jersey state titles. Also noteworthy, at the time of his passing in 1979, Haas had amassed a then-national secondary school record of 409 victories.

A U.S. Marines

Born in Montclair, New Jersey, Haas graduated from Colgate University in 1941 and, following that, served a four-year stint in World War II with the U.S. Marines. Upon discharge in 1945, he began his Chatham coaching career.

Beginning in 1952, and until his retirement from coaching in 1978, Chatham's 16 NJSIAA titles included two occasions when the school captured four successive championships (1952-56; 1967-70). It was during the 1967-70 seasons that the team recorded what was then a national unbeaten winning streak of 52 matches.

Chatham recorded six undefeated seasons under Haas, and he was named New Jersey's best coach on three occasions. He retired with a career record of 409-70-58. In tribute, the school's soccer field is named in his honor, and the MVP of the Morris County playoffs is annually presented with the Otto Haas Award.

The Man

"I know that message made the rounds of the school the next day and was as an effective lesson regarding sportsmanship as one could deliver." –John Rennie

Haas product John Rennie's comments help in describing the role the Chatham legend played in his community. "He was loved and respected for how well he managed all he had to deal with as coach and administrator. He helped a lot of people and for many, he was a father figure."

Rennie recalled an incident that confirmed for many the high standard that Haas established for Chatham's soccer players. "I remember one game where a Chatham player got into an argument with one of the referees. At halftime Otto simply helped the player get his uniform shirt off and ushered him to the school bus where he stayed for the second half. I know that message made the rounds of the school the next day and was as an effective lesson regarding sportsmanship one could deliver."[85]

Mentoring Others

Upon his 1961 graduation from Temple University, where he earned All-America honors playing for coach Pete Leaness, Gene Chyzowych served as assistant coach under Otto Haas. Two years later, Gene took the coaching position at Columbia (NJ) High School, where he shaped his own soccer-coaching legacy.

John Rennie had an opportunity to access the Haas-Chyzowych relationship: "Gene was an excellent player and was intent on helping us improve our technical ability through the introduction of various drills while Otto, not resisting Gene's approach, was of the opinion, 'If we are successful doing it my way, why change things.' I am certain he appreciated Gene's good intentions and also certain he recommended him for the Columbia (NJ) High School soccer job."[86]

Some attributed Chatham's early successes to the fact that the school did not field a football team. When football was introduced in 1960, it was thought that a sharing of the small school's athletic manpower would greatly impact its soccer team. "We'll be fine," Haas assured everyone, and they were, as the team recorded a 17-2 season, including capturing the New Jersey Group III title.

Attesting to Haas's professionalism, John Rennie noted that when Chatham decided to restart football, Haas in his AD role made certain the school hired the best football coach it could find.

A year later, John Rennie scored 30 goals in 15 matches before embarking on an injury-shortened playing career at Temple, followed by a lengthy coaching career that included directing Duke University to the NCAA title in 1986.

Gene Chyzowych – A Columbia High School Legend

Possibly, brother Walter earned greater soccer national acknowledgement, but Eugene "Gene" Chyzowych also cut a wide swath through the U.S. game as a player, coach, and advocate of the game.

Gene Chyzowych (right) was a coaching legend at New Jersey's Columbia High School.

The Leaness Influence

Born in the Ukraine, Gene survived World War II as a displaced person and eventually settled in Philadelphia, where he became a standout soccer player, first at Northeast Catholic High School and later under coach William "Pete" Leaness at Temple University.

The Chyzowych playing career was marked by championship play in the American Soccer League with various teams in the 1950s and 1960s, including the Philadelphia Ukrainians and the New York Inter teams. He also coached in the ASL with the Newark Ukrainians (1973) and the New York Apollo (1976).

For a brief time (1972-73), he served as president of the ASL as well as the USMNT coach in 1973.

Constructing Columbia Powerhouses

... he was the school's founding [volleyball] coach and led the team to a 248-match unbeaten streak...

Following graduation from Temple, his search for a teaching job brought him to Northern New Jersey, where in 1961 he served the aforementioned apprenticeship under Otto Haas.

In 1964, and eager to replicate Chatham's soccer success, Gene was named boys coach at Maplewood's Columbia High School. The following year he took the step of doing something that was a new concept for soccer—he established a feeder system, with the creation of the Cougar Soccer Club.

As with his brother, in 1971, Gene honed his coaching skill through enrollment at the USSF Coaching School. There, he was among the first American coaches to earn an A coaching license from German coach Dettmar Cramer.

Until he was forced by health issues to resign his coaching in 2013 (he passed in 2014), his Columbia teams were annually a soccer power in New Jersey, racking up 24 conference titles, 16 sectional titles, 13 Essex County championships, and four NJIAA titles. Under Gene, over 200 Columbia players earned All-NJ honors, 28 players were accorded NSCAA All-America honors, and five had earned USMNT caps.

With his 758-216-73 (.724) coaching record, Gene Chyzowych ranks first nationally in career victories in public high school annals. Terry Michler at Christian Brothers (MO) College with over 1,000 wins and Miller Bugliari at The Pingry (NJ) School with 818 (and counting) have achieved their records at private schools.

Chyzowych's coaching success also extended to girls volleyball. In 1977, he was the school's founding coach and led the team to a 248-match unbeaten streak before losing its first match in 1988.

His soccer success spawned a coaching tree composed of ex-players who became highly successful college coaches, including Dave Masur (St. John's University [NY]) and Lenny Armuth (Drew University [NJ]), along with such established New Jersey high school coaches as David Donovan (Delbarton), Marty Berman (Seton Hall Prep), and Jack Weber (Verona).

The First Soccer Camps

In 1966, Gene and brother Walter, along with Montclair's Lenny Lucenko and Pratt's Wayne Sunderland, founded one of the nation's first residential soccer camps, The All-America Soccer Camp.

Named to the NSCAA Board of Directors in the 1980s, Gene was a force in the organization's promotion of secondary school soccer, serving on its All-America committee for many years and also chairing the startup of a seasonal approach to national rankings of high school boys and girls teams.

Outside of his NSCAA contributions, the well-respected coach was a member of the national high school federation's rules committee for many years and also aided in the formation of the New Jersey State Youth Soccer Association in the 1970s. He, along with Miller Bugliari and others, conducted coaching licensing programs for the NJSYA for many years.

Soccer Honors

Gene Chyzowych was inducted into the New Jersey Interscholastic Coaches Hall of Fame in 1986. In 2002, he was honored with the presentation of the Frank McGuire Foundation Award for his coaching accomplishments in the Metropolitan area. Columbia High School named its soccer field in his honor, and he was inducted into its Hall of Fame in 2004.

For his service to the secondary school game, he was the recipient of the NSCAA Robert W. Robinson Award in 1999, and he was inducted to the organization's Hall of Fame in 2009.

Miller Bugliari – A Pingry Institution

If one ranks secondary school coaches in terms of longevity, then The Pingry School's Miller Bugliari, as of 2020, is at the top of the list. Not only do his 52 years of service at the New Jersey private school eclipse others in the soccer coaching community, but as of 2020, his 878 career coaching victories rank second only to Christian Brothers College (MO) coach Terry Michler's more than 1,000 wins.

Pingry soccer coach is shown in his office strewn with soccer memorabilia with Juventus captain Giorgio Chiellini.

Pingry School Longevity

...he [Bugliari] was hired by New York Giants football team for what has been a nearly century-long position as head of its chain crew for its home games.

The Pingry School has played a substantial role in the coach's life with his family having had a long affiliation with the school.

It was at Pingry that soccer coach Frank West noted an energetic youngster playing touch football and coaxed him into playing soccer. In addition to playing sports (basketball and baseball were his other pursuits), Miller graduated with a firm commitment to achieve the same level of excellence in teaching and coaching that he had experienced at Pingry.

With that in mind, and following his 1953 graduation from Pingry, Bugliari enrolled at Springfield College, where he majored in physical education and journalism and graduated *cum laude*. Nicknamed "Bugs" by his teammates, he also excelled as a three-year soccer center midfielder for coach Irv Schmid.

Following a four-year hitch in the U.S. Army, Miller returned to Pingry in 1960 to teach biology and coach a variety of teams. In 1959, he succeeded West as soccer coach.

According to interviews with players, as shared in the 2015 book published by Pingry (*The Lives and Times of Miller A. Bugliari*), the coaching change was transformational for the Pingry players. The new coach, who placed an emphasis on fitness, by his own example, conducted training sessions that emphasized mastery of soccer's techniques.

The aforementioned book offers various insights into Miller's personality that, over a long period of time, has been marked by a series of high jinx and pranks. His multifaceted career includes ownership of a summer camp that offered bare-bones accommodations and life-changing experiences to wealthy children. His purchase of a used bullet-proof Cadillac (no Carfax included!) provided an instrument of enjoyment on many occasions. Miller's attention to detail was invoked in 1974 when he was hired by the New York Giants football team for what has been a nearly century-long position as head of its chain crew for its home games.

Exemplary Coaching Record

The Bugliari coaching record was achieved in New Jersey's highly competitive Union County region against both private and public high schools.

Entering the 2020 season, the career record of 878-125-76 (.849) included 25 combined state championships at the private and public school levels and 25 county championships. Along the way, Pingry has finished undefeated on 25 occasions. In 1983 and 1989, the Bugliari name was honored when he was named NSCAA secondary school COY.

In 1977, in addition to his classroom and coaching responsibilities, Pingry named the affable "Bugs" as director of alumni fundraising. As a measure of his effectiveness, monies were raised to upgrade The Miller Bugliari 1952 World Cup Field (which has hosted World Cup practices for the 1995 Italian National Team, the 2002 United States National Team, and the 2013 Ecuadorian national soccer and baseball teams). Also, in 2017, The Miller A. Bugliari Athletic Complex was opened and features eight squash courts, two basketball floors, and a weight room.

In addition to his dedicated work on behalf of Pingry, Miller has contributed to the game both regionally and nationally.

Honors

Named an NSCAA COY in 1983 and 1989, Bugliari was recipient of the NSCAA Honor Award in 1999 and in 2006 was inducted into the group's Hall of Fame. In addition, in 1996, he was the first recipient of the NSCAA's Robert W. Robinson Award for service to the secondary school game.

Earlier, he was named to the New Jersey Youth Hall of Fame (1989), and Pingry inducted him to its HOF in 1991. He was honored by his alma mater by induction to the Springfield College HOF in 2004, and, in 2014, he was inducted into the New Jersey State High School Hall of Fame.

Manny Schellscheidt – The Games the Teacher

He first came to the United States in 1963 to visit his aunt in New Jersey, and, except for a soccer-related visit back to Germany, Manny Schellscheidt has contributed much to the game in his adopted country as a player and coach.

Playing for Elizabeth SC

Manny shared that his day job paid $75 weekly, he earned another $75 each Sunday.

As mentioned, the 1963 visit to his aunt resulted in his signing and playing some matches for the Elizabeth Soccer Club. Impressed with his play, in 1964, the club made all the arrangements, including a job with a tool and die company, for his return to the United States.

Manny Schellscheidt counsels a Seton Hall University player. He coached Pirate soccer for 24 years.

Frequently, U.S. semi-professional soccer play, prior to the NASL days, is dismissed as unimportant. But for many players of that era, that was not the case. Asked to its impact on his wallet, Manny shared that his day job paid $75 weekly, and he earned another $75 each Sunday.

He recalled that by January of 1966, he had saved enough to buy a used Volkswagen Beatle and then expended $30 ("I could fill my tank for $3!) to travel to Los Angeles to visit a friend.[87]

In June of 1966, and for the next year, Manny returned to his homeland to earn the German DFB's highest coaching license.

Returning to New Jersey in 1967, he pulled the strings from the midfield for Elizabeth SC for the next several seasons. He combined with other stalwarts (some, like Carlos Metidieri, flown in each week to play) to lead Elizabeth to U.S. Challenge Cup titles in 1970 and 1972.

In 1971, as holders, Elizabeth represented the United States in the CONCACAF Cup and hosted Mexico's Cruz Azul FC at their Farcher's Grove home field. The story has a visiting player standing on the battle-worn pitch and inquiring as to where the match was to be played. After all, the visitors' home field was the famed Azteca Stadium in Mexico City. Nevertheless, the match ended a scoreless tie, with the North Americans later losing away, 2-0.

Having first met Al Miller at John McKeon's Pocono Sports Camp, Schellscheidt left Elizabeth and, in 1973, signed as player-assistant coach as Miller formed a new NASL Philadelphia franchise. The Atoms, led by Miller ("a great motivator and organizer") would, in Cinderella fashion, capture the NASL title in their first season of operation. The German transplant also credits GM Bob Ellinger with a great marketing effort ("We drew 22,000 our opening match!").

He noted that in the case of the Atoms sojourn and with other of his later soccer ventures, his New Jersey employer generously granted him leaves of absence. He mentioned that his Atoms salary was $1,000 a month. The team's foreign players earned $500 a month plus use of an apartment and car.

While his playing career was noteworthy, it was his reunion with and enrollment at the USSF Dettmar Cramer-led coaching schools that helped propel his soccer coaching career.

Coaching U.S. Soccer

"Walter [Chyzowych] took on both jobs. I thought it was too much for anyone to do that."
–Manny Schellscheidt

When Cramer left USSF late in 1973, the national team head coaching position was in a state of flux. After leading the Rhode Island Oceaneers to the 1974 American Soccer League title, in February 1975, Schellscheidt assisted interim USMNT coach Al Miller.

1975 was a very busy year for the coach because, in addition to his U.S. team duties, he was player/coach for the new NASL Hartford Bicentennials. At the completion of the NASL season, Schellscheidt was in charge as the U.S. team suffered losses in Seattle and Mexico.

As mentioned, one subject that involved USSF was the matter of filling the USMNT head coaching position along with hiring someone to direct its coaching education department. Schellscheidt recalled a meeting that involved Federation President Gene Edwards, Al Miller, Gene Chyzowych, and himself. "I was very interested in taking on the coaching end of things and proposed a salary to do so. I didn't think I wanted to be national team coach. Well, of course, Walter [Chyzowych] took on both jobs. I thought it was too much for anyone to do that."

With a total player payroll of $65,000, the 1975 Hartford team struggled to compete, going 6-16 that year before improving to 12-12 the second season. By 1978, the team folded after averaging about 3,500 spectators per game.

Taking a breather from his Hartford duties, Manny was one of three coaches who led the Club America Team that participated in the three-team 1976 Bicentennial

Cup Tournament, managing the team in the 1-3 loss to England at JFK Stadium in Philadelphia.

Following Hartford in 1977, he coached the New Jersey Americans to another ASL title.

Those 1975 matches were the first of many U.S. Soccer coaching positions to be held by the transplanted German over the next four decades. Probably his longest stint was assisting Angus McAlpine with the 1982 U-20 men's team. On the bubble to make the team roster was 15-year old Tab Ramos. "He was the best one versus one player we had on the roster," recalled Schellscheidt. "I knew him from our New Jersey ODP."

The team's final tune-up was a match at Dillon Stadium in Hartford. Whatever the circumstances, Ramos had forgotten to pack his soccer shoes. "We borrowed a pair from one of the players who played in the preliminary game. Eventually the starter ahead of him was injured and Tab replaced him and had a great game. It was agreed – he should be on the roster."

Unfortunately, just before the team was about to embark for the CONCACAF U-20 Tournament in Guatemala, it was discovered that Ramos was not a U.S. citizen. The fact that his father held citizenship paved the way for his son to join the team.

Also unfortunate was the fact that Schellscheidt's job prevented him from joining the team, his role assumed by George Tarantini, then-coach at North Carolina State.

In 1983, the McAlpine-Schellscheidt duo was preparing the U.S. men for Olympic play in 1984. Seeking to have a good showing as host country, 36 friendly matches were played by the USMNT. Unfortunately, in changing its rules to allow professionals on team rosters, FIFA resulted in a decision by USSF to replace its basically U-23 roster with players from various NASL teams. In the process, by 1984, the Federation also changed coaches, with McAlpine being replaced by Alketas Panagoulias. Meanwhile, Schellscheidt was tabbed to lead the 1983 Pan American Games team in Caracas, Venezuela, where, in August, it would exit after the first round, as did the United States at the 1984 Olympics.

The McApline-Schellscheidt coaching team was reunited in 1985 as the U.S. U-17 team journeyed to China to play in that inaugural age-group event. Once more the team failed to make it out of first-round play.

Youth Soccer Tributes

Says Al Miller: "Manny is a good man, was an excellent youth coach, helped a lot of young men in the game and was an asset in New Jersey soccer. Dettmar chose him out of the coaching schools to be the national youth coach and suggested I support that decision when he left the U.S. to go coach Bayern Munich."

Throughout his career, Schellscheidt served the U.S. youth game. He was a USYSA Region I ODP coach for 25 years and its head coach in 1987-97. In that time span, he coached the Union Lancers of New Jersey to two straight McGuire Cup U-19 national championship titles (1987-88). His Lancers' assistant coach was Bob Bradley.

Often mentioned is Schellscheidt's ability to identify talent, and that included future coaches such as Bob Bradley. "We often held our ODP tryouts at Princeton where he coached and one day I encouraged Bob to get involved as we were always looking for coaching help. He then joined me coaching the Lancers. In my mind he is one of the best in our country. He is a real student of the game."

His involvement with U.S. Soccer resumed in 1994. Due in part to the elevation of Bruce Arena as USMNT coach in 1998 and his appreciation of Schellscheidt's effectiveness as a mentor of young players ("He's a hidden gem," quoted Arena), the Schellscheidt focus was on development of U-14 age-group players.

Standing on Two Feet

Coincidental with the demise of the U.S. tool and die industry due to outsourcing, in 1988 Schellscheidt took his first full-time soccer job coaching the Seton Hall University men's team.

Except for having to master the intricacies of the NCAA Rule Book, it was an enjoyable experience with the school located but a 12-minute drive from his Union (NJ) home.

Over his 24-year tenure at Seton Hall, the team won two Big East Conference titles and entered the NCAA Division I Tournament on eight occasions.

"If I had to stand on two feet to earn a living I would prefer to do it coaching soccer" was his response when asked to summarize his collegiate coaching experience.

Such responses are a frequent hallmark of Schellscheidt; there are many more to share.

The Outstanding Pennsylvania Soccer Coaching Community

Pennsylvania's coaching community has had a long history of promoting the sport of soccer.

From the 1900s, when Doug Stewart solidified soccer matters in Philadelphia, such Keystone State stalwarts as Walter Bahr, Bob Dunn, John Eiler, Pete Leaness, Charlie Scott, and Don Yonker later took up the cause.

But as the game exploded in the state, especially at the secondary school level, other individuals emerged that continued the legacy created by the state's earlier founders. The names of Jim Egli, John McKeon, Bob Robinson, and Jeff Tipping left their imprint on soccer in the Keystone State. Meanwhile, a contiguous area in central Pennsylvania became the birthplace of several coaches who not only impacted soccer in their locales but eventually would have a national influence on the game.

Bob Robinson – Master Organizer

... the NSCAA High School Long-Term Achievement Award ... was renamed the Robert W. "Robby" Robinson Award in 2001.

Known affectionately as the "cellar dweller" by his wife Kate and his four children, it is obvious when chronicling his career that whatever Bob Robinson was involved with in his Wayne, Pennsylvania, basement has resulted in good outcomes for the Keystone State in particular and U.S. soccer in general.

For whether it was his contributions to his school, community, state, or the National Soccer Coaches of America, Robby's record of accomplishment ranks near the top when his lifetime accomplishments are assessed.

Lower Merion High School

Robby played a bit of football at Interboro High School before enrolling at West Chester State University, where his undergraduate years included witnessing the 1961 soccer team capturing the NCAA title under coach Mel Lorback.

Graduating in 1965 with a degree in math, Bob began a 32-year teaching career at Lower Merion High School. A talented administrator, he eventually ascended to coordinate the school district's K-12 match curriculum.

In 1967, the energetic Robinson got his soccer feet wet when he assisted with the school's junior varsity team and a year later was named varsity coach, a position he assumed for the next 23 seasons.

His 214-119-65 coaching record includes winning the first of five Central League championships his first season. The team later captured two Pennsylvania Interscholastic

Bob Robinson, founder of the Pennsylvania Soccer Coaches Association, received his honor award from Ray Buss in 1998. Later, in 2001, he was inducted into its Hall of Fame.

Athletic Association (PIAA)District titles, while in 1987, the Aces were PIAA champions. That state title was sandwiched between 1984 and 1988 PIAA semi-final losses. In 1984, Rob was named the NSCAA Mid-Atlantic and the Pennsylvania Soccer Coaches Association (PSCA) COY.

Part of his coaching success at Lower Merion resulted from his 1976 work in co-founding and coaching the Radnor Soccer Club. The club's program included indoor soccer play at the Lower Merion gymnasium, the very floor that produced basketball great Kobie Bryant some years later.

It should be noted that the Radnor Soccer Club included boys and girls teams. Daughter Chris played on the boys high school team at Radnor High School because the PIAA had not sanctioned girls' soccer in the 1970s. When younger sister Amy got to Radnor, she played on that school's first team, and in her senior year she was the team MVP. Earlier, brothers Tom and Jeff had graced the Radnor soccer rosters.

Wearing Several Soccer Hats

In addition to coaching Lower Merion's soccer team, Rob was also involved in the growth of soccer outside his community. In 1972, he founded the Pennsylvania Soccer Coaches Association (PSCA) and was its first executive secretary, serving in that position until 1979. In this role, Rob was instrumental in creating the first Pennsylvania All State Soccer Team (1972) and the PIAA state-wide playoff system (1973).

At the time of the PIAA's founding, there were 19 leagues and 140 schools actively playing soccer in Pennsylvania. By 1988, 55 leagues and 376 Pennsylvania secondary schools were playing soccer and competing in PSCA events.

He was also co-founder, past-treasurer, past-president, and first executive secretary of the Southeastern Pennsylvania Soccer Coaches Association.

In 1972, it was West Chester coach Mel Lorback who convinced Robby to utilize his familiarity with numbers to run for the NSCAA treasurer position. Elected, thus began a 40-year-long involvement with an organization that was retitled the United Soccer Coaches in 2016. Rob served on the NSCAA Executive Committee for 25 years as treasurer (1972-92), vice president (1992-95), and president/past president (1995-97). His last assignment was as the NSCAA Convention Manager (1997-2012), where he coordinated an event that had grown to attract 10,000 soccer aficionados to its annual confabs.

Accolades

In addition to his attention to detail, Bob Robinson's accommodating personality has endeared him to countless friends in the soccer coaching community.

Perhaps most telling of the many awards he has received was the fact that the NSCAA High School Long-Term Achievement Award, first established in 1996 (he was its third recipient in 1998), was renamed the Robert W. "Robby" Robinson Award in 2001.

In addition, the NSCAA has honored Rob with two of its most prestigious awards, including the Honor Award in 1998, and he was inducted into its Hall of Fame in 2001.

In 1989, the Southeastern Pennsylvania Soccer Coaches Association awarded Rob its Bob Dunn Award for service to the soccer community. Meanwhile the PSCA honored its founder with presentation of the Honor Award in 1989, and he was inducted into its Hall of Fame in 2001.

Finally, in recognition of its longest serving soccer coach, Lower Merion High School inducted coach Robinson into its Athletic Hall of Fame in 2011.

Retired from teaching in 2005, Robby and Kate moved from their Wayne residence to a new home in Berwyn, where there is no basement but a comfortable second-floor office full of coaching-related memorabilia and a lot of memories of a soccer life well-lived.

Meanwhile, at the same time Robinson was organizing things in the central part of the state, a number of important soccer coaches had begun to also make their mark.

Dr. John L. McKeon – A Soccer Workaholic

If there was a soccer organization that was involved in promoting soccer beginning in the 1950s, there was a good chance that Dr. John McKeon was among those leading its efforts. If there was a soccer organization that needed a helping hand, there was a good bet that McKeon was involved in its affairs. His early coaching career was at the University of Bridgeport (CT), but beginning in 1966, he spent the next 22 years teaching and coaching at East Stroudsburg (PA) University.

With his move to East Stroudsburg, McKeon succeeded another coaching legend, John Eiler. In all, he coached soccer 29 years, with a combined record

John "Doc" McKeon cut a wide swath in U.S. soccer circles during his long career in the game.

of 215-130-29. His ESU teams competed in nine NCAA post-season tournaments, and he produced seven All-American players, including goalkeeper Bob Rigby, who was the first NASL player to grace the cover of *Sports Illustrated*.

In addition to soccer, he also coached track at East Stroudsburg.

A Soccer Workaholic

Beginning in 1965, the workaholic served a seven-year term on the NCAA Soccer Rules Committee, including six years' service as recording secretary. In 1972, McKeon headed the ISAA Senior Bowl Committee and a year later ascended to the

NSCAA presidency. In 1974 and in recognition of his contributions to collegiate soccer, McKeon was named the third recipient of the ISAA Bill Jeffrey Award. Years later, in 1995, and in acknowledgement of coordinated work with the National Intercollegiate Soccer Officials Association, he was inducted into its Hall of Fame.

For his long and varied service to the organization, and to soccer in general, McKeon received an NSCAA Honor Award in 1988.

In the 1970s, his service to USSF included publishing *Soccer Monthly* magazine (Francisco Marcos, editor). He also oversaw ticket sales for the 1974 World Cup, with the U.S. ticket sales for the event outstripping every other non-competing country in terms of total sales.

For 16 years, McKeon was also a member of the U.S. Olympic Committee.

Gravitating to the NASL, he was a head scout for the Montreal DeManic for many years and later a special assistant for the Tampa Bay Rowdies.

He wrote numerous articles and gave many lectures and presentations on soccer and physical education. In 1968, he co-authored with Springfield's Irv Schmid and his brother, Mel, the textbook, *Skills and Strategies in Successful Soccer,* which was used in college classes throughout the nation and went through six printings. He also oversaw the publishing of Dettmar Cramer's soccer coaching manual that went through 12 reprintings.

NSCAA Executive Director

During his tenure, the NSCAA Convention attendance numbers tripled ...

In addition to his presidency of NSCAA, beginning in 1980, McKeon began a 12-year term as the organization's executive director.

His appointment as the first "full-time" executive director was a bit misleading. Working from his Stroudsburg (PA) home, McKeon worked at keeping the affairs of the association in order on a full-time basis but on a part-time salary. He succeeded Bob Cal Berkeley coach Bob DiGrazia in the post.

Inheriting a membership numbering around the 2,000 mark, McKeon's term of office saw the organization expand to over 10,000 members by 1992, when he turned the reins over to the "real" first full-time executive director, Jim Sheldon. During his tenure, the NSCAA Convention attendance numbers tripled, the number of marketing agreements helped keep fiscal matters in the black, and the association All-America and COY programs also were significantly expanded.

Honors

The former track athlete was chosen to receive the Double D Award from Drake University in 1974, given to individuals who distinguished themselves in their careers after leaving college. He was inducted into the Drake Athletic Hall of Fame in 1973, the University of Bridgeport Athletic Hall of Fame in 1986, and East Stroudsburg University Athletic Hall of Fame in 2001. Also, in 2001, he was recipient of the Walt Chyzowych Award, and in 2002, he was inducted into the Connecticut Athletic Hall of Fame.

He also earned numerous Coach of the Year Awards at the national, regional, and conference level.

The McKeon Mentoring Process

"He was so respected that if he got behind you, you pretty much had the job." –Bob Dikranian[94]

During his 29-year soccer coaching career, coach McKeon acquired the nickname "Doc" and was noted for serving as mentor to an array of later soccer coaching notables.

With John McKeon's fingerprints all over the U.S. soccer community, that paid dividends for many of his former players.

Among his Bridgeport graduates who entered coaching with a boost from their former coach were Bob Dikranian (Southern Connecticut), Jim Kuhlman (Fairfield), and Bill Brew (Quinnipiac).

Jim Lennox's career also received a boost from McKeon. Graduating from Stroudsburg in 1966, Lennox received a call from the good "doctor." Seems John had arranged for the eager Lennox to earn his master's degree while serving as his freshman soccer coach. Among his subjects for his thesis were then-East Stroudsburg undergrads Jay Hoffman and Jay Miller.

Later the McKeon network paid one more dividend for Lennox. In the summer of 1969, McKeon phoned Lennox and informed him that he was to take the coaching reins at Mitchell (CT) Junior College. Not to apply for the job, "but take it." Seems John's recommendation had been accepted by retiring Mitchell coach, Warren Swanson![95]

Layton Shoemaker (Messiah College), Ron Quinn (Xavier), and McKeon's successor at East Stroudsburg, Jerry Sheska, were other coaching notables who spent time honing their coaching skills with "Doc."

The Jays – Miller and Hoffman

The coaching careers of the two Jays, Miller and Hoffman, also attest to the McKeon influence.

Jay Miller first established his coaching reputation at ELCO (Pa.) High School.

Miller enrolled at East Stroudsburg University (ESU) in 1966 to major in health and physical education. As noted, in his sophomore year, Jay was asked by the coach to monitor the visit of Jay Hoffman. Not only would their ESU playing careers be joined but also their later work with U.S. Soccer.

As for his time with McKeon, Miller's initial response was: "What can I say, he was Doc. He could talk to you on any level but basically he was an intellectual in his field. I think what I took away from him was the idea that there is a career out there for you. Now go out and get it!"[96]

While serving as vice-president of USSF, McKeon invited Jay to dine with England's Alf Ramsey when that World Cup-winning coach visited this country in 1971. He also helped Miller and others land tickets to the 1974 World Cup in Germany.

It was also "Doc" who introduced Miller to the National Soccer Coaches Association and encouraged his attendance at the organization's annual conventions.

"I know one time I lost a girlfriend when I took a trip with him!" –Jay Hoffman

Previous to his 1968 ESU enrollment, McKeon's recruitment of Hoffman consisted of having

Jay Hoffman was a protégé of John McKeon and enjoyed a long, successful career in the game.

viewed his Conrad Weiser High School team in a Berks County playoff game the previous fall.

But over his four-year Stroudsburg career, the relationship grew. "As with many college students, we were all looking for direction. John took me under his wing," Jay recalled. "He was passionate about the game, had soccer friends all over the place. He might call me to go up to Hartwick to view Al Miller's team playing or phone and say, 'Let's go to the city and visit the USSF offices.' You didn't want to disappoint him and I know one time I lost a girlfriend when I took a trip with him!"[97]

McKeon also served to widen the Hoffman soccer sphere of influence by hiring him at the Pocono Sports Camp when John served as director of soccer instruction. The camp's staff also included such notables as Al Miller, Timo Liekoski, Bill Killen, Bill Muse, and Bob Dikranian.

Hoffman also cites his Stroudsburg coach as being well educated, well-spoken, and an excellent man-manager. His office door was always open. But he was also very demanding. "He was an excellent kinesiology teacher and make no mistake, he expected you to attend class and do the work."

Following graduation in 1972, Jay credits McKeon for looking after him. "I was working at Bethany Children's Home as the recreation director. I'm scheduled to teach one day and John phones and tells me to be back to Stroudsburg at 3 p.m. that afternoon. I race up there, meet him at the admissions office and I ended up as his grad assistant on my way to my master's degree. It's a Friday. I ask him – 'when do we start?' He says – 'Monday!'"

It was also through the McKeon coaching network that Jay landed his first collegiate coaching position at Alderson-Broaddus College (WV) in 1973.

James Egli – A Western PA Stalwart

… "coach Jim is known as "The Father of NAIA Soccer."

While Bill Jeffrey, John Eiler, and Walter Bahr are legendary figures in upstate Pennsylvania intercollegiate soccer, further west, Slippery Rock University coach Jim Egli established his own coaching identity.

A graduate of East Stroudsburg State University, where he played football, basketball, and baseball, Egli succeeded another Stroudsburg graduate, John

Eiler, as Slippery Rock coach in 1956 and coached Rock soccer for the next 30 years.

The NCAA staged its first men's tournament in 1959, and correspondingly, the National Association of Intercollegiate Athletics (NAIA), spearheaded by coach Egli, was playing its first national tournament on the Slippery Rock campus. For his role in hosting the 1959 and 1960 tournaments, coach Jim is known as "The Father of NAIA Soccer."

In 1965, and in honor of his early advocacy for NAIA soccer, Egli was the initial inductee into the NAIA Soccer Hall of Fame in the Meritorious Service category.

Coach Jim Egli staged the first NAIA national championship tournament at Slippery Rock University.

Slippery Rock Soccer

Egli compiled a record of 250-143-38 during his career, with his greatest successes coming in 1973-76, when he led the team to four consecutive PSAC and NAIA title games.

In 1973, Egli was named NAIA National Coach of the Year, though it was the following year, 1974, that Slippery Rock recorded a 17-1-1 record and won its only Pennsylvania State Athletic Conference title. The seasonal record stood at the Rock for 35 years.

Egli's teams finished with winning records in 22 seasons, and during his 30 seasons at the helm of the program, he coached 35 All-Americans, including Slippery Rock Hall of Famers Kamal Houari and Art Rex. Rex, a two-time NSCAA All-America, succeeded Hank Steinbrecher as coach at Appalachian (NC) State. He coached there from 1981-97, winning four Southern Conference titles. He has been active in player development for the North Carolina Youth Soccer Association as well as a staff coach for U.S. Soccer.

In honor of the fact that many consider Jim Egli the "Father of Rock Soccer," the college conducts its intercollegiate soccer matches on James Egli Field. Egli was inducted to into the Slippery Rock Hall of Fame in 1986.

Following his passing in 2011, then-coach Mike Bonelli offered, "Coach Egli defines what Slippery Rock Soccer has been and will continue to be for all years. I never had the pleasure of meeting coach Egli, but after spending time with many alumni it is clear he had a positive impact on so many on and off the field."[98]

Jeff Tipping – A Fine Player and Creative Coach

Jeff Tipping's soccer career has been embellished with a number of geographic stops following graduation from Hartwick (NY) College, with part of his playing career and a large portion of his coaching career taking place in the Allentown, Pennsylvania, community.

A Stellar Playing Career

It was a fortuitous occurrence that brought Jeff Tipping from his native Liverpool, England, to the United States.

In 1974, Hartwick College, through its unofficial scout Francisco Marcos, was looking to stock its roster with a talented player, and Tipping was searching for a place to continue his education. That year, they discovered each other at an English schoolboys match. Both have subsequently left their marks on the U.S. soccer scene.

Leaving his beloved Everton FC in 1974, the solid center back started four seasons for Hartwick coaches Timo Liekoski and Jim Lennox. Tipping played in three College Cups, including the 1977 season, when he, as the tournament's MVP, helped lead the Warriors to the NCAA Division I Men's Soccer title.

Jeff Tipping has played an honored role in the U.S. game both as a player and coach.

From 1978-82, Tipp played professionally with the New York Eagles and the Pennsylvania Stoners of the American Soccer League. In 1980, the three-time ASL all-star captained the team to the ASL championship.

While his playing career was important, it was in the coaching and coaching education realm where Jeff would leave his mark on the U.S. game.

Leaving a Coaching Legacy

"My six grandchildren all know how to play chess because of Jeff Tipping." –Steve Erber

Following the success in professional soccer, Jeff attended graduate school at Syracuse University where, for a semester, he assisted men's coach Alden Shattuck and aided in the startup of the Orange women's soccer team.

In 1982, Hartwick coach Jim Lennox hired Jeff as his assistant coach, and for the next four seasons, he was the team's chief recruiter. During his apprenticeship, the team reached two NCAA Division I College Cups. He was also active as an Olympic Development coach for the New York State West and Eastern Pennsylvania programs.

He utilized his Hartwick experience and his newly acquired FA Preliminary Award when he became soccer and golf coach at Muhlenberg (PA) College in 1986. During his 16-year tenure, he coached the Mule soccer teams to a 225-71-21 record. That included eight NCAA Division III soccer tournaments, including a Final Four appearance in 1996. On four occasions, Tipping was named regional coach of the year. Along the way, the soccer and golf teams captured three conference titles, and the golfers also gained entry to an NCAA tournament. In addition, Tipping was instrumental in guiding the new Muhlenberg women's soccer team to a successful start.

His AD Recalls Tipping

Asked to recall Tipping's influence at Muhlenberg, former athletic director Steve Erber shared the following: "When I was hired as the AD at Muhlenberg in 1996, Tipp was ten years into his first head coaching career, and just coming off a Final Four finish in the DIII NCAA tournament. Soccer was far and away the most successful team at the school, historically."

"Working together and getting to know him I began to realize that this man is much more than a 'coach,' and his calling is really teaching and educating. He was very advanced in the technical and strategic parts of the game, and what he delighted in was passing that knowledge onto others. I think he viewed his players as students, and more than just athletes. He had the requisite personality and charm to get his students, and others, to listen and learn."

"I remember he had three requirements to play on his teams ... every one, in addition to all the typical team rules and regulations, had to learn to play chess, to ballroom dance, and to tie a bow tie. When he told me that, I knew he was special. If I had known that when I was coaching, I think I would have mimicked him. My six grandchildren all know how to play chess because of Jeff Tipping."

"When he left Muhlenberg in 2002, he told me he was dismayed by how the balance required for success in college athletics had become so tilted toward recruiting and away from coaching expertise. He wanted to teach. He never wanted to be a salesman. He was the ideal person to then become the NSCAA Director of Coaching."[99]

The Tipping Tree

Three of his former Muhlenberg players have enjoyed long coaching careers, with one, Sean Topping, having in 2002 succeeded his mentor at the Allentown campus. As of the 2019 season, he has amassed a 176-103-32 record that included bids to five NCAA Division III Tournaments.

In 2019, Tim O'Donohue finished his best season at the U.S. Naval Academy, as the Midshipmen recorded a 12-4-1 mark. He earlier had coached 10 seasons at Stevens (NJ) Tech, where he led the school to a 165-21-23 record, including nine NCAA Division III tournament appearances. Beginning in 2011, he served five seasons assisting coach Ray Reid at Connecticut.

Meanwhile, Brian Kelley, after first assisting Tipping at Muhlenberg, garnered his 100th coaching win in 2018. That included four seasons at Defiance College (OH) and seven years as headman at Worcester Polytechnic Institute (MA).

Honors

In 2002, Jeff Tipping was named the first fulltime NSCAA Director of Coaching (see Academy chapter). Jeff brought several coaching education experiences to the position. They included having earned the U.S. Soccer A License in 1995, finishing the UEFA A and Irish FA licenses in 2008, and having received the FIFA Futuro Coaching Education Award in 1992 and the FA Generic Tutor Award in 2010.

He was inducted into the Lehigh Valley Soccer Association Hall of Fame in 2006, and Hartwick and Muhlenberg colleges have inducted him into their Halls of Fame. He was also presented the National Soccer Hall of Fame's Billy Gonsalves Award for Services to Soccer in 1989. Jeff had the National Diploma translated into Spanish and taught by Latino staff, most notably Marco Santillan. In recognition of his service to the Latin American soccer community, Tipping, in 2003, was awarded the Latin American Soccer Coaches Association (LASCA) Award for "Unlimited Contribution to the Latin Soccer Community." Lastly, the National Intercollegiate Soccer Officials Association Honor Award for Services to Soccer was awarded to him in 2010, and he was the recipient of the coveted NSCAA Honor Award in 2014. In 2021 he was further honored with induction into the United Soccer Coaches HOF.

Upstate New York – A Soccer Hotbed

While the metropolitan areas of New York and New Jersey were the center of strong ethnic leagues and produced players who subsequently became noted coaches of soccer, the upstate New York area, led by legendary coaches Fred "Doc" Holloway at SUNY Cortland and Huntley Parker at SUNY Brockport, also produced its share of coaching legends.

Chronologically, Army coach Joe Palone was a contemporary of Holloway and Parker, and his West Point teams battled theirs for early New York soccer supremacy.

One of his former players, Francisco Marcos, brought coach Al Miller's career in focus when asked his place among early upstate soccer coaching stalwarts. He said of the Hartwick College legend, "He's certainly at the top of the coaching fraternity that brought soccer coaching in the USA into the modern era; his early pro success paved the way for American coaches to get in, and succeed, at the that level of play. When you evaluate him, he is probably the most complete coaching/administration individual in last 50 years of the American game having been an All-America player, a championship coach, the national team coach, USSF general manager, a general manager at the indoor game—he's done it all in unparalleled fashion."[100]

Those names are among many who graced the sidelines of upstate institutions as the Empire State led the way in sponsorship of the sport at the secondary school and university levels of play. That includes competitive play for women once the Title IX floodgates demanded equal opportunity for women, where Aliceann Wilber and Terry Gurnett led their institutions to national prominence.

Not only did coaches in the upstate cities of Albany, Syracuse, Rochester, and Buffalo have long histories in the game of soccer, but with noted coaches leading the way, its leaders produced players of national prominence, some of whom have gone on to remarkable coaching careers of their own.

Let's start with Joe Palone.

West Point's Joe Palone[101]

"Upon the fields of friendly strife are sown the seeds that upon other fields, on other days, will bear the fruits of victory." –General Douglas MacArthur

Perhaps no other individual incorporated those ideals in his coaching more than did the late Joseph Patrick Palone of West Point.

In establishing an exemplary soccer record at Army, his approach to coaching was possibly a bit unorthodox compared to today's more modern and systematic approach to player training. But the methodology was always in harmony with the objectives of the Academy—namely, to graduate young men who, through their soccer experience, learned valuable leadership lessons that they themselves would impart after leaving West Point.

As the Depression hit, it wasn't the norm for high school graduates to consider college, but Palone opted to try to overcome its economic challenges ...

His Early Years

Born in April 1903 and raised in the western New York village of LeRoy (best known as the home of Jell-o Foods), Joe lost his father in his infancy, and the family struggled fiscally during the ensuing years.

As the Depression hit, it wasn't the norm for high school graduates to consider college, but Palone opted to try to overcome its economic challenges by enrolling in the physical education program at what is now SUNY-Cortland.

Between his studies and a variety of part-time jobs, there was little time left for the hard-working youngster to engage in Cortland's intercollegiate athletic program. "Baseball was my best sport. I played during the summer with McGraw, N.Y., and was able to help me support myself through Cortland."

Upon graduating from Cortland in 1931, the energetic Palone took his first teaching position at Belmont (NY) High School. There is little evidence that Joe ever engaged in soccer prior to taking the Belmont position, but it was reported that he was a successful coach of not only that sport but also of basketball and baseball.

Arrival at West Point

Coach Palone took a circuitous route to West Point.

At one point, while teaching physical education at Belmont in the late 1930s, he introduced to his classes an Army-recommended regime of 11 fitness exercises.

One day, after being drafted in 1940 and sent to Fort Shelby (MS), a drill instructor asked for volunteers to lead the fitness exercises. Palone raised his hand, and his impressive leadership qualities came to the attention of the camp commander, who recommended Palone's transfer to West Point, there to oversee Plebe fitness. By 1944, Joe had earned an appointment to the Point's Physical Education Department, a position he held until his retirement in 1980.

A Typical Day

In October of 1974, reporter Alex Yannis of the *New York Times* best captured the typical rigorous daily regime followed by Palone during his Physical Education tenure. Taking a moment to put his feet up (he had spent the morning teaching volleyball), the coach shared with Yannis that in addition to his coaching he also taught boxing, golf, and soccer in the instructional program. In addition, he gave oversight to a 24-team intramural basketball competition.

Checking his watch, he told Yannis he had to leave, "We are playing Air Force in an hour and I want to get together with my boys before the game starts." Yannis also reported that the coach's office walls were adorned with photos of all his soccer captains plus one of the late-astronaut Ed White, the first man to walk in space. The Air Force match? Army won, 3-1.

Summers? Palone's assignments included oversight of the physical training of the incoming Plebe classes. This included early morning marching by the yearlings wearing full combat gear up and down the undulating West Point campus.

Taking Charge of Soccer at West Point

Beginning with the 1950 season, Army soccer under Palone would not endure another losing campaign!

As part of his initial duties, Palone was assigned coaching of the Plebe teams in soccer and baseball.

In soccer, he first served three seasons under coach Colonel G.F. McAneny before taking over as head soccer coach in 1947. And for the next 23 years, it was Joe Palone in charge of Army soccer.

Commencing in 1950, and for the next three seasons, Army soccer recorded two unbeaten seasons on the way to a cumulative 25-1-3 record. In each of these years, the Cadets were named Eastern Intercollegiate Champions. Of great interest was the fact that in each of the three seasons, victories were recorded over the U.S. Naval Academy.

Also of note is the fact that once the NCAA Soccer Tournament was initiated in 1959, and beginning in 1963 and through the 1975 season, West Point was selected to play 10 times. On four consecutive occasions (1963-66), the Cadets were Tournament semifinalists.

Joe Palone is carried off the field in 1978 following his last game as Army coach. Fittingly, it was a 1-0 victory over Navy.

Palone, who once modestly proclaimed that the day he retired "would be the saddest day of my life," coached his final game in November of 1978, and it was a victory over Navy. He departed having compiled a 226-80-37 record (a .713 winning percentage). During his tenure, 18 Army players were selected to NSCAA All-America teams. Listed among the 1967 All-Americans was Michael Palone.

During his career, coach Palone contributed to intercollegiate soccer through service on the NCAA Rules Committee and on the Intercollegiate Soccer Association of America (ISAA) Rating Board. On the rules front, and possibly due to the fact that he was far less a traditionalist than others, he favored the kick-in from touch that ruled play for many years in the 1950s. He was also a proponent of adopting (for a short spell beginning in 1958) a semicircular (yes!) penalty area. Also, games were played in 22-minute quarters!

As rating board chair, one recalls Monday evening phone calls to the Palone residence to discuss Joe's weekly ISAA New York State ratings. Unfortunately, they generally had to interrupt his weekly poker games. Between puffs on his favored cigars and giving attention to the card game, we did get the rating business completed!

Many thought Joe Palone was a perfect fit for West Point, and stories abound related to his time as soccer coach at the institution.

Palone Coaching Methodology

"Failure is Not a Destination!" –West Point Maxim

Upon reflection, former Army players Bob Behncke and Joe Casey shared that their former coach's greatest strength was that he had formulated a plan for West Point soccer and stuck to it. "He had us in a 3-3-4 formation," recalled Bob, and he and Joe agreed that Palone's Army teams were encouraged to think offensively—to attack. "I played as a sweeper behind the front four," recalled Behncke. "Joe always emphasized that once the ball was lost we high-pressured and once we won it, we were to spread the field."

In addition, the "Palone System" included prescribed functional roles for each position. Casey shared, "I think Joe had a facility for knowing what he expected from each of the players in each position and who could fulfill that spot. And in many cases, he took athletic players who had relatively little soccer experience and slotted in where they could be effective. Not that we didn't have some very good players but Joe knew how to identify others to support those who would see most of the ball."

Casey also allowed that training sessions were rarely focused on development of technique but rather on what might be termed "pattern play." "The playbook we had, outlined typical forms of ball and player movement and, in particular, emphasized attack play from the width of the field. We scrimmage a lot (and on the Clinton game field!) with the emphasis on getting the ball wide. And once the ball was played in, coach would holler – 'Shoot! You can't score if you don't shoot the ball."

Obviously, the fitness level of the Army players, when abetted by the free substitution rules then in effect, had its impact in many matches. This writer recalls his 1959 University of Rochester-Army match where waves of Army subs eventually won out, 4-2.

Behncke recalled that Palone's military-related strengths included his ability to organize well, to communicate effectively, and to delegate. The coach also imparted to his charges a West Point maxim: "Failure is not a destination!" "We learned that if we persevered, we would find a way to be successful," summarized Behncke, who served a 24-year career as an Army officer that included a tour in Vietnam.[104]

Honored in His Retirement Years

One of coach Palone's finest West Point moments occurred in 1978 when he was honored with induction as a member of that year's graduating class.

On October 27, 1995, at halftime of an Army-Holy Cross match, the Academy announced the establishment of the Joseph M. Palone Scholarship.

The day's printed program contained the following tribute: "Friends, graduates and associates are extremely proud of coach Palone and have come to celebrate his return to West Point. Coach Palone's leadership, service, character, and contributions to his profession reflect the highest tradition of the Corps of Cadets and the Unites States Military Academy – Duty, Honor, Country."

He passed away seven years later, on September 9, 2002, at age 92. In recognition of his outstanding overall contributions to West Point, coach Palone was inducted posthumously to the West Point Athletic HOF in 2004 and to the United Soccer Coaches HOF in 2020.

Al Miller – An Influential U.S. Soccer Coach[105]

Al Miller, one of the most influential American coaches of the last 60 years, began his love affair with soccer by playing with a rubber soccer ball noon hours at a one-room school house in Ono, Pennsylvania (population 50).

The words highly competitive, analytic, creative, and reflective are easily ascribed to Miller, who has successfully served the game of soccer in a variety of capacities over his 80-plus years.

Aided by a Referee

It was at Jonestown (PA) High School that he played in the first soccer game he ever saw. By his senior year, a growth spurt and increased skill saw him emerge as the team's star striker. He concluded his final season by scoring the winning goal in the regional championship.

The referee in that game was Werner Kraheck, who coached the Reading (PA) Americans, a team in the very competitive Philadelphia amateur league. In part because of his desire to Americanize the sport and, in larger part, because Miller had talent, Kraheck invited him to join the team.

Later, it was Kraheck who recommended him to East Stroudsburg State (PA) University coach John Eiler.

East Stroudsburg and John Eiler

Miller received letters from John Eiler, each containing the same message: "You were the best leader I ever had on any of my teams!"

Eiler's only enticement included a mailed application form.

Nevertheless, Miller enrolled and for four seasons starred (and captained) the East Stroudsburg soccer and baseball teams. In soccer, Miller was twice accorded All-America honors.

"I could have focused on a baseball career. But I have to say that Eiler was the reason I decided to focus on soccer. He was a very straight guy. He was a real professional physical educator. By that I mean he had the ability to teach most anything and do a good job. We'd call him and others of his generation 'generalists.'"

In terms of his practice organization, Eiler also finished each of the sessions with a series of sprints. In his first year, in an effort to impress and because of his natural competitiveness, Miller tried to finish first each time. "The older guys were trying to rein me in, but I yelled the F-word at them and continued to outrun them."

After practice and knowing that Eiler frowned on swearing, Miller was thinking the worst when he was told to report to the coach's office. "He closed the door, sat me down and told me he liked the way I took charge of the situation. What a confidence boost that was for me."

Later in his career, when he was honored with induction to the East Stroudsburg Hall of Fame and the U.S. Soccer Hall of Fame, Miller received letters from John

Eiler, each containing the same message: "You were the best leader I ever had on any of my teams!"

One thing Miller took away from his time with the Stroudsburg mentor was that once a rule was established, you had to stick with it, no matter what the circumstances. "There were a lot of older guys, some returning from military service and so having a beer or smoking were part of their routine. But they never wanted to get caught doing so by Coach Eiler."

That Eiler mandate included bed checks for his players. On one occasion, that meant leaving one of the team's best, but tardy, players home for an important match.

Miller recalls that in the locker room following the win, the coach reminded the group that no one individual player is ever bigger than the team.

Rebuilding New Paltz

Upon graduating, with soccer coaching jobs limited, the married Miller persevered until he eventually landed a soccer coaching position at SUNY-New Paltz in 1961.

What the athletic director hadn't told Miller was that for two years the team had never won a game. With half of his job working in admissions, the innovative Miller utilized the position to recruit some quality players (including Gene Ventriglia, who played on the U.S. Pan American team and the 1968 Olympic qualifying team). In 1965 won the SUNY Conference title over traditional powers coached by Huntley Parker (Brockport) and Fred Holloway (Cortland). A win in the NCAA Atlantic Coast Tournament further cemented the rebuilding process.

Elevating Hartwick College Soccer

"We did things that weren't being done back then. Made game programs, had a national anthem singer, fenced off the field, and had a refreshment stand. It was like a small college football program." –Al Miller

Indirectly, his New Paltz success came to the attention of Hartwick College AD Jim Konstanty. Jim had been the National League MVP in 1950 while pitching for the Philadelphia Phillies.

Hired in 1966, the AD and the new coach hit it off immediately. "He thought like a professional," was Miller's appraisal of his new boss. "He told me to give him some ideas about how to improve things and he'd see what we could do about them.

We really started promoting the program. We did things that weren't being done back then. Made game programs, had a national anthem singer, fenced off the field, and had a refreshment stand. It was like a small college football program."

Miller also noted that among the innovations was the staging of indoor soccer tournaments during the off-season. Here he credits his student manager,

Al Miller's achievements at Hartwick were indicative of the great soccer success he would enjoy throughout his career.

Thom Meredith, with taking care of their organization. Of course, during his post-Hartwick soccer career, Thom has worn more hats than the Queen of England!

"We traveled to Europe after my first year and brought a sports reporter with us, who wrote fantastic stories about us. It really got the community behind us. And all of a sudden we had people tailgating before our games, buying tickets in advance."

Oneonta became known as "Soccer City USA." Miller's Hartwick teams included players Timo Liekoski, Francisco Marcos, and Alec Papadakis.

Miller's record at Hartwick was 64-12-3 and included a 1970 NCAA Final Four appearance and a 14-1 record. He was inducted into the Hartwick College Hall of Fame in 1995.

Miller is best remembered as the first American to coach in the North American Soccer League. Leaving Hartwick following the 1972 season, he quickly put together a roster for a new league franchise in Philadelphia called the Atoms, who won the NASL title in their first season.

He later coached the Dallas Tornado, Calgary Boomers, and Tampa Bay Rowdies in the NASL and then, with the collapse of the NASL, turned to the indoor game, where he was involved in managing two indoor franchises in Cleveland (the Force and the Crunch). The latter team was successful on the field and at the box office.

Miller, who briefly coached the U.S. national team in 1975 and served as national team general manager in 1988, was inducted into the National Soccer Hall of Fame in 1995.

As with many of his contemporizes, Miller's coaching was influenced by Dettmar Cramer.

The Hartwick Coaching Legacy[106]

What is remarkable about Hartwick College, whose student body averaged about 1,500 students, was the wide swath it has carved for itself in the U.S. soccer landscape.

Timo Liekoski had earned All-America honors under Al Miller and succeeded him as 'Wick coach in 1973. Hartwick continued its ascent under Liekoski, recording a 30-9-7 (.728) record that included three more NCAA appearances, including a Final Four appearance in 1974.

Succeeding Liekoski was Jim Lennox, who led Hartwick to the 1977 NCAA Division I title and compiled a 318-163-43 (.648) record before his retirement in 2002.

Miller and Liekoski were soccer coaching pioneers in that they left the relative comfort of the Hartwick campus to coach at the then-emerging but by no means secure professional game in the United States. Each had nearly identical 20-year careers at that level of the game.

Other 'Wick Coaching Alumni

Terry Fisher assisted Liekoski with the NASL teams in Houston and Calgary and Dominic Kinnear with the San Hose Earthquakes. Today, Terry oversees the affairs of the Washington State YSA.

Eddie Austin enjoyed a long administrative career in the Tampa Bay area, first with the 1975 NASL champion Rowdies and later with the MLS Mutiny. It was with the Mutiny that the former 'Wick All-America received the MLS Director of Operations Award in 1998 and 2001.

Glenn Myernick, following an eight–year NASL playing career, served as head coach of the MLS Colorado Rapids from 1997-2000, leading the team to an appearance in the MLS Cup his first year.

Perhaps the most professional coaching involvement has been that of Dominic Kinnear (1985). Following an 11-year MLS playing career, he has enjoyed a 13-year coaching career in the league. Highlight of his eight years was as head coach of the Houston Dynamo, leading the team to consecutive MLS Cup titles in 2006-07.

Among those former Hawk players who gravitated into professional soccer were Davie D'Errico, who played eight years in the NASL and five in the MISL; Doug Wark (six NASL teams; four MISL teams); Billy Gazonas (Tulsa and Calgary in NASL, New York and Kansas City in MISL); Steve Jameson (Rochester Flash); Keith Von Eron (Baltimore Blast); and Gary Vogel (Minnesota Kicks).

Ken Peterson assisted David Hasse and later coached at SUNY-Oswego for 36 years while Bill Killen and Bill Muse each assisted Miller. Killen moved on to coach at CCNY, Yale, Akron, Old Dominion, and MacMurray (IL). Muse coached Princeton from 1973-83. Later, Alden Shattuck assisted Liekoski before moving on to Syracuse and then Maryland as head coach, and his brother Jape Shattuck later assisted Lennox before coaching at Harvard. Another Lennox assistant, Greg Moss-Brown, later served as assistant or head coach at a number of schools, including at Emory (GA). Other Lennox assistants who moved on included Tom Duffy (William and Mary assistant) and Carl Rees (Fairfield).

A number of former Hartwick players have parlayed their successful playing careers into coaching positions, including Ian McIntrye (SUNY Oneonta, Syracuse); John Bluem (Fresno State, Ohio State); Dave Gregson (Emory-Riddle, FL); Mike Harrison (Aston Villa youth GK coach); Matt Kern (Sewanee; Wofford; UNC-Ashville; Hendrix College (AR); Mark Mettrick (Loyola, MD, Gettysburg); Bryan Scales (UMass Lowell and Cornell); and Geoff Bennett (Rhode Island and Colorado College women).

At the secondary school level, Hartwick's two first-team All-America players, Tony Martelli (Washingtonville [NY] and West Point) and Tony Elia (Saugerties [NY]), have enjoyed long, successful coaching careers.

While the coaching accomplishments of various Hartwick alumni are noteworthy, none have achieved the overall administrative accomplishments of 'Wick grad Francisco Marcos.

Terry Gurnett – A Program Builder[108]

Former UR AD Jeff Vennell, in portraying Gurnett as a "great coach, better guy," recalled how he involved his players in maintaining the positive team culture so important for continued success.

Terry Gurnett's path to soccer coaching acclaim at the University of Rochester (NY) was not what might be termed a smooth, logical progression.

He did play for some accomplished coaches, and he wasn't the star player for any of them but rather was a team member who admits that it was the positive team experience that he most enjoyed being part of.

Coach Terry Gurnett held his teams to a high standard.

As for his subsequent coaching success, he modestly attributes that to being at the right place at the right time.

From Player to Coach

... for an initial stipend of $250 and for the next 33 years, UR women's soccer fortunes soared.

Raised in Spencerport, New York, he calls himself an average high school student who shared goalkeeping duties on coach Ron Broadbent's stellar NYSPHSAA Section V champion teams of 1971-72.

Near graduation, he had designs on joining the U.S. Marines. That is, until his father, who had lost his own father and brother in earlier armed conflicts, steered him to Monroe (NY) County Community College. There he studied accounting and tended goal for coach Joe Mancerella's strong NJCAA national tournaments teams.

It was following a UR-MCC scrimmage where, as he recalls, "I had a good day," that UR coach Tom Connor approached Terry about matriculation at Rochester.

"Everything changed" was how he phrased his 1974 enrollment at the academically competitive upstate institution. While he enjoyed his time in goal for Connor's Yellowjacket teams, of more importance academically, he discovered an aptitude for computer science programming and became a Dean's List student.

In the spring of 1977, it was when sorting out his student loan payments that he was offered a junior accounting position in the bursar's office. That fall, a group of women approached coach Connor about starting a soccer team. Connor approached the neophyte Gurnett about coaching the ladies, and for an initial stipend of $250 and for the next 33 years, UR women's soccer fortunes soared.

Forming a Coaching Methodology

Relying on his past player-coach relationships, the fledgling coach incorporated coach Broadbent's emphasis on the soccer fundamentals with doses of Mancerella's organizational excellence and his compassionate approach to player development into his coaching. He also admired and incorporated Connor's enthusiastic attitude but did not adopt his "beer on the bus ride home" approach to player management.

That didn't mean that he was not searching for new coaching ideas. He efficiently received an in-house coaching tutorial in the person of then-Yellowjacket men's coach George Perry. "I'd watch his practices and over time, he effectively shared his ideas relative to information contained in the NSCAA Academy program." He credits that exposure, along with attendance at the NSCAA annual conventions, with further refinement of his coaching methodology.

Whatever his approach, it paid early dividends for, by the 1985 season, Rochester women's soccer had ascended to a number one national ranking among NCAA Division III teams.

Asked to define his style, he shared that for the most part, his on-field approach differed little in how he would have coached male athletes. "I always treated the women with respect. That included never embarrassing them as that would result in a group lost of trust in. And, I always worked on the team concept."

He recalls that he generally withheld use of the term "team." "I would inform the group until I saw something that indicated 'they were a team,' I would say, 'You are not a team until I say you are a team.' Generally something like a comeback win or overcoming a favored opponent would be enough for me to say to the group, 'Today you became a team!'" That acknowledgement was always awaited by his charges.

Former UR AD Jeff Vennell, in portraying Gurnett as a "great coach, better guy," recalled how he involved his players in maintaining the positive team culture so important for continued success. "His ability to build a sense of team is illustrated by his on-campus recruits who visited on weekend overnights. He would ask the student host and other team members who interacted with the recruit if she was the type of player and personality who would fit well on the UR team. If they had any reservations, he would cease recruiting that prospective student."[109]

The National Title

Until 1986, the penultimate championship for New York teams was ECAC regional tournaments.

That season, when the NCAA staged its first Division III tournaments for women, the coach recalled, "there was no feeling like it" as Rochester defeated neighboring William Smith, 1-0, at Cortland.

On the way to the title, the UR coach had to demonstrate some quick off-field maneuvering. That year the team was on its way to a first-round match versus Mt. Holyoke when Terry questioned the bus driver as to the expected arrival time to the Massachusetts school. "We're not going to Massachusetts," informed the driver. "My paperwork has us going to Saratoga Springs, New York!"

Apparently UR AD Don Smith had signed paperwork with a Skidmore College destination. Terry asked the driver to make a rest stop, and there he phoned the Greyhound bus company and identified himself as 'Mr. Don Smith' and asked that the trip be rerouted to South Hadley, Massachusetts.

With that, the trip continued with all concerned cautioned that what took place on the bus remained on the bus! Or failing that, and per the coach's edict, they could walk home!

A year later, Rochester retained the title on its Fauver Stadium turf, upending Plymouth State 1-0. In all, from 1986 forward, Rochester qualified for 19 NCAA Tournaments and six ECAC post-season competitions. That included a 1991 appearance in the championship match, a 2-0 loss to Ithaca College. In 1991, the NCAA declared Gurnett the NCAA Division III Women's Soccer Coach of the Decade for the 1980s.

Also beginning with its University Athletic Conference membership in 1986, Rochester women's soccer has captured 12 UAA titles, the most of any conference member. The UAA has acknowledged the UR staff for its coaching award on five occasions.

High-Quality Student-Athletes

Obviously, the Gurnett coaching accomplishments (he ended his career in 2010 with a 422-135-66 record) demanded that he recruit high-quality student athletes to the River Campus.

The process itself was enhanced when he assumed a role in the UR alumni relations office that included travel to various parts of the country. That assignment coincidentally followed news that Notre Dame and Penn had interviewed Gurnett for their coaching positions. A later career move to oversee UR athletic development efforts included a 25 percent time allotment for his soccer coaching.

Thirty-three UR players were accorded All-America honors during the Gurnett tenure, and from 1999 to the time of his 2010 retirement, every one of his teams had earned the NSCAA's Team Academic Achievement Award. Two student-athletes, Ashley Van Vehten and Loren Cerauci, were awarded Fulbright Scholarships in the early 2000s.

Several Gurnett disciples have, upon graduation, had soccer coaching on their resumes. These include Penny Waderich (Monroe County Community College); Nikki Izzo Brown (West Virginia); Jill McCabe (St. John Fisher); Abby Heister (RIT; NC youth soccer); Cherise Galasso (WPI soccer and basketball); Cheryl Cole (Paul Smith plus basketball); Libby Tobin (Duquesne); Joanna Tomasino (Indiana [PA] and SUNY-Albany); and Jennie Deprez (assistant UVA and Cornell).

Giving Back to the Game

In addition to giving back to the game in the form of his former players who have entered the coaching field, in 2010, Gurnett received a Letter of Commendation from the NSCAA at its annual convention in Philadelphia. It was awarded based on his longtime service to soccer, both on and off the field. That service has included national chair of the NSCAA All-America Committee, member of the Division III Ranking Committee, and member of the ECAC Women's Soccer Tournament Selection Committee.

In addition to all the accolades, the understated coach was selected the NSCAA Northeast Region Coach of the Year in 2005 and the New York State Coach of the Year in 2005 and 2006.

While he demurs and credits other events in his life to his success, there is little doubt that Tom Connors' phone call and a $250 initial salary stipend have paid huge dividends specifically for the University of Rochester and its women's soccer program and for the sport of soccer in general.

Aliceann Wilber – Setting New Benchmarks

She may have been the farmer's daughter, but everyone in women's soccer has come to know her.

We are referring to Aliceann Wilber, who founded the women's soccer program at William Smith College (NY).

Little could she have known when attending Penn Yan High School in upstate New York that much of her life's work took place in Geneva, just 17 miles north.

Aliceann Wilber became the first woman soccer coach to collect 600 wins in 2021. It was just one of many honors to befall the William Smith coach.

In high school she professed a love for sports but interscholastic competition was not part of the offerings in the late 1960s. Instead, her physical education teachers arranged sports days with other area schools. On those occasions, for one day the young ladies focused on various sports on a seasonal basis.

The Gibbs sisters [Vallie, Amy, Martha, Aliceann, and Lyn) were raised on a farm in Penn Yan, which is located on scenic Keuka Lake. It was evident to her father that he had a daughter who loved to exercise. To hone her interest in the balance beam, he built a wooden version that occupied space in the family living room. Her high school physical education teacher, Mary Schleiernacher, also encouraged her sport interest. On one occasion, she took her young charge to Cortland to view gymnastic practice on the SUNY campus.

SUNY-Brockport

Realizing she had a love of children and admiring the lifestyle of Scheiernacher and other of her physical education teachers, Aliceann enrolled in that major at SUNY-Brockport in 1969.

Her interests included adaptive physical education and athletic training.

She did not appreciate the chauvinistic sports scene at the upstate school. "As one of two students who were the first females ever to work in the training room I remember that breaking that barrier was difficult as initially overt actions made it clear we were not welcomed there. I worked with two of the men's teams who were very prominent – wrestling and basketball - and quickly learned that if I wanted anyone to come to my taping table, I needed to tape better than the guys."

While offered a graduate assistantship by the school, Wilber set it aside to begin her teaching career at West Valley High School, located in the southwestern part of New York. There, she taught K-12 physical education and, with Title IX now in force, coached girls' soccer, basketball, volleyball, and track and field.

Starting William Smith Soccer

With scant soccer coaching experience, Aliceann noted Smith's posting of a part-time position to start a women's soccer team.

Upon her father's passing in 1978, Aliceann returned to Penn Yan to help her mother run the farm. At the time, William Smith, the women's college of Hobart College, was expanding its athletic program in part to meet the demands imposed by Title IX legislation.

With scant soccer coaching experience, in 1980, Aliceann noted Smith's posting of a part-time position to start a women's soccer team. Hired, her first four years reflected the difficulties she faced trying to establish the fledgling program. Its cumulative 14-35-1 record included a first game loss to Wells College, 9-0.

She recalls two incidents of those startup seasons. "One game I motioned to a player to report in as a sub. As she was about to enter the game she looked at me and said – 'Which way are we going?' Another time our goalie upon being scored on for about the fifth time screamed 'I can't take this anymore!' while running down the field and across heavily traveled Route 5 and 20! I turned and looked at the other players on the bench and they all were looking down at their shoes. I don't think they knew whether to laugh or cry."

By 1984, and through hard work, the Herons dramatically turned things in the right direction with a 8-5-1 record. The college, likely recognizing it had a coaching gem in its midst, granted Wilber increased recruiting monies. By 1988, just nine seasons after the program's inception, William Smith, in recording 18-2-1 record, was the NCAA Division III champion.

Behind the Surge

Wilber's taxing schedules were the result of a reminder shared with her by North Carolina's Anson Dorrance: "You are your schedule!"

Exhibiting the same determination to become the best in the Brockport training room, the committed coach decided early in her coaching career that to be the best you had to "get in the belly of the beast." Namely, you had to beat the best.

She also realized that by adding tournament play to the regular schedule, such exposure would toughen the team's resolve. Thus when the NYSAIAW asked for schools to host their tournaments in the early 1980s, William Smith had its hand up.

"I remember that prior to my first season, when William Smith was a club team, that Cortland, then a power in New York State, beat us 20-0 and this was recorded in the NSCAA record book. It seemed a bit unfair…"

Cortland, then one of the most dominant programs in the entire country, was the beast that needed to be scheduled. As an up-and-coming program taking on a legendary one, these competitions had a charged air about them. Finally, in 1987, after beating them 1-0 in an NCAA game, their very direct, but highly successful coach, Chris Malone, gifted me with this comment: 'I am sick that I have the better team technically and tactically and lose to a team that wants it more!'

In part, Wilber's taxing schedules were the result of a reminder shared with her by North Carolina's Anson Dorrance: "You are your schedule!" The end result is that the annual achievements by Heron teams have placed them at the top of the NCAA Division III heap.

The mother of two remarked that the 1988 title was in large part due to the team's resolve following a 1-0 loss to Rochester in 1986 in what was the first NCAA DIII tournament. "I remember them saying in that locker room, 'We're winning it next year!'"

Following the 2019 season, William Smith had appeared in 30 NCAA post-season tournaments. The team won its second national title in 2013 and counts 13 semifinal round appearances on its resume. Since 1995, the college has competed regionally in the UCAA and Liberty Conferences, winning 17 titles.

Wilber has collected a closet full of coaching accolades in her career. They include being named the United Soccer Coaches National Coach of the Year awards five times. She and her staff have won nine regional USC coaching awards and similar Liberty League COY awards on 14 occasions.

Other Wilber benchmarks include being, in 2021, the first woman in Division III to collect 600 career wins. If one discounts those first four losing seasons, her W-L percentage is 82 percent.

Those figures are buttressed by the fact that William Smith has attracted and nurtured 50 players who have achieved All-America recognition. Seventeen players have been recipients of Academic All-America honors.

All of the Wilber accomplishments she credits to recruitment of quality players along with exposure to soccer coaching guru Graham Ramsey.

The Wilber Philosophy

Aliceann's initial attraction to teaching remains in force, namely, as a vehicle for helping young people achieve their goals. "I don't think I ever wanted to strictly 'coach.' I just wanted to teach and all that it entails. Coaching is perhaps a specialized form of teaching."

One concern in women's collegiate soccer is the number of women whose coaching involvement is short-lived. Now in her 41st year at William Smith, Wilber's perspective on that is worth consideration: "I think that many women who were involved as players of the game received a certain joy from playing that, once they became older and more challenged for time and choices, didn't quite feel the same when coaching. For coaching longevity, I believe that you must love teaching more than you loved playing."

"In teaching you find your joy in shaping people's lives. In my case, soccer is the medium for that to happen. There is a lot to that process but players will respond as long as they know you care for them. I think caring is key."

In sharing that, she admits that the coaching environment is changing. Citing the recent dismissal of several celebrated coaches (North Carolina women's basketball coach Sylvia Hatchell being one), she admits that coaches have to be very careful. "We have to be contemporary and take nothing for granted. And be more aware of the necessity of understanding more of legalities than we have previously needed to involve ourselves with. We are dealing with an entitled generation of kids and parents and things don't always align when it comes to team sports."

The Wilber Coaching Tree

That fact is more compelling when one notes that William Smith's academic focus is on the liberal arts.

In stating her soccer-related concerns, it is obvious that Aliceann's influence on her William Smith ladies is substantial if only viewed from the number of her players who are contributing to the game. That fact is more compelling when one notes that William Smith's academic focus is on the liberal arts.

The Smith notables in coaching include Mindy Quigg at Ithaca College; Tatiana Korba at Stevenson (MD) University; Laura Burnett-Kurie, head coach, and Zoe Eth, assistant coach, at Gustavus Adolphus (MN) College; Whitney Frary at St Olaf (MN) College; and Madeline Buckley, assistant coach at Bowdoin (ME) College.

Other Soccer Contributions/Honors

Wilber is a 34-year member of the United Soccer Coaches organization. In 2013, she was elected to serve on the organization's Board of Directors as the Women's College Representative. She later served in the same capacity on its Advocacy Council. Concurrently, she heads the Women's Division III All-America Committee.

Service stints on the NCAA Women's Soccer Sport Committee are also another valued soccer experience on the Wilber resume.

In 2002, as a result of her significant work for intercollegiate soccer, she was the first woman to receive the Bill Jeffrey Award. In 2019, as further acknowledgement of her overall contributions to the United Soccer Coaches organization and the game of soccer, she and Dr. Colleen Hacker became the first women inducted to its Hall of Fame.

She has also been inducted to the William Smith College Hall of Honor and the West Valley Central School Hall of Fame.

David Sarachan – Loyalty as a Hallmark[112]

Dave Sarachan's soccer career has seen him earn All-America honors as a player and later, in addition to serving as a head coach at the intercollegiate and professional levels, has helped best define for others the role of the assistant coach.

The Player

"Dan [Wood] had a profound influence on me and without his belief in me, my career as a student, professional player and coach could have taken me down a different path." –Dave Sarachan

At Brighton High School in suburban Rochester, New York, the diminutive Sarachan (5 feet as a freshman) was fortunate to play under former SUNY-Cortland All-America graduate Clarence Mepham (who himself played for coaching legend Fred Holloway). Installed as a winger as a freshman, he credits the coach with giving him initial confidence that led to his captaining the team when it won the 1972 New York State Section IV title his senior year.

He also credits observing Carlos Metidieri play with the hometown Rochester Lancers in the early 1970s with influencing his development. Twice, the diminutive Brazilian led the NASL in scoring.

In moving on to Monroe County Community College in 1973, David joined a soccer program that coach Joe Mancerella had elevated to NJCAA national prominence. "He had an eye for soccer talent and he got the most out of it with his empathetic nature," Dave recalls. "He taught us to behave, how to prepare while allowing us to be ourselves on the field. The guys wanted to play for him." In that environment, his game thrived and Sarachan twice earned NJCAA All-America honors.

Cornell University coach Dan Wood had mined Monroe CC rosters for talent,

Coach Dan Wood impacted the career of Dave Sarachan.

and in 1975, Sarachan joined the Big Red soccer team. "Massive" was how the skillful striker framed Wood's impact. Sarachan's statement on the occasion of the 2020 passing of Dan Wood captures the coach's impact on his career: "Dan had a profound influence on me and without his belief in me, my career as a student, professional player and coach could have taken me down a different path. He was a brilliant guy, fabulous teacher, passionate devotee to detail in soccer and golf and a wonderful human being."

In part led by three Mighty Mites, Sarachan, Joe Mui, and Einar Thorarinnsson (all in the 5'6" range), the Big Red entered NCAA post-season play in 1974 and 1975. Both Sarachan and Mui earned All-America honors. With Dave as the team captain, the 1975 squad captured the first Ivy League title in school history.

After two seasons playing for the Lancers and four playing in the MISL, the Sarachan playing career ended and his coaching career began.

Coaching Progression

"Bruce looked at me with one question: 'Where have you been?'" –Dave Sarachan

The Sarachan soccer-coaching career began at Cornell in 1983 when he assisted Wood successor Jack Writer.

The following fall, he began his long association with Bruce Arena as his assistant at the University of Virginia. The first meeting of the two was not encouraging. "Traveling to Charlottesville, I arrived an hour late. As our paths crossed, Bruce looked at me with one question: 'Where have you been?'"

"I was like a sponge" was how he recalled his four seasons of working with Arena. By 1987, he had been exposed to the nuances of planned training sessions, scouting, recruiting, and budgeting as well as refining methods that complemented the workings of the head coach.

With the UVA experience in hand, in 1988, the eager young coach began a 10-year stint as Cornell headman. Highlights of his tenure included two NCAA Tournament appearances and an Ivy League title.

Arena and the professional game beckoned in the fall of 1997 and another Arena-Sarachan coaching relationship began with the MLS DC United franchise. When Arena left following the 1998 season, his assistant aided coach Tom Rongen when they paired to win the 1999 MLS Cup.

Following the MLS triumph, Sarachan was hired to assist coach Arena with preparations of the USMNT for the South Korean 2002 FIFA World Cup.

Assisting Bruce Arena

Of course, the Arena-Sarachan pairing was a success, as, for the first time, the U.S. men advanced to the quarterfinal round before bowing to Germany, 1-0.

In reviewing his relationship with the man who many rank as our country's most successful coach, the Rochester native cites that while many may rate Arena "difficult,' he views the man's personality through a different lens.

"He can be 'tough' at times, 'soft' at other times," states his coaching ally. "He can be funny and he can be anti-social. He can be self-deprecating one minute and show his ego side later. Most of the people who surround him swear by him or can't stand him," was Sarachan's analysis following 30-plus years of working as his loyal number two man.

Dave cites loyalty—and honesty—as two essential traits assistants must possess if they are to maintain a successful relationship with the headman. And those qualities have to be invoked with the right sense of timing and sensitivity.

"Many times players may not have accurately interpreted that the message of the head coach. That's when the assistant can step in and reframe it in a way that preserves the essence of the coach's intent and, in that manner, keep things on an even keel."

Sarachan's analysis also focused on the mutual respect that must exist if a coach-assistant relationship is to continue to evolve. "Sometimes there must be hard, painful conversations that have to take place between coaches. Challenges have to be made and accepted as the partnership matures. Whatever has been the case between Bruce and myself, I guess we have a 'Yin-Yang' sort of thing going and it has worked for us."

But what, in his estimation, accounts for the notable coaching successes Bruce Arena had enjoyed?

Based on their long association, Sarachan has concluded that the man is a "master builder. He has a keen eye for talent and understands how teams are constructed. Further, he knows how to manage rosters. Bottom line, he is a competitive guy and is just a winner. Oh – I forgot to mention, it always helps when you have better players!"

Following his World Cup experience, Sarachan's career was focused on coaching involvement at the professional level of play.

World Cup Qualifying

U.S. Soccer, seeing its national team headed for non-qualification for the 2018 World Cup, prevailed on Bruce Arena and his sidekick, Dave Sarachan, to make matters right. Short-lived, the team's demise marked the first defeat the coaching pair has suffered, though post-2018, it did allow for Dave to serve as interim UNMNT coach for one year.

CHAPTER VI

ESTABLISHING THE GAME IN FOOTBALL COUNTRY

Demonstrating equal parts persistence and political savvy, it was through the efforts of several committed individuals that soccer was established in the schools and clubs of the U.S. South and Southwestern regions.

A pioneer role in the launch of Southern soccer has to be credited to Dr. Marvin Allen at the University of North Carolina. His identification of Anson Dorrance as his successor, when coupled with the emergence of Clemson under Ibrahim Ibrahim, provoked other Atlantic Coast Conference schools to devote greater resources to both men's and women's soccer.

Paralleling the advancement of the intercollegiate game, coaches Bill Holleman and Bob Sims led the way, first in its private schools, then in its public schools. Today, the South's share of outstanding players is testament to states from Virginia to Florida having caught up with other regions of the country.

While focused on coaches and their contributions to soccer's popularity in various locales, much of the credit to its establishment in Texas has to be credited to a latecomer, Lamar Hunt. Much of the interest and eventual popularity of soccer flowed from his investment in the NASL's Dallas Tornado franchise. That team's coaches and players played significant roles as soccer established a solid foothold in the schools and clubs throughout the Longhorn State.

As we shall see, the individual coaches cited in this section of the country were but the tip of the iceberg, as soccer found acceptance in other regions of the country as well.

Southern Soccer's Growth

The Maryland Juggernaut

The players' solution: Leave the table before the bill came.

In the post-World War II time frame, coach Doyle Royal and the University of Maryland Terrapins were *the* force in Southern men's soccer.

Following graduation from Maryland in 1943, Royal entered World War II service with the U.S. Army. During the conflict, he participated in the Normandy Invasion as well as the Battle of the Bulge. In the latter battle, he earned the Silver Star for destroying a German tank with a hand grenade.

In 1946, he returned to his alma mater to coach men's soccer, and later, men's tennis. He also served as assistant dean of students for 35 years.

Beginning in 1946, Royal's soccer teams dominated Atlantic Coast Conference play, winning 16 consecutive ACC titles (17 in all). The 1968 Terrapin team shared the NCAA national title with Michigan State, following a 2-2 tie in the championship game.

As coach of two then-minor sports, his teams operated on somewhat meager budgets and, at the time of his passing at age 101, one of his former players recalled Royal's personal generosity that stretched those dollars.

In the mid-1970s, the alumnus remembered being hungry all the time on spring break tennis trips across the South, when players were each given a $10 daily food allowance. It wasn't enough for young athletes, and most of the players had run out of money by the time they gathered at a restaurant for dinner.

The players' solution: Leave the table before the bill came. Coach Royal always picked up the tab. "He never complained," the player recalled.

Reportedly, as a Washington (DC) native, Royal was well connected with government Foreign Service agencies and used that network to aid in recruiting foreign students to both his soccer and tennis teams.

Tennis was his avocation, and he was reported to have won a USLTA regional title in his 80s.

When he retired following the 1973 season, his Maryland teams had compiled an overall 217-58-18 (.771) record. By the 1970s, with Clemson joining Maryland, North Carolina, North Carolina State, and Virginia, the ACC became a very competitive soccer conference.[113]

Dr. Marvin Allen – Gentleman Coach

As tribute to his mentor, Marvin Allen, who always wore a coat and tie while on the UNC sideline, today his successor [Dorrance] dons a tie while coaching.

While known by his middle name throughout his professional career, Ernest Marvin Allen was born in North Carolina and graduated from the University of North Carolina (UNC) in 1938. During his undergraduate years, he played on the UNC club soccer team and was reported to have scored the first goal in team history. He joined the UNC physical education department in 1940, after attaining his M.A. degree from the school, and later completed his doctorate at Penn State in 1960.

As with many others, Marvin served in World War II, commanding a minesweeper in the Pacific Theater. He returned to service during the Korean conflict and retired from the U.S. Navy with the rank of commander.

Marvin Allen was a pioneer coach in the Southern part of the country.

Coaching Dorrance and Berson

Upon returning to UNC in 1946, Allen started the UNC men's intercollegiate program and, during his 20-year career, achieved a 148-68-14 record.

As a neophyte coach, Ray Alley traveled to UNC practices run by coach Allen. Marvin outlined his practice sessions in a black notebook and allowed Ray to copy the sessions. At the time, both Anson Dorrance and Mark Berson were members of the team, Anson in the midfield and Mark serving as the Tarheel keeper.

Ray utilized the Allen workouts while coaching his boys youth team. "I did that for most of my season and so as far as my coaching education was concerned I have to credit Marvin Allen as my soccer mentor."[114]

Dr. Allen is also credited with hosting the first ever North Carolina Independent Schools Athletic Association boys championships on the Chapel Hill campus.

In 1970, the UNC men were among the first college teams to take an international tour, when Francisco Marcos led the Tar Heel team on one of his first European junkets. Other coaches and their teams soon followed the UNC lead.

Leading the NSCAA

President of the NSCAA in 1962 and active in ISAA as well, the gentleman coach was presented the NSCAA Honor Award in 1969. That year was also memorable, as UNC soccer defeated Atlantic Coast Conference power Maryland for the first time.

His post-war membership in the NSCAA included outreach work for the organization in the South, where it sought to attract new members. He and Dinty Moore were reported to have conducted coaching clinics as part of that initiative. As president, he was an early advocate for hiring a full-time person to orchestrate the group's affairs, though financing the concept postponed its implementation for a few years.

In 1975, Dr. Allen enlisted one of his former players, attorney Fred Parker III, to serve as the NSCAA attorney *pro bono*, as legal issues emerged in connection with the enforcing compliance of the group's code of ethics within the coaching community.

Indicative of the closeness of the NSCAA coaching fraternity at the time, coach Allen recruited several of Huntley Parker's former SUNY Brockport players to Chapel Hill both to earn their master's degree and to assist coaching Tar Heel teams. Those individuals included Fred Taube (SUNY Cortland), Bill Utter (UNC-Greensboro), and Doug May (RIT and Nazareth College).

Anson Dorrance

Perhaps coach Allen's greatest contribution to the game was his keen assessment and 1976 recommendation to UNC Athletic Director William Copey that one of his former players, Anson Dorrance, be appointed his successor. In retrospect, Anson states, "I guess that he [Allen] saw something in me that even I didn't see in myself."

At the time, Anson was enrolled in law school and had the promise of a secure future as an attorney in his father's oil business in hand. But as he attempted to juggle his law studies with coaching the UNC men, it became evident to him that his true passion was in the area of coaching and he, with wife M'Liss's support, set aside his study of the law.

As tribute to his mentor, Marvin Allen, who always wore a coat and tie while on the UNC sideline, today his successor dons a tie while coaching.

As for Dorrance's teammate, Mark Berson, he would also contribute to the establishment of Southern soccer.

Dr. I.M. Ibrahim

...coach Walt Chyzowych spoke for other conference coaches when he credited Ibrahim with sparking interest in the rise of ACC soccer. "He's the one who got it going," said the respected Wake Forest mentor.

Whether it was coincidence or not, Doyle Royal's retirement as Maryland coach ushered in another era of Atlantic Coast Conference soccer. For, in 1972, in his sixth season as Clemson (SC) University coach, Israeli-born Ibrahim steered the Tigers to the first of eight consecutive conference titles. In fact, Clemson recorded an unbeaten (38-0-2) ACC record from 1972-79.

Recruiting Foreign Talent

The 1972 ACC title was the first of 13 conference titles for Ibrahim-coached teams. Perhaps more impressive is the fact that Clemson qualified for the NCAA Tournament in 17 of his 28 seasons as coach, including four College Bowls during the 1970s. Leading those teams were Guyana recruits, Clyde Browne and Clyde Watson. The former was a four-time ACC Player of the Year. Later, Nigerians Godwin Obueze, Benedict Poppola, Nnamdi Nwokocha, Damian Ogunsuyi, and Adudarie Otorubio were among the foreign players who were accorded ACC Player of the Year honors and made Clemson a consistent national title contender.

The highlights of Clemson soccer were the NCAA Championships won in 1984 and 1987. Two American-born players, Bruce Murray and Eric Eichmann, starred on those teams. Murray was recipient of the Hermann Award in 1987, and both went on to star for the USMNT.

Murray shared with Ray Alley that he and other players knew of coach Ibrahim's superstitious nature and, related to that, began a pregame ritual whereby they dropped coins along the sidelines patrolled by the Tiger coach. In time, the coach would see and retrieve one and, especially after team victories, began to associate the wins with the "lucky coins." Bruce and others watched this routine with amused interest as the scenario repeatedly unfurled during their careers. 116

Sometimes criticized for his initial recruitment of international players to Clemson, South Carolina, the flamboyant Ibrahim defended his recruitment policy by pointing out that the community was devoid of

Dr. I.M. Ibrahim trod the Clemson sidelines for 28 seasons while setting new standards for other ACC schools to attain.

any soccer when he located there for graduate study. He later sought to Americanize his roster, with Murray and Eichmann among those who were attracted by the program's winning tradition. Ibrahim was accorded ACC Coach of the Year honors five times, including 1990 and 1993, when the Tigers won the last of it 13 ACC titles. Upon his retirement in 1995, Ibrahim's coaching record stood at 388-102-31 (.774) and was the fifth winningest record among college coaches.

Elevating ACC Play

While Doyle Royal established a benchmark for a handful of schools to try to emulate, many point to Ibrahim as elevating ACC play to a whole new level during the 1980s. And before his passing in 1994, coach Walt Chyzowych spoke for other conference coaches when he credited Ibrahim with sparking interest in the rise of ACC soccer. "He's the one who got it going," said the respected Wake Forest mentor.

The ACC hired full-time coaches who focused not only on fielding competitive teams but also on developing other aspects of their programs. Duke hired its first full-time coach in John Rennie, and by 1986 he had taken the Blue Devils to an

NCAA soccer title. While Virginia's Larry Gross moved to North Carolina State, his replacement, Bruce Arena, soon had the Cavaliers winning five of the 17 NCAA titles won by ACC teams. Gross, in turn, was succeeded by Argentine George Tarantini. While Anson Dorrance eventually focused on coaching women, his record with the North Carolina men included an appearance in the Final Four. The very successful Elmar Bolowich subsequently succeeded Anson. Meanwhile, Wake Forest built its program by hiring former USMNT coaching legend Walt Chyzowych.

In time, as with Ibrahim, who has his name imprinted on the Clemson soccer facility, all ACC schools have dedicated soccer stadiums for the sport, and many of the coaches have founded highly successful soccer camps that have educated thousands of young players in the nuances of the game in "The ACC Way."

Unfortunately, it was during the early 1970s that another Southern school that featured black soccer players on its roaster ushered in what was perceived as a race-related occurrence that reflected poorly on the national administration of the sport and its coaches.

John Rennie at Duke

As with many of his colleagues, John Rennie's coaching career involved a series of fortuitous events that led to his eventual ascendency as one of the game's most successful tenures while soccer coach at Duke University.[118]

Chatham High School/Temple University

Raised in the prosperous New Jersey suburb of Chatham, John was a standout high school soccer, basketball, and baseball player.

In soccer, Rennie came under the influence of two of the early soccer-coaching pioneers, Otto Haas and Gene Chyzowych. As a senior in 1960, John set a school record when he scored 30 goals in 15 games for coach Haas's Chatham (NJ) High School team.

It was Chyzowych, a Temple University grad, who helped arrange a scholarship for Rennie to attend his alma mater. While the grant included room and board, on-campus rooms were under construction his freshman year. So for a year, John resided with Gene's parents in the inner city of Philadelphia. While John didn't

Coach John Rennie led Duke to the upper echelons of ACC and national Division I play.

understand Ukrainian and the parents knew little English, the relationship survived until university housing opened.

At Temple, John came under the influence of Owl Hall of Fame coach Pete Leaness. While Leaness produced three dozen All-America players during his tenure, John Rennie's promise (he scored six goals in his first varsity match) did not result in such honors, and a senior-year knee injury ended his Temple soccer-playing career.

College Coaching

Rennie frequently scouted metropolitan soccer matches with Columbia professor Sunil Gulati and soccer columnist Paul Gardner.

The route from high school to college coaching was one not frequently traveled, though, while teaching at Sayerville High School, John Rennie had noted that Hackensack High School coach Bob Seddon had moved on to coach at the University of Pennsylvania.

Following completion of his master's degree, Rennie took a combined soccer and swimming coach position at the University of Massachusetts, Dartmouth,

238

in 1971. In 1972, Rennie led the team to a 12-4-3 season and was named NAIA New England COY.

By coincidence, while attending a friend's wedding, John had met Columbia University AD Ken German. In part, that meeting, coupled with his success at UMass, Dartmouth, led to his being hired, in 1972, as Columbia's men's coach.

Despite winning but four matches in his first three seasons, the new coach did meet one of the AD's major concerns: he was able to quell the number of fisticuffs that had annually marred Columbia matches.

In trying to elevate Columbia's on-field play, Rennie frequently scouted metropolitan area soccer matches with Columbia professor Sunil Gulati and soccer columnist Paul Gardner. By 1978, led by two talented English products, Steve Charles and Barry Nix, the Lions recorded a 13-2-1 season that saw the team win the Ivy League title and defeat Hartwick and Rhode Island on the way to the NCAA quarterfinal round.

Duke University

Now with Ivy League credentials on his resume, in 1979, Duke University hired Rennie to lead its fully funded men's soccer program.

John credits Duke with joining other ACC schools in placing more emphasis on soccer as an important fall sport. In 1980, Duke became the first ACC team to defeat perennial conference power Clemson. It earned Rennie the first of five ACC COY awards.

By 1982, Duke entered the NCAA DI final versus Indiana with a 22-0-1 record, only to lose to the Hoosiers in a record eight-overtime match. Four years later, the Blue Devils captured the University's first national athletic championship with a 1-0 win over Akron.

By the time of his retirement in 2007, coach Rennie had led Duke to five ACC titles and to a like number of NCAA College Cup appearances and accumulated a 399-153-33 coaching record.

Included in the team's success has been a wealth of individual honors. Flooding the trophy cases at Duke are numerous Coach of the Year awards and plenty of player accolades. Rennie was voted NSCAA National Coach of the Year in 1982, ACC Coach of the Year in 1980, 1983, 1987, 1997, and 1999, and South Region Coach of the Year in 1982, 1983, and 1997.

Rennie has been honored with induction into the North Carolina Soccer Hall of Fame (2011), the United Soccer Coaches Hall of Fame (2012), and the Duke Athletics Hall of Fame (2013).

A Wide Range of Soccer Contributions

During his 28-year career as Blue Devil coach, the New Jersey native has seen the ACC emerge as the most dominant soccer conference in the country, with seven schools since 1981combining to win 17 NCAA titles. He himself has served as the chairman of the NCAA Division I Soccer Committee.

While Rennie initially returned to the Northeast to recruit players [including six who have been named Hermann Trophy recipients], he has seen soccer recruitment expand to other regions of the country. "I credit that [soccer's growth] to the fact that many former NASL and other professional players remained in the country and began to play prominent roles in developing players in their regions. In particular that includes the Southeast. Today coaches find good players throughout the Southeast as a result."

In addition to his success as a field coach, the Rennie imprint on the game has included development of the 7,000-seat Koskinen Stadium on campus, while his Duke University soccer camps were among the nation's largest.

His involvement in the growth of the sport in his region has included playing a leading role in the Olympic Development Program as well as involvement in the sport at the club level. This has included time as a member of the USSF regional coaching staff and as DOC for the North Carolina Youth Soccer Association. In his home city of Durham, Rennie and his players have helped develop the local soccer club, which now counts over 4,000 players on its roster

Also of note are the number of former Rennie-coached Duke players who have become soccer stalwarts subsequent to their graduation.

Bruce Arena at Virginia

While Bruce Arena's career that began at Virginia in 1978 overlapped Rennie's and other ACC coaches as well, during his tenure, which ended in 1995, he further raised the bar as far as conference soccer was concerned.

While his expansive recruiting network included attracting stellar players such as Claudio Reyna from New Jersey and Jeff Agoos from Texas, he also played an important role in the construction of the modern campus soccer facility, Klockner Stadium.

Beginning in 1983, and for the next 12 seasons, the Cavaliers were the dominant ACC men's team, capturing nine regular season and five tournament titles with Arena accorded COY honors on seven occasions.

By 1989, when he had relinquished his lacrosse coaching duties, Arena's team shared the first of its NCAA national titles with Santa

Bruce Arena interviewed following one of Virginia's five NCAA DI championship victories.

Clara. Two years later, UVA would capture the first of four consecutive national Division I titles.

Off-field, the UVA coach headed the ACC soccer committee for several years and served six years on the NCAA Division I soccer committee.

At the end of his Virginia coaching career in 1995, Arena had built a program that won 95 percent of its matches and set a new standard of achievement for ACC soccer.

More on Arena's stellar coaching career later in the book.

Bill Holleman's Multifaceted Roles[119]

When he concluded his 38th season as soccer coach, Bill Holleman had an overall coaching record of 652-184-43, which is among the best in secondary school annals.

Bill Holleman is one of those U.S. soccer coaches whose contributions to the growth of the sport have been multidimensional.

Whether it has been on the development side of the game, his remarkable coaching record, or the administration of the sport, he made an impact both regionally and nationally.

Campbell and Catfish

Holleman's introduction to the game took place at Campbell (NC) College, where he came under the influence of James "Catfish" Cole. Playing as a winger, Bill's four-year career ended in 1967, following a loss in a NAIA regional tournament to the eventual titlist, Quincy College. In 1968, he entered coaching at the Ravenscroft (NC) School. Bill spent 10 years there as a teacher, soccer coach, and athletic director. His 1977 and 1978 teams captured North Carolina Independent Schools state championships.

It was while at Ravenscroft and seeking to gain more experience for his players that he made an important connection that played into a later important life experience. He met Hank Steinbrecher when Hank was the then-Warren Wilson (NC) Junior College coach. Thus, a coaching relationship was formed that would later play long-term dividends for coach Holleman.

As with other U.S. builders of the schoolboy game, Bill became its advocate in the Raleigh community. It was exemplified in 1972 when he conceived of and was one of the original board members of the Raleigh Soccer League, predecessor to the Capital Area Soccer League (CASL). CASL was cited recently as impacting some 15,000 members. Led at one point by Charlie Slagle, CASL has hosted U.S. Soccer international matches as well as NCAA Championships at its stadium site. Bill also was the founder and served four times as president of the North Carolina Scholastic Soccer Coaches Association.

Among his former Ravenscroft products is coach Lee Horton. Holleman recalls that Lee had no soccer experience when he entered school as a junior in 1972, but upon graduation was an All-America goalkeeper. Subsequent to his playing at UNC for coaches Marvin Allen and Anson Dorrance, since 1984, Horton has worked his coaching magic at the Charlotte Latin School, leading the school to 13 North Carolina Independent Schools Athletic Association titles while accumulating over 1,000 coaching wins.

The Lovett School

In 1979, the Holleman family moved to Atlanta, where Bill began a 14-year tenure as athletic director and men's soccer coach at the Lovett School. There he coordinated and supervised 60 interscholastic teams in 15 sports. Bill's Lovett soccer teams won state all-classification championships in 1984, 1985, 1986, and 1989.

He also formed the highly competitive Concorde Soccer Club, leading its teams to state and regional championships. That included its U-16 appearance in the John D. Niotis U-16 USYSA National Championship tournament. One of his Lovett players, John Cocking, played on the 1985 U.S. U-16 team that played in China and later played for Anson Dorrance at North Carolina.

On to World Cup '94

It was while at the 1993 NSCAA Convention in Baltimore that the Hollemans met with Hank Steinbrecher (then CEO of US Soccer). With the 1994 World Cup in its planning stages, they expressed an interest in getting involved in that process.

Granted a leave of absence by Lovett, Bill first landed a spot on the planning group that focused on meeting the off-field needs of the 32 World Cup teams. He then moved on to Detroit to assist with the 1993 US Cup Tournament played at the indoor Pontiac Stadium venue. That competition proved to FIFA that an indoor grass field could last the 23 days demanded for World Cup play. When Tom King left Detroit for another WC role, Holleman became the 1994 Venue Executive Director for the Detroit site.

Bill Holleman.

Upon completion of the 1994 event, Bill and wife Kay accepted an assignment as president of the Birmingham Olympic Soccer Organizing Committee. "It was a unique opportunity for that city to enhance its image which had suffered as the result of the earlier racial uprisings," shared Bill. "So the city and area companies went out of their way to 'make things happen.'" One of Bill's soccer coaching friends, Preston Goldfarb at Birmingham Southern, helped align the school to serve as the site for the Olympic Village. In the process of hosting its 11 matches, Birmingham ticket sales tripled those sold at the other three Olympic soccer sites combined. Further, the opening match between the United States and Argentina attracted the largest crowd (83,810) in Legion Field history, and that includes any attendance for the annual Alabama-Auburn football games played there. "Best of all," concluded the proud venue chief, "we ended up with a surplus of $5 million in Birmingham coffers!"

Following his national soccer successes, Holleman returned to his first loves, soccer coaching and the NSCAA.

Robert "Bob" Sims and Georgia Soccer

"Bob Sims was a true gentleman. He gave his heart and soul to high school soccer in Georgia."
–Bill Holleman

If there were a soccer wasteland in the United States, then Bob Sims found it in the state of Georgia when he was appointed to start a soccer program at the Westminster Schools in Atlanta in 1958.[120]

Three years after indoctrination to the sport, there were 20 teams spread across the state engaged in soccer play, and one year after his retirement from Westminster in 1992, 156 high school teams were playing soccer in the Peachtree State.

A perusal of Sims' resume leaves but one impression on the reader: Bob truly deserves the label of the state's "Father of High School Soccer."

Bob Sims led the way as secondary school soccer was established in Georgia.

Starting From Scratch

With nary a soccer book in the local branch of the Atlanta Public Library, its staff located some in New York City, and they became the basis for Sims's initial immersion in the sport. His first squad recorded a 5-3-1 season, playing the only two other Georgia schools and other college/club teams in the area. It would be the first of 34 straight seasons of non-losing soccer for the Westminster Schools.

Sims' soccer education included outreach to two individuals also promoting soccer in the Atlanta area, Clyde Partin and Phil Woosnam. Partin had started the program, while Woosnam was establishing professional soccer with his leadership of the Atlanta Chiefs soccer franchise. Partin introduced the novice coach to membership in the NSCAA and, beginning in 1959, Sims attended every January convention through 2009, annually returning home with copious notes and diagrams. Woosnam spent time chalking blackboard sessions with the highly engaged schoolboy coach.

Advocating for the Game

...it took 15 years of arm-twisting to move boys soccer from an all-classification tournament to an enrollment-based classification tournament.

Two personality traits benefitted coach Sims as he became a principal soccer advocate for the sport—namely, persistence and a meticulous attention to detail.

By 1960, Bob, along with Partin and Dan Kennerly from O'Keefe High School, began making annual trips to the Georgia High School Association (GHSA) meetings to lobby for the acceptance of high school soccer as a recognized sport. Six years later, the GHSA approved the request for the 1965-66 year and, in 1969, appointed him soccer coordinator and tournament chairman, a position he held through 1993. As such, he not only created leagues but also, for the duration of his office, tracked and recorded all manner of league results, officials' reports, and other valued statistical information. He also served as the principal source for high school soccer information for Georgia media.

Not wishing to butt heads with fall football, Sims tirelessly sought to move soccer to a spring season. In 1979, after eight years of lobbying, that move was approved by the GHSA. The GHSA establishment of a state tournament for girls was achieved in 1992 after five years of lobbying, while it took 15 years of arm-twisting to move boys soccer from an all-classification tournament to an enrollment-based classification tournament. Three years later, a similar arrangement took place for girls state tournament play.

Promoting Sportsmanship

Alongside Bob Sims' service that elevated school soccer in his home state was his work to support the goals of the NSCAA in his region. His was an annual effort to recruit coaches to join NSCAA in order to see their players and programs recognized at a national level while also allowing for greater exposure for more Georgia players.

Specifically, he was the organization's Southeast high school representative for five years and was a member of the *Soccer Journal* Committee for eight years. He would be the Georgia representative on the NSCAA All-America Committee for many years and shared his archives with the History & Records Committee as it began to compile histories of the secondary school play. He also served on the Robert W. Robinson High School Long Term Achievement Award Committee for numerous years and was its award recipient in 1997.

In the late 1970s, as the NSCAA began to address the issue of ethical behavior, the ever-vigilant Sims began an effort to convince GHSA to establish a sportsmanship award for teams receiving no yellow or red cards for the season. It took six years of backroom work before an award was established. In 1983, the award was renamed the Robert Sims Sportsmanship Award. In the 10 years that Westminster Schools were eligible for the award, it was its recipient on five occasions.

Westminster Schools Soccer

The Westminster Schools varsity boys soccer program, in 34 seasons from 1958 through 1992, achieved a 316-83-19 record. The Wildcats qualified for the GHSA State Tournament in 17 of the 27 years they were eligible and captured state titles in 1966, 1967, 1976, 1982, and 1983.

Some of Sims' standards shared with his players included:

- Hard work and fun can co-exist beautifully.
- The health and well-being of the player trumps all other concerns.
- Sportsmanship and ethics enable victory with honor.
- Competing with great passion is necessary to experience the height of joy upon victory and the depth of agony upon defeat.
- Never exploit inferior competitors; build the esteem of inferior competitors.
- Positive reinforcement works.

- Repetition works; KISS principle.
- Always credit the opposition.
- Respect everyone, especially the officials.
- Call home to check on any injured player.
- If a player is in the hospital, the coach is at the hospital.
- If you want something done right, quietly go about doing it.
- Players always win games; coaches always lose games.
- Leadership is service.

Sims' former players presented a proclamation from the school's Board of Trustees on the occasion of his retirement in 1993. It read in part: "Coach Sims showed humor and grace under pressure, and a human approach to coaching and dealing with young men that made playing for him a pleasure. We thank him for the opportunity to play under his leadership and note for the record that Coach Bob Sims is not simply the father of soccer at The Westminster Schools, yet also the father of Georgia High School Soccer."

Coach Bill Holleman locked horns with Westminster teams when coaching the nearby Lovett School and shared, "Bob Sims was a true gentleman. He gave his heart and soul to high school soccer in Georgia. I also recall that his wife Marie was right by his side every step of the way!"

Honors

The list of involvements and accolades for the highly respected Sims reflects both the breadth and quality of his commitments to the game of soccer. They include the following.

- Northside YMCA (Atlanta, GA): Charter founder of its youth soccer program, 1966; member and chair of its soccer board, 1966-86
- National High School Athletic Coaches Association National COY, 1975
- National Federation of High Schools, Soccer Rules Committee charter member, 1970-76; committee member, 1981-85
- NSCAA Region IV High School Coach of the Year, 1981
- Atlanta District Amateur Soccer League board member for 12 years; president 1982-83
- NSCAA South Region High School Coach of the Year, 1983

- Coach, Army/NSCAA National High School All-Star Game, 1984
- Georgia STAR Teacher of the Year on four occasions
- Georgia High School Association Meritorious Service Award, 1993
- The Westminster Schools Athletic Hall of Fame, 1993
- Georgia High School Association established the Bob Sims Sportsmanship Award, 1993-present
- The Westminster Schools Outstanding Science Student Award named the Bob Sims Award, 1993-present
- Georgia State Soccer Association Hall of Fame, 2001
- The Westminster Schools established Bob Sims Tournament, 2001-present
- United Soccer Coaches 60-year Membership Pin, 2019

Anson and April – Builders of the Women's Game

As Title IX sped up and guaranteed more opportunities for women, Anson Dorrance's pioneering efforts as coach of the University of North Carolina (UNC) women established new standards for other coaches of women to strive for. In large part, today's great parity in NCAA Division I women's play is a tribute to the benchmarks Dorrance established.

One measure of coaching effectiveness is the end product of that effort. In a sense, April Heinrichs personifies what the North Carolina mentor has long endeavored to produce—namely, women who were talented, competitive players and who, upon completion of their playing careers, found places to contribute to the U.S. game.

Anson Dorrance – An American Soccer Icon

Among the many accolades tossed his way, possibly the one most valued by iconic UNC women's soccer coach Anson Dorrance was the one attributed to Dean Smith, its famed men's basketball coach.

When queried about the Tar Heels athletic program and the court team's place in it, the late coach candidly reminded that, to his thinking, his teams were second to Dorrance's, noting, "This [UNC] is a women's soccer school."[122]

Foreign Influences[123]

In 1970, and familiar with being uprooted, student Dorrance transferred to UNC and 50 years later has become a honored fixture on the Chapel Hill campus. He was born in Bombay, India, and, due to his father's ties, grew up in many places, including Ethiopia, Kenya, Singapore, and Belgium. The family also had stops in Oakland (CA), White Plains (NY), and, every three years, stays at the maternal homestead in Lewisburg, North Carolina.

His early sporting interests were focused on such British sports as boxing, cricket, field hockey, rugby, and tennis. Additionally, in finishing his secondary school education in Switzerland, the youngster was exposed to recreational soccer and skiing.

It was in 1970, when enrolled at St. Mary's College in San Antonio, that Anson was first introduced to competitive soccer while playing on the college team that was fortified with children of South American missionaries. He transferred to UNC the following spring and joined coach Marvin Allen's men's team, where he became a three-time All-ACC selection.

Indicative of whether that decision has been impactful, today, when the name of "Anson" is mentioned in American sporting circles and attesting to his huge influence on the development of U.S. Soccer, it denotes but one person.

Anson Dorrance wears an ever-present tie in tribute to his former coach, Marvin Allen.

Marvin Allen's Intuition

Perhaps one of UNC coach Marvin Allen's greatest contribution to the game was keen assessment of individual potential. In 1976, it was his recommendation to the UNC AD William Copey that Dorrance be appointed his successor.

Named to start the women's program by Copey in 1979, and for the next nine seasons, Anson patrolled the sidelines as coach of both the UNC soccer men's and women's teams.

Until he singly focused on the women's team in 1989, Dorrance's coaching of the men cannot be overlooked. During his 12-year tenure, the UNC men recorded a 125-65-21 record, including an appearance in the 1987 NCAA College Cup semifinals.

But, of course, it is his success as coach of the Tar Heel women that has brought rightful comparison to UCLA basketball coach John Wooden in terms of the number of national championships won. On that basis alone, North Carolina's 21 NCAA titles dwarfs UCLA's by nearly a dozen!

In terms of his geographical influence on a sport, the UNC dynasty has influenced the emergence of women's soccer through the Atlantic Coast Conference and can be attributed to the upsurge in scholastic and club soccer play in the southeastern part of the United States. While his success has been attributed to his keen eye for soccer talent and his reputation (in 1991, *Soccer America* acknowledged him as one of the 20 most influential soccer persons over the last 20 years!) allows him seemingly "his pick of the soccer litter," he has tended to recruit close to Chapel Hill. A peek at his 2020 team roster revealed that 25 of its 35 players hail from southeastern states.

Three best-selling books have added to the Dorrance influence. They include *Training Soccer Champions* (1996), *The Vision of a Champion* (with Gloria Averbuch, 2005), and *The Man Watching* (with Tim Crothers, 2006). The coach has no details as to the number of books sold, though he does report that sales spike when the Tarheel women annually advance in NCAA post-season play.

In addition, his UNC summer camps have annually sold out, with their receipts helping fund the salaries of his three assistant coaches. The team's media guide lists 28 individuals supporting various facets of the Carolina women's program!

The Competitive Cauldron

"But then I got to the University of North Carolina, and it was O.K. to want to be the best."
–Mia Hamm

Maybe most impactful has been the influence of the Dorrance approach to the coaching of his women athletes. A voracious reader (he may have 10 books on varied topics open at once), over time he has, along with various soccer exposures, partially formed the basis of his approach to coaching women from such readings.

As Title IX legislation opened up competitive athletics for women, how coaches, the majority of them male, would approach the actual coaching of their female athletes, was to a large extent an unknown.

Not unlike other soccer-coaching pioneers of another era whose approach mirrored that of their predecessors, there were few precedents for Dorrance and others to fall back on when it came to coaching women.

But relying in part on how women ("they want to be valued as persons first") reacted to his approach to teaching, Dorrance arrived at a set of coaching principles that buttressed his approach and, most importantly, has willingly shared his beliefs with others in the U.S. coaching community. By attentiveness to such matters as framing of his words (his vocabulary includes some salty phraseology!) and body language, he has perfected those communication skills.

Definitely most telling was his confidence that women athletes could overcome their need for group acceptance in the team setting and become serious competitors trying to earn their PT (playing time). It was through observing the training methods of UNC coaching legend Dean Smith that he introduced what he labeled his "Competitive Cauldron." Basically, it applied measurement to players' success in a series of competitive settings.[124]

Most importantly, through a well-formed and balanced approach, he was able to consistently achieve group harmony between what are, in many ways, conflicting priorities. Namely, the individual desire of players to compete for playing time and their collective need to cooperate if group success is to be achieved.

UNC great Mia Hamm remarked about the Dorrance competitive training regime in a 1998 *Sports Illustrated* article: "I grew up always good at sports, but being a girl, I was never allowed to feel as good about it as guys were. My toughness wasn't celebrated. But then I got to the University of North Carolina, and it was O.K. to want to be the best."[125]

Core Values

Underpinning the on-field approach to coaching women, coach Dorrance developed a set of core values that every Tarheel athlete ascribes to once she dons Carolina blue.

Culled from his various readings (these include such writers as George Bernard Shaw, John Donne, Thomas Duxton, Desmond Morris, Reynolds Price, Jason Elliot, Victor Frankl, William Damon, Gregg Easterbrook, and Carol Gillingham), these ideals form the emotional and psychological approach that have led to the consistently high performance of the UNC women over four decades.

The values include adherence to the following overriding statement: "I will excel athletically by committing myself to performance excellence, team success, and continual improvement." Players are reminded that in accepting the challenge they will embrace certain team principles termed core values:[126]

- We don't whine. The truly extraordinary do something every day. They have remarkable self-discipline and everyday have a plan to get better.

- We want these four years of college to be rich, valuable, and deep. This is that the focused individual is here for the right reason: To get an education.
- We work hard. The individual embodies the "indefatigable human spirit" and never stops pushing. We are relentless in training.
- We choose to be positive. Nothing can depress or upset this powerful and positive life force.
- We treat everyone with respect.
- We care about each other as teammates and as human beings.
- When we don't play as much as we would like we are noble and still support the team and its mission.
- We play for each other.
- We are well led. This is the verbal leader on the field that is less concerned with popularity and more concerned about holding everyone to their highest standards.
- We want our lives to be never ending ascensions but for that to happen properly our fundamental attitude about life and our appreciation for it is critical.

Initial UNC Team Tactics

Alongside Dorrance's psychological approach to coaching women was his initial tactical approach to UNC team play, which emphasized individual and collective speed. That included a rapid transition (called "reckless fury" by the coach) to a systematic application of high-pressure tactics to win back the ball defensively once it was lost.

To implement that philosophy, UNC played a 3-4-3 alignment and, particularly with its three forwards, flooded opponents in their defensive third of the field. Such pressurizing recognized that female players at the time weren't as capable as men of releasing Tar Heel pressure by playing long and accurate passes. Once the ball was won, the team had three strikers, not two, in position to attack.

Over time, Dorrance has adopted various systems of play (4-3-3, 3-5-2, 4-3-3) tailored to the playing strengths of his rosters. In stating that, UNC on-field success is still predicated on high pressure and quick transitional play that demands consistent individual and collective effort.

Of course, as women's play has improved, the effect rate for Carolina NCAA titles has been somewhat diminished. After winning 15 of the first 17 NCAA titles, from 1981-97, UNC has captured "only" six of the next 22.

In addition to the NCAA team titles, the coach is proud that 19 UNC players, beginning with April Heinrichs in 1984 and 1986, have been named as national collegiate players of the year.

In 2003, *Sports Illustrated* declared UNC women's soccer as college sports' greatest dynasty.

USWNT

Well-known is the fact that beginning with his appointment as coach of the fledgling U.S. women's national team in 1986, the Dorrance coaching philosophy also proved dominant on the then-emerging women's international soccer stage.

That appointment took place following a 1985 USSF encampment in Dallas, where a panel examined candidates for possible appointments to manage its national teams. "In retrospect, the method they used played right into my strengths," Anson recalled. "I coached a team in a match, evaluated it following the match and made a soccer-related talk to the group. I have no problem with any of those aspects of coaching." Anson believes that one examiner, Walt Chyzowych, was an important ally in his being named coach of the U.S. women's team.

U.S. coaching legend Walter Bahr had earlier accompanied coach Anson Dorrance and the USWNT to China in 1988 when FIFA staged a women's championship tournament. "They [FIFA] were trying to figure out if a FIFA Women's World Cup would be a worthwhile event. The large crowds and the competitiveness of the women's teams convinced them to move forward with the World Cup format for women. I liked what I saw in terms of how our women played. Michele Akers was great and Mia Hamm, 15 at the time, was a very promising player," Bahr stated. "I particularly was impressed with how our women played. They did not rely on physical force. Rather they played my kind of soccer, 'thinking soccer.'"[127]

Led in part by nine UNC players, the U.S. team won the inaugural 1991 FIFA Women's World Cup Tournament held in China. In choosing the team, Anson, in addition to evaluating a player's technical, tactical, and psychological components, placed an emphasis on that individual's ability for self-discipline along with her capacity to positively impact the total team effort.

Dorrance lauded April Heinrichs for her leadership role in achieving the 1991 title, as she influenced the reserve players to "buy into" the selfless component the coach feels is vitally important in achieving team cohesiveness.

In choosing Tony DiCicco and Lauren Gregg as his USWNT assistants, he added two personalities different from his own, qualities he values as important for persons in such roles.

No fan of U.S. Soccer officialdom, Dorrance short-circuited the organization's normal hiring practices when he announced at a 1994 team training session both his retirement and the appointment of DiCicco as his successor. With normal protocol breached, U.S. Soccer agreed to the appointment with a private understanding that Dorrance would become the organization's overseer of a national program for women's player development. Of interest is that that commitment was unfilled until April Henrichs assumed that role in 2011. It wasn't until 2008 that U.S. Soccer named Anson Dorrance recipient of the Werner Fricker Award that honors individuals for their contributions to building the game in this country.

Dorrance's influence has been felt in the number of his former players turned coaches while he has also chimed in as a member of the NCAA Rules Committee.

Foreign Influences

Asked about the influence of foreign soccer play on his coaching methodology, the long-time UNC mentor acknowledges that his initial interest in the international game was in the individual techniques of great players such as George Best and Johan Cruyff. "I tried to study the game at its basic level of 1 v. 1 play and impart that information to my players," formed the basis of his interest at the time.

With the advent of exposure to international coaches, his favored disciples include Arsenal's Arsene Wenger, Manchester City's Pep Guardiola, and Liverpool's Jurgen Klopp. Most recently, the physical training methods of Dutch coach Raymond Verheijen have intrigued him.

Plenty of Acknowledgements

When asked to what he ascribes his coaching success, Dorrance replies somewhat simplistically, "I am an expert at competition." He can obviously back up that comment as he has accumulated a combined coaching record of 1,043-140-63 and, along the way, has garnered countless acknowledgements for his outstanding contributions to the game.

The first award was the 1996 Walter Chyzowych Award. It was followed by induction into the U.S. Soccer Hall of Fame (2008) and United Soccer Coaches Hall of Fame 2018). He was also the recipient of the United Soccer Coaches Bill Jeffrey (2007) and Honor (2010) awards. Earlier, in 2002, UNC had inducted him into its HOF. In 2005, he was named to the North Carolina Sports Hall of Fame.

Possibly U.S. Soccer's presentation of its Werner Fricker Award best honors Anson Dorrance for his overall impact on the game. It is annually presented to an individual who has been a builder of the game.

April Heinrichs – From Player to Builder[128]

When her basketball coach at Colorado Mesa University learned that the University of North Carolina was offering April Heinrichs an athletic scholarship, he informed her, "You'll never play there."

As the history of her subsequent soccer career has unfolded, that quote will live in infamy. Unfortunately, that dismissive quote needs clarification as the court coach thought UNC's aid offer was for basketball, not soccer.

In any case, in a wide-ranging interview, April traced the events and persons who impacted her playing career and subsequent substantial life in coaching and administrating soccer.

A Heavenly Match

"I credited him with always having a reason for why he was doing something. His listening, in turn, allowed his players to 'find their voice.'" –April Heinrichs

Supported by a modest, caring family as a youth, April was encouraged to engage in a variety of sports. But at Littleton's Heritage High School, her focus narrowed to playing soccer and basketball.

In the fall of 1982, her club soccer team played in a tournament at Brown (RI) University. Impressed with her play, a club coach from Virginia alerted UNC women's coach Anson Dorrance of her potential.

When asked of Anson's hallmarks as a coach, April was quick to name his recruiting prowess at the top of his aptitudes. After watching her play indoors, the astute coach offered her a half scholarship and, if she became an All-America player, she'd receive a full ride.

Dorrance has long acknowledged his three-time All-America performer as one of the most competitive of those many Tarheel women he has mentored in his 43-year coaching career. That quality, when coupled with skill, enabled the coach-player duo (she termed the relationship as one "made in heaven") to win three NCAA titles and the plucky striker to be acknowledged as college Player of the Decade for the 1980s by *Soccer America*.

April and Anson combined to capture the initial FIFA world title in 1991 in China.

She credits herself and her teammates with fine-tuning Dorrance as he transitioned serving as coach of both the UNC men and women. "I would say that Anson was a little 'rough around the edges' when it came to coaching women," she recalled. Of all the many qualities she valued about America's premier coach of women, ("demanding; caring; competitive"), the one that stands out was his ability to communicate. "I was always one to question things we did on the field. Anson was never offended and I credited him with always having a reason for why he was doing something. His listening, in turn, allowed his players to 'find their voice.'"

Her exposure to Dorrance also fueled her own competitive juices and that of other UNC women. She credits the coach with granting them "permission to compete," with the group impacted by what the coach termed his Competitive Cauldron coaching regime.

Post-UNC Coaching Influences

Following graduation, April played professionally (1987-89) in Italy, first for Juventus ("a bad contract") and then for Prato. She credits the two seasons

257

as exposing her to another way of doing soccer, including refinement of her understanding of the defensive side of the game. She also learned to speak Italian!

During this period, another U.S. coach, John Ellis, impacted her soccer life. Better known as the father of former USWNT coach Jill Ellis, John has long served the game in the Washington, D.C. area. In addition to offering summer camps, he has principally served as a soccer consultant for various club teams in the region.

He is credited by April with guiding her through her formative years as a coach. It was while in his employ that she and other staff met for morning tutorials where they presented their camp lesson plans. She particularly valued the Ellis instructional emphasis on relating all coaching back to the attacking and defending principles of the game. Ellis also offered valued feedback to his camp instructors. "I recall him watching me doing a session and later sharing that I was monotone in my voice."

It was also at this developmental phase of her coaching career that April exposed herself to the coaching schools offered by U.S. Soccer and the NSCAA. In earning the highest license or diploma offered by the groups, she refined the planning process needed for successful instruction. She also valued the exposure to the instructional styles of various staff members. "I also liked the commonality that took place among those taking the courses. We all became friends."

She also remarks that soccer is unique among sports in offering courses for aspiring coaches to improve their methodology. "It was a great experience for me. I don't know about others, but I would have paid double for it!"

Subsequent to her playing career, April Heinrichs has played important coaching and administrative roles in soccer.

USWNT

Heinrichs's U.S. Women's National Team play began in 1986, coinciding with Dorrance becoming the first full-time women's national team coach.

Over the next six seasons, the team became better supported, organized, and competitive.

Leading up to the first FIFA-sponsored Women's World Cup Tournament, Heinrichs formed part of a devastating threesome, labeled by the media as the "Triple-Edged Sword." Besides April, it included Carin Jennings-Cabarra and Michelle Akers; in 1991, the trio helped the team capture the inaugural FIFA Women's World Cup in China. She captained the team and, during her USWNT career, earned 46 caps and scored 35 goals.

The Busy 1990s

In addition to the FIFA Women's World Cup, the 1990s saw April juggling intercollegiate coaching with increased USWNT responsibilities.

Princeton (1990), Maryland (1991-95), and Virginia (1996-99) were her collegiate coaching stops. In 1995, Tony DiCicco asked her to assist him with the USWNT.

She termed college as the most professional environment in coaching. "I liked the cyclical nature of the job, along with having the ability to shape the lives of the athletes I dealt with. Thank goodness for email as it helped me communicate with my assistants (Jill Ellis for many of those years) and keep in touch when away on national team duties."

As for her time with DiCicco, April cited several coaching lessons taken from her relationship with the late coach. "He was always well-prepared and he brought more professionalism to the team. When you are doing two-a-days it isn't easy to keep players focused. But Tony was highly creative and no two practices were ever the same." In addition, she liked the fact that he brought in specialists who addressed the team in such matters as nutrition and mental preparation. He also spliced in video presentations of high value.

Her ability to manage these responsibilities is reflected in the fact that she was Atlantic Coast Conference COY at Maryland in 1995 when the team earned its first NCAA Tournament appearance. Four more NCAA appearances took place while she was at Virginia.

Under DiCicco, the USWNT finished third in the 1995 World Cup and later earned the gold medal in the first women's Olympic soccer tournament in 1996. This was followed by a second FIFA Women's World Cup trophy win at the Rose Bowl in 1999. She also found time to coach the U.S. U-16 youth national team following the 1996 Olympics.

Uncovering USWNT Talent

April mentions one challenge that women face in accepting high-profile coaching assignments—the realization that "it's lonely at the top."

That was the reality when she became the first female coach of the USWNT in 2000. Over her five-year reign, the U.S. women finished third at the 2003 FIFA Women's World Cup and won the gold at the following year's Olympics in Greece.

As national team coach, having an eye for sometimes latent talent that can survive at the highest level of play can be a real asset. Heinrichs mentioned two cases in point.

An unfancied Shannon Boxx was 25 years old and had never been capped when April, having followed her tenacious midfield play in the Women's United Soccer League, called her up for the U.S. team in 2003. By the 2004 Olympics, she made six starts for the gold medal-winning team and the following year, 2005, finished third in the balloting for FIFA Player of the Year. By the time she retired in 2015, Boxx had been capped 195 times!

It was in observing ODP play one year that April was impressed by a youngster who "weighed all of 100 pounds." In Heather O'Reilly's case, the athleticism and determination were evident. The question was, as she aged, could her skill be still existent against more formidable opponents? The 16 year old answered that question as she scored four goals and assisted on seven others as the U.S. team won the 2002 FIFA U-19 Women's World Cup gold medal. Three years later, at age 19, O'Reilly was named the youngest player ever to play for the USWNT and scored the decisive goal in the Olympic semi-final match. Upon her retirement, O'Reilly had earned 231 caps.

The coaching lessons? Persistence is a valued commodity in players as exemplified in the case of Boxx. Meanwhile, in terms of player development, coaches need to reward and acknowledge talent in players such as O'Reilly. Such individuals, no matter where they are physically, can carry on and "play up" in age group competitions.

USWNT Technical Director

In large part, the legacy of Heinrichs's work is focused on keeping U.S. women's soccer on top internationally.

In 2007, April switched to a third role in her career. That year she joined the U.S. Olympic Committee, where she served as a Sportfolio Leader. There, she oversaw all team and technical sports. In 2011, she returned to U.S. Soccer for her second stint as the USWNT Technical Director.

Eight years later, she shared an overview of the progress women's national teams had made during her tenure: "I'm so proud of the growth of our Women's Youth and Senior National Teams program. We have grown from a few full-time staff in 2011 to full-time coaches at every age group from our WNT, to U-23s and every birth year from our U-20s down to U-14s. What I'm most excited about and proud of is that we finally articulated and implemented our USA style of play in attacking and defending. You can now look at every team in our system and see the USA way of playing. You can see we had a philosophy, our coaches are on the same page and our players move seamlessly from team to team. The full-time staffing began with the U-17 and U-20 teams in 2013. In 2015, we progressed to hiring coaches responsible for identifying and developing talent at every birth year. That year also coincided with the appointment of Jill Ellis as the USWNT coach."

"In addition to adopting a common system of play for all age groups (U-14s to U-20s to our WNT), we increased the number of international games played by each youth team commensurate with those played by their age groups in Europe and Asia. This allowed us to keep pace with the rest of the world's ability to develop players every birth year."

In large part, the legacy of Heinrichs's work is focused on keeping U.S. women's competitive internationally. She counsels: "While we won the 2019 FIFA Women's World Cup, Europe and Asia, in particular, have quickly developed competitive women's teams that operate in soccer-friendly cultures. This development has included the fact that in several age groups, their teams have been exposed to more competitive games than ours."

A Lingering Issue

One major issue facing our men's and women's national teams is player identification. Under April's scheme, identifying talent should be birth year-specific, led by our full-time youth national team coaches and then supported by the talent identification department. In short, it is hoped that our country can pinpoint players like Shannon Boxx, Heather O'Reilly, and Rose LaVelle earlier, ask them to "play up" as youth players, give them more international games at a younger age, and accelerate their development through our vertically integrated youth national team program.

Since 2019, April has become a FIFA High Performance Expert/Consultant and has been involved in a FIFA Global Ecosystem Analysis project focused on player development programs with its member nations. Each high performance expert is assigned to work with the technical leadership of several countries to map all facets of their player development programs over the previous five years in an effort to write a global report on player development critical success factors. Stymied by the pandemic, at the time of her interview, April was working "virtually like the rest of the world" to connect with 13 countries around the world.

Recognition

In 2019, April Heinrichs was presented the Werner Fricker Builder Award by U.S. Soccer in recognition of her important contributions to the game as a player, coach, and administrator.

In 1998, April was the first woman player inducted into the U.S. Soccer Hall of Fame. Prior to that, in 1986 and 1989, she was named U.S. Soccer's Female Athlete of the Year.

Harking back to her Colorado junior college coach's comment that she'd never make it in basketball—he was correct. But boy, has she made it in spades in soccer!

Building the Game in the Southwest

Few would have predicated that soccer would gain a foothold in the football-mad southwestern part of the United States. But, beginning in the late 1960s and continuing to the present, that area has produced competitive teams and players at every level.

The sport, especially in Texas, saw accelerated growth take place at the professional and secondary school levels of play.

Lamar Hunt's Influential Impact

Many credit an NFL owner, Lamar Hunt, with his funding of the 1968 NASL Dallas Tornado team, as spearheading the growth of soccer in the region. During its rein, the team brought successful coaches Ron Newman (1969-75) and Al Miller (1976-80) to the area. Former players Jim Benedek, Kyle Rote, Jr., and Mike Renshaw not only performed but also remained in the area to play roles in soccer's development. Benedek, in particular, initiated the men's soccer program at SMU and remained Mustangs coach until 1984.

Lamar Hunt is credited by many for elevating the sport of soccer in the Southeastern part of the U.S.

In 1980, one of the most competitive international youth tournaments, the Dallas Cup, debuted. Since then, highly talented teams continue to travel to Dallas each spring to compete for the title. Teams from Brazil have been dominant, winning 12 titles lead by later stars Edmilso, Edu, and Gil. Among other later stars who appeared in the Cup competitions were David Owen, Wayne Rooney, David Beckham, and Hakeem Olajuwon, the latter with a Nigerian youth team.

Gordon Jago, who relocated to Dallas to coach the MISL Dallas Sidekicks for over a decade, oversaw the staging of the Dallas Cup competitions beginning in 1983 and extending to 2013.

The careers of two Dallas area coaches, Guy Greening and Schellas Hyndman, are reflective of the area's role in the growth in the U.S. game.

Guy Greening – From Beginning to Winning[129]

Guy Greening was born, raised, and fell in love with soccer in the midst of the football-crazed state of Texas.

And he is not ashamed to admit that part of his coaching style was formed by his exposure to a legendary football coach at Garland High School. It was also at Garland that Greening was first exposed to soccer and influenced by a Hungarian expatriate, Steve Johannes. Nearby Richardson High School was coached by Jim Benedek, another Hungarian.

Taking the Duncanville Reins

Following graduation from North Texas State University, where soccer was played at the club level, Greening was hired in May of 1978 to be the first head coach of the boys varsity and junior varsity soccer teams at Duncanville High School (DHS), a Dallas suburb.

Prior to his hire as a health teacher, a club soccer program had existed for three years. At the time of Greening's appointment, soccer had not been adopted as a sanctioned sport governed by the Texas University Interscholastic League (TUIL).

The club team had trained at a local park and was organized and coached by parents. It was those parents who, in January 1978, formed an advocacy committee

Guy Greening, coach at Duncanville HS, has also aided in developing other facets of secondary school soccer in Texas.

(Duncanville Citizens for Soccer) with the goal of adding soccer as a school-sanctioned sport. When one of the parents was elected to the school board, the die was cast. Much to the dismay of the DHS athletic director (a former football coach, as are most of the ADs statewide), soccer was to begin in fall of 1978 as a school-sanctioned sport.

No Startup Roadmap

There were no guidelines or roadmap for Greening when he took on the DHS challenge. In the first few years, he singly served as coach for both the boys varsity and junior varsity teams.

On the positive side, he was given an adequate budget to start the program. He had to learn budgeting as he equipped the team with new equipment and uniforms.

He also had to learn the art of organization. It was here that he recalled observing Garland football coach Chuck Curtis and how he structured things. "I liked the way he organized the team, how he treated the players. I have to say that I initially modeled my approach to coaching on his example."

Administratively, that even included obtaining a bus driver's license, as he was in charge of transporting the team to its away matches!

Team Building Around Football

...it commenced after Thanksgiving and continued through the end of the following January. It was the only way to share fields and not interfere with football in the fall and spring.

Once he had a handle on the administrative side of things, Greening focused on building the DHS team structure.

Fortunately, he inherited a very well organized and competitive club program that included a varsity level team and two junior varsity teams. After conducting tryouts, the new coach settled on two teams of 18 players each—one varsity and one junior varsity.

In order to spread his coaching between the two teams, the group was combined for technical and fitness training but divided for tactical training. Here the coach had to count on team leadership from within the varsity team when he shared his coaching with the JV team. He also implemented a grade monitoring system as part of the team's off-field culture.

The Texas soccer season was arranged around football. In 1978, it commenced after Thanksgiving and continued through the end of the following January. It was the only way to share fields and not interfere with football in the fall and spring.

The Duncanville field was known as the "Toilet Bowl" because it didn't drain very well. And, it was football-sized. Greening eventually prevailed on the AD to expand its width from 53 to 60 yards!

Marketing Duncanville Soccer

... Greening's first DHS team recorded a 12-game undefeated district season and established a championship tone for the program.

The first home game was marked with pomp and circumstance as the new coach sought to make an impression that soccer was going to become an important sport in Duncanville. Invited to the game were the school's administrators, people from the local soccer community, and even North Texas State professors who had encouraged his soccer career.

In addition, youth players served as ball boys at every home match, and the team was well supported by the local soccer association. On his own, Greening published a game program.

Going into the 1979 season, DHS soccer was a decided underdog relative to established programs in north Dallas. Along with skill development, there was a strong emphasis on fitness by the new coach. The physical training paid off, as the newcomers won several games with strong second-half performances. The end result was that Greening's first DHS team recorded a 12-game undefeated district season and established a championship tone for the program.

The next four seasons (1980-83) were similar in that they were all designed to prepare for ultimately competing in state-wide tournament competitions.

TUIL Sanction and Formation of the TSCA

Over time, and with the advent of girls soccer, the clinics annually attract upwards of 5,000 coaches ...

While Guy Greening was successfully initiating Duncanville soccer, he was also intent on statewide development for the sport.

The Texas Soccer Coaches Association stages clinics every fall. Shown here is a group photo of those attending its 1996 fall clinic.

In 1981, and without permission from the DHS administration ("I thought I might lose my job!"), he authored a letter to the TUIL requesting that it consider sanctioning soccer. This prompted a TUIL study that led to the adoption of soccer during the 1982-83 school year. The first state championship was held in Austin, Texas, in the spring of 1983. With the official season situated in the winter months, there have been many frigid soccer games in Texas, but not usually cold enough to cancel play.

In 1982-83, Greening was one of 20 coaches who met in Austin and formed the Texas Soccer Coaches Association, and he twice served as TSCA president. The TSCA initially staged coaching clinics at the annual TUIL championships. The sessions featured such coaches as Schellas Hyndman, April Heinrichs, Colleen Hacker, and Gary Avedikian and generated revenue for the new association.

Eventually, the TSCA clinics were moved to fall, where they preceded the start of the school season. Over time, and with the advent of girls soccer, the clinics annually attract upwards of 5,000 coaches and are held in Georgetown, Texas. That community also annually hosts the UIL boys and girls championships.

Professional Advancement

"I was with the Tornado the week they played the great New York Cosmos," Greening recalled.

Coach Greening has been privileged to expand his soccer knowledge through a series of fortuitous life experiences.

He recalls that when the NASL was alive and well, the Dallas Tornado franchise, as a marketing ploy and led by coach Ron Newman and later by Al Miller, sent players like Mike Renshaw to Duncanville to share soccer insight with players and coaches. At one point, the Tornado also sponsored an area coach to spend a week with the team as it prepared for an opponent. "I was with the Tornado the week they played the great New York Cosmos," Greening recalled. "Can you imagine watching all the training sessions, sitting in on team strategy meetings. What an experience!"

Beginning in 1980, Guy enrolled in the USSF coaching schools; he eventually became the first Texas-born coach to earn the A license. As part of the USSF experience, he met Tom Fleck and later helped staff his soccer camps. He also earned his NSCAA National Diploma as he advanced his coaching know-how.

He also recalls serving as a liaison for U.S. Soccer and meeting Pele when the Brazilian team was based in Dallas during the 1993 Gold Cup Tournament. A year later, as part of World Cup 1994, he helped administratively when the city hosted the South Korean team.

Establishing the DHS Soccer Tradition

As a result of DHS successes, teams began to recognize that if Duncanville was in a tournament, then getting to the championship would likely go through them.

Over time, coach Greening developed a year-round program at DHS.

He created a successful template for preseason and the format for tryouts and added in other in-season and off-season activities. Coupled with its on-field successes, the program was run with integrity and brought tremendous attention to the school and the community.

After a few seasons, in addition to league play, DHS began to stage or participate in competitive regular-season tournaments as a means to challenge his teams. As a result of DHS successes, teams began to recognize that if Duncanville was in a tournament, then getting to the championship would likely go through them. The coach recalled, "We established the moniker, Duncanville - The Winning Tradition."

That formula was founded on an attacking mindset that evolved in terms of its tactical approach based on the collective skill of the team. "We played a variety of formations, eventually focused on a 3-4-3 which squeezed play by using the offside trap," Greening explained.

1986 was a milestone year for DHS soccer when the team won the TUIL State Championship and, as a reward, Greening was allowed to hire his first assistant coach! In addition, that year he coordinated with some of his former players to launch the Arsenal Soccer Club, where he served as the club's first director of coaching. Arsenal was the very first soccer club in southwest Dallas County and eventually grew to become the largest club in the North Texas area.

The Duncanville Legacy

In 21 years of DHS coaching, Guy Greening never had a losing season, amassing a 371-72-28 record. DHS soccer was in the *Dallas Morning News'* top 10 rankings every year and made the NSCAA top 20 several times. He was named NSCAA National Coach of the Year in 1992.

Included among 60 players who moved on to play at collegiate and other levels were such former DHS standouts as Parker Cowand, Tony Soto, and Chris Hayden. Parker was in the U.S. National Team pool at one time and later become an NSCAA All-America selection at Midwestern State. Soto, at age 17, was the youngest player selection to the U.S. Olympic team in 1995 and earned All-America honors for coach Schellas Hyndman at SMU. Hayden starred at North Texas State, played for the indoor Dallas Sidekicks, and served as the director of player development for the MLS FC Dallas franchise.

In the summer of 1999, Greening left Duncanville and become the head coach at the new Flower Mound (TX) High School. When he retired from Flower Mound in 2009, he could take some credit for the fact that both the boys and girls teams won UIL titles in 2018 and 2019.

Greening finished his 30-year coaching career with an overall 485-138-48 record. He was named to the inaugural Texas High School Soccer Hall of Honors in 2010 and the Duncanville High School Hall of Honor in 2011.

Schellas Hyndman – A Success at Every Level

Upon his resignation from Grand Canyon in the spring of 2021, the fact that in a day's time he received over 200 messages from soccer friends is indicative of the high regard that he is held within the U.S. soccer community.

While Schellas Hyndman's coaching accomplishments place him in an elite position in the U.S. coaching fraternity, he also holds the distinction of being the only Chinese-born coach to have achieved coaching notoriety in this country.

A Transitory Early Life

Born in 1949 in post-war Shanghai, China, to a Russian-French mother and a Portuguese father, the family first relocated to the island of Macau before a Mao edict banning all non-Chinese from citizenship forced them in 1957 to board a ship headed to the United States.

Settling in Springfield, Ohio, Schellas did develop confidence and acceptance when as a teenager he joined the Dayton Edelweiss, a German senior soccer club. The team's coach, Jon Wagenbach, also officiated college soccer, and on one occasion, the young midfielder fortuitously tagged along to view a Ball State-Eastern Illinois match. A post-game meeting with Eastern Illinois coach Fritz Teller eventually led to the Panther coach offering Hyndman a scholarship.

Eastern Illinois, Then Brazil

"He guided me, held me accountable. We had some uncomfortable conversations as part of his concern for me." –Schellas Hyndman

First was the matter of Schellas qualifying academically. "I know I had to a least get the minimum ACT score and boy, was that exam hard. When Coach Teller called me with the results, I asked him my score. 'You squeaked through,' was his reply."

Hyndman joined a talented freshman class, and the group experienced immediate success, beating Davis & Elkins (D & E) College in the final to capture the 1969 NAIA title. Turned out that the player giving him a close marking in the title match was D & E's Hank Steinbrecher, later the U.S. Soccer Secretary General!

Schellas Hyndman coaching at SMU and with the MLS FC Dallas team helped elevate play in one of the nation's largest cities.

Schellas credits Teller with increasing his knowledge of the game. That included an awareness of team tactics and also how to maximize the individual talent within a team through players' alignment on the field. More importantly, the coach became a father figure for Hyndman, as his own father had passed away. "He guided me, held me accountable. We had some uncomfortable conversations as part of his concern for me."

Graduating with a degree in physical education in 1974, Hyndman earned a master's degree from Murray State (KY). He was also playing professionally with the ASL Cincinnati Comet team when the owner asked him if be had interest in a teaching opportunity at the American School in Sao Paulo, Brazil.

By 1975, he was utilizing his Portuguese language and soccer skills to teach for the next two years at the Escola Graduada School. He also served as an *estagio* with the Sao Paulo Futebol Clube. He basically was serving as an apprentice coach with the club's first team. "At times the coach would have me scout opposing teams and he would then use my findings to address that individual's play at halftime and following the match."

Elevating Eastern Illinois Play

Upon returning to the United States in 1976, he landed a graduate assistantship at Eastern, where he assisted the soon-to-be retired Teller with the team.

Named coach in 1978 at age 28, Hyndman led the Panthers to a third-place finish in the NCAA Division II Tournament. A year later, the team finished second to Alabama A & M. 1981 was an important year for Hyndman. Eastern was now a NCAA Division I team and, led by three-time All-America player Damien Kelly, it reached the Division I College Cup, where the team finished third. The young coach was named NSCAA COY and was pursued by several prominent schools.

"I was really happy at Eastern. After all, they had been so supportive of my career," he recounted. But in 1984, he moved to Southern Methodist as coach. "I really enjoyed Eastern and was nervous about what lay ahead at SMU, especially if things went wrong."

Establishing Southern Methodist Soccer

In 1987, SMU football received the so-called "Death Penalty." It turned out that it was a blessing for the soccer program.

In moving to SMU, Hyndman landed in Dallas, an area rich in soccer talent. But with just three full scholarships, the new coach found that sometimes that aid didn't allow him to compete for its very best players. In particular, the ACC teams saw Dallas as a happy hunting ground—and were fully funded. "I remember recruiting Jeff Agoos. I asked him why he chose to go to Virginia. 'I want to change my area code was his reply.'"

In 1987, SMU football received the so-called "Death Penalty." It turned out that it was a blessing for the soccer program. AD Bob Hitch made the Mustangs a fully-scholarshipped program, and all-university fall events were now centered on soccer matches.

Beginning in 1984, and for the next 24 seasons, SMU was an annual contender for the national Division I championship. Special players like Daniel Hernandez (NSCAA POY in 1997), 2001 Hermann Trophy recipient Luchi Gonzalez, and All-American Kevin Grimes were abetted by a host of other talented players. Under Hyndman, 20 SMU players were accorded All-America honors.

In 2000, SMU reached the College Cup and finished third. The following year was Hyndman's best chance to capture the title. The Mustangs were unbeaten going into the NCAA tournament and had been ranked first throughout the season. With a roster that featured five players who were drafted by the MLS, SMU hosted St. John's and suffered a 2-0 loss. "They say that all losses are the same, but this one hurts to this day. We had our home all set for a victory party and I can remember coming home to see my five-year-old daughter all in tears."

In 2005, in Schellas's next-to-last season, SMU lost to eventual champion Maryland in the semifinal round. 2006 concluded with SMU having produced a combined 368-96-38 record during the Hyndman reign, including an 80-11-7 record in post-season play. Individually, he received NSCAA regional COY honors on five occasions and was Western Athletic Conference COY eight times.

On to MLS and Its Demands

"One year I kept track and due to one soccer event or another, I stayed 132 nights in hotel rooms. The job was full of stress and, as we know, stress is a killer." –Schellas Hyndman

In 2008, Schellas, having previously turned down the job, was named FC Dallas coach. His much earlier premonition that "things could go wrong" materialized with the professional appointment. But it took five years for things to unravel.

In that role, there were some on-field successes, particularly in 2010 when he coached the team to the MLS Cup final and was league COY. In 2011, FC Dallas became the first MLS team to win an away match in Mexico when it defeated UNAM, 1-0, in CONCACAF Champions League play.

Schellas admits that he wasn't prepared for the demands of the job, particularly from its emotional stresses. In his words, he went from SMU, where many viewed him "The Godfather of Dallas Soccer," to a position where he was constantly in the public eye and perceived as "fair game" when criticism of his coaching was the issue.

On one occasion, while dining in Seattle, a Dallas fan stopped by his table and apologized for having been a 'Schellas hater.' Turns out he was a vice-president of a Dallas bank. The coach thought to himself: "I wonder what he would say if I went to his bank and publicly berated him for his job performance?"

In retrospect, the competitive/perfectionist coach found the Dallas position more than he had bargained for. "The tension affected our family life. I remember by daughter asking me if I'd promise her one thing; that I would make her high school graduation. It was to take place on a Saturday night. In promising her that, in the back of my head I knew that with the MLS playing schedule not yet released, there might be a problem with my promise. As it worked out we had to play on Friday night in Denver and Sunday in Los Angeles. By arranging flights, I was able to honor all commitments!"

"One year I kept track and due to one soccer event or another, I stayed 132 nights in hotel rooms. The job was full of stress and, as we know, stress is a killer."

He resigned his Dallas position in 2013, having coached FC Dallas to a five-season 63-58-14 record. He felt he was in the worst physical condition of his life, and he and his family agreed that he would take a year off from any coaching to recover his health and their well-being.

In 2015, at the behest of Grand Canyon University AD Mike Vaught, he rejoined the collegiate soccer coaching community and by the 2018 season had the Lopes in the Division I soccer playoffs.

Presiding Over NSCAA

It was while coaching SMU in 2000 that Schellas began a six-year commitment as an NSCAA officer. "You ask me to do a coaching session, no problem. But I had no experience in terms of running meetings and all the many things involved in running a volunteer organization," he said in reviewing matters. NSCAA president in 2005, he heaps credit on the late Jim Sheldon for mentoring him when he moved through the officer chairs.

He also was appointed to serve on the NSCAA Academy staff by the late Mike Berticelli in 1999. He is presently an active NSCAA Director of Coaching Emeritus. He was effusive in his praise for the Academy's foresight in adding talented female staff members April Heinrichs, Janet Rayfield, Laura Kerrigan, Felicity Day, and Nancy Feldman to the staff. "What great teachers and role models these women have been!"

Looking back on his career, Hyndman is thankful for the many coaches who have supported him as well as proud of the number of his former players who have continued to contribute to the game.

Career Acknowledgements

In 2001, Eastern Illinois honored Schellas Hyndman with induction into its Hall of Fame. He was also enshrined into the Walk of Fame in 2007 at Pizza Hut Park in Frisco, Texas. In 2015, Hyndman was inducted into the Southern Methodist University Hall of Fame, and in 2020, the United Soccer Coaches (formerly NSCAA) inducted him into its Hall of Fame.

Three Women Soccer Pioneers

Three women soccer coaches deserve accommodation as they have made significant impacts during their lengthy careers in the game.

Two, Becky Burleigh and Kim Wyant, are Floridians. Becky lived on the West Coast of Florida while Kim was raised in the Miami region of the state. The third member of the group, Nancy Feldman, was raised in New England. Burleigh retired in 2021 following a lengthy coaching career that was marked by becoming the first woman coach to win the NCAA Division I championship. Wyant, following time as a USWNT player, is today the only woman known to be serving as coach of a men's intercollegiate team. Trouper Feldman has made significant contributions to the game both on and off the field in over her quarter century of coaching.

Becky Burleigh – Soccer Early and Often[131]

Blessed with an inquiring mind and with a series of valuable soccer-related experiences, Becky Burleigh, the recently resigned University of Florida women's coach, was propelled into the upper echelon of Division I soccer coaches.

Entering the 2020 season, the ever-smiling and upbeat Gator coach had accumulated over 500 victories that ranked second among coaches of Division I women's teams. Among the wins is the 1998 NCAA title.

But, in many ways, her professional success is no surprise. It is the result of a series of soccer networking experiences that, when coupled with a progressive attitude, has fueled her rise to soccer prominence.

Pereira Expands Her Network

Burleigh began playing soccer when her family located to Tarpon Springs, Florida. Across the street from their home was the community soccer field.

From age 10 through high school, the talented midfielder played on a Florida championship USYSA club team, Palmer's Marina Barracudas, which included goalkeeper Katie Braman. An NSCAA All-America selection, Braman was recruited

In 1998, Becky Burleigh was the first woman to lead a team to the NCAA Division I title.

by Methodist (NC) College coach, Joe Pereira, who also expanded his interest to Becky Burleigh. (Incidentally, Pereira had played for coach Hank Steinbrecher at Warren Wilson College.)

A three-time All-Dixie Intercollegiate Athletic Conference choice as well as an All-South selection (and a Phi Beta Kappa graduate to boot!), Burleigh helped lead the Lady Monarchs to four conference titles and advancement to the NCAA Division III semifinals her senior year. It is of note that, as a senior, she played not in her customary midfield spot but, at six feet tall, became the team's goalkeeper and earned 12 shutouts.

More importantly, Pereira, as head of the North Carolina women's Olympic Development Program, assigned the eager freshman Olympic Development Program coaching responsibilities. He also lined her up for what annually became 10 weeks of work at various summer soccer camps, where she continued to hone her coaching skills. One such camp was at the University of North Carolina, where she played in the off-hours with USWNT stalwarts as Carla Overbeck, Linda Hamilton, and Carin Gabarra. She does not discount the importance that introduction had on her ability to better access talent when coaching at Berry College and at Florida.

Continuing Berry's Successes

"He [Charles] had observed my session and at dinner that evening complimented me for including throw-ins as part of my presentation. I was 'riding high' the rest of the week!" –Becky Burleigh

While working the Duke University soccer camp, Becky had met Berry College coach Ray Leone. In 1989 and set to depart Berry, Ray recommended the 21-year-old Burleigh as his replacement.

Berry had established a strong soccer program led by such men's coaches as Brett Simon, Mike Parsons, and Bob Warming, and in her five years at Berry, the young coach added to that tradition, leading the women's team to NAIA titles in 1990 and 1993. The final season included a 3-1 win over ACC power Virginia.

It was also during this period that Burleigh added to her soccer resume through attendance at both USSF and NSCAA coaching schools. Specifically, she recalls that exposure to such teachers as Jeff Tipping, Barry Gorman, Anson Dorrance, Jerry Smith, and Clive Charles proved invaluable.

In particular, she recalled receiving early affirmation of her coaching ability from Charles. "I considered him a real idol. One day I was assigned the topic, coaching set pieces. He had observed my session and at dinner that evening complimented me for including throw-ins as part of my presentation. I was 'riding high' the rest of the week!"

Starting Florida's Program

So it was not the average 26-year-old's resume that University of Florida AD Jeremy Foley examined as he sought to hire a coach to initiate the Gator women's soccer program in 1994.

Rather, Burleigh's nine years of informal and formal coaching experience and Foley's willingness to invest in promising young coaches (he'd hired basketball coach Billy Donovan at 31 years of age) led to her 1994 hire.

Her ODP exposure, coupled with Florida's full allotment of scholarships, enabled the Gators to assemble a stable of talented players ("we had more better players" was how she framed the move from Berry) that by 1998 included all-time NCAA leading scorer Danielle Fotopoulos as well as later USWNT hero Abby Wambach.

It was Fotopoulos's goal that led to the 1-0 win over North Carolina in the 1998 NCAA title match. In only her fourth season, Burleigh became the first woman soccer coach ever to lead a team to the national title.

During her tenure, Florida has won 14 Southeastern Conference titles and 12 SEC tournaments on its way to play in 22 NCAA Division I tournaments.

The Burleigh Approach

"I am not afraid to search out others for help and take their advice and also call on outside experts and find out their approaches to their professions." –Becky Burleigh

Her "glass is half-full" positive approach to life allows her to evaluate her first losing, injury-riddled season (2018, 7-10-4) with a forward-looking mindset. "I think everybody should go through such a season as you learn you have to stick to your principles whether you are winning or losing. ... I look at it [the season] as one where everybody found out a lot about themselves."

Key to her past successes, she believes, has been an ability to benefit from making inquiries of a wide variety of professionals both inside and outside the realm of athletics. "Right down our hallway at Florida I can call on such great coaches as Mike Holloway [track] and Mary Wise [volleyball] as questions arise."

"I am not afraid to search out others for help and take their advice and also call on outside experts and find out their approaches to their professions. I think that not everyone is comfortable in asking people, but if you identify people you respect, you can learn from them as well and continue to evolve as a coach."

In large part, her success story has been constructed based on the fact that coaching skill is founded on mastery of human relationship issues, and answers to that topic are continually emerging.

Meanwhile, when asked to identify her most positive coaching moment, she declines to choose just one. "My best coaching moments arrive each year when we host our alumni weekends. There I can marvel at the evolution of our former players and the people they have become."

That, in the end, over and above wins and losses, says it all.

Update: In the 2022 spring season, Becky Burleigh resigned as women's coach at the University of Florida. She last served as interim coach for the NWSL's Orlando Pride.

Nancy Feldman – A Long, Successful Coaching Career[132]

When asked what had been the key to her relatively lengthy soccer coaching career, Boston University (BU) women's coach Nancy Feldman paused for a bit before noting that at every stop on her journey she had the good fortune to have mentors who offered ongoing encouragement.

About to enter her 26th year at BU in 2020, she noted that unlike some women coaches who drop out of coaching, in part because they have not had a support structure in place, she can trace her successes in coaching back to those who have "had her back" at each of the stops in her career.

Soccer in Needham (MA)

"She was terrific with young athletes for someone just starting her career." –Bonnie May

Adam Caputo, Joe McDermott, and Vernon White are not household names in U.S. soccer, but collectively, the triad organized youth soccer for young girls in Needham (MA) in the early 1970s. Nancy was one of those youngsters who they recruited off a town tennis court. In short order, in 1976, Needham HS physical education teacher Carol Bamberry, buoyed by Title IX legislation, organized the emerging talent and started the girls high school soccer program. The young women sought to achieve the same success enjoyed by the Needham boys under coach Don Brock.

After graduating in 1979, Feldman's subsequent soccer playing career at University of Massachusetts-Amherst under coach Kalekeni Banda was waylaid due to knee injuries. Also, her academic major in public health had not enabled her to attain her intended goal of entrance to medical school.

Marking time following her graduation from UMass in 1983 and seeking to find a new career direction, Feldman found that coaching a girls varsity team at Danvers (MA) High School and a boys JV team at Kennett (NH) High School resonated with her. And so it was off to Smith College in 1986, where study in its Exercise and Sport Studies Program was coupled with coaching/mentoring experiences with soccer coach Jim Babyak and basketball coach Bonnie May. The latter was impressed with the young coach, noting, "She was terrific with young athletes for someone just starting her career."[133]

Nancy was also able to find time to assist Banda when he led the UMass women to the NCAA DI soccer final in the fall of 1987.

The NSCAA Academy

"I came away from the course having a solid foundation in the teaching process"
–Nancy Feldman

In January 1986, the aspiring coach described her enrollment in the NSCAA Academy Program in Cocoa Beach, Florida as an important step in the advancement of her soccer-coaching career. The only woman candidate (out of an estimated 70 coaches), she recalled that prior to the course that she, not having been a physical education major, had not been exposed to many of the major topics at the course, particularly those focused on coaching methodology. "I came away from the course having a solid foundation in the teaching process," she recalled. Between Tom Fleck making her feel welcome to the course and exposure to instructors like Bob Gansler, she further solidified her coaching resume.

In 1988, the embedded New Englander took on coaching soccer and softball at Lake Forest (IL) College. Her confidence was bolstered when the soccer squad reached new heights and captured the Midwest Conference title her second season. She credits AD Mike Dau with making the two-year experience most enjoyable.

Returning to New England and Plymouth State, she acknowledges the five-year tenure (1990-94) at the New Hampshire college was another career-building experience. There, veteran basketball coach Phil Rowe and other staff helped reinforce Nancy's coaching instincts. She made AD Steve Bamford look good, as his hire led Plymouth women's soccer to five straight NCAA Division III appearances. In 1994-95, Feldman-coached soccer (15-1-2) and basketball (21-7) teams earned NCAA DIII Tournament appearances. Her Plymouth coaching accomplishments were acknowledged with selection as the New England DIII COY in 1991 and 1993, and, in 1993, she also received the New England Women's Intercollegiate Soccer Association (NEWISA) Service Award.

The Boston University Challenge

In January of 1995, her father, Chet Feldman, read a *Boston Globe* story indicating that Boston University was transiting its women's club soccer team to varsity status. With her father's urging and a 75-9-7 record at Plymouth buttressing her credentials, Nancy was hired to direct the school's transition to Division I status.

In the lead-up to the team's first season, she recalls meeting with every club team member in the spring of 1995 and indicating the different expectations that would be in play in the transition to intercollegiate competition.

The Feldman approach to attaining the right team culture is based on her experiences at Camp Huckins (NH), first as an enrollee and later as a staff member. "The leaders at Huckins were able to create a value based family-type atmosphere every summer," she recalled. "We have tried to have that as our goal for women's soccer at BU."

Respected for her initial efforts, the hard-working Terrier coach was honored with the first of her subsequent 11 COY awards in 1997 when her colleagues voted her America East COY, and that same season she was named New England Women's Intercollegiate Soccer Association (EWISA) DI COY. By 2000, BU won the first of its 13 regular season and tournament titles and entered NCAA Division I play for what was the first of 14 appearances by a Feldman-coached team. Ten were earned as America East's representative and, since 2013, four have represented the Patriot League. It should be noted that, at Plymouth, Nancy served on the NCAA Division III Selection Committee from 1992-95, and at Boston she served on the NCAA Division I Soccer Committee.

Getting back to the longevity and success of her coaching career, she again attributed it to those individuals who have supported her. "Coaching is an emotional career. It has its 'ups' and 'downs.' You need to be able to rely on people who have been successful and from time to time who can offer you a perspective on things." She cited the impact of women Region I ODP leaders Sue Ryan and Charlotte Moran as two such individuals, noting that the ODP experience advanced her coaching of more talented youth players.

She feels that women soccer coaches in other less compassionate environments often don't succeed because of the lack of support mechanisms. "Unfortunately I also feel that in many cases they are not extended second chances. I think there is a bias that hampers women coaches and we need to overcome that attitude if more women are to have longer coaching careers."

Accolades/Honors/Service

"Nancy Feldman is a world-class coach, educator, and role model. ..." –Lesle Gallimore

For many U.S. coaches, their off-field contributions have been as impactful as their coaching accomplishments. And that is the case for Nancy Feldman.

Holder of the NSCAA Advanced National Diploma and a USSF B License, the BU coach was appointed as a United Soccer Coaches Academy staff member by

DOC Jeff Tipping in 1998. There, she has been able to share her coaching expertise with many aspiring candidates much like herself back at Cocoa Beach in 1986. She credits fellow Academy staff members Peter Gooding, Jeff Vennell, and Doug Williamson with encouraging her Academy work. In 2011, she received the Mike Berticelli Award for her outstanding contributions to the United Soccer Coaches' educational component.

Along with her work with the Academy program, the "Feldman Touch" has also applied when she served the NSCAA (now United Soccer Coaches) as national chair of its Women's All-America Committee from 1989-95. She also has chaired its Convention Education Committee. The later group seeks to align the educational component (speakers, etc.) of the annual convention. In 2018, the BU coach was acknowledged with presentation of the United Soccer Coaches Long-Term Service Award.

In 2018, she was also honored by WAGS (Women and Girls in Soccer) with the presentation of its Women's Soccer Award of Excellence Award. This acknowledged the BU coach's work as chairperson for the City Kicks, a non-profit organization for urban and underserved middle school girls in the Boston area. In presenting the award, then-United Soccer Coaches President Lesle Gallimore noted, "Nancy Feldman is a world-class coach, educator, and role model. She has consistently dedicated herself to promoting and advocating for women and the women's game."

Related to her BU soccer coaching responsibilities was another accolade that was reflective of the Feldman commitment to excellence. That was the 2008 presentation to her of the Scarlet Key Award by Boston University for her significant overall contributions to university life.

Ten years later, on December 11, 2018, in honor of her 25th season as BU women's soccer coach, the city of Boston declared the day as "Nancy Feldman Day."

Upon reflection, the medical field's loss of Nancy Feldman has been U.S. soccer's gain!

Update: Nancy Feldman resigned her position as coach at Boston University in the spring of 2022. Her 33-year career as a woman coach is one of the longest in intercollegiate soccer coaching annals.

Kim Wyant – Assuming a Unique Role[134]

"In a future ready organization, 'talent' is increasingly a metaphor for capability—at the right place, at the right time and equally, at the right price." -Gyan Nagpal

Kim Wyant's soccer career reflects all phases of the quote, with the added note that, in several instances, her immersion in the game was, if not historic, significant.

Kim Wyant has taken on a unique challenge coaching the NYU men's soccer team.

The latest impact came in the fall of 2015 when she, under somewhat dire circumstances, was named coach of the New York University men's soccer team. In that role, she is the only NCAA female coach of a men's team.

A USWNT Pioneer

While she indulged in other sports, Wyant had a late start on the soccer field. It wasn't until her junior year at Hialeah High School (FL) that the school initiated girls soccer. Her ball-catching ability prompted her to become the team's goalkeeper.

By her own admission, Kim was a bit of a "lost kid in Miami" by the time of her high school graduation, only to be rescued by a scholarship offer from University of Central Florida coach Jim Rudy. Women's collegiate soccer was making a transition from Association for Intercollegiate Athletics for Women (AIAW) to NCAA-sponsored play at the time. In 1982, as a freshman, Wyant started in the nets in the first NCAA Women's Soccer Tournament championship final. Despite being on the losing end of a 2-0 defeat to North Carolina (the first of Anson Dorrance's 21 titles), Wyant was named Tournament MVP. In her senior year, she was named an NSCAA first team All-American.

While it may seem a bit informal in its execution, by 1985, Wyant achieved another milestone when at that year's Sports Festival in Louisiana she was chosen to become a member of the first USSF women's national soccer team. "I think it was Mike Ryan [the first USWNT coach] who stood in front of all the players, and read the 16 names that had been chosen for the first Women's National Team," Wyant said. "I don't know if I was nervous ... just emotional. Things are done differently nowadays. Back then, they just read the names in front of everybody. Here's the team."

In 1985, in Jesolo, Italy, Wyant was the team's starting goalkeeper as the team went 0-2-1. In 1986, she recorded the team's first win, a 2-0 shutout against Canada, in Blaine (MN). Two days later, she suffered an ACL injury that eventually limited her USWNT appearances to 16 matches. Her greatest playing success, however, arguably would come later with the Long Island Lady Riders.

Making Soccer "Work"

"It was the best decision I made in terms of my soccer career," she said of the move from her native South Florida to the metropolitan New York area.

Upon graduation from UCF with a Bachelor of Arts degree in psychology, Kim made a commitment to soccer as a livelihood and was seeking in various ways to earn a living in her chosen field.

Whether playing for the next eight seasons with the USWNT or working with youth teams or coaching at camps (including at the late Tony DiCicco's), she made it happen.

It was in 1998, while in her first coaching position at Florida Atlantic University, that the conduit she was seeking opened in the form of a generous joint venture contract offered by the Jacob family to play for and work in the front office of the W-League Long Island Rough Riders. "It was the best decision I made in terms of my soccer career," she said of the move from her native South Florida to the metropolitan New York area. It offered her the soccer stability she was seeking. In addition to playing, she had the opportunity to help the team make budget in a very tight soccer marketplace.

Wyant would play for the Lady Riders for nine years, helping lead the squads to W-League Championships in 1995 and 1997. Beginning in 1995, she was acknowledged as W-League Goalkeeper of the Year for four consecutive seasons and was honored as the MVP in the 1997 Championship Series and was a two-time All-Star.

Following retirement in 2003, Wyant was named general manager of the Lady Riders, and her teams twice received W-League Organization of the Year honors. By 2006, while having survived competition from the New York Power franchise of the short-lived Women's Soccer Association (WSA), Kim's lifestyle was refocused.

Meanwhile, the Wyant coaching resume was building. In addition to her head coaching stint at FAU (1995-98), she assisted Sue Ryan at Stony Brook University in 2000 and coached and assisted at Dowling College (2003-05).

In 2008, Wyant received the Special Recognition Award from the National Soccer Hall of Fame for her contributions to the USWNT, and her stellar playing career has culminated in inductions into the United Soccer League (2004), the UCF (2010), and the inaugural Long Island Soccer Player (2013) Halls of Fame.

Family and Soccer

With the birth of her first child, Alexandra, in 2006, and her second, Danielle, in 2008, Wyant's soccer involvement was largely focused on coaching a U-12 girls team near her Garden City home.

By 2011, and for the next five seasons, she was back in action assisting NYU women's coach Michelle Canning while also serving as coach of the New York Athletic Club women's team. Thus, she had a working relationship with NYU when the challenge of assuming the coach of its men's team occurred one game into the 2015 season.

"No matter the coach, male or female, stepping into the program that has their coach leave one game into the season was going to be an enormous challenge and I think that [the challenge] is what intrigued me the most," Wyant said. "There is also the challenge of gaining respect and doing a good job."

Meeting the NYU Challenge

"The first 48 hours were crucial," Kim said in assessing the coaching transition that took place in 2015. "It was a messy situation. Joe [Behan] had recruited all the players on the team. I imagined things happening such as me being introduced to the team and them getting up and walking out! There was anxiety for sure.

"My assistant Paul LeSueur was very helpful. We agreed we'd do everything we could to keep the ship afloat. Obviously we had to act calmly. 'Fake it to make it' was one way of putting it. We needed to stabilize things while putting ourselves in the players' shoes. And while doing this we had to earn the immediate respect of the team.

"Of course, while we were getting things settled, there was the 'elephant in the room,' my being a woman coaching a men's team."

As she assessed matters prior to accepting the position, Kim sought Jim Rudy's counsel. He reminded her that she had "paid her dues" and was qualified for the job.

Rudy's endorsement recognized that his former star was no stranger to the psychology of team dynamics. And she fell back on those experiences as she settled in directing NYU affairs, noting, "One of my first jobs was a simple one; I had to learn the players' names!"

In terms of helping evaluation of players, in addition to her observations, she formed a five-player council and asked each member to submit starting lineups as well as two key substitutes. This procedure allowed the staff to develop a sense of internal team dynamics, including its leadership. When coupled with their own evaluations, the process proved of great value to Wyant and her staff.

Of course, there was some player pushback as the squad adjusted to the coach, if not overtly. While she adopted a phrase, "We are all in this together," in three instances, player behavior resulted in either dismissal or 'timeouts.'

While the team won five of its remaining 16 matches, six of the losses occurred in the very competitive University Athletic Conference. UAA is an eight-team conference with teams located from Boston (Brandeis) to Atlanta (Emory) and westward to Missouri (Washington University). As a measure of NYU's improvement, the team's combined UAA record for Wyant's first three seasons was 4-16-1; the last two seasons, the Violets combined for a 6-6-2 league record, including 2018, when a 12-4-3 record earned the team its first NCAA Division

III Tournament appearance since 2010. The 2018 post-season bid was the fourth earned by NYU during the Wyant era.

Off the pitch, in 2015, the Violet team was given the Sportsmanship Award from the New York Metro Intercollegiate Soccer Officials Association (NYMISOA). "I guess that while I have been able to instill my teams with the right competitive attitude, underneath I still do not personally deal well with losses. They still eat me up."

Upbeat about her NYU experience, the enthusiastic coach has embraced the opportunity to recruit to an academic institution that is not only a widely known national university but also one whose brand is one that extends internationally. She termed NYU a "hot university," and that is reflected in the fact that the school's annual applicant pool numbered 100,000-plus in 2021, which makes NYU the number one private university in applications received.

In taking the reins one game into the 2015 season, the new job has offered a test in terms of dealing with the team's practice and game facilities. For training sessions, the team practices at the Pier 40 facility off the West Side Highway, a 30-minute drive from campus. Games generally are wedged into Manhattan College's Gaelic Field, 90 minutes away.

Perspective

"It will be exciting to talk to you 10 years from now and to see where we've come and where we're going." –Kim Wyant

In an interview with Michael Lewis, Wyant put her current situation in perspective: "I was not sure I would be making history because there are definitely other women who have coached men's sports in the NCAA. But I just knew the enormity of the moment because there's just more interest in women being in leadership roles in society. I knew this was going to be different because women were not coaching men's soccer in the NCAA. I knew it was going to be magnified because of the media environment we're in."[135]

Meanwhile, Kim Wyant's time in soccer has taught her to accept what cards are dealt her and move forward one day at a time.

"I want to continue to make a difference," she said in her Lewis interview. "I am very happy at NYU and I still have a lot of work to do. I am always thinking, what's going to be my next move and how I am going to be prepared for it? It will be exciting to talk to you 10 years from now and to see where we've come and where we're going."

Update: Kim Wyant's unique role was matched in the spring of 2022 when the University of Chicago appointed Julianne Sitch to coach its men's team. Both NYU and Chicago are members of the University Athletic Association.

CHAPTER VII

ADDING TO A MIDWESTERN SOCCER TRADITION

In examining soccer's evolution in the Midwestern region of the United States, one is obliged to first acknowledge the city of St. Louis and its long history in the game.

That tradition was invigorated in the post-World War II period by coach Bob Guelker. His oversight of the city's Catholic Youth Council CYC youth program and its successes would serve as a template for other U.S. communities as youth soccer play surged beginning in the 1960s and 1970s.

But it wasn't just for youth soccer alone that Guelker is renowned. His enormous energy and perceptive vision for the sport had national implications as well.

There were other regional cities where a soccer tradition existed, but in the states of Indiana, Illinois, and Ohio it remained for Jerry Yeagley and a host of other largely transplanted coaches to establish new centers of soccer excellence beginning in the 1950s.

These stories were not isolated instances where coaches played multi-dimensional roles as soccer became imbedded but would be replicated in other more-western regions of the country.

The St. Louis Contribution to U.S. Coaching

When U.S. soccer migrated westward, it seemed to have made its greatest impact on the city of St. Louis, Missouri.

Home to a variety of ethnic groups who settled in various enclaves within the city, soccer, as one pundit put it, seemed to naturally fit into the developing culture of the city: "It is a working man's sport in a working man's town."[136]

What stands out today is that not only did the city keep the sport alive in this part of the country, but also the 950 individuals (with nicknames ranging from "Apples" and "Ducky" to "Red" and "Toots") enshrined in the St. Louis Soccer Hall of Fame helped create a center of excellence in the game perhaps unmatched in the sport's history.

From that group, 29 have been further honored with elevation to various national soccer halls of fame. Included are 23 former players/administrators, three coaches, and three referees.

In terms of the two USSF-sponsored senior events, since 1935, St. Louis teams have captured six U.S. Open Cup and 11 U.S. Amateur Cup titles. On the intercollegiate soccer scene, St. Louis colleges have won 11 NCAA Division I men's championships and two at the Division II level. Meanwhile, beginning in 1967, in National Junior College Athletic Association (NJCAA) men's play, 12 St. Louis-area teams have recorded first-place finishes. Extending the swath of St. Louis soccer influence eastward to Quincy, Illinois, it was with a roster stocked with St. Louis players that Quincy College captured a record 11 NAIA men's soccer titles.

All this continued success was the result of certain individuals and institutions building on a solid foundation formed in the early part of the 20th Century by earlier soccer activists.

Ethnic Communities

At one time, USSF, with its finances scraping bottom, prevailed on the Kutis team, abetted by a few guest players, to form the basis of the 1958 U.S. National Team ...

It was natural that the English, German, Irish, Italian, Scot, and various ethnic groups found comfort and a means of preserving their cultural heritage by congregating in various geographic areas of St. Louis.

Perhaps the most well known was the Hill section of St. Louis, where such baseball luminaries as Yogi Berra and Joe Garagiola grew up and, incidentally, played soccer in their youth. In 1935, when they were 10 years old, the St. Louis Central Breweries team won the first of what were six U.S. Open Cup titles won by city-based teams.

By the 1950s, the Kutis Funeral Home was sponsoring a series of powerful St. Louis senior soccer teams that prevailed in one U.S. Open Cup (1950) and six U.S. Amateur Cups (1952, 1956-61). Of importance was the fact that six of the players who manned the roster of the 1950 U.S. World Cup team were seasoned by their play in local senior team competitions. Coached by Penn State legend Bill Jeffrey, the Mound City group included goalkeeper Frank Borghi, defender Harry Keough, midfielders Charlie Colombo and Bob Annis, and forwards Gino Pariani and Frankie "Pee Wee" Wallace.

At one time, USSF, with its finances scraping bottom, prevailed on the Kutis team, abetted by a few guest players, to form the basis of the 1958 U.S. National Team when it competed for a place in that year's World Cup tournament in Sweden.

Bob Guelker – Builder Extraordinary

Synonymous with the successes enjoyed by various segments of St. Louis soccer was the name of Bob Guelker.

While his playing credentials are obscure, there is little question that, beginning in 1946 as executive secretary of the Catholic Youth Council for the Archdiocese of St. Louis, he has to be credited with the growth of the game at the youth level in the city.

Coach Bob Guelker is shown with St. Louis University All-America player, Carl Gentile. Gentile starred on Guelker's 1965 national championship team.

Guelker utilized the city's churches as the building blocks for youth soccer competitions. Thus, the St. Ambrose Parish on the Hill south of the city organized soccer play for its largely Italian parishioners. St. Philip Neri did the same for its northside Irish congregation. On the southside, Immaculate Heart of Mary parish was home to a Hispanic segment of the population.

While the CYC program sponsored youth activity in a wide range of sports, it was reported that, by 1963, its soccer program alone numbered nearly 8,500 participants spread over nine age group leagues.

Retired U.S. Soccer CEO and CYC product Dan Flynn offered a perspective on Bob Guelker's role with the organization.

Mound City Senior Soccer

Flynn and other youth players were also the beneficiaries of having older Mound City senior players to model in terms of their development.

He recalls that youth players gathered Sundays at the city's Mullaly Field to watch its three-game senior schedule. He noted that when George Mihaljevic's White Star team played Kutis SC, standing-room crowds were the rule. George was also well known for his coaching school, where the emphasis was on individual technical development.

And the city's love of the game was extended to an appreciation of international play. Dan, whose professional life included working in sports promotion for Anheuser-Busch, noted that, beginning in 1955, the company and others in the St. Louis community annually raised funds to import such international teams as Borussia Dortmund, Everton, Glasgow Celtic, Liverpool, Manchester United and Manchester City, Nottingham Forest, Sheffield United, Saarbruecken, Sochaux, and Wolverhampton to the city for summer stays.

Included in their visits were youth clinics by the players and coaching sessions by the team managers. The culminating event was an exhibition between the visitors and a CYC senior all-star team coached for many years by Bob Guelker.

The End Products

The CYC program was abetted by equally-competitive school play (again sponsored by schools such as St. Louis University High School and Christian Brothers College High School) and produced an abundance of players subsequently populating the rosters of the region's colleges.

As evidence of the quality of its products, beginning in 1946, St. Louis teams have won an unprecedented 23 McGuire Cup competitions, emblematic of national under-19 youth soccer supremacy.

It was St. Louis University that first became the beneficiary of the city's thriving youth soccer programs. In 1958, the school agreed to hire SLU grad Guelker (at little or no salary or budget!) to initiate its intercollegiate men's soccer.

In 1959 and, in one of the great stories that permeated the U.S. sports scene, in its second season, the Billiken team lost but one match on its way to winning the first NCAA College Championship held at the University of Connecticut. With the best graduates of the CYC farm system manning its rosters, SLU under Guelker subsequently won NCAA titles in 1960, 1962, 1963, and 1965.

Having left SLU in 1966 to initiate the men's program at Southern Illinois University-Edwardsville (SIUE), the well-known Guelker was appointed to coach the U.S. National teams at the 1971 Pan American Games and the 1972 Summer Olympics. [Of note was that the majority of the 1972 team roster consisted of players from the two St. Philip Neri teams that captured the 1968-69 McGuire Cups.]

In 1972, his SIUE team captured the first NCAA Division II title, making him the only collegiate coach to win each inaugural NCAA men's soccer tournament. By 1979, SIUE had elevated its program to Division I, and that year, the Cougars gifted the coach with his sixth NCAA title. Upon retirement, he had achieved an overall record of 311-77-26 (.783).

Guelker and Coaching Education

As noted, Bob Guelker's coaching of the USMNT's in 1971-72 was just part of his leadership of the USSF as he served as the organization's president from 1967-69. He is also cited as chairing the Federation's Junior Cup and Olympic development committees. It was his earlier presidencies of both the Missouri Soccer Federation and its senior soccer association that led to his USSF leadership roles.

It was in 1969 that the Missouri administrative dynamo, recognizing the need for a coherent approach to coaching education, proposed that USSF, in conjunction with NSCAA and ISFAA, hire Dettmar Cramer to bring his coaching philosophy to the United States.

It is reported that the organizations ponied up $1,000 each (nearly $9,000 today) and that underwriting helped secure the hire of Cramer. Ever the politician, Guelker's "sweetener" to NSCAA and ISFAA was that the coaching schools would be held on college campuses, thus providing a new revenue stream for those institutions.[138]

As noted, coach Guelker's almost herculean efforts respected all organizations that had soccer development as a primary objective, and he envisioned enhancement of coaching education as something that should have been a cooperative venture by the organizations cited.

As will be seen, that was not to be the case and added to the distrust between elements within the greater coaching community and USSF, later U.S. Soccer.

Guelker Honored

The acknowledged master soccer builder was the recipient of numerous soccer honors, including having the Catholic Youth Council of St. Louis conducting its annual "Bob Guelker Soccer Tournament" in his honor. He was inducted into the St. Louis University Hall of Fame in 1979; in 2009, he was named to SLU's Half-Century Team. Other inductions include those into the National Soccer HOF (1980) and to the St. Louis Soccer HOF (1986). Posthumously, he was honored with induction into the National Soccer Coaches Association of America's HOF (1993) as well as the SIUE Athletics HOF (2005).

With his legacy as one of the game's national founders intact, Bob Guelker remained at SIUE until his death in 1986 at age 62.

Coach Harry Keough

Harry Keogh first attracted attention as a gifted national team and Kutis SC player, but his coaching contributions were also noteworthy.

Off the field, he worked for the U.S. Postal Service and also offered his service as a volunteer coach in the CYC program. Of interest was that his Spanish-language fluency enhanced his role within the USMNT.

In 1967, after a short stint at Florissant Valley Community College, Harry took over from Bob Guekler

Harry Keough is a St. Louis playing and coaching legend.

at St. Louis University. Under his tutelage, and abetted by assistant coach Val Pelizzaro, the SLU team shared the Division I title his first season and subsequently won the NCAA post-season competitions in 1969-70 and 1972-73.

One of the players on the last two championship teams was Joey Hamm, another St. Philip Neri product. It was while in New York City to be honored as an NSCAA All-America player that Joey, Keough, and Fred Schmalz got lost on their way to dine at the famed Mama Leone's Restaurant. Hamm found the directions by popping his head into a Chinese restaurant and inquiring its location—in Chinese! Turns out that, in addition to being a standout midfielder, Joey was an expert linguist.

Keough hired soccer players to work at the USPS during holidays. Hamm was one of such players and eventually became a full-time employee.

Flynn on Keough

"He being such an outstanding guy, you just did not want to disappoint him by your play."
–Dan Flynn

Dan Flynn proved a valued resource when asked about coach Keough's methodology.

It was reported that Keough training sessions were organized around small-side play, where the legendary mentor imparted technical or tactical lessons. There was some thought that, as other collegiate teams became better organized, SLU teams were "caught up with" as the 1970s decade unwound. This, following the fact that the Billikens' last NCAA title was won in 1973.

The start of the 1973 season marked the debut of Dan Flynn in SLU colors, but the season itself was delayed a bit as the SLU team took an extended U.S. State Department-sponsored trip to South America. Over a two-week time frame, the team met similar college-age teams in Colombia, Chile, Uruguay, and Brazil (playing in Sao Paulo and Rio) and wound up with a match in Mexico City.

Whether factual or not, Flynn (and most others) focused on the man's humanity. "He was a humble, decent human being," noted Dan, who played at SLU from 1973-77. In terms of coaching style, Flynn noted that Keough, much like his former USMNT teammate Walter Bahr, believed 'less was more.' "He did not overcoach. He very much emphasized that soccer was a 'thinking man's game.' He would make subtle adjustments for the team during the game, things that made sense. In defending, he would emphasize the position of your feet and body angle, such that you forced a player in the right direction. If an opposing player was known for his speed, he would give you ideas as to how to let him use his speed to your advantage, not his."[139]

Flynn also credited his SLU coach with taking on all comers in terms of scheduling matches. "He believed that there were a lot of good life lessons learned from taking on a good, hard schedule." Thus, the Bilikens annually played teams from UCLA on the West Coast to Connecticut on the East Coast.

"Harry still loved to play and generally we'd end practices with small-sided games that he was part of. Communication was no problem with Harry as he was easy to talk to." Flynn concluded with an ultimate compliment: "He being such an outstanding guy, you just did not want to disappoint him by your play."

Upon his retirement in 1982, the understated, easy-going soccer legend had compiled a 213-50-23 (.785) record.

Honors

Harry Keough has been honored with selection to five halls of fame, including the inaugural St. Louis Soccer HOF (1972), the National Soccer Hall of Fame (1976), the St. Louis University Athletic HOF (1995), the National Soccer Coaches Association of America HOF (1996), and the Missouri Sports Hall of Fame (2009).

Coverage of St. Louis soccer would be inexact without acknowledging to the long list of coaches who have left their mark on their region.

DAN FLYNN — FROM PLAYER TO ADMINISTRATOR[140]

"I am optimistic for the future of the game in this country." –Dan Flynn

Flynn's appreciation of soccer's international influence was first heightened when he took his first flight to Mexico to view play in the 1970 World Cup. That and the aforementioned trip with the St. Louis University team to South America in 1973 played a role in his later careers in the corporate world—and in soccer itself.

Dan Flynn.

With aspirations for a professional career derailed by a serious knee injury, Dan Flynn entered the corporate world by becoming the assistant to Anheuser-Busch President Dennis Long beginning in 1978 in its sports marketing division. At the time, the company was fighting to increase its share of the beverage market. Assigned to develop strategies in the young adult marketplace, Dan's success landed him, at age 32, the presidency of Anheuser-Busch, International in 1987.

It was while representing Anheuser-Busch's interest in sponsoring World Cup 1994 that Flynn intersected with U.S. Soccer CEO Hank Steinbrecher. At a point, he was attracted back to the game, leaving Anheuser-Busch in 1991 to become Venue Executive Director for the Chicago WC site. Following the 1994 event, he served U.S. Soccer as its Chief Administrative Officer, then, in 2000, became its CEO/General Secretary.

He had watched as U.S. Soccer, following its phenomenal success in promoting the 1994 World Cup, missed a second marketing opportunity when there had been no television coverage in this country of the 1996 Olympic soccer competition. He credits Steinbrecher with persistence in bidding for the 1999 Women's World Cup. "I knew that events like World Cups and Olympic events are global events and the marketing values in them are immense," noted Flynn. The 1999 event attracted huge crowds and increased television ratings. Best of all, before 90,000 fans at the Rose Bowl (the largest crowd ever to watch a women's sporting event!), the U.S. team won, and the U.S. Soccer budget for the event finished in the black.

As U.S. Soccer's CEO/Secretary General, Dan has seen the country host the 2003 FIFA Women's World Cup (profit of $11 million) and served as a director for the successful United States/Mexico/Canada bid to host the 2026 World Cup. He had a short stint on the disabled list for a heart transplant in 2016 before retiring in 2019.

"Brick by brick, a lot of people have contributed to build soccer in this country," was how he viewed matters in 2021. "We have solid professional leagues, our women's national team is world champions and our men and women players have options here and abroad to fine-tune their play. I am optimistic for the future of the game in this country."

Growing Midwestern Soccer in Indiana and Illinois

Dr. Joe Guennel's Contributions

While Bob Guelker was overseeing soccer matters in St. Louis, a transplanted Easterner, Dr. Joe Guennel, was spearheading soccer growth beginning in 1950 when he organized the Midwest Collegiate Conference. From 18 Midwest colleges playing soccer that year, by 1972, nearly 70 colleges were sponsoring the sport. 141

He also started soccer at the University of Indiana, coaching the club team from 1949-60. Springfield College graduate Terry Jackson briefly succeeded him as IU club coach. In turn, it was left to Jerry Yeagley to patiently elevate the IU club program to varsity status and subsequent national intercollegiate prominence.

Guennel also became involved in senior league soccer administration in Indianapolis before leaving Indiana to work his soccer magic in the Denver area.

A tireless promoter of the game, he edited the *Midwestern Soccer News*, and later, upon moving to Denver (he was a geologist by training), he edited the *Rocky Mountain Soccer News* beginning in 1961.

Charlie Matlack at Earlham

Following being named an All-America player while performing at Haverford (PA) College, in 1943, Charlie Matlack began coaching as an assistant at Ursinus (PA) College. In 1954, after completing his Ph.D. in linguistics, he joined the faculty at Earlham (IN) College to both teach and establish its soccer program.

His teams became a force in the Illinois-Indiana Soccer Conference. The National Association of Intercollegiate Athletics (NAIA) became the organization that sponsored soccer competition for Earlham and a substantial number of other small colleges. In 1963, Earlham was declared NAIA national co-champion. A leader both in his conference and in NAIA athletics, Matlack was elected president of NAIA in 1971.

Led by numerous St. Louis products, Quincy College became a national force in NAIA play, and, beginning in 1966, captured a record 11 NAIA titles.

For his efforts to promote soccer in Indiana, within NAIA as well as the NSCAA, Matlack was the recipient of the NSCAA Honor Award in 1981.[142]

Bob Baptista – Sportsman

Dr. Robert Baptista was a Chicago native who contributed to the growth of the game while coaching at Wheaton (IL) College.

After playing as a Wheaton undergrad, he and his wife spent three years developing the athletic program at Roberts Wesleyan (NY) College before returning to coach soccer at Wheaton in 1951.

Bob Baptista (left) presents former player Cliff McCrath with the NSCAA Honor Award in 1985.

Extraordinary Ethical Conduct

Perhaps one incident informed the soccer coaching community of the model behavior of coach Baptista.[143]

It occurred in 1964 in the Michigan/Illinois/Indiana Athletic Conference championship game played at Wheaton against Lake Forest College. Dick Triptow, the Lake Forest coach, thought he saw the Wheaton's winning goal score through a hole in the side netting, but went along with the ref's call. It was after the game in the locker room that coach Baptista heard one of his players say that he also thought the ball went through a hole in the net and the goal shouldn't have counted.

Bob's moral character and integrity came to the forefront. He knew a certain fan always stood behind the goal for the games and he decided to call him. Sure enough, he said the ball definitely went through a hole in the net. Upon hearing this, Bob phoned coach Triptow and told him that the goal should not be counted and that they should replay the game. Triptow told him that he had already collected the gear from the players and he didn't want to take another trip to Wheaton for a replay. Bob told him that Wheaton would travel to Lake Forest for the rerun, which they did, and this time the game was "legit" and Wheaton won.

Not only that, but Wheaton's President, Dr. V. Raymond Edman, was overseas serving in the military at the time and read about it in the *Stars and Stripes* daily newspaper. So, ironically, the whole incident was the "game heard round the world."

Soccer Service

Highly organized, Baptista served for many years as the executive secretary of the Midwest Soccer Association (MSA). The MSA was an amalgam of college teams irrespective of soccer emphasis. Thus, the Baptista coaching record of 104-52-22 included the 1959 victories over then-soccer powers St. Louis and Michigan State.

He headed the NCAA Rules Committee (1967-71) and, as a means of promoting the game regionally, assumed Joe Guennel's role as editor of the *Midwestern Soccer News*. While completing his Ph.D. at Indiana University, his doctoral dissertation ("History of Intercollegiate Soccer in the United States") was another contribution to the game.

He is believed to be the only soccer coach to have served as a college president, serving in that role at Sterling (KS) College and later at Taylor (IN) University. He was presented the NSCAA Honor Award in 1975.

Wheaton's Joe Bean[144]

"Football's loss was soccer's gain" might best describe coach Joe Bean's good fortune as he made the switch from the gridiron to the soccer pitch way back in 1959 at East Stroudsburg (PA) State University (ESU).

Upon entering ESU in 1958, he became the starting fullback for interim coach George Ockershausen. However, Jack Gregory, upon taking the head coaching reins the following year, did not invite Bean back for fall practice!

So sophomore Bean turned out for the ESU soccer squad, where he fell in love with the game. Legendary coach John Eiler and upper-class mentor Al Miller eased the transition to the new sport.

"Coach Eiler was perfect for me as he was a good teacher of soccer skills. Al, of course, was an All-American player and captain of the team," shared Bean of his first soccer experience.

Bean was effusive of his experiences with John Eiler.

"He was highly-disciplined in his approach to coaching. He worked through his practices, one drill leading to the next. He had a very mellow disposition and when he spoke, everyone listened. I guess you could say he was a 'gentleman coach.'"

Among Eiler's responsibilities, he also served as the school's Dean of Students. As such, he and wife Betty lived in an apartment in Joe's dormitory. With a chuckle Joe paused, "I guess you could say that Coach Eiler ruled us on and off the field!"

Joe Bean compiled one of Division III's most outstanding records during his 38-year coaching career at Wheaton College.

Mike Schmidt

In 1961, Joe (and wife Shirley) moved to Ohio University to get his master's degree while assisting in soccer. When soccer was dropped as a sport, Bean was assigned to assist coach Bob Wren with the Bobcat baseball squad.

Playing third base on the 1962 squad was none other eventual baseball HOFer, Mike Schmidt.

The 1960s were a period of expansion for collegiate soccer, and in the fall of 1962, Joe was hired to initiate the sport at Quinnipiac (CT) College. Before leaving three seasons later, he led the team to a 20-9 record. It was while playing Gordon College that he struck up a life-long friendship with its coach, Cliff McCrath.

In 1965 Bridgeport hired Joe Bean to succeed John McKeon as coach. "I knew John a bit as we frequently were battling to recruit the same players." Both men later assumed important roles in the expansion of the NSCAA. Under Bean, Bridgeport went 31-15-2 and in his final season; only a 1-0 loss to coach Joe Machnik and LIU kept the team from reaching the 1968 NCAA semifinal round.

Succeeding Baptista

In 1969, Wheaton College hired Bean to succeed Bob Baptista.

In his 38 seasons at the Illinois institution, Bean led the school to two NCAA Division III championships (1984, 1997) while finishing as runner-up on two other occasions. Upon retirement, he was the first collegiate coach to have won 600 games (607-185-56). During his tenure, Wheaton captured 23 conference titles. In 2010, the College Conference of Illinois and Wisconsin (CCIW) named its annual coaching award in his honor.

Perhaps most noteworthy was Wheaton's 66-match winning streak achieved over the 1996-98 seasons. It broke the 60-year record of 65 matches established by coach Bill Jeffrey's Penn State teams in the 1930s.

He was inducted into the Wheaton College Hall of Honor in 1990, and, upon his retirement, the school's soccer facility was named Joe Bean Stadium.

Forty-four Wheaton players have earned All-America honors, including Steve Long and Bret Hall, who both played for the NASL's Chicago Sting franchise.

In addition to his coaching, Bean aided in the promotion of soccer in his region while serving as the editor and secretary-treasurer of the seasonal *Midwestern Soccer News* for 17 years. This was in addition to founding Premier Soccer Camp, the Midwest's largest camp of its kind at the time.

NSCAA and Other Contributions

The Bean records of contributions to the growth of the game of soccer are both many and varied.

Elected NSCAA president in 1978, he oversaw a rewrite of the organization's constitution and by-laws while in office. Ten years later, he was the recipient of the coveted Honor Award and also was inducted into the NISOA Hall of Fame. In 1991, and commemorating the NSCAA's 50-year anniversary, Bean and Tim Schum collaborated on publishing a book celebrating the organization's history. Crowning his accomplishments was Bean's induction into the NSCAA Hall of Fame in 2007.

Jerry Yeagley[145]

His Early Mentor

"I just wanted to be like Barney" was Jerry Yeagley's summation of how he first came to follow his Myerstown, Pennsylvania, hero into soccer coaching.

Yeagley, of course, is one of the game's great collegiate coaches, having founded the men's program at Indiana University in 1973.

Barney Hoffman was the Myerstown High School physical education teacher and oversaw the town's playground in the summers. As an elementary school student, Jerry rode his bicycle to the playground, where every day there were lots of soccer balls waiting to be given some love.

"He would work with us on our technique while emphasizing the individual principles of play," recalled Jerry in a January phone call from his Bloomington, Indiana, home. "He also encouraged us to be creative, try new things and experience the joy and beauty of the game."

Jerry Yeagley's patience paid off as Indiana University's soccer established itself as one of the nation's exemplary programs during his tenure.

To further expose his charges to good soccer, the coach gassed up his battered Studebaker and drove them to see college soccer games at both his alma mater, West Chester, and Penn State.

West Chester and Mel Lorback

In describing his role on the team, the good-humored Yeagley noted he was "a piano carrier, not a piano player!"

It was at West Chester in Yeagley's senior year (47 students were in the senior class) when Myerstown defeated Upper Darby to become the smallest school ever to capture the Pennsylvania high school soccer title.

Watching the match that day was West Chester State coach Mel Lorback. He later enticed both Jerry and teammate Billy Fulk to matriculate at the suburban Philadelphia school.

"I have to say that my decision to major in physical education and become a coach had a lot to do with Barney Hoffman and the example he set," said Yeagley. "I know my parents had other thoughts as far as my studies were concerned, but they saw my passion and allowed me to follow my dream."

The contrast between coaches Hoffman and Lorback couldn't have been more pronounced. "Mel had been in the Navy and his practices were quite regimented. At the onset of practice the team would circle and one of us at a time would be called on to put the rest of the team through a predetermined set of calisthenics labeled red, green and blue. At times, Mel would be up on a scaffold, overseeing matters. While we warmed up there'd be two bags of soccer balls, but they were not taken out until the various exercises were completed. As opposed to Barney, Mel wanted the ball to move forward quickly. We call it direct play today."

"I guess the things Mel and Barney had in common were that they were both short in stature and both earned our respect."

Jerry played at right fullback and in describing his role on the team, the good-humored Yeagley noted he was "a piano carrier, not a piano player!"

The 1961 Ram team went 13-0 during the regular season and earned three more wins in NCAA play, including a 2-0 win over Bob Guelker's home-standing St. Louis team in the championship final.

On to Indiana

He is also proud that, in 2009, when the NCAA announced its half-century team, he was selected as the group's coach.

In 1963, following completion of his master's degree at the University of Pittsburgh, Jerry joined the Indiana University Physical Education faculty as an instructor and soccer coach.

The "soccer coach" segment of the job meant oversight of a club team. And for the next 10 years, that competitive designation remained in place.

Did he ever get discouraged that it took that long for the Hoosiers to become an intercollegiate team?

He recounted, "You know I actually look back and I realized that I learned a great deal from the experience," citing that he learned to be patient and positive throughout the process. "We played as a club team in the Midwestern Soccer Conference. I tried to change the club's culture, gradually using only undergraduates. My wife Marilyn washed the uniforms, the players and I lined the field, put up the nets and tried in various ways to publicize our matches."

Indiana AD Bill Orwig was lukewarm about adding another sport (the last sport added had been gymnastics some 25 years before), but Yeagley's patient approach began to pay off.

First, one of his players, Jeff Richardson, became the Student Association president just as student activism became more strident in the late 1960s. Jerry credits Jeff and club captain Gary Fresen with extraordinary work on behalf of the varsity soccer initiative. That included staging a successful student referendum on the issue of varsity status. It didn't hurt that retired Indiana Past President and revered Chancellor Herman Wells became an important advocate for adding soccer.

Indiana Soccer Takes Off

In 1973, the Indiana Athletic Board approved the addition of men's soccer as a varsity sport, and for the next 31 seasons, Hoosier soccer achieved recognition as one of the top Division I programs in the country. Over those decades, Yeagley guided Indiana to 28 NCAA tournaments, played in 12 College Cups, and captured NCAA Division I national titles on six of those occasions.

Since the conference was formed in 1991, Indiana has won 10 Big Ten Championships under Yeagley.

His overall career record stands at 544-101-45, and he is the NCAA Division I all-time winningest coach. Along the way, his and the teams' ethical approach to the game has resulted in his being awarded NSCAA National Coach of the Year six times and Big Ten Coach of the Year five times. He is also proud that, in 2009, when the NCAA announced its half-century team, he was selected as the group's coach. He was also pleased that two Indiana players, Angelo DiBernardo and Armando Betancourt, were also honored.

With all that he had going for him at Indiana, was he ever pursued to leave Indiana?

"Well, in the early 1980s some folks at the Montreal Monique of the NASL flew Marilyn and me in for an interview. There was no offer and they told me to take two weeks to think about it. By then Marilyn and I realized that we loved seeing young boys turn into men under our watch more than trying to meet the challenge of coaching at the professional level." Al Miller, when he was at Dallas, had earlier approached him about coaching at the professional level. Miller appealed by saying, "We need more American coaches in our league."

Coaching Reflections

Over the course of his tenure, coach Yeagley has been constant in seeking improvement in his methodology.

Looking back, he fondly recalls that, despite their different coaching philosophies, he and coach Lorback became fast friends. "Underneath the veneer, Mel was one of the warmest guys you'd ever want to meet."

He admits that he suffered perhaps his toughest defeat in 1979 when the Hoosiers, ranked number one in the country and having shut out 18 opponents, lost to Walter Bahr's Penn State team 2-0 at State College.

He admitted to learning a couple of coaching lessons from Bahr. "Before one of our games with Penn State, I shook hands with him and wished him 'good luck.' He stood for a second, looked at me and said, "Don't ever wish an opposing coach that – simply say, I hope we have a good game!"

On another occasion, Jerry had his assistant Don Rawson return a call to Walter, inquiring of Indiana's practice time on the Penn State field. Later Bahr sidled up to Jerry and reminded him: "Admirals only talk to admirals!"

He worked also to upgrade the coaching education of his fellow Indiana soccer coaches by inviting famed German coach Dettmar Cramer to the Culver Military Academy for a two-day clinic. "He was an impressive coach. He stayed with us and enjoyed a game of ping pong in our basement."

Jerry did add to his coaching expertise by observing the coaching methods of two Indiana colleagues, basketball coach Bobby Knight and swim coach Jim Councilman. He shared that, "Bobby rarely allowed anyone into his practices but on occasion I snuck in. I don't think there was anyone who taught the principles of the game better than he did. He excused physical mistakes, but never mental errors." He and Knight enjoyed some golf and tennis competitions, and, on occasion, each invited the other to address their teams.

Councilman was one of the great innovators in competitive swimming. "I would attend his classes and learn things that were applicable to my coaching, particularly in the area of psychology of coaching, as well as in the application of scientific principles to coaching."

Marketing/Development Work

From 1983-96, the staging of the in-season Adidas/MetLife Classic annually exposed Indianans to top-quality soccer. This author recalls NSCAA marketing committee meetings with former MetLife executive Ivar Quigley. MetLife was utilizing soccer as part of its marketing strategy. Unfortunately, our coaches' group wasn't finding the right avenues to expose Met/Life to our membership. He frequently mentioned how pleased the company was with the exposure the company received through its sponsorship of the Indiana tournament. Again, Jerry's attention to detail was a winning formula as far as MetLife was concerned.

Following his retirement from Indiana in 2004, Jerry's excellent interpersonal skills have been utilized on a volunteer basis by the Athletic Department's development office. It is in large part due to his groundwork that the University is undertaking a $9 million upgrade to its soccer facility. Included will be the new Richardson-Fresen locker room area honoring the work of the two undergraduates who spearheaded the varsity soccer proposal.

Coach Yeagley is also proud of the host of former IU players who have been able to "give back to the game."

Coaching Honors

In 1982, West Chester University named Yeagley as recipient of the Distinguished Alumni Award. In 2000, he was honored with selection to its Athletics Hall of Fame. From 1987-89, the affable coach received three prestigious awards: the Bill Jeffrey Award in 1987 for his contributions to intercollegiate soccer, induction into the Pennsylvania Athletic Hall of Fame in 1988, and induction to the U.S. Soccer National Soccer Hall of Fame in 1989. Later, he was recipient of the National Soccer Coaches Association of America Honor Award in 1997 and inducted into the group's Hall of Fame in 2008.

Soccer immortal Pele presented coach Yeagley with the NSCAA Honor Award in 1997 in Cincinnati.

These various acknowledgements reflect the impact Jerry Yeagley has had on the game of soccer in this country, and to think that it all began on the playgrounds of Myerstown, Pennsylvania.

Fred Schmalz – Evansville's Ace Coach[147]

There are few other American-born coaches who have impacted soccer as has retired University of Evansville coach Fred Schmalz

Born and raised in the St. Philip Neri parish of St. Louis, Fred cut his soccer teeth on the church's Catholic Youth Council team and further honed his play at Laboure High School.

As to the coaching Schmalz received at either stop, he replied with a chuckle, "It was ridiculous. It was minimal. We were organized by say a Father Burke or by an interested parent, but that was it." He did recall attendance at CYC team practices by Bill Looby, a great player with the Kutis FC teams of the 1950s.

Fred Schmalz is another St. Louis area soccer product who has made numerous contributions to soccer's progress both in the Midwest and nationally.

Fred's soccer life took a fortuitous turn when he enrolled at Quincy College in 1962. Prompted by Schmalz and others, the school started soccer in 1964. Coach Frank Longo didn't exactly have to show his team that the ball was round, as a dozen former St. Louis all-district players formed an experienced first-year Hawk nucleus.

Fred played for three seasons, including the first campaign when Quincy was unbeaten (8-0-1). The team went 9-2-1 under new coach Roger Francour the next year and then, in 1966, was unbeaten (13-0-0) as it captured its first of 11 NAIA championships.

Recalling coaching lessons from his play at Quincy, Schmalz credits Frank Longo as a man who knew how to organize things. "He was a physical education teacher who was hired to coach basketball and so there was not a lot he could offer in terms of our technical improvement. But there are tactical similarities between the sports and that proved to be a coaching strength of his."

Fred also noted that Longo had coached at McBride High School prior to coming to Quincy. While there, he had observed the soccer coaching success of Jack Mackenzie at Augustinian High School. Frank has to be credited with luring Mackenzie to replace Francour in 1969. It would be a successful hire, as for the next 43 years, Mackenzie fielded nine more NAIA national championship teams.

First Coaching Posts

Following graduation from Quincy, Fred spent 1968 assisting coach John MacKenzie at Western Illinois University. Unlike Quincy, Western's first team had but four experienced players and scored four goals all season.

In retrospect, the Western experience exposed Schmalz to the variety of methods MacKenzie utilized as he focused on improving the technical ability of his inexperienced roster. "John was an excellent teacher. We did a lot of ball work. We also had to show a lot of patience as it is not an easy season when you go 1-9."

Hired in 1969 to introduce men's soccer at the University of Wyoming, Fred recruited St. Louis goalie Ray Remstedt to Laramie. Ray became a two-time All-America selection, and his face graced the 1970 cover of the NCAA Rules Guide. Unfortunately, Wyoming dropped the sport in 1972.

Following Wyoming and for the next seven seasons, Schmalz never lost a conference match while guiding Davis & Elkins College (D & E; West Virginia) to a 91-21-5 record and six trips to the NAIA Final Four. In the 1974 title game, D & E lost to Quincy, 6-0.

Directing Evansville's Soccer Fortunes

"Finally we asked him for his thoughts. 'I'll be keen to go' was his reply." –Fred Schmalz

The Schmalz coaching career at Evansville University began in 1979. By his retirement in 2002, Fred had accumulated an overall collegiate career record of 403-196-56 in 33 seasons, including a 23-year mark of 302-165-49 with the Purple Aces.

At the time, he ranked third in victories among the nation's active Division I coaches and also stood fifth in all-time Division I wins.

That success didn't happen by accident but through dogged work on the recruiting trail at both home and abroad.

Olympic Development Program

"He [Banks] was a tremendous physical player with speed. He was a Jim Brown-type with ball control." –Fred Schmalz

"When I talk to younger coaches today they shake their heads," recounted Schmalz in a spring 2020 interview. "They can't believe the amount of energy we [coaches] devoted to areas outside of our coaching."

He was referring to the uncompensated times outside his Evansville coaching duties that he spent furthering the sport of soccer.

Among Fred's early accomplishments was, while at Davis & Elkins, orchestrating the organization of the West Virginia Youth Soccer Association as part of the United States Youth Soccer Association (USYSA) effort to give administrative oversight to the explosion of the game at the youth level.

One personal accomplishment was, in 1978, earning his USSF A Coaching License under Walt Chyzowych. Appointed to the Coaching School Staff in 1980, Fred and other staff members were subsequently involved in a player identification initiative labeled the Olympic Development Program (ODP). Initially sponsored by USSF, it has subsequently been underwritten by USYSA.

Beginning in 1980, Schmalz has been instrumental in organizing ODP activities in Region II, basically the Midwest region.

Among such undertakings was arranging for one-week camps for talented youth players ages 12 through 19. Playing for their state teams, the teams then played matches against other state teams in their regions. Through such play, individuals could be identified for possible elevation to USSF national age group teams.

As with any such talent search, there are always stories involving players who never quite reached his or her potential. Schmalz' favorite story involved a player from Bettendorf, Iowa, named Tavian Banks. "He was a tremendous physical player with speed. He was a Jim Brown-type with ball control. One year he led the Iowa ODP team to our inter-regional championship almost by himself."

Unfortunately for the sport of soccer, Banks accepted a football scholarship to the University of Iowa. During his senior campaign of 1997, Banks rushed for 1,691 yards and scored 17 touchdowns, a then-school record, as were his 33 career touchdowns. Drafted in the fourth round by the Jacksonville Jaguars, a serious knee injury effectively ended his NFL career after four seasons.

Schmalz was one of those coaches who aided Region II DOC Bob Gansler. Other Region II staff coaches included Steve Adlard, Jim Lauder, Gary Parsons, and Ron Wigg.

In 1998, he was the recipient of the first Ron Wigg Award, the highest honor presented by the Region II Olympic Development Program.

Another Schmalz involvement was his participation as a regional coach in a series of annual U-23 select team competitions known as summer U.S. Olympic Sport Festivals. Schmalz was the first person to coach gold medal-winning teams from separate regions in such competitions, with his Region II/IV (1990) and Region II (1991) teams both finishing on top. Cobi Jones and Lexi Lalas were among the 1990 group who started on the 1994 U.S. World Cup team.

Since his retirement from Evansville, the energetic and committed Schmalz served as the first director at the area's 10-field Goebel Soccer Park. As noted, he has also served as the Evansville SC's DOC.

Recognition

In 1988, Fred was presented the Intercollegiate Soccer Association of America's Bill Jeffrey Award for his contributions to intercollegiate soccer.

His induction into the Missouri Valley Conference Hall of Fame Class of 2011 marked the sixth such honor for Schmalz. Others include inductions into the Quincy University (1993), Indiana Soccer (1997), Davis & Elkins University (2003), University of Evansville (2003), and St. Louis Soccer (2009) Halls of Fame.

Growing Midwestern Soccer in Ohio

Soccer's progress in the post-World War II era in certain Midwest states was based on existing legacies in their cities (Chicago and St. Louis in particular). Meanwhile, in other Midwest states such as Ohio, advancement of the game was due in large part to the groundbreaking efforts of several influential coaches.

The state of Ohio utilized the talents of transplanted individuals from the Eastern seaboard. Four, Cliff Stevenson, Bob Nye, Gary Avedikian, and Jay Martin, were Springfield College graduates, while Mickey Cochrane arrived from the Baltimore area. Of the six coaches to be cited, only Stu Parry was a native of Ohio.

All these coaches contributed their talents not only to produce competitive teams, but, as will be seen, also spent time and energy to leave varied soccer legacies in a state where scholastic and intercollegiate football had ruled the day.

Oberlin's Cliff Stevenson

One individual who lent a spark to Ohio's soccer development was Springfield College graduate Cliff Stevenson. He was ambitious, highly organized, and charismatic. Upon graduation from Springfield in 1952, he became varsity soccer and lacrosse coach and director of physical education at Oberlin College. Prior to the Stevenson appointment, under coach Ben Collins, Oberlin was the standout team in the Buckeye State.

Beginning in 1952, Stevenson continued the school's soccer success, recording three straight unbeaten seasons before a loss to Kenyon ended the school's 42-match unbeaten streak. The coach's enthusiasm for the game was reflected in the fact that a reported 78 undergrads turned out for places on the 1955 team. All-America midfielder Joe Molder later surfaced as coach at Columbia University from 1958-70.

One undergrad attracted to Oberlin because of its soccer prowess was Stu Parry. He later established one of the Midwest's first soccer dynasties at Akron University.

In eight years at Oberlin, Stevenson's teams were 48-16-7 and captured four Midwest Conference championships. In lacrosse, the beat was the same: a 56-12-4 record with three undefeated seasons and four Ohio Collegiate Association titles.

Stevenson left Oberlin in 1960 and embarked on an equally successful coaching career at Brown University.

Stu Parry – Putting the Zip in Akron[148]

At Oberlin, Stevenson's coaching success attracted the attention of an Akron (OH) high school student named Stuver Parry. Stu enrolled at Oberlin in 1953 and scored five goals in one match for the undefeated Yeoman team (9-0-1).

In 1954, and following military service, Parry transferred to the University of Akron where, prompted by his father, he started a club soccer team. Building on recruits from the city's ethnic leagues, Akron became a varsity team the following year, led by student coach Parry.

By 1961, the Zips had arrived competitively, beating St. Louis before a crowd of 15,000 at the city's Rubber Bowl Stadium. Over his 16-year tenure, Parry and Akron became a force

Stu Parry started what has become one of the Midwest's most competitive Division I soccer programs at the University of Akron.

in NCAA play. Coach Parry was also be credited with introducing indoor soccer play during the winter months as a means to sharpen the technical skills of his players. Other coaches such as Al Miller soon incorporated off-season indoor play in their regions of the country.

Parry became involved with the NSCAA, serving as its president in 1968.

Mickey Cochrane – Coach and Historian[149]

Cornelius Rice Parsons Cochrane, Jr., now in his 10th decade, is like the Energizer Bunny. He takes a licking and just keeps on ticking!

Most recently, in February 2020, his dream of finding a home for all the Bowling Green sports memorabilia he and former Bowling Green State University (BGSU) sports information director Don Cunningham had collected was realized when the University unveiled a modern, interactive, ongoing display inside its Stroh Center.

Informally known as "Mickey," Cochrane has never met a soccer ball, a pair of shoes, a game program, or an admission ticket he didn't want to secure and store for future display.

Cochrane's career as coach of soccer and lacrosse has been honored, but it is his role as a self-taught chronicler/preserver of both sports that will stand as his legacy.

Mickey Cochrane is shown with then-USSF historian Sam Foulds breaking ground for the Oneonta Hall of Fame.

Education on the Run

Born in Flushing, New York, on March 13, 1930, the Cochrane clan moved nine times because Cornelius, Sr. traveled about the country, setting up governmental centers for FDR's Social Security Administration. Due to the various relocations, his academic record did not grant him entrance to his father's alma mater, Amherst College. Instead, Mickey attended Oberlin (OH) College, an institution that made history of sorts when, in 1935, it became the first Midwestern college to sponsor soccer.

At Oberlin, Mickey majored in physical education and, like many, would be termed a generalist in the field. Oberlin's curriculum equipped its undergraduates with a fundamental pedagogical foundation that then enabled them to apply that knowledge to a multitude of sports.

During his subsequent careers at Johns Hopkins University (1953-64) and BGSU 1964-77), in addition to coaching soccer and lacrosse, he at times also coached wrestling, baseball, volleyball, and track. His Hopkins tenure was interrupted when he coached soccer at the Brooke Army Medical Center at Fort Sam Houston (TX) from 1955-57.

In retirement, he chaired the Historical Committee of the Oberlin College Heisman Club from 1988-95. He was also a member of the Oberlin College Athletic Hall of Fame Committee from 1986-95 and was inducted into it in 1998.

Following graduation from Oberlin in 1952, he earned his M.A. from the University of Maryland.

Quick BGSU Improvement

The effervescent Cochrane is known as the father and architect of the BGSU men's soccer and lacrosse programs. He initiated each in 1966, after serving as club coach of the sports the year before.

Cochrane noted that, when he arrived at Bowling Green, both sports were little known in the Midwest. The BGSU president at the time, William Jerome, came from Syracuse, New York, and upstate New York had been a hot bed of lacrosse largely due to the historical influence of Native American tribes.

Jerome granted Cochrane 10 out-of-state scholarships and sent him East to find players, especially if they could play two sports. Fortunately, he found that many athletes competed in soccer in the fall and lacrosse in the spring.

By 1972, in just seven seasons after the sport's inception at BGSU, the Falcons qualified for the first of two consecutive NCAA Tournaments. The next year the team was named Ohio Collegiate Soccer Association champions.

By the time he stepped down from his coaching duties in 1977, Cochrane had compiled a 13-year record of 68-56-14 at BGSU, including a 61-39-10 mark over his final 10 seasons.

The Cochrane coaching philosophy was stated in Cliff McGrath's 1978 NSCAA Honor Award presentation. Cliff stated, "Athletics has a lot to do with how you handle things. They're great preparation for the highs and lows of real life because you can't control everything ... so you learn to cope with anything."[150]

Preserving NSCAA Memorabilia

At Hopkins, and aided in part by his open, youthful countenance and further enhanced by his willingness to take on numerous assignments, Cochrane soon became an important cog as the NSCAA began to play a more important role in the development of the sport.

Noted for his integrity and organizational acumen, he was named as a member of the first NCAA Tournament selection committee that shaped the sport's inaugural tournament in 1959. For this effort, he received an NSCAA Letter of Commendation in 1964 and in 1969 was elected the association's president.

His term was marked by membership unrest, as a younger element, many of whom were recent recipients of USSF coaching licenses, was displeased with the organization's failure to grow the game, particularly in terms of clinic offerings. His calm, reassuring manner forged a compromise by appointing many of the disgruntled members to a newly constituted clinics and development committee.

In 1978, when he was the recipient of the NSCAA's prestigious Honor Award (the association's highest prize signifying lifetime service to the sport), Cochrane's forethought to collect and preserve every manner of soccer memorabilia was acknowledged. It was also for his work in the records and other artifacts preservation of soccer history that was the basis for his receiving the ISAA's Bill Jeffrey Award in 1984. At the time, that honor acknowledged his work in helping establish the now disbanded National Soccer Hall of Fame, in Oneonta, New York.

Annual NSCAA (now United Soccer Coaches) Conventions were marked by Cochrane displays of memorabilia, especially chosen for that year's meeting. As usual, Mickey stationed himself nearby to educate the uninitiated to the theme of the exhibit.

Many attendees to NSCAA conventions fondly recall viewing Cochrane's annual displays, usually located near the high-traffic registration areas. Those exhibits always contained a small sign reminding viewers of a sacred Cochrane stratagem: "Don't throw it away!"

Interest in Artifacts

Those exhibits always contained a small sign reminding viewers of a sacred Cochrane stratagem: "Don't throw it away!"

Cochrane credits the family's eventual settlement in Bethesda, Maryland, as sparking his interest in sports memorabilia.

Living within relative proximity of such Civil War battlefields as Manassas, Antietam, and Gettysburg and viewing reenactments by Union veterans sparked an early interest in that conflagration by the inquisitive youngster. Mickey recalls retrieving spent *minie* balls fired by soldiers on various sites he and his father visited. Later, he visited shops to purchase various items of Civil War memorabilia.

With an abiding interest in American history, on occasion he visited Ford's Theater, site of Lincoln's assignation, and then followed the escape trail taken by John Wilkes Booth, his killer.

In 1953, it occurred to Cochrane that the NSCAA had achieved little in the way of preserving its history.

At the time, the diligent Cochrane had collected personal troves of stamps and other items (that included a Coca Cola sign he bought for $5 and sold for $150!) alongside his Civil War collection. Soon, every manner of NSCAA-related stuff was annually deposited in the Cochrane basement and garage. With the history of intercollegiate soccer tied to the first game played at Philadelphia's Haverford College, for a time, the Cochrane/NSCAA collection was stored there.

The mindset of any collector is: Where and when can I off-load what I have and share it with others of similar interest?

That opportunity presented itself in the early 1980s when, led by Al Colone, the city of Oneonta began a drive to establish a soccer hall of fame in that upstate New York community. Encouraged by the city's Wright family, initial space was secured. Cochrane recalled being contacted regarding his collection: "I received a phone call that I had two weeks to box everything we had and get it to Oneonta. My wife [Patricia] and I got it done. Eventually, of course, they constructed [in 1999} a wonderful building that housed and displayed artifacts from every level of soccer, youth, professional, college, referees. While it lasted, it was a wonderful way to preserve the game's heritage." Unfortunately, due to finances, the Oneonta HOF closed its doors in February 2010.

All of the NSCAA-related material housed at Oneonta was forwarded to the organization's headquarters in Kansas City. That is, all but one item. That was a soccer ball signed by soccer legend Pele in Columbus, Ohio. "He was awaiting back stage to be introduced and I came upon him almost by accident. I asked him to sign the ball and he inscribed it 'Good luck to the US Soccer Hall of Fame.' I think of it as an item that doesn't necessarily belong to any organization and so have kept it for now."

Honored by Bowling Green

Through the years, Cochrane has received a multitude of awards. For his many years of service at BGSU, he received the Honorary Alumnus Award in 1987, followed by his induction into the BGSU Athletic Hall of Fame in 1993. In addition, the Bowling Green soccer field was named in his honor.

Cochrane was named USILA Lacrosse Coach of the Year in 1970 and Ohio Soccer Coach of the Year in 1969 and 1972. In 1995, he was inducted into the Ohio Lacrosse Hall of Fame.

Cochrane received Ohio Collegiate Soccer Association COY recognition on two occasions (1969 and 1972). He was bestowed the OCSA's Honor Award in 1989. He also is a member of the NSCAA Hall of Fame, Class of 1995.

Mickey is also proud of his successor at BGSU and other Falcon soccer alumni who have gone on to contribute to the game.

Bob Nye – Wooster's Finest[151]

Robert "Bob" Nye was one of those Springfield College graduates whose career included introducing the game to virgin soccer territory of Ohio in the 1960s.

He not only helped implant soccer in the state but also parlayed his professional experiences in the game of golf to the benefit of the NSCAA.

From Springfield to Wooster

Bob was one of the members of coach Irv Schmid's 1957 Springfield College's National Championship soccer team that went on to carve a name in the game of soccer. He first served as a physical education instructor at Bloomfield (NJ) High School from 1958-64, where he coached soccer, basketball, and golf. Two of his Bloomfield players, Jeff Vennell and Bill Muse, subsequently enrolled at Springfield and later played significant roles in the growth of soccer.

The Nye family departed the East Coast in 1964 for the College of Wooster (OH), where Bob was charged with initiating soccer, coaching golf, and managing the school's L.C. Boles golf course. In 30 years as Wooster soccer coach, he compiled a record of 269-188-41 and coached 16 NSCAA All-America players. Wooster qualified for 10 NCAA Division III Tournaments, recording a fourth-place finish in 1977.

College of Wooster's Bob Nye (center) is one of those transplanted Easterners who was hired to launch a soccer program in Ohio.

One of the pioneer coaches in the Buckeye State, in 1969, he was credited with distributing what he termed "starter kits" to area schools. These items included balls, uniforms, and other soccer equipment to help schools kick-start the sport. In 1970, he was named the Ohio Collegiate Soccer COY.

Borrowing From Golf

Tabbed by then-NSCAA President Mel Lorback, Bob Nye entered the organization's officer ranks in 1976 and by 1981 was serving the first of a two-year term as president. He was one of 18 former Springfield graduates to serve in that role.

Nye's two-year presidency coincided with the implementation of a new NSCAA constitution. The Board of Directors now included the six officers, eight regional representatives, and three at-large representatives. NISOA's Dr. Ray Bernabei shared his management expertise in finalizing the new document that mirrored that of the officials' association in terms of spreading out the individual workload of its leadership group.

It was during earlier service with the Golf Coaches Association of America that Bob introduced a trade show in conjunction with that organization's annual meeting. His role in staging a similar exhibit of soccer merchandise at the NSCAA convention has been covered in the chapter detailing the evolution of the NSCAA Convention. For his efforts, Nye was awarded a NSCAA Letter of Commendation in 1980. For his long and meritorious service, he was later the recipient of the 1992 NSCAA Honor Award and in 2021 was inducted into United Soccer Coaches HOF.

Honors

For his contributions to his local community, Bob Nye was inducted into the Wayne County (OH) Sports Hall of Fame in 1980. Other honors include Ohio Soccer Officials Association Merit Award, 1990, and Ohio Collegiate Soccer Association Honor Award, 1992; in the same year, he was inducted into The College of Wooster Athletic Hall of Fame. And in 1999, Springfield College selected him to its Hall of Fame.

In 2002, Golf Week magazine presented coach Nye with its annual Father of the Year Award. It put him in pretty rarified air. Among the previous recipients were Jack Nicklaus and Earl Woods.

Robert Elwood "Bob" Nye passed away in 2014 at age 81.

Gary Avedikian – Master Marketer[153]

Gary Avedikian's establishment of one of the country's model secondary school soccer programs can be attributed to the keen eye of his wife's grandmother.

That occurrence was in 1973 when Betty Probert informed Sue Avedikian to alert husband Gary that Centerville (OH) High School was searching for a soccer coach to start its boys soccer program.

Granny had visited the Avedikians often and fell in love with soccer and the teams Gary coached for a combined 10 years at East Hampton and Vinal high schools in Connecticut. Avedikian's soccer coaching was in combination with teaching social studies.

Avedikian played for coach Dale Harper at West Hartford's Conard High School. Harper had been a roommate of Springfield College soccer coach Irv Schmid and encouraged Gary's enrollment there. But, after playing junior varsity soccer his first year, a serious knee injury ended Gary's thoughts of further soccer participation.

A Progressive Community

The merger of Avedikian's soccer experience, imagination, and work ethic with a progressive Centerville community was a recipe for a soccer success story unrivaled in U.S. secondary school annals.

Centerville was an upper-class Midwestern community of 24,000 nestled in the Dayton suburbs. The economy of the area was supported by thriving companies such as General Motors and National Cash Register as well as by the military installation at Wright-Patterson Air Force Base.

Gary Avedikian developed one of the nation's most progressive secondary school soccer programs in Centerville, Ohio.

Once informed of the job, Gary contacted the head of Centerville's popular youth soccer program as part of an investigative process. That person started the ball rolling that concluded with Gary being offered a teaching-soccer coaching position. He and wife Sue pulled up stakes and moved to Ohio in 1973.

Plenty of Success

In the early 1970s, the state of Ohio was virgin territory for the sport of soccer.

Upon his hire, the Centerville AD requested that Avedikian submit a list of all soccer-related equipment he needed to start the new program.

"I remember there was not one store in Dayton, Ohio, that supplied soccer equipment. That included shoes. I contacted a store back in Hartford and ordered Puma shoes." That the shoes were in the school's black and gold colors was a clue as to the new coach's marketing mentality!

On-field success was immediate; in fact, the school never came close to a losing season over Gary's 14-year tenure. His overall Centerville record stood at 222-36-

29 when he departed in spring of 1987. The team captured 11 straight Western Ohio League titles from1977-87 and won 10 sectional titles and seven regional crowns. Centerville reached the Ohio State semifinals seven times, including in 1984 when it won the Ohio State Division I title.

The Centerville Game Experience
Centerville soccer became a must-see outing.

In addition to the five-man coaching staff prowling the team's sideline, every match featured 12 well-outfitted Bobby-Soccers serving as ball persons and in other game-related capacities. "These positions became highly-prized," said the now-retired coach. "We'd have 200 girls trying out over three days for the 48 spots. Those that didn't make the varsity team cut performed similar functions at the games of our three junior varsity teams." The uniforms for the four Bobby-Soccers squads alone came to $7,000!

Of course, there was the usual cheerleader corps, and also the school had a precision dance team that performed at some halftimes for home matches. Avedikian recalled that the dance team was such an attraction that at one of its performance the Parents Club of the Coeds brought in a helicopter to dry out the field so their show could take place!

Centerville played night games and over the Avedikian era averaged 2,300 spectators. In time, as the crowds grew, season tickets were sold as were reserve tickets to the prime seating areas. There was also VIP seating in the press box with that facility climate-controlled and with restroom availability. Centerville soccer became a must-see outing.

Avedikian traveled to and hosted high school teams from neighboring states along with the more traditional local rivals. On one occasion, he recalled, he arranged to fly an assistant to Cleveland to scout a playoff opponent!

Summers found Centerville underclassmen attending Jerry Yeagley's soccer camp at Indiana University, with the upper classmen enrolling at the Tampa Bay Rowdies Camps. It was at the latter camp that Avedikian's networking hooked him up with Mick Hoban of Nike. Beginning in 1977, all the clothing and equipment involved in the Centerville soccer experience featured the Nike swoosh. That included the varsity team's Gortex rain suits paid for by one of the parents.

Not mentioned was the Parents Club's oversight of concession stands and sale of game programs. The game programs included numbering such that, at halftime, prizes were awarded based on those holding such special publications. One prize included participation in penalty kick competitions.

The group also organized the post-season team banquet. Gary recalled that the Centerville principal had had an opportunity to attend a similar function hosted by Cincinnati football power Moeller High School. "He came up to me after one of our banquets and said, 'Yours is much better than theirs!'"

Gary credits wife Sue with supporting him on all that went into making Centerville soccer what it was. "Nobody outworked Sue and me. A lot of what we did was of a permanent nature that was there after we left. I remember one time it was agreed that we needed to plant shrubbery around the stadium. We dug the holes, planted the shrubs, watered them just like everyone else who cared to work on the project."

Perhaps indicative of the soccer's influence in Centerville were events surrounding the construction of a new stadium.

Ohio State Men's Soccer

"'I think you need one more goal scorer up front.' I bit my tongue. It was frustrating." –Gary Avedikian

Seeking a new challenge, Avedikian left Centerville in 1987and was hired as men's coach at Ohio State University. AD Rick Bay informed him going in that there were no soccer scholarships but promised that when an impending Big 10 soccer league was formed, the issue would be addressed. Nine years later, in 1996, he was granted nine-and-a-half awards, all based on tuition waivers. In terms of real value, the monies amounted to three-plus scholarships.

As influential as Gary Avedikian was at Centerville, he found that overcoming the lack of dedicated scholarship money and other roadblocks eventually deflated his ideas of making a dent in the big sport mentality at Ohio State.

"One year I had a good striker lined up from St. Louis and needed just a little more money to close the deal. I went to the AD Andy Geiger and pleaded my case. It was no deal. Later the next season he was standing by me on the sideline observing and said, 'I think you need one more goal scorer up front.' I bit my tongue. It was frustrating."

In 1992, the Buckeyes were challenging for the Big 10 crown and needed a win over Wisconsin to seal the deal. Ahead, with minutes to go, a late giveaway in the final third gave the Badgers a tie and a later win. "I think the other coaches knew the battle I was fighting," Gary said in reference to the fact that they voted him Big 10 COY.

On one occasion he identified an alumnus affiliated with Pennzoil who was willing to underwrite a new scoreboard at the soccer facility. When the athletic department's development office found out about the proposal, they tried to divert the monies to women's basketball, and the deal died. Other ideas by the persistent coach (soccer stadium upgrades, etc.) also never found traction.

By the spring of 1997, Gary had to reflect that, until new properly funded coach John Bluem arrived, the O-State game with Cleveland State in 1987 had attracted the largest crowd (3,118) ever to view a Buckeye soccer match. The coach shared that part of the game's attraction was that his loyal Centerville parents had donated four airline tickets for a halftime raffle.

In 1997, Avedikian returned to coaching soccer and teaching social studies at first Chillicothe and then Hillard Davidson high schools. Upon retirement in 2003, his cumulative coaching record stood at 443-195-79.

Other Soccer Contributions

*"They were more interested in listening to someone who could inform them how to win games than learning about how to grow the sport." –*Gary Avedikian

Prior to ascending to the NSCAA presidency in 1994, the Avedikian name was associated with other administrative success stories.

In the late 1970s, he was part of the organization's Partners of the Americas exchange program. It was a program where American soccer coaches traveled to Brazil to experience two weeks embedded in its soccer culture. Later, various NSCAA coaches arranged similar experiences for their Brazilian visitors. "I remember a student assembly at Centerville where two of them whacked the ball from one foul line of the gym to the other. That impressed our students."

At another time, Centerville also hosted an NSCAA/US Army clinic on its campus that featured Walt Chyzowych and an all-star coaching staff.

In 1974, the proactive Avedikian was a founding member of the Ohio Scholastic Soccer Coaches Association. Subsequently, at Centerville and Ohio State, he helped organize the annual meetings of the group.

On ascending to the NSCAA's Executive Committee, he was remembered for advocating for uniformity of dress (similar blue blazers, grey slacks) for all officers. Perhaps used to having no pushback for his Centerville budgets, he overlooked the fact that the organization monies only went so far!

Any regrets? Gary served as a clinician at various conventions, sharing his soccer marketing initiatives at Centerville. Referring to those sessions, he sensed a less than enthusiastic response. "They were more interested in listening to someone who could inform them how to win games than learning about how to grow the sport."

Jay Martin – Collegiate Soccer's Winningest Coach[154]

"Luck is a residue of design." –Branch Rickey, Ohio Wesleyan University, Class of 1904[155]

In the midst of an interview charting the various milestones in his stellar coaching career at Ohio Wesleyan University, John "Jay" Martin III, in an attempt to minimize his many accomplishments, stated, "Let's face it, I have just been lucky."

When researching the Rickey quote, it turns out that, over time, it has been modified to include the words, "hard work." Thus, "Luck and hard work is the residue of design."

The latter revision is probably more appropriate to describe the energy and foresight of Jay Martin.

The Gene Pool

If one's gene pool is any predictor of success, then the fact that Jay's maternal grandfather, Leo Murphy, and his father, John "Jack" Martin, were former professional baseball players had to play a role in Jay Martin's athletic successes. Jack's father, John, eventually headed the Boston City Fire Department, where he formed the first scuba unit to help combat fires on the Boston docks.

Jay Martin set a goal for himself to be the best soccer coach he could be, and as far as Ohio Wesleyan University is concerned, he has accomplished that objective.

Jack supported his family of 10 children through his career with New England Telephone and, over time, coached his oldest son Jay and other siblings in every one of their youth sport endeavors.

Not unexpectedly, Jay's first competitive sports experience involved baseball. His unbeaten CYO team roster included several who signed professional baseball contract. Also on the teams was NHL Hall of Famer Robbie Ftorek.

Jay's Higham High School career was marked by immersion in athletics and neglect of academics. A catcher in baseball, he also played basketball and some soccer.

In retrospect, he was fortunate to be greatly influenced by Higham basketball coach John Barker. Unabashedly, he states that Barker's coaching style has greatly influenced his own: "He was empowering. He always wanted to know how players felt about things. He valued you and your opinions. In this manner, he got players' commitments to the team." In Martin's junior year, Higham reached the state semifinals played at Boston Garden.

It was coach Barker who first steered Martin to soccer. "He told me to turn out for either cross country or soccer in order to get myself in shape for basketball.

I didn't see myself running around in my underwear on those cold New England falls so I played a couple of years for coach Peter McGregor's team."

Springfield College's Impact

"I was never a good player but I always had in mind, 'I may not be great, but I will be a great soccer coach.'" –Jay Martin

Barker's alma mater was Springfield College and, unfortunately, Martin's bid for admittance was initially denied: "I was just a terrible student in high school."

Again, his one-year stay in 1968 at Dean Junior College in Franklin (MA) proved fortuitous. He earned all As and Bs in the classroom and, along with playing soccer and basketball, joined the Dean lacrosse team.

Admitted to Springfield's physical education program as a sophomore transfer, Jay, by NCAA rules, was allowed to practice but not play. In his junior year, he played junior varsity soccer under coach Ray Cieplik and the first of two years of basketball under Ed Bilik.

In his senior year, he made coach Irv Schmid's soccer squad, starting two games. Out of that exposure came a Martin resolve: "I was never a good player but I always had in mind, 'I may not be great, but I will be a great soccer coach.'"

Obviously, lessons were to be learned from his exposure to Springfield's coaches and physical education faculty. "Ray was a relationship guy. Irv was more an organized, well-prepared guy who seemed to treat stars like my roommate Tony DiCicco a bit differently from others on the team. Ed Bilik was a lot like Irv, very well organized with his practices set out to the minute on small note cards. There were several other professors who shared their ideas with us. In some cases I recorded their ideas; in other cases I would hit the delete button."

Lessons From Helmut Schoen

"He [Schoen] said that the creative players were never going to become ball winners and so you needed to play an aggressive, hard-working player next to them to do that job." – Jay Martin

A bit of a politician, Martin was president of the Springfield physical education majors club in 1970-71. In that role, he served as a distribution point as job openings were forwarded his way by a Springfield administrator. One such opportunity was a position as a director of sports for the YMCA in Munich, Germany. Jay applied and Springfield grad Bob Jones agreed to hire Martin.

One small hitch. Upon graduation in 1971 and holding draft #41, Dame Fortune tapped him on the shoulder when, at his draft physical on June 4, 1971, it was discovered that he was claustrophobic and therefore draft exempt.

Two days later, he was on his way to Germany. Over the next four years, his stays in Germany left several indelible marks on his career.

As sports director, he taught several sports at the YMCA—all in German.

The early 1970s marked the heyday of the great Bayern Munich teams of Beckenbauer, Mueller, Maier, and others. With his class schedule allowing for free mornings, the eager Martin would travel to view Udo Lattek conduct Bayern training sessions. "Today there will be 4,000 people at the practices; then there would be 20."

Once again, Martin was at the right place at the right time as one frequent attendee at the sessions was German national team coach Helmut Schoen. In time, the young American was able to pick the soccer brain of one of the world's most famous coaches.

He found Schoen to be a rather laid-back individual who was an acute student of the game. "I learned the science and art of coaching from Schoen. For instance he shared with me how to align players according to their playing characteristics. He divided players by their personalities labeling the creative players as 'pink shirts' and the fighters as the 'dirt boys.'" Martin continued, "He said that the creative players were never going to become ball winners and so you needed to play an aggressive, hard working player next to them to do that job."

"Did You See It?"

Jay Martin wasn't the only American coach with a Helmut Schoen anecdote.

Seems that the late Penn State coach Walter Bahr's wide swath of coaching friends included FIFA staff coach Peter Kirchrath, who shared with him a story involving the German coach. Kirchrath was a FIFA staff coach who had introduced coaching schools in Turkey and Peru. One day, he found himself assisting the legendary Schoen.

Schoen was not one to either share or ask others for advice on coaching matters. But one day, Peter found himself next to Schoen watching a national team scrimmage. When, atypically, the tight-lipped German boss said, "Did you see it?"

Kirchrath shared with Bahr that he was so dumbstruck that all he could do was reply with a "yes." He also shared with Bahr: "To this day I don't know what he [Schoen] was talking about. But I dared not want him to know that I hadn't saw 'it.'"[154]

In that post-1971 period, German basketball was in its infancy, and Martin, in addition to serving as player/coach with the Munich semiprofessional team, traveled around the city lecturing and staging basketball clinics.

Eventually, Germany has been able to produce its share of international stars such as Dirk Novitske and others. Jay attributes that incremental basketball growth to the fact that teams' 12-man rosters were restricted to only two foreign players. "Think about it. If the NASL had been truly interested in growing American soccer and had similar rules, it would have helped the development of our players and our national team a great deal."

After returning to Ohio State in 1973-74 to earn his master's degree, Martin was offered a contract by the American International School at Dusseldorf. In addition to teaching, he played on the city's basketball team. Jay also found himself within easy travel distance of a host of Bundesliga teams and was able to view Ajax and the other great Dutch teams of that era.

In reviewing the impact of his time in Germany, Martin confesses that he always felt confident that he could become an excellent coach of any sport. "But I have to say that my immersion in the German soccer culture confirmed for me that I wanted to become the best soccer coach I could be."

Setting Records at OWU

Returning to the states in 1975, Martin continued his studies for the Ph.D. at Ohio State. Opportunity again presented itself in a somewhat unique manner when, in 1976-77, Martin served an internship with OWU Director of Athletics Dick Gordin. In the spring of 1977, Gordin appointed him to a search committee that was seeking to hire a combined soccer and lacrosse coach. At a point, Gordin, recognizing that Martin's resume would soon include a doctorate in addition to experience in both sports, encouraged him to throw his hat in the ring.

Thus began what has been a 43-year OWU relationship for Jay Martin.

When measured by coaching victories, Jay Martin has accomplished his goal of becoming a superb coach for, as of 2020, he is the winningest coach in NCAA men's soccer history and the first to reach the 700-win mark. Heading into the 2020 season, he had guided his 42 Battling Bishop soccer teams to a 723-150-74 record.

In addition to leading OWU to NCAA Division III titles in 1998 and 2011, his teams have reached the Division III semifinals nine times, finishing second on two occasions. He also served a six-year stint on the NCAA Division III selection committee, including four years as committee chair.

He has been the NCAA Regional Coach of the Year 16 times and named NSCAA National Coach of the Year in 1991, 1998, and 2011. In 2000, Martin received the Ohio Collegiate Soccer Association's Honor Award, only the fourth time that award was bestowed since the association's founding in 1949.

Beyond coaching, Martin was elected president of the National Soccer Coaches Association of America in 1996. In addition, he was named editor of the NSCAA's *Soccer Journal* in January 2003, becoming the publication's third editor since its establishment in 1950. He received the organization's Honor Award in 2007 and was inducted into its Hall of Fame in 2019.

Before becoming OWU athletics director in 1985, Martin's lacrosse teams posted an eight-year record of 104-34, winning four Midwest Lacrosse Association titles and earning six NCAA playoff bids. Twice Martin was named MLA Coach of the Year.

Oh, and in his spare time, he was color analyst of the Major League Soccer's Columbus Crew for nine seasons.

Coach Martin, in achieving his personal coaching objective, attributes lessons not only learned in Germany but from a number of U.S. models. He is also proud of the number of OWU players who have chosen soccer coaching as an avocation.

CHAPTER VIII

THE EMERGING FACE OF WESTERN U.S. SOCCER

In tracing the impact of soccer coaches in the Western areas of the United States, it is evident that their roles in the Rocky Mountain region differed from the contributions of those coaches on the West Coast where the game had been established in the early 1900s.

In the Rockies, the trail-blazing efforts of Joe Guennel cannot be discounted in launching the game, though others, including outsiders Lou Sagastume, Horst Richardson, and Marcelo Curi, as well as Denver native Theresa Echtermeyer, have subsequently left their soccer imprints in the Denver environs.

There are many similarities between the establishment of soccer on the West and East Coasts of the United States. As with the East Coast, the migration of various soccer-playing ethnic groups to West Coast cities aided in the organization of the sport beginning early in the 20th Century.

However, and similar to the refinement of the game on the East Coast, the contributions of several coaches who improved the existing West Coast soccer culture have been noteworthy. Many have cited the University of San Francisco's Steve Negoesco as "The Father of West Coast Soccer."

Not far behind in the quality of their regional and national influence have been coaches Bob DiGrazia, Julie Menendez, Lothar Osiander, and Steve Sampson in the Bay Area and Terry Fisher, Ralph Perez, and Sigi Schmid in the Los Angeles region. Meanwhile, the twin influence of Cliff McCrath and Lesle Gallimore in the Pacific Northwest cannot be discounted, nor can the Coast's Karl Dewazin's progressive contributions related to youth soccer issues.

Thus, as will be seen, the many varied contributions of coaches to the evolution of the game in the Western part of the United States has created a soccer culture second to none in the country.

Rocky Mountain Soccer

Most appropriately, he became the first soccer person named to the Colorado Sports Hall of Fame. At the 1991 ceremony, Joe Guennel commented, "It's rewarding, but the thing that pleases me the most about my induction is its reflection of the sport's stability. It's part of the fabric of the community now."

Joe Guennel Works His Magic

If there were an individual in the sport of soccer who might be best described as its "Johnny Appleseed," G.K. "Joe" Guennel's name would come to the fore.[157, 158]

Born in Germany but reared in Pennsylvania, Joe spent periods of his life in Indiana and Colorado, where his tireless attempts to grow the game are the stuff of legends. After spending a segment of his professional and soccer life in the Midwest, he was transferred to Colorado by Marathon Oil in 1961. Called the "Father of Soccer" by many Coloradoans, his involvement was spread across all sectors of the game.

Never a player himself, it was while serving in the U.S. Army and stationed in Germany that he first viewed that country's youth enjoying the game. It became a lifetime goal of his to provide U.S. youth with similar experiences.

His Colorado efforts began in Littleton, where he founded a five-team youth league. He soon coordinated his organizational efforts with Dutch-born John Meyer who had in 1961 formed the Colorado Junior Soccer Association. When Meyer left the state in 1963, Guennel took the Colorado Junior Soccer Association (CJSA) helm and expanded youth soccer programming for the next 16 years.

Of interest was that due to his work in the formation of Colorado youth soccer and also his service with U.S. Soccer, Guennel was later credited with spearheading the formation of the United States Youth Soccer Association in 1974.

Joe Guennel (left) receives the NSCAA Honor Award from Mickey Cochrane in 1962.

As a measure of the Guennel impact, 20 years after his arrival, the CJSA program involved 41,000 boys and girls, including 9,000 members of the more competitive and nationally affiliated Colorado State Youth Soccer Association teams.

Mirroring his earlier commitment to develop senior soccer in Indiana, as president of the Colorado State Soccer Association, he began to promote senior play in the Rockies. Most recently, the state's 10-league adult recreation program fields 250 male, female, and co-ed teams encompassing 6,000 players.

And not to overlook the needs of the emerging intercollegiate game, Guennel is credited with becoming the commissioner of the Rocky Mountain Intercollegiate Soccer League. By 1992, Colorado was fielding 15 varsity and 15 college club teams for men and women.

Taking on Other Initiatives

Guennel was not one to let others do the "heavy lifting" so essential to taking organizational ideas from concept to reality. He pushed for increased field usage and field development, imported needed equipment from suppliers in more mature soccer areas, and was a constant presence with Denver-area media. He also coached and shared his coaching knowledge by staging clinics for players and coaches and did the same for referee development. Seeking to develop a soccer culture in the state, Guennel was credited with bringing European teams to play exhibitions so that newcomers could develop an appreciation of the sport played at its highest levels.

Coincident with his drive to establish youth soccer was his campaign to have soccer recognized in the Colorado high schools. Decisive was the 1971 decision by the Colorado High School Activities Association to sanction soccer. This push also involved mobilizing lobbyists to battle school boards and school administrators to invoke Title IX in the 1970s. Again, and adding a chapter to the "Guennel Success Story," Colorado High School Athletic Association (CHSAA) activity had mushroomed from fewer than 20 teams in 1971 to 115 teams by 1992. The Colorado High School Coaches Association was also Joe's brainchild and continues to the present to promote the high school game in the state.

With increased play came the need for more, better-trained officials, and Guennel is credited with founding the Rocky Mountain Soccer Officials Association and the Soccer Officials Association of Colorado, the latter an affiliated group with U.S. Soccer.

Guennel's national endeavors to support soccer included 12 years of service with the U.S. Olympic Committee and being an active NSCAA member. He was presented the NSCAA Honor Award in 1963 and posthumously inducted into its Hall of Fame in 1999. Earlier, in 1980, he had been named to the U.S. Soccer Hall of Fame.

Most appropriately, he became the first soccer person named to the Colorado Sports Hall of Fame. At the 1991 ceremony, the then-retired Joe Guennel commented, "It's rewarding, but the thing that pleases me the most about my induction is its reflection of the sport's stability. It's part of the fabric of the community now."[159]

Coach Horst Richardson – Educating Through Soccer

His formal job at CC was teaching in the German department. Concerned not only with his players' formal education, Horst also saw in soccer coaching a means to expand their out-of-classroom educational experiences.

Want to learn what holistic soccer coaching in all about?

Then maybe a study of the 50-year career of retired Colorado College (CC) coach Horst Richardson might give one a perspective of how to meet the many player demands at an academically challenging institution. In 2019, Horst and Helen Richardson published *The History of Men's Soccer at Colorado College, 1950-2015*. Perhaps the book's legacy to the greater soccer coaching community is how taxing coaching can be in terms of all that is entailed in the development of a

Horst Richardson coached Colorado College soccer for 50 years.

soccer program. The resilience, perseverance, commitment, and creativity of the Richardsons in the retrospective contain lessons far beyond the normal coaching Xs and Os.[160]

Strengthening Player Relationships

Possibly its isolated Rocky Mountain location was instrumental in allowing for the development of unique relationships between the coach and his players. For until 1982, when it became an NCAA Division III institution, Colorado College, as an unaffiliated team, played primarily Division I-level schools. Arranging schedules meant travel to Kansas, Minnesota, Utah, New Mexico, and California for matches. Travel did not abate when the Tigers began Division III play as CC teams were forced to trek hundreds of miles each season to find Division III competition. Whether in Horst's VW bus, their own vehicles, or later on various modes of transportation, the squads' relationships and memories were strengthened on these long trips.

Some of the anecdotes are humorous. One such example is when a player pulled down Horst's shorts while he addressed the team (he didn't flinch but simply finished his talk and calmly pulled them up!). Some are poignant, as is the

336

recounting of a favorite player's death on the day the individual was inducted into the Colorado College Athletic Hall of Fame.

His formal job at CC was teaching in the German department. Concerned not only with his players' formal education, Horst also saw in soccer coaching a means to expand their out-of-classroom educational experiences. Not only did the usual seasonal journeys enhance the CC soccer involvement, but on several occasions the coach also arranged team excursions to Europe, the Far East (China and Japan), and Central and South America. In each instance, the players' on-field experiences were matched with itineraries that also included valued off field experiences.

Professor Richardson

To a degree, Richardson's approach to his classroom teaching mirrored that of his coaching. Though it focused on sharing lessons on the German language and its culture, perhaps he became best known on campus for the annual student play that was performed in German.

Ongoing in his half century of coaching was instilling in his players a sense of community service. This continued when, in 2016, the Horst and Helen Richardson Scholarship fund was established to support coaches serving the soccer communities in the Colorado, New Mexico, and Arizona regions. It was in these areas where the Colorado College men's soccer program regularly conducted volunteer projects and soccer clinics for Native American communities.

Enduring are the long-term relationships that were established by the Richardson family with the players themselves. Prior to or following CC games, wife Helen hosted the group for team-bonding meals. As an offshoot of that socialization, the coach was able to later enlist team support and helped establish an endowment that annually enhances the CC soccer team budget.

A Lengthy Soccer Coaching Career

A U.S. Soccer A licensed coach, Horst guided CC to seven conference championships in the Joe Guennel-instituted Rocky Mountain Intercollegiate Soccer League.

Born in Nürnberg, Germany, during World War II, Richardson immigrated to California in 1955 and attended the University of California-Riverside for his bachelor's and master's degrees before earning his Ph.D. in German from the University of Connecticut.

After assisting CC founding coach Bill Boddington in 1965, Horst took the team reins the following year. When he retired in 2014 following his 50th season as CC coach, Richardson had compiled a 537-304-71 record that ranked fourth among active Division III coaches. Tiger teams earned NCAA playoff bids 19 times during his tenure, including playing St. Louis University in the 1966 national championship. A U.S. Soccer A licensed coach, Horst guided CC to seven conference championships in the Joe Guennel-instituted Rocky Mountain Intercollegiate Soccer League. Richardson earned NSCAA regional Coach of the Year honors five times, including 1992, when CC was 18-2-2 and reached the NCAA Division III semifinals.

Richardson's involvement with the NSCAA and U.S. Soccer dates back to 1966. During the course of his career, he has served on the *Soccer Journal* editorial board, chaired its International Coaching and Bill Jeffrey Award committees, served as a regional representative, hosted one of the first USSF licensing courses taught by Dettmar Cramer, and accommodated NSCAA Coaching Academy courses on the Colorado College campus. He also was a member of the ISAA ratings boards.

In 2000, he received the NSCAA's prestigious Bill Jeffrey Award for longtime achievement in college soccer.

"Few soccer coaches have done as much as coach Richardson to elevate the profile of American soccer," current CC head coach Scott Palguta said. "Of course, there were many, many wins in his 50 years at Colorado College, but there were also a great number of soccer camps, clinics, coaching seminars, and community service hours."[161]

The comment, in part, alluded to the fact that Horst formerly served on the District 11 school board in Colorado Springs. In 2005, he was recognized by the Colorado Springs Sports Corporation as winner of the F. Don Miller Award for his commitment to athletics in the local community. For several years, Horst served as the State Coach of Colorado, offering course for state coaching licenses and clinics for aspiring coaches. In 2014, the Colorado Soccer Association presented him with a Lifetime Achievement Award and inducted him into its Hall of Fame.

Career Honors

In 2021, Horst Richardson completed his career hat trick of receiving the three most prestigious United Soccer Coaches awards with his election to the organization's Hall of Fame. The trio included the aforementioned Bill Jeffrey accolade and the organization's prestigious Honor Award, presented in 2018.

In acknowledging the Hall of Fame citation, he noted, "This is an award for myself and my wife, Helen, who has been with me every step of the way. We are completely overwhelmed. I was stunned when I received the Honor Award in 2018. I never expected to be recognized at that level. Induction into the Hall of Fame certainly trumps that. Receiving the call was like a bolt out of the clear blue sky."

"Not many coaches have had the pleasure of coaching at a place like Colorado College," Richardson said. "I have had the pleasure of coaching so many wonderful young men along the way, and I certainly share this award with them. Having my son Erik play for CC (1988-1992) and then coaching the team with him were highlights of my coaching career."

It was left to one of his former CC players and past president of United Soccer Coaches, Jay Engeln, to have the last word: "Horst was my coaching mentor and I am most grateful for the opportunities he provided me at Colorado College. His name will forever be synonymous with CC men's soccer."[162]

Lou Sagastume and Air Force Academy Soccer

Seeking to upgrade his coaching expertise, in 1980 the ambitious young coach began pursuit of the English FA full coaching badge. In 1982, Lou became the first American to earn the coveted coaching license.

It is apparent from researching Lou Sagastume's coaching career that it was his good fortune that his appointments in many cases were, in part, orchestrated through the actions of his former players rather than an aggressive pursuit of the same by the confident but laid-back former Guatemalan native.[163]

Following his senior season at the University of San Francisco, where as an All-America player he captained the Dons to the 1966 NCAA title, Lou coached the city's St. Ignatius junior varsity team to an unbeaten season. It was those players

Lou Sagastume's coaching career began on the West Coast and moved to the Air Force Academy in 1979.

who requested that he be named the varsity coach. From 1968 through 1972, the popular coach compiled a 65-6 record in leading the school to three league titles.

It was at St. Ignatius that the team overwhelmed an overmatched Serra High School team coached by Dick Cullen. Years later, upon the matriculation of son Chris at the Air Force Academy, Dick reintroduced himself to his former adversary. Chris (1993) and brother Rich (1999) each earned team MVP awards playing at Air Force.

Chico State and Don Batie

It was in 1972 that two former St. Ignatius players, brothers Dave and Mark Stahl, recommended that Chico State coach Don Batie hire Sagastume as his assistant. In addition to the coaching experience, Lou earned his master's degree as the Wildcat team compiled a two-year 29-3 record.

In 1977, it was Chico player Laurie DeGhetaldi who was influential in landing him his first head coaching position at San Francisco State. In his two seasons at the helm, he led the Gators to a 21-8-0 record and to two NCAA Division II Tournament berths (losing to Seattle Pacific's Cliff McCrath each time), and he was named the Far West Conference COY in 1978.

Seeking to upgrade his coaching expertise, in 1980, the ambitious young coach began pursuit of the English FA full coaching badge. In 1982, Lou became the first American to earn the coveted coaching license. The FA coaching curriculum opened his eyes. "I never quite understood in a certain situation on the field why I might have dribbled the ball when I may have been better to have passed it. That course answered a lot of soccer 'questions' for me."

Later, in 1989, and prompted by his former USF teammate Lothar Osiander, he enrolled in the USSF coaching schools and received his A coaching license.

The Air Force Academy

The esteem in which his players held Sagastume was again revealed in 1979 when another former St. Ignatius player and U.S. Air Force Academy graduate, Second Lieutenant Greg Schultz, encouraged his application for the Academy soccer coaching position.

In offering the job to Lou, AD Colonel John Clune shared that if he were to take the position, there were no monies available for moving expenses. That issue appeared to be a deal breaker until a Schultz-led USAF alumni group in San Francisco staged a fundraiser to pay for the coach's move.

In the mid-1970s, Lou had combined with the Stahl brothers to operate a soccer camp in the boys' hometown of Livermore, California. At one of the camps, Lou talked to a youngster who indicated he specifically wanted to become a left back. "I watched him play and even at a young age, he was a natural, even making overlapping runs on occasion." Years later, Mike Nutter became a four-year starter for Air Force.

The Record

As with his friend Horst Richardson at Colorado College, the Air Force coach played a schedule heavy on air miles. In his first year at the helm, the Falcons played a typical schedule that featured matches in California, Florida, Illinois, Missouri, Nevada, Ohio, and Utah.

Upon his retirement in 2007, Sagastume had compiled a 282-188-43 record in his 28 seasons at Air Force and an overall record of 303-195-43 in 30 seasons. During the 2006 season, he became the 25th coach in Division I history to reach the 300-

win plateau. Teams under his guidance were responsible for 14 of the 16 double-digit winning seasons in Academy history, nine of 23 conference championships, and four of the program's 10 NCAA Tournament appearances.

Well respected by his peers, the Falcons coach was twice named Mountain Pacific Sports Federation COY and NSCAA Midwest COY. He also earned a similar award from the Rocky Mountain Intercollegiate Soccer League.

Among those players on his USAF soccer rosters were sons Ryan (1997-2000) and Marcus Sagastume (2001-04). Ryan operates his own business, and Marcus utilizes his USAFA training flying for Fed Ex. The Fed Ex position was landed with the help of then-company pilot Chris Cullen.

Elevating Latino Coaches

Lou has been a leader in trying to help mainstream Latino coaches into the American coaching education system. To that end, he formed the Latin American Coaches Association in 1994. In recognition of his work, that advocacy group presented its annual award to Sagastume at the 2020 United Soccer Coaches Convention.

He explained the reason behind the formation of the LACA: "I think that various U.S. coaching organizations have to recognize that Latino soccer is 'street soccer,' not 'prescriptive soccer.' USSF's failure of Teofilo Cubillas at its coaching school was bothersome. He certainly had a great deal to offer as a coach of the game is concerned. That he couldn't pass a test of some sort exemplified the need to find a way of integrating the Latino soccer culture into that of this country." He cites Bora Milutinovic with offering an example to Latinos of how to integrate their coaching expertise into the U.S. soccer culture.

"I am hoping that there can be a better integration of Latino soccer coaches and its culture into mainstream American coaching. I think that each will benefit. So far there is still work to do."

Theresa Echtermeyer – An Understated Achieving Coach

"Overall I don't see big differences between my boys and girls teams. ... The main thing, whether they're boys or girls, is to be consistent and send a clear message." –Theresa Echtermeyer

She has been a year-round coach of soccer for over 25 years, invested in a pro soccer franchise, produced championship teams and quality players at the high school and club levels, and is considered an expert coach of coaches.

We're talking here about Denver's Theresa Echtermeyer, coach extraordinaire and a significant force in the growth of soccer in the Rocky Mountain region.[164]

The First Challenge: Youth Coaching

Echtermeyer had little idea as to how things would evolve when, in 1992, she began to coach teams and instruct at camps for Real Colorado Soccer Club. Obviously, she made an impression for, in 1994, she was named the club's recreational DOC, responsible

Theresa Echtermeyer is among the nation's most successful combined youth and secondary school women coaches.

for the training and oversight of coaches and players for the program's recreational teams, ages 5-18. She continued in that role until 2005, when she moved to a similar position with Highlands Ranch Soccer Association/Littleton Soccer Club. From 2015 to the present, she has been reaffiliated with Real as its director of recreational soccer. In 2007, and in recognition of her contributions to youth soccer, Colorado Youth Soccer named Theresa girls recreational COY.

Denver Lady Cougars

With the objective of allowing the better women players to continue their play at a more competitive level, in 2000, Theresa became an investor in a United Soccer League (USL) franchise.

Echtermeyer served as owner and coach of the Denver Lady Cougar team that competed in the USL's second division. By her last season, the team was known as the Real Colorado Cougars. Saddled with extensive and expense travel costs, following the 2005 season, the team folded. As Coach, Theresa led the Cougars to a 22-21-9 record that included a Western Division title in 2002.

That year, the USL awarded her its Archie Moylan Award for her great courage and outstanding humanitarianism.

As her commitment to a career in coaching evolved, Echtermeyer sought to hone her expertise, earning the NSCAA National Diploma (1994), the NSCAA

Advanced Diploma (1998), and its Premier Diploma (2002). She also obtained her USSF B Coaching License (2000) and its Youth Coaching License (2001).

High School Coaching

Along with her commitment to Real, in 1993, Echtermeyer began coaching girls teams at Green Mountain High School. In 1997 and 1999, the school captured the Colorado 5A girls championships. The titles were the first of five titles for Echtermeyer-coached teams. In 1997, 1999, 2005, 2011, and 2013, she was recipient of Colorado 5A COY awards.

In 2000, she was hired by former NSCAA president Jay Engeln to coach the girls and boys teams at the newly opened Mountain Vista High School.

In a 2011 *Soccer America* interview, she discussed the dual coaching role:

"Overall I don't see big differences between my boys and girls teams. I actually see it from team to team. Teams take on certain personalities and tendencies."[165]

"I have some teams where the reins need to be tight. Other teams are more self-disciplined, self-motivated and you don't need to put the hammer down as much. The main thing, whether they're boys or girls, is to be consistent and send a clear message."

"Let them see why you're doing something. The days of coaches saying, 'jump this high because I say to jump this high' are over."

"For me, getting the players to buy in, take ownership of their team and their team's goals, that's how I get the most out of my boys and my girls."

As for parents' reactions to her coaching both sexes at the school or youth levels, Theresa noted, "I think if they see you're knowledgeable and competent, they don't look at your gender first. I think the parents appreciate having a strong female in front of their sons. I know that a lot of these boys might be working for women someday, so that's not a bad thing."

In her 21-year Mountain Vista coaching career, her boys teams have reached the Colorado state finals twice (losing in overtime in 2010 and 2015) and her Golden Eagles girls team have captured four state titles (2005, 2011, 2013, 2017).

The End Product: Notable Players

An examination of the teams' accomplishments is in itself testimony to the end product of the Echtermeyer coaching impact. But related, of course, were the players who led the competitive teams. To that point, possibly no other U.S. coach at the secondary school level has produced as many notable players at the secondary level of play and beyond.

The most noteworthy Green Mountain product was Aleisha Cramer. After helping lead Green Mountain to state championships in 1997 and 1999, she played four season at BYU and had the potential to become one of the USWNT's best talents. A 1999-2000 Gatorade National POY and a four-time NSCAA All-America selection, in 1998, she became the third youngest woman ever to suit up for USWNT. While playing for BYU she was cited as "the most impactful player in college soccer" by April Heinrichs. Citing Sunday play as her reason, in 2002, having already earned 20 caps, she retired from further USWNT play.

In like fashion, three other Mountain Vista products have distinguished themselves. First was Chelsea Stewart. She was a stalwart on the 2005 Golden Eagles state championship team and earned NSCAA All-America honors in 2007 and 2008. She has played professionally in Germany and currently has earned 40 caps performing for the Canadian WNT.

Gabbi Miranda also starred on Mountain Vista's championship teams of 2011 and 2013. She was named the Colorado Gatorade POY in 2013 and was a three-time NSCAA All-America choice. She and Stewart were on the 2013 UCLA team that won the 2013 NCAA Division I title.

Mallory Pugh also played for Mountain Vista and was part of the 2013 state championship team. She was named the 2014-15 Gatorade National Player of the Year, the 2014 NSCAA Youth Girls National Player of the Year, and the 2015 High School Female Athlete of the Year by the Colorado Sports Hall of Fame. In 2016, at age 17, she made her first appearance with USWNT and subsequently earned 75 caps. As of 2021, she has played for the Washington Spirit and the Sky Blue FC, and she is currently playing for the Chicago Red Stars of the NWSL.

There are few high schools that can lay credit for the development of three players who have played Major League Soccer. Recently retired Taylor Kemp (Maryland) played 100 matches for DC United and at Mountain Vista was a 2009 High School boys Parade All-America selection. After being named the 2010-11 Colorado Gatorade Boys Soccer Player of the Year, Amadou Dia played at Clemson. Both he and Graham Smith (Denver) have suited up for Sporting KC.

TOPSoccer

U.S. Youth Soccer's TOPSoccer is a community-based training program for all athletes with intellectual, emotional, and/or special needs. The program strives to provide soccer opportunities for players to develop at their own pace in a safe, fun, and supportive and inclusive environment.

Theresa has worked with the Colorado TOPSoccer program as a volunteer, coach, and director. Many of her teams and players have been TOPSoccer volunteers over the years. In many cases, their initial volunteer involvement has led to their becoming engaged as volunteer and/or paid coaches of the games at various competitive levels. A win-win for TOPSoccer and the game of soccer in general!

Instructing at Coaching Schools

"Coach education is a different animal from coaching players and she, certainly, is a leader in the female "Coach Education Game" –Jeff Tipping

In addition to her youth and high school coaching, Echtermeyer's coaching expertise has been shared with aspiring coaches at United Soccer Coaches Academy programs.

Since joining the Academy staff in 2002 under DOC Jeff Tipping, she has not only been involved in instructing at Academy residential courses but also has been featured in now-United Soccer Coaches-produced videos on various topics. Theresa has also been a featured clinician at the January conventions.

Asked to comment on Theresa's coaching, Tipping named her a pioneer in coaching education. Further, he noted, "She has a great personality, an excellent sense of humor and knows her coaching education stuff. Coach education is a different animal from coaching players and she, certainly, is a leader in the female 'Coach Education Game' and she can go toe-to-toe with any male educator. She is, certainly, in the top 20 of female coach educators and has the courage and knowledge to mix it up with male educators about an issue. She is a top-class instructor with a lot of energy and a good vision of what American soccer can be."[166]

Theresa is also concerned about identification and mentoring of more women soccer coaches.

Marcelo Curi – A Soccer Entrepreneur

Chelo's expertise was also shared with boys and girls in the Colorado Olympic Development Program, where he oversaw the development of striker Casey Connor.

Marcelo Curi is known as "Chelo" to his many soccer friends, and his life's travels have taken him from Cuba, where he was born, to Spain in exile, and finally to the United States, where the family settled in the Long Island community of Garden City, New York. [168]

A National Championship

It was a life-long friend and fellow Garden City graduate, Kevin Gannon, who preceded Chelo to SUNY-Brockport and recommended him to then-coach Bill Hughes. In 1974, the pair were key members of the Golden Eagle team that captured the first NCAA Division III championship.

Drafted 19th by the NASL New York Cosmos in 1977, Curi and other Americans rode the bench that season. But it was a Cosmos-related off-field situation that was a life-changing event. It occurred when Curi volunteered to do a clinic at a New Jersey prep school where George Tarantini served as coach. "While we winged it, I got a lot of satisfaction doing it. I think that's when I made up my mind that I wanted to go into coaching. Also, when we finished they gave me a check for $200 so that was good money at the time!"

Marcelo Curi is shown following his induction into the SUNY Brockport Sports Hall of Fame.

When former Cosmos Dave Clements was appointed Denver Caribou's coach in 1978, he persuaded the lefty midfielder to join the team. Unfortunately, that year the team moved to Atlanta!

Marking time, Chelo received his teaching certificate and, that fall, began a 13-year career coaching the Regis College men. Indicative of progress made, when he assumed the job, the Rangers frequently were lopsided losers to the Air Force Academy. In Curi's final season, 1989, the Rangers were 3-0 victors over the Falcons.

Curi's playing career ended following the 1981-82 indoor season with the Denver Avalanche, where his 19 goals were the MISL team's third best.

Coaching Club and Schoolboy Soccer

Beginning in 1982, in addition to coaching Regis, Chelo became DOC with the Striker SC. By 1999, the Striker club had morphed into Storm SC and was owned by the MLS Colorado Rapids. Among the Striker products is Nat Borchers, who was a member of the MLS championship teams at Real Salt Lake and the Portland Timbers.

1999 also marked the year Chelo began a 20-year career teaching Spanish and coaching the boys team at Cherry Creek High School. He led the Bruins to the 2010 CHSAA 5A title. The Cherry Creek alumni list includes Miguel Jaime, a 2013 NSCAA All-America choice and the Gatorade POY for Colorado that year.

Chelo's expertise was also shared with boys and girls in the Colorado Olympic Development Program, where he oversaw the development of striker Casey Connor. Connor would play 16 seasons of professional soccer and earned 19 caps for the USMNT.

World Cup '94

"Can you imagine being able to hang around a player like Fernando (by 2000 he was European POY)? When I went to check out of my hotel, he picked up the tab. It didn't get any better than that." –Marcelo Curi

In 1994, Chelo's combined Spanish language and soccer background landed him a position serving as the World Cup liaison with Argentina. In that role, he was charged with looking after all the team's many off-field arrangements. On one occasion, and with the team stationed at Babson (MA) College, Chelo arranged for

Babson coach John Anderson's wife to shorten Diego Maradona's game shorts to his specifications!

In overseeing the team affairs, Chelo became close friends with fellow lefty Fernando Redondo who, in 1995, while playing for Real Madrid, invited Curi to spend a month living in Madrid. "Can you imagine being able to hang around a player like Fernando (by 2000 he was European POY)? When I went to check out of my hotel, he picked up the tab. It didn't get any better than that."

Appointed to oversee Argentina's team at the 1996 Atlanta Olympics, he didn't get a chance to renew his friendship with Redondo. Seems coach Daniel Passarella hadn't selected him based largely on the length of Fernando's hair!

But in addition to his varied coaching roles, Curi's major soccer contribution to the Denver area has been his promotion of the Coerver Camps.

West Coast Soccer – Developing a Winning Culture

Steve Negoesco – A Soccer Lifer

"I always felt I had a mission to put the game on the map by: 1) playing attractive soccer; 2) playing clean soccer, and 3) if possible, winning." –Steve Negoesco

Soccer was his passion. To some degree, it saved his life, and to a large degree, it dominated his life.

We are talking here about Steve Negoesco, who was born in New Jersey, grew up and began to master the game in Romania, returned to the United States following World War II, and, to many, is the most influential individual in terms of the growth of the game on the West Coast.

A Will to Survive

When his mother died months after his birth in 1925, his seafaring father sent him to live with his aunt and uncle in Romania. It was there that he fell in love with soccer. In 1940, the Nazis imprisoned him when Germany occupied Romania. Savvy beyond his years, he befriended and impressed his guards with his soccer skill and "arranged" his escape.

That story, along with a myriad of others, was shared with his University of San Francisco players to instruct that no mater the circumstances, the will to survive can prevail.

Following World War II, in 1945, he returned to the United States and, in 1947, enrolled at the University of San Francisco. There, he came under the influence of West Coast soccer legend,

Steve Negoesco at one time was noted as coaching as many as a dozen teams in the San Francisco area!

USF coach Gus Donoghue. While earning a degree in biology, he co-captained the 1950 team that tied Penn State at the Soccer Bowl. As a senior, he became the first West Coast player accorded first-team All-America honors.

Coaching Carousal

Upon graduation in 1951 and for the next decade, in addition to teaching biology at Giannini Junior High School, Negoesco was making soccer coaching his primary focus. Cited once as giving oversight to 10 teams at the same time, he focused on youth coaching with the Hakoah Soccer Club along with playing and coaching the San Francisco Italian Athletic Club.

In 1961, Hakoah became the first West Coast team to capture the U-19 James McGuire Cup. In 1962, and for the princely sum of $300, USF hired the 37-year old Negoesco to succeed Donoghue.

"To be perfectly honest, I never got into this with the thought of winning games," Negoesco told the *San Francisco Chronicle* in 1995. "I wanted to develop the college game to be palatable to people. I always felt I had a mission to put the game on the map by: 1) playing attractive soccer; 2) playing clean soccer, and 3) if possible, winning."[169]

But, of course, under his tutelage, USF did win. In fact, he became the first collegiate coach to win 500 games, ending his 40-year career with a 544-172-66 record. The Dons captured 22 conference titles and qualified for 32 NCAA championships, including winning the 1966, 1975, 1976, and 1980 NCAA titles. In 1976, he achieved a rare U.S. coaching "double" when the SF Italian Athletic Club won the U.S Open Cup.

"The King of West Coast Soccer"

"I also think he was able to utilize the game for social good in the sense that he was able to show that various nationalities could be taught to work together for a common goal." – Joe Dugan

What was the coaching methodology that allowed USF soccer to fashion a national presence at the intercollegiate level?

Joe Dugan, who played for the coach from 1988-90, and Lou Sagastume, a player from his 1960's team, offered their perspectives:

"Steve had his own coaching 'style,'" said Sagastume. "He had a few favored technical drills that he started every training session with. Sometimes a friend of his would stop by and they would start chatting and we'd just continue until he realized that we'd gone on too long with a particular exercise."[170]

"Once the game started, he would go up in the stands and let the team play. At halftimes, he would meet with the team and share his thoughts. He said he sat apart from the team as he didn't want to be distracted from concentrating on the game."

Fagan and Sagastume agreed that the coach preferred more experienced soccer players and was constantly scrutinizing San Francisco's cosmopolitan soccer scene looking for same. Lou had come to the city from Guatemala and noted that, over time, the USF roster included players from Nigeria, England, Brazil, Colombia, Norway, Greece, Venezuela, and Ireland. One Peruvian player, Alec Toledo, eventually became the country's president.

Dugan noted that, in short order, USF came to enjoy a reputation as a "foreign-dominated team."

"I think that Steve was a very experienced coach. He set some guidelines for the players but basically, in terms of style, he trusted his players to be able to demonstrate an advanced system that placed an emphasis on speed of play."

"I also think he was able to utilize the game for social good in the sense that he was able to show that various nationalities could be taught to work together for a common goal," said Dugan. "I know that he thought that ideally it would take 40 matches for a team to mature and achieve its potential. I guess in evaluating his coaching, he was able to speed up that process while merging the talents of players from a number of different soccer cultures. It wasn't easy, but he made it look so."

Both former players agreed that basic to Negoesco's coaching success was that he cared for people. "I know that he gave everyone a chance to prove themselves," offered Dugan. "He cared for his players as if they were his own children. In addition to playing quality soccer, there were life lessons imparted as part of the process, things about life's priorities. When he shared stories about growing up in Romania, there was a lesson in terms of developing a perspective on things."[171]

Honors and the Final Word

"He is an alumnus who lived our values as a coach educator, earning the affection of his players, motivating them to the highest levels of performance and prepping them for lives of meaning and purpose." –Father Paul Fitzgerald

By the time of his passing in 2019, the USF coaching legend had accumulated a host of coaching honors, including the following.

- Member of University of San Francisco Hall of Fame (1959)
- Member of the California Soccer Federation North Hall of Fame (1970)
- Negoesco Stadium at USF, dedicated in his honor (1982)
- Commended by United States President Ronald Reagan (1983)
- West Coast Conference Coach of the Year Award (1993)
- Lifetime Member National Soccer Coaches Association (1995)
- NISOA Merit Award (1996)
- West Coast Conference Award (2000)
- San Jose Earthquakes Recognition Award (2001)
- The Bill Jeffrey Award (2002)
- U.S. Soccer National Soccer Hall of Fame (2003)
- NSCAA Hall of Fame (2003)
- Bay Area Sports Hall of Fame (2010)
- WCC Hall of Honor (2011)
- West Coast Conference Hall of Honor (2011)

USF President Father Paul Fitzgerald's summary comments seemed to capture the essence of the man's life: "Coach Stephen Negoesco's personal story is forever intertwined with that of his longtime academic home, the University of San Francisco," Fitzgerald said. "He is an alumnus who lived our values as a coach educator, earning the affection of his players, motivating them to the highest levels of performance and prepping them for lives of meaning and purpose. His unique style of coaching emphasized skill development and game savvy during practices, then he empowered his team to take responsibility and run themselves during matches. He will be forever remembered and long missed."[172]

Lou Sagastume – A Successful Soccer Adaption[173]

... in 1961, the youngster's love for soccer had waned. ... He credits Negoesco with never giving up on him.

As a measure of the importance of soccer in his life, Luis "Lou" Sagastume, then 14, on the occasion of leaving his native Guatemala for the United States, first packed his soccer shoes. Arriving in San Francisco in 1958, he was the youngest player chosen to play for Club Guatemala in San Francisco's senior division's third league. Thus began a significant playing career that evolved into a likewise noteworthy career in coaching.

Lou Sagastume's soccer career was impacted by coach Steve Negoesco.

San Francisco Youth Soccer

Lou recalls being a standout youth player for his Guatemalan youth team, Crismo Atoyac. With his new friend, Manuel Torres, he honed his English language skills while also utilizing his advanced soccer skills to educate his mostly neophyte Lincoln Junior High School teammates in the basics of the game. He credits another friend with aligning him with the Teutonia youth team that won the state title game played at Kezar Stadium.

Sagastume and his Lincoln teammates formed the core of the none-too-prolific Herbert Hoover Junior High School soccer team. In fact, due to a part-time job he held, coach Harvey only asked him to show for games.

The club scene was where good soccer was played, and it was there that he met an individual who had a major impact on his life.

Hakoa Soccer Club

As noted, the Hakoa SC was well established in the city, and its youth club was under the direction of coach Steve Negoesco. Unfortunately, when the coach asked Lou to join the youth team in 1961, the youngster's love for soccer had waned and he turned down the invitation: "I guess I was disappointed in how soccer was being supported by the city. In Guatemala, even youth soccer drew crowds." He experimented with basketball and swimming but in 1962 rejoined Hakoa.

He credits Negoesco with never giving up on him. In his first match back with Hakoa, he scored the winning goal in the state final before a packed Balboa Stadium crowd. That outing restored his love for the game. Thus began a life-long Sagastume-Negoesco relationship.

USF and Steve Negoesco

Sagastume credits Steve Negoesco not only with providing him a soccer scholarship to the University of San Francisco but also with helping him land his first coaching job and inspiring him to become a teacher.

Lou noted that Negoesco knew every kid who played soccer in the Bay Area and credits him, along with Ernie Flebush, as the two coaches who were responsible for the development and oversight of youth soccer in San Francisco. Thus, when he was appointed head soccer coach at the University of San Francisco in 1962, the Romanian had a built-in pipeline to the city's best players.

In 1962, the newly appointed coach offered the talented midfielder a half scholarship, with other assistance coming from a work-study job. At one point, that consisted of coaching the JVs at the city's private St. Ignatius Preparatory High School.

At USF, Lou intended to study engineering, but through Steve's mentorship and guidance, he chose to major in Spanish.

During his three varsity seasons, USF achieved a combined 34-3-1 record, with the crafty Guatemalan wearing the number 10 jersey and pulling the strings from the midfield. Elected captain his final two seasons, in 1966, the Dons captured the first of Negoesco's four NCAA championships, defeating Long Island University. Following his senior season, Sagastume was named to the NSCAA All-America team.

Following USF graduation, Lou immediately turned to coaching, though he also continued his playing soccer with senior teams representing the San Francisco Athletic Club, the Greek American Club, Union Espanola, and Hakoa—all coached by Negoesco.

In 1969, Sagastume became the first American player to be drafted into the NASL when the new Oakland Clipper franchise chose him. He saw action in exhibitions against the Israeli National Team, Dynamo Kiev, and Santos (and Pele!). It was a hamstring injury suffered in the Israel match that ended his dream of making the 1972 U.S. Olympic team.

Eventually, and having been mentored by Steve Negoesco, Lou Sagastume turned to coaching, including a long tenure at the U.S. Air Force Academy. That phase of his career is covered in another chapter in the book.

Bob DiGrazia – Another Gentleman Coach

"He figured out how to upgrade the program at Cal until they were as competitive as UCLA and USF. He didn't quit trying to develop the game." –Steve Negoesco

One of the key figures in the growth and development of the game on the West Coast was Bob DiGrazia. His tireless work was fueled by his passionate love of soccer.

In addition to his successful coaching rein at the University of California at Berkeley, DiGrazia is recalled for lending exceptional organizational acumen to his university, to college soccer in general, and to the NSCAA in particular.[174]

Bob DiGrazia engaged in soccer as a successful coach and administrator of the sport.

Standout Athlete

He was born and raised by immigrant parents in San Francisco and at an early age exhibited athletic excellence. Quick of foot, DiGrazia was an all-conference soccer player at Balboa HS and the three-time city champion in the 100-yard dash. He also earned all-star accolades at San Francisco College before entering the U.S. Navy. Following service, he entered Cal-Berkeley, where he played on the Bear soccer team, earning NSCAA All-America honors in 1950.

In graduate school at Cal, he continued his soccer play, starring for the city's Olympic SC team that twice was the California State Amateur Champion. He also was selected to San Francisco City all-star teams that competed against visiting international teams such as Glasgow Celtic, Grasshoppers, and Manchester United.

Following graduation, he assisted with the Cal soccer team before assuming the part-time head coaching position in 1953. He taught full-time at Foothill Middle School, a position he held for over 20 years.

Coach/Soccer Promoter

His 27-year coaching tenure is the longest in Bear history. Highlights included taking Cal to its first two NCAA tournament appearances in 1960 and 1977. Following the 1977 season, he was named the Far West Region Coach of the Year; fifteen DiGrazia players were named to the All-America team, including three-time choice, Dan Salvemini.

Steve Negoesco, the former USF coach, said: "We used to play together when we were young, at the Olympic Club in 1950. ... He figured out how to upgrade the program at Cal until they were as competitive as UCLA and USF. He didn't quit trying to develop the game."[175]

That included organizing what was believed to be one of the first summer soccer camps held on a college campus.

NCAA Rules Committee

Well respected in the collegiate soccer community, in 1962, DiGrazia was named to the NCAA Rules Committee. He became one of the few coaches who served the full nine years on the committee and, following the end of his term, was presented the coveted NCAA Medallion for his service.

One of the committee activities that brought DiGrazia into prominence was his role in hosting the first of two NCAA University Division Soccer Tournaments in the San Francisco area. The organization and promotion of the first event, in 1966, was well attended, as Negoesco's University of San Francisco team won the first of its four national championships.

Berkeley was again selected to host the 1977 affair. DiGrazia utilized his extensive Bay Area network to promote the tournament, and for many years it was the most successful in NCAA soccer history, with more than 11,000 watching the final when Hartwick College became the smallest institution ever to capture the national title.

Stabilizing the NSCAA

"Perhaps the most notable of all are the years of tireless devotion he rendered to this organization when for all intents and purposes he was the National Soccer Coaches Association of America." –Cliff McCrath

As the NSCAA expanded in the post-World War II era, it became evident that there was a need to establish a funded position to oversee its ongoing affairs. Following an ill-fated attempt to fill the position, in 1969, the well-organized DiGrazia was named to the post.

During his 12 years of service to the NSCAA, DiGrazia computerized business matters of the association and, acting in concert with the newly-appointed treasurer, Bob Robinson, solidified the backroom operation of the organization. Under their direction, the association recorded some of its largest membership increases.

Prior to his passing in 2006, when asked what he thought were the most significant events that took place during his dozen years as executive secretary, the quiet and reserved DiGrazia listed the following:

Reorganization of the association under the new constitution in 1980, when the Executive Committee was replaced with the National Advisory Board;

the growth of the national convention;

change in the editorship and management of *Soccer Journal*; and

increased marketing ventures and sponsorships.

DiGrazia cited another undertakings that was of special interest to him during his tenure. Namely the Partners of the Americas program.

Post-1981 Accomplishments

In 1981, DiGrazia stepped down from his NSCAA role to become associate director of athletics at Cal-Berkeley. There, the affable and long-standing Berkeley alumnus worked in development for six years.

Later, following his university retirement, he was named the executive director of the California Coaches Association. There his responsibilities were quite comprehensive, since the office gave oversight to all sport coaches in the state of California.

His significant contributions to NSCAA were recognized when he was bestowed the Honor Award in 1983. In chronicling his career, Honor Award chairman Cliff McCrath stated, "Perhaps the most notable of all are the years of tireless devotion he rendered to this organization when for all intents and purposes he *was* the National Soccer Coaches Association of America. ... for 12 years he carried the bulk of responsibilities attendant to the day-to-day administration of our program."[176]

In 1991, in honor of his long service, Bob DiGrazia was named to the Cal-Berkeley Athletic Hall of Fame, and in 2010, he was posthumously inducted into the NSCAA Hall of Fame.

Julie Menendez – A Born Fighter for Soccer

When researching the athletic career of the late Julius ("Julie") Menendez, one has to hark back to the adage, "If you want to get something done, ask a busy man!"

In many ways, his career looks a lot like other coaches in the post-World War II era who were involved in various aspects of soccer beyond chalking up the usual Xs and Os, but with one exception.

Toughing It Out

Though the highlights of his soccer entanglement took place on the West Coast, his career began in East St. Louis, where he was born in 1922 to immigrant parents; his father worked in the area's zinc mines. Among Julie's Mound City friends were later baseball greats Yogi Berra and Joe Garagiola.

The exception noted was that the tough neighborhood led Julie to become an expert boxer as a youth, eventually becoming the city's Golden Gloves flyweight boxing champion in 1942. Entering the Navy in 1943, he served as an aviator and continued to box, retiring undefeated when he left the service in 1946.

Upon release, he continued his pugilistic career and to play senior soccer in St. Louis. In 1946, he was crowned national Golden Gloves champion at 147 pounds. His amateur career included bouts in New York's Madison Square Garden, and when he turned professional, his bouts included a preliminary match prior to the 1947 Rocky Graziano-Tony Zale middleweight title bout in Chicago Stadium.

San Jose State University Successes

Relocating to San Francisco, he played soccer in the city's First Division from 1947 through 1950 and utilized the GI Bill and his boxing skill to attend San Jose State University. During his undergraduate years, he also served as the boxing coach at nearby Santa Clara University. He graduated *magna cum laude* from SJSU in 1950 and earned his master's degree from Stanford University in 1951. Asked in later years how he spent his spare time, he replied he enjoyed reading a dictionary.

Menendez joined the San Jose State coaching staff in 1953 as an assistant boxing coach, and a year later, in 1954, he revived its men's soccer program that had been disbanded in 1943.

He had little initial success with the soccer team, but in seven seasons as the Spartans' boxing coach, he directed the team to the 1958, 1959, and 1960 NCAA Championships and coached 15 NCAA boxing champions. 1960 was the final year that the NCAA sanctioned boxing as an intercollegiate sport.

1960 also marked a milestone in his boxing career, as Julie was named coach of the U.S. Olympic boxing team. Competing in Rome, light heavyweight Cassius Clay was among three American gold medalists.

Elevating Spartan Soccer

Off-field, the coach kept things "light," frequently leaving the players transfixed with his endless assortment of card tricks. –Gary St. Clair

Apparently energized by a Menendez adage posted in the locker room ("The difference between being good and great is a little extra effort"), San Jose soccer turned things around beginning in 1963, when the team earned the first of its 11 NCAA Tournament berths.

In 1968, the team, led by three All-America players, Manni Fernandez, Fred Nourzad, and Ed Storch, compiled a 13-1 record and advanced to the NCAA semifinals before losing to eventual co-champions, Maryland.

The trio joined the 23 All-America players who donned San Jose colors. In 1968, Fernandez was named winner of the Hermann Trophy and went on to play with the 1972 U.S. Olympic team. Eventually, he turned to coaching, and he led the Presentation (CA) High School girls to 17 league titles. Among his players was Aly Wagner, who starred for the USWNT from 1998-2008.

In his 36 seasons as the San Jose State men's soccer coach, Menendez's teams won 295 games and had 22 consecutive winning seasons from 1963 through 1984.

His successor, Gary St. Clair, who played for him from 1970-73, described him as a "players' coach," knowledgeable but unruffled on the sidelines. Off-field, the coach kept things "light," frequently leaving the players transfixed with his endless assortment of card tricks.[177]

Growing the Game

He found time to author Soccer, *a book about coaching the sport ... and also produced instructional films on soccer.*

Many recall his deep, commanding voice that underpinned an ability to take on and lead various soccer initiatives.

Well respected in the soccer coaching community and known for adhering to his motto, "The standards of sport are never compromised," coach Menendez was the chair of the NCAA Soccer Rules Committee from 1968 to 1975. He was awarded a coveted NCAA Medallion for his outstanding organizational service. He found time to author *Soccer,* a book about coaching the sport and also produced instructional films on soccer.

In 1972, he became the first person to coach Olympic teams in two sports when he assisted fellow St. Louis colleague Bob Guelker with the U.S. soccer team at the Germany games. That team included former San Jose players Manni Fernandez and Jim Zylker on its roster. In 1976, he was named head coach of the Olympic team that fell short of qualifying for the Canadian soccer event. Between soccer- and boxing-related assignments, Menendez was well traveled, having visited 22 foreign countries during his career.

Coach Julie Menendez received the NSCAA Honor Award in 1984. Wife Doris and HA chair Cliff McCrath were present.

A professional physical educator, Julie served as a past president of the California Association of Heath, Physical Education and Recreation, Santa Clara County. He also served on the Minneapolis Conference of Physical Fitness, the predecessor to John F. Kennedy's President's Council on Physical Fitness.

During the 1970s, he served as a color analyst on San Jose Earthquakes broadcasts. Oh, and in his spare time, his creative energies patented a golf-teaching device!

Acknowledgements

"... a quiet genius in all the right ways." –Cliff McCrath

His honors included the NSCAA Honor Award (1984), induction into the San Jose Sports Hall of Fame (1996), the Spartan Legend Award (2001), and induction into the Multi-Ethnic Sports Hall of Fame and NSCAA Hall of Fame (2018).

Cliff McCrath captured the essence of the man when, upon presentation of the 1984 NSCAA Honor Award, he summarized, "Yes, Julie is a lot of things: indeed he is a multi-talented, multi-faceted man among men. He is an outstanding coach; a better-than-average author; an honest and exemplary citizen; an achiever; a counselor; a sensitive and pensive teacher; a gold medal athlete; a decent and thoughtful father; a loving husband; a humorist of sorts; a quiet genius in all the right ways."[178]

Lothar Osiander – Committed to the Game

"He brings to the table the same level of passion to his current boys teams as he did to the national and Olympic teams and the same is true whether he is teaching a State "D" Coaching Course or the "A" licensed course on the National level." –Bob Gansler

Listening to Lothar Osiander recreate the highlights of his soccer life is like watching a movie that jumps from one interesting focus to the next but always concludes with a happy ending.[179]

And there have been a number of noteworthy soccer achievements by this naturalized citizen and U.S. soccer coach that have left their imprint on our country's soccer ascendancy.

German Soccer Memories

"We grew up outside Munich and in the post-war period due to the war the fields we played on were miserable. There was no formal youth soccer, just pickup soccer and being a teenager, I played against older guys. The thing I remember is that they thought for some reason drinking water was a no-no. We had no soccer boots and had but two soccer balls; one to practice with, one to use in any games the older guys arranged."

His German education focused on skills needed in the hospitality industry. With the aid of an uncle living in San Francisco as a sponsor, the family landed in San Francisco in 1958.

San Francisco/Steve Negoesco

"Rare was the promising player who escaped his notice." –Lothar Osiander

Lothar's soccer passion was sated by play in the very competitive San Francisco Soccer Football League, where his speed and ball skills attracted the attention of University of San Francisco coaching legend Steve Negoesco.

Unable by age restrictions to ply his waiter skills, and following a year's hiatus at a junior college, Osiander, in 1965, accepted one of the first USF soccer scholarships offered by the Romanian-born coach.

Regarding Negoesco, Lothar offered: "He knew the game and, most importantly, he knew how to recruit. The cosmopolitan culture of the city made it a hotbed for soccer. There were four games every Sunday at Balboa Park and Steve was always on hand to view the games. Rare was the promising player who escaped his notice. He also developed a pipeline to good Norwegian players."

As for the coach's training sessions, Lothar noted that the USF team shared a field with the football and baseball teams. "Frequently our practices were small-sided games. That's all we had space for."

Negoesco utilized Osiander's quickness as a right-winger but at times switched him and the other wide player during matches. "Of course, that is a bit of the norm today, playing a left-footed player of the right side, and vice-versa. But Steve did that in the 60s."

"We all respected Steve Negoesco. I think the fact that there were over 1,000 persons at his funeral reflected that."

The Northern California Soccer Football League

It was in the NCSFL, once his playing days subsided in 1970 ("I moved from striker to the midfield and then sweeper"), that he turned to coaching.

NCSFL President Rudy Studnik appointed him coach of the league's all-star team. Seeking to grow the game, Rudy scheduled the all-stars to play international teams as Bayern Munich, the Swiss Grasshoppers, and Mexican teams UAM and Chivas.

"I scouted all the league, talked to all the good players and we got together a very competitive team that held its own against these teams. One time Walt Chyzowych brought the U.S. National Team to play us and we beat them. I think that added to Walt's opinion of me as a coach."

Part of the Osiander coaching success resulted from his affiliation with the Greek-American SC. A social club with a huge interest in the game, it financed a highly competitive senior team that won five consecutive NCSFL titles and captured National Open titles in 1985 and 1994.

What was it like coaching a senior team? Turns out that when working full-time as a waiter at Graziano's, a fashionable San Francisco restaurant, Lothar arranged his schedule to train the team twice weekly. "While Greek in name, we had a lot of nationalities on the roster, probably only a couple of Greeks. We paid them $25 a game but only if they showed for practices. They loved the game and they didn't mind that rule. We practiced all over the place, baseball fields, wherever. It was year-round."

Among the players were Nigerians Andy Atuegbu and Godwin Odiye, who each achieved All-America status at USF. In 1989, when the team represented the United States in the CONCACAF Champions Cup, they and a number of non-American players were not with the team when it lost 5-1 to UNAM in Mexico City.

Cramer and the Coaching Schools

"We all became 'Little Cramers!'"–Lothar Osiander

Lothar was one of the first West Coast coaches to earn his USSF A coaching license under Dettmar Cramer.

As for many coaches, it was a life-changing experience. "You knew he was a tough guy. At 18 he had been a paratrooper in the war. He was just great. I remember Lenny Lucenko wrote down all his sessions. That book became our guide in the coaching schools. His [Cramer's] coaching became our coaching. We all became 'Little Cramers!'"

Beginning in 1974, and for the next 20-plus years, Lothar traveled the country as one of Walt Chyzowych's (Cramer's successor) coaching staff. Noted as an

Lothar Osiander was a dedicated teacher, on and off the field.

excellent instructor, Lothar shared that it didn't happen by accident. "Outside the school settings, I worked on my technique so that when I had a session on dribbling, I could provide a good picture for the candidates."

He credits Chyzowych with first identifying and then inspiring a talented cadre of staff coaches. "We all knew he was a great player but he was also an excellent teacher." And fun. "At the end of the day we'd all gather to have a wine with him and he'd write down the next day's coaching assignments on a cocktail napkin. His legacy lives on through the lives of his coaching staffs."

By 1978, as part of a U.S. Olympic committee drive to improve the country's international competitive standing in all sports, the USOC staged summer sports festivals. Chyzowych eyed the U-23 competitions as a means to help identify talent to man national team rosters. The four teams were chosen regionally, and Osiander was placed in charge of the western region. "I knew all the good players and traveled on my nickel to see those who were recommended to me by others who I trusted." The position lasted for 10 years.

Coaching the National Team

Impressed with his coaching and organizational successes and reeling from failure to win a place in the 1982 Mexican World Cup, in 1986, U.S. Soccer hired Osiander as national team coach, principally to prepare a team for the 1988 Olympic Games.

After a first-round comeback of historic proportions versus Canada, the team easily qualified for South Korea, where a 1-1-1 record did not qualify them for second-round play. "We simply did not have enough preparation time. Also the main senior focus was on indoor play and, with MLS struggling to survive, coaches of those teams were reluctant to release their players to us."

Prior to a pre-arranged turnover of the team to Bob Gansler, Lothar led off the first World Cup qualifying round with a tie and a win over Jamaica. When Paul Caligiuri's goal propelled the United States to the 1990 WC in Rome, 11 of the players on the team roster were holdovers from the 1988 Olympic team.

Lothar remained on as coach of various U.S. Soccer teams before leading the U-23 team to a gold medal at the 1991 Pan-American Games in Cuba that included a win over archrival Mexico. Subsequently, the team easily qualified for the 1992 Olympics in Spain. While critics faulted the coach for not playing the team's leading striker, Steve Snow, as usual, there was more to the story than met the eye. Osiander shared that Snow was nursing a cruciate injury and was in no shape to play. Unfortunately, in his absence the team suffered a 2-1 loss to Italy before 64,000 at Barcelona's famed Camp Nou Stadium. The loss effectively ended its medal chances, after which Osiander's contract was not renewed.

The Osiander Approach

... the savvy coach shared that it is no secret to coaching success: identify good players with character.

His post-national team work has included coaching the Los Angeles Galaxy as it entered first season Major League Soccer play in 1996. He took the team to the first MLS Cup and, after creating a 2-0 lead, fell to Bruce Arena's DC United team in overtime, 3-2.

Following a later stint with the San Jose Earthquakes that ended his MLS work in 2001, Lothar scratched his coaching itch by leading various Bay Area youth teams. He has been successful coaching San Ramon's Tri-Valley Soccer Club U-16 and U-17 teams that captured first-place medals in notable competitions as the Surf and Nomad Cups.

He has been impressed with the speed of play at the youth level. "In my playing days you worked the ball slowly, trying to beat players one on one. These kids today play a lot of one-touch soccer all over the field."

Queried as to his approach to successful youth coaching, the savvy coach shared that there is no secret: identify good players with character.

"I spent a lot of time scouting games. I like to evaluate a player's personality. Is he part of a team's commonality? Does he work for other teammates? Is he a good citizen to begin with? Does he understand the responsibility involved in being a good team member?"

"I've found that such individuals are more at ease and receptive to coaching."

Ever the politician, Lothar reminded, "If the team is at ease, the parents are at ease. And you want the parents to be happy because in case of youth soccer, they have to foot the bill."

Perhaps the quote of former National Team coach Bob Gansler on the occasion of Osiander's reception of the 2007 Walt Chyzowych Award speaks to the man's coaching strength: "He brings to the table the same level of passion to his current boys teams as he did to the national and Olympic teams and the same is true whether he is teaching a State "D" Coaching Course or the "A" licensed course on the National level." Indeed.[180]

Steve Sampson – Impressive Credentials[181]

It seems when reviewing details of their coaching careers, individuals love sharing memories about matches long past but clear as a bell's ring in their retelling today.

And so it was with one-time United States men's soccer coach Steve Sampson as he recreated events leading up to the World Cup qualifier on November 9, 1997, at the famed Azteca Stadium in Mexico City.

With the U.S. Soccer treasury full, Sampson elected to isolate the U.S. team at California's Big Bear Mountain Resort for 10 days. Big Bear's 7,000-foot altitude nearly matched that of Azteca's and that, along with demanding training sessions, increased the collective team stamina and team confidence as it headed to the crucial qualifier.

Clearly the underdog, the U.S. chances were further dampened when Jeff Agoos was red-carded in the first half. But Sampson's training strategy paid off: "We battled and as the game wore on and as we started to string passes together late in the game, the 120,000 disgruntled Mexican fans started to shout 'Ole' after each successive pass."

At game's end, the 0-0 tie represented the first time a U.S. team had earned a point in Mexico. Coaching Mexico that eventful day was former USMNT mentor Bora Milutinovic. "I think because I knew how he would have his team play certainly helped us," said Sampson, referring to his long relationship with the well-traveled Serbian coach.

Despite the fact that the tie cemented Mexico's place in the World Cup, none of the Mexican team or officialdom showed for the post-game meal hosted by Bora. The Mexican coach was fired the next day.

Known on Many Campuses

Raised in Los Altos (CA), Steve earned accolades playing three sports at Homestead High School. He sharpened his play and his Spanish language proficiency playing with an all-Hispanic youth team before enrolling at UCLA in 1974. The Bruins under coach Terry Fisher reached the semi-final round of the NCAA Tournament that season.

Steve left UCLA and enrolled at Foothill JC where, following a red shirt season, he earned junior college All-America honors playing for George Avakian.

He finished his career within a few miles from home when he enrolled at San Jose State in 1977, where he played for coach Julie Menendez. Now a junior academically, the 19-3 1977 Spartan team was bound for the NCAAs until ruled out because of play of an ineligible player. A knee injury then ended Steve's senior season.

Initial Coaching Positions

His UCLA salary was $2,500 for the season, and tutoring Spanish was one of the side jobs he took on to make ends meet.

After SJSU, and as with most novice coaches, Sampson scratched out a living coaching high school and ODP soccer, assisting Avakian at Foothill and, at the same time, earning his master's at Stanford.

Steve described his time (1982-86) serving as assistant coach to Sigi Schmid at UCLA as a "phenomenal experience. He allowed me to grow as a coach, gave me plenty of latitude and valued my opinion." His ODP experience was invaluable in that he could recruit for the Bruins in Southern California and in the Pacific Northwest. His UCLA salary was $2,500 for the season and tutoring Spanish was one of the side jobs he took on to make ends meet.

In the fall of 1985, UCLA captured its first NCAA Division I title. Earlier, in 1984, Steve was granted time off to work with the Los Angeles Olympic Committee as the outlying sports coordinator for the sites at Annapolis, Harvard, and Stanford. "The first job assignment was to set the draw for the Olympic soccer tournament. I was given one month to put the draw in Pasadena together." The position introduced him to Alan Rothenberg and FIFA Secretary-General Sepp Blatter. Of course, the overall success of men's soccer at the Olympics was pivotal in FIFA's awarding of the 1994 World Cup to the United States.

By 1985, he was a full-time UCLA employee and, in addition to his coaching, was assigned to assist the associate athletic director for business. Among his projects was oversight of the remodel of the men's basketball locker room. Among the UCLA side benefits was the ability to view the techniques of several legendary coaches such as Al Scates (volleyball), Ron Ballatore (swimming), and Valorie Field (gymnastics). He also acquired a signed copy of John Wooden's famed Pyramid of Success.

By 1986, Sampson was ready to become a head coach, and Santa Clara agreed. Following his Santa Clara successes he was onto coaching at the international level of play.

U.S. National Team Coach

"First Americans do not generally respect CONCACAF soccer. They don't realize that many of those team rosters are comprised of full-time professionals playing on competitive teams in Europe or elsewhere." –Steve Sampson

With Milutinovic's resignation as USMNT coach leaving the job open, Sampson filled the USMNT breach, serving as interim coach of the USMNT B national team, as early in 1995 it suffered 0-1 away losses to Belgium and Costa Rica.

Steve Sampson is shown in 1995 as head coach of the USMNT with assistants Clive Charles and Milutin Soskic to his right.

The results were encouraging enough that U.S. Soccer retained him on an interim basis as the team prepared for the USA Cup in June followed by the Copa America Cup the following month.

The U.S. team captured the June tournament with a 3-2 win over Nigeria and a 4-0 victory over Mexico at RFK Stadium. The loss represented the worst defeat ever suffered by Mexico to a U.S. team. The tournament concluded with a tie against Colombia in Miami.

Following the USA Cup, the United States participated in the Conmebol-sponsored Copa America Cup. The outing in Uruguay was marred by a confrontation between the U.S. team and the U.S. Soccer organization. Knowing of the Federation's sudden influx of cash from the 1994 World Cup, the players were holding out for increased compensation. With an interim status already placing him in no-man's land in terms of his standing with the team, Sampson threw down the gauntlet on the Friday before the Sunday, July 8, match with Chile.

"I had scheduled a 5 pm meeting with the players and five minutes before the start of the meeting no one had showed. I was furious but my assistant Clive Charles prevailed on me to wait. The players arrived and I told them in no uncertain terms that I wanted their respect and full committed effort from them." They agreed.

Two goals from Eric Wynalda sparked a historic 2-1 win over the Chileans. The victory represented the first-ever triumph by a U.S. team over a South American team on their home soil. Six days later came a 3-0 win over Argentina that had the Uruguayan fans in support of the American team and Maradona congratulating the team afterwards on its performance. Another win over Mexico (via PKs) sent the team to the semifinals, where it lost to Brazil, 1-0.

The team's play encouraged U.S. soccerdom that good things were in the offing for the team as it sought qualification for the 1998 World Cup in France. But Sampson, now signed as head coach, saw the lead-up as a "contentious time. First Americans do not generally respect CONCACAF soccer. They don't realize that many of those team rosters are comprised of full-time professionals playing on competitive teams in Europe or elsewhere. Also at the onset of the MLS, many of our U.S. players came home from Europe to play in a far less competitive league. And finally, from 1996 onward, we rarely had full teams for every preparation match."

Thus, the importance of the November 1997 match with Mexico was that it cemented the U.S. place in the World Cup in France.

Unfortunately for the coach, there were what turned out to be unrealistic expectations as the USMNT headed for France. And Steve's MLS coaching stint was also revealing in its coaching demands.

Back to the College Game

Following that, the Samson family moved from Los Angeles to Avila Beach on the central coast of California. For several years he coupled his vast soccer knowledge with Spanish fluency to stay in the game as a soccer color commentator in the United States and Mexico.

In 2015, the still energetic Sampson returned to the coaching ranks as head men's coach at Cal Poly University. Subsequently, he has directed the Mustangs to two Big West appearances and one NCAA tournament appearance, led by several Cal Poly players who have been drafted by MLS teams. He stated that in returning to college coaching he again has enjoyed mentoring young men. He also acknowledged that the school's San Luis Obispo's beauty, quality of life, and close proximity to the Pacific Ocean have been an added bonus.

Impacting Los Angeles Soccer Development

Sigi Schmid – A Massive Coaching Contributor

… many point to Schmid's facility to evaluate talent and then to apply the right dose of coaching to allow that ability to reach its potential as the basis for his success at UCLA and beyond.

Sigi Schmid's German heritage steered him to soccer, and his accomplishments in the game have left a legacy that few U.S. coaches can match.

Coach Sigi Schmid (foreground) is shown with Seattle Sounder staff including current coach Brian Schmetzer to his right (Seattle Sounders Photo).

Whether as player and later coach at his alma mater, UCLA, as mentor for U.S. national teams, or as leader of three Major League Soccer franchises, Schmid achieved a record for success that marks him as one of the modern game's most successful coaches.

A Talented Player

As a youngster, Schmid was encouraged by his parents to strike a balance between his soccer and academics. AYSO founder, Han Stierle, and a local coach, Joe Bonchonsky, also spotted his skill and fostered his play.

Hugely successful UCLA coach Dennis Storer (103-10-10 during his tenure) had a proven talent for assessing player talents and merging rosters and, seeing Sigi's skill, plugged him into the lineup for four years. Three of Storer's career losses occurred in the NCAA playoffs to St. Louis University, with Schmid on the defeated 1972 and 1973 teams. Schmid's final season was played under one-year coach Terry Fisher.

Post-graduate years included earning his MBA in accounting at USC and continuing to play in the Greater Los Angeles Soccer League. He also was a part-time assistant to Fisher's successor, Steve Gay. When Gay left following the 1979 season, Schmid put his accounting degree in mothballs and, in 1980, begin a 19-year UCLA coaching career.

Huge Success at UCLA

Possessed of a competitive spirit that at times boiled over, and with a penchant for soccer detail, many point to Schmid's facility to evaluate talent and then to apply the right dose of coaching to allow that ability to reach its potential as the basis for his success at UCLA and beyond.

Beginning in 1983, UCLA under Schmid made 16 straight NCAA tournament appearances as the team recorded a 322-63-33 record. In total, UCLA fielded 42 players who earned All-America honors under Schmid's tutelage. Led by All-America choices Dale Ervine and Paul Caligiuri, the Bruins captured the first of three national titles in 1985.

Brad Friedel, Chris Henderson, Cobi Jones, Mike Lapper, Joe-Max Moore, and Billy Thompson were All-America selections and led the team to its second title in 1990. Five more All-America choices, Carlos Bocanegra, Seth George, Josh Keller, Tom Poltl, and Matt Reis, led the way as UCLA won the 1997 championship.

UCLA's Contributions to the USMNT

Perhaps more importantly, 15 of Schmid products manned various USMNT World Cup rosters beginning in 1990, when Paul Caligiuri's goal sent the U.S. team to its first World Cup appearance since 1934. Chris Henderson, Paul Krumpe, and David Vanole joined him on the 1990 team.

When totaled, the UCLA soccer dynasty has seen nearly 2,500 USMNT appearances by Bruin players, with Cobi Jones' 164 caps leading the way. Caligiuri (114), Bocanegra (110), Joe-Max Moore (100), Friedel (92), Frankie Hejduk (84), and Eddie Lewis (81) also made significant contributions to the national team efforts.

Also attesting to the quality of Schmid players, when the MLS began operations in 1996, and for the next four seasons, 23 UCLA players were drafted.

U.S. Soccer Calls

In addition to giving oversight to the UCLA program, Sigi joined Steve Sampson and Timo Liekoski as assistant coaches to Bora Milutinovic when the USMNT prepared for the 1994 World Cup. The team roster included five UCLA grads, with Mike Lapper joining Caligiuri, Friedel, Jones, and Moore on the squad that reached the second round of play.

In 1999, U.S. Soccer named Schmid coach of the U.S. U-20 team that reached second-round play of the FIFA World Cup tournament held in Nigeria.

On to the MLS

Upon his MLS departure, Schmid had accumulated the most wins (320) in league history and, in 2019, the league renamed its annual coaching award the Sigi Schmid Coach of the Year Award.

In 1999, Schmid began a nearly 20-year career coaching professional soccer.

As the late Glenn Myernick shared one time, coaching at the MLS level has its own set of challenges. Asked the difference between coaching at the college level and training his then-Colorado Rapids team, he noted that the season began in February and concluded in December, "This [coaching] is not a sprint; it's a marathon!"

Schmid enjoyed instant success when he left UCLA in 1999 to coach the Los Angeles Galaxy. The team finished 17-9 and he was named MLS COY. Alexi Lalas noted that Schmid created a new environment that demanded 100 percent commitment by the players every day. The competitive spirit mentioned? Following a 2-0 loss to DC United in the MLS Cup, Sigi's dismissive comments about the officials resulted in a fine and a suspension.

The highlight of the 2000 season was the Galaxy's capture of the 2000 CONCACAF Champions' Cup. Led by two former UCLA players, Cobi Jones and Sasha Victorine, in 2001, LA won the U.S. Open Cup after losing to San Jose in the MLS Cup.

Success followed in 2002 when Schmid led LA to the MLS "double," winning the Supporters Shield for the best season record and following that with a 1-0 win over New England for its first MLS Cup.

The 2003 season was the team's first losing season, and though the team was in first place midway through the 2004 (and his fifth in charge) season, the Schmid messaging had lost its impact, and he was released, having compiled a 79-53-32 record.

Schmid returned to the MLS in 2006 to coach the Columbus Crew. By his third season, the team completed another "double," and his resume now included a second COY accolade.

In 2009, Schmid returned to the West Coast as coach of the new MLS Seattle Sounders FC. There he lasted six-plus seasons. From 2009 to 2016, Schmid led the Sounders to seven playoff appearances, four more Lamar Hunt U.S. Open Cup titles, and the MLS Supporters Shield in 2014. Long favoring a defensive style of play, Sigi spent some time in 2015 embedded with FC Roma, studying their counter-attacking play.

Following a mediocre 2015 season and a slow start in 2016, the Sounders and Schmid parted ways, and he was replaced by his assistant, Brian Schmetzer. After an announcing gig with ESPN, he returned home to the Galaxy in 2017, but the combination of the club's playing fortunes and his lingering physical issues resulted in his departure by fall 2018.

Upon his MLS departure, Schmid had accumulated the most wins (320) in league history and, as noted, in 2019, the league renamed its annual coaching award the Sigi Schmid Coach of the Year Award.

Mr. Nice Guy – Schmetzer

"Sigi's memory and knowledge of the sport was better than anybody's, still to this day. He could remember everything." –Brian Schmetzer

Brian Schmetzer followed Sigi at Seattle and has taken the Sounders to new heights. In a 2021 *Soccer America* interview, he was quick to credit Schmid with helping form his coaching style.[182]

"Sigi was the guy with the knowledge. Sigi could remember training sessions, he could remember players, he could remember games, particular plays in a certain game about where he took this tactic and did this and that. Sigi's memory and knowledge of the sport was better than anybody's, still to this day. He could remember everything." He also credits Sigi, a fellow German, with giving him the experience factor of what MLS is truly like.

Possibly most telling was Brian's personal comment: "Sigi wasn't just a great coach. He's a really nice man, really super-nice man, always willing to help. Just generally a nice guy."

Sigi never saw a soccer ball that he didn't want to kick. Also, unfortunately, he did not pass up a meal that he didn't want to consume. Plagued by overweight and associated heart issues, he passed away on Christmas Day in 2019 while waiting for a heart transplant.

Sigi Schmid's imprints remain through the roles that many of his players continue to play in the game.

Ralph Perez – Living His Dream

Reflecting on his long and varied career in the growth of the U.S. game, current University of Redlands (CA) coach Ralph Perez states that "I am totally living my dream." On another occasion he reiterated, "I've had a great run . . . sometimes you have to pinch yourself a little bit."[183]

Playing at SUNY Oneonta

Growing up in the predominantly Hispanic community of Brentwood, NY, Perez took his soccer and basketball talents to the State University of New York's Oneonta campus in 1970.

While his basketball fortunes would ebb ("I sat on the bench and that later enabled me to empathize with what substitutes have to deal with") in time his soccer immersion become all-encompassing. He shared, "I never realized before enrolling what a great soccer hotbed existed in Oneonta. Every Hartwick game drew crowds and by my junior year we were attracting great crowds ourselves."

Coach Ralph Perez is living his dream at the University of Redlands.

Following a 4-7 season in 1970, and aided by a full-court recruiting campaign by coach Garth Stam (aided by Francisco Marcos), by 1972 the Red Dragons defeated Hartwick 3-0 before an estimated crowd of 8,000 fans on their way to the NCAA College Division title game, where they lost 1-0 to Bob Guelker's SIU-Edwardsville team.

By senior year, Perez' starting role was hard-earned, as Oneonta's only loss by 1-0 to Hartwick eliminated the team from the NCAA Division I playoff.

Moving to California

"Probably there is no other sport that educates coaches as does soccer." –Ralph Perez

With a teaching degree in hand and his professional playing career set aside ("I just wasn't good enough"), Perez followed Horace Greeley's advice and moved west to California in the fall of 1974. He landed a teaching job in East Los Angeles and then, aided by Hartwick friend Terry Fisher, landed a part-time soccer coaching position at Whittier College.

That previous summer, he enrolled in the USSF Coaching School, where he earned his C license: "I really had no idea of what coaching was about but in that week I now had a solid foundation of how to approach coaching." By 1977 he had achieved his goal of obtaining his A license and the following year was tabbed by Walt Chyzowych to join the USSF Coaching School staff.

His master's thesis ("The Uniqueness of the USSF Coaching School") at Whittier was based on his Coaching School experiences. He explained: "Probably there is no other sport that educates coaches as does soccer. Coaches of other sports may attend clinics or land assistant jobs and learn to coach that way. But soccer has had the schools where young coaches can receive instruction from experienced mentors."

Coaching With Gansler

"From his [Gansler] presence, (impeccable, never a hair out of place!) to his organization, everything is planned." –Ralph Perez

After one year assisting at Cal-Fullerton, his first full-time job was at Cal-State Los Angeles in 1978, where he initiated the men's program. By 1980, he had developed a pipeline to talented players in the LA area and in his third season taken the city school to a conference title and a bid to the NCAA Division II Tournament.

Moving on to the University of Santa Clara (1981-85), his tenure was marked by a NSCAA Far West Coach of the Year Award in 1983. By 1989, his successor, Steve Sampson, had guided the Broncos to the NCAA Division I title.

Ralph also started women's soccer at Cal State San Bernardino in 1988.

Adhering to earlier advice never to shut a door when opportunity knocks, in 1989 he utilized his USSF connection and joined USMNT coach Bob Gansler as assistant coach for the U.S. Under-20 men's team. That group's fourth-place finish at the FIFA U-20 Tournament earned some international respect for the United States. A majority of that team roster helped the U.S. qualify for the 1990 Italian World Cup.

Ralph feels that coach Gansler has never received proper credit for his role in guiding those teams. While serving as his assistant in Italy as well as observing his teaching at the coaching schools, he admits to being a charter member of the Gansler fan club: "From his presence, (impeccable, never a hair out of place!) to his organization, everything is planned. He may have a training session early in the week but he has an idea as to how it will be fit into an overall weekly coaching scheme. With Bob, everything has a natural coaching flow to it."

Following Italy, it was Bora Milutinovic in as USMNT coach, and Perez pivoted to replace Mike Berticelli at Old Dominion (VA) University. Honored as regional COY in 1991 as ODU captured the Colonial Athletic Conference title, the Perez' ODU record includes a 4-0 win over Berticelli's Notre Dame team.

With the startup of MLS, the Perez name was affixed to various teams, primarily as assistant to noted league coaches.

At Redlands and Upon Reflection

"... along the way you have gotten to know such great people and you want to stay in the game and continue those relationships." –Ralph Perez

With over 40-plus years in the game, and now approaching 70, Ralph Perez shows no signs of slowing down, as in 2020 he entered his 15th season as coach of the NCAA Division III University of Redlands team.

Since returning to his Division III roots (Oneonta was playing at the Division III level when he enrolled), Ralph has directed the Bulldogs to a 208-67-21 record that has included six bids to the DIII Tournament and nine conference titles. On three occasions (2011, 2015, 2016) he was been United Soccer Coaches Regional Coach of the Year.

Asked about his future plans, Perez replied enthusiastically, "I still love coaching. Each season offers another challenge. You can think you've planned for every game and then it throws you a curveball. You have to adjust on the fly. Further, I think coaches can make a big difference in players' lives. And being around young people keeps you young. Also along the way you have gotten to know such great people and you want to stay in the game and continue those relationships. As I've said, I sometimes have to pinch myself in terms of how lucky I've been."

The Perez Tree

As noted earlier, Ralph's Puerto Rican heritage aided his coaching career, particularly when recruiting.

He shared that his Spanish fluency is passable. "It probably would have been better but my parents favored us speaking English, but only when we visited our grandparents was Spanish dominant."

He first recalls the language as being influential when he recruited Guatemalan Carlos Juarez and Mexican Martin Vasquez to Cal State Los Angeles. Smiling, he recalled, "I think speaking their native tongue made the parents comfortable with what I was selling."

Both players have gone on to long soccer coaching careers. Juarez has assisted or coached several U.S. Soccer national youth teams as well as assisted Jurgen Klinsmann with the USMNT from 2011-16. Vasquez is perhaps the only player to have played for both Mexico and the United States and has been affiliated with various MLS teams, including serving as head coach of Chivas USA in 2010.

Speaking of family, one of Ralph's regrets is that his brother Ray has not been along for his coaching journey. Long-time coach at Brentwood High School on Long Island, Ray passed away in 1995. Ray's soccer legacy includes mentoring current UConn coach Ray Reid as a high school player.

One Redlands's product, Richie Marquez, enjoyed a four-year stint with the MLS Philadelphia Union team.

Still giving back to the game, Perez recently spliced in a two-hour preseason training session with the 2019 Brentwood team. "I had a large group and I had to do it on the fly. I kept them busy for two hours." He doesn't know if it was the basis for the team's later success or not, but Brentwood recorded an unbeaten 22-0 season and won the New York State Class AA title. Post-season, coach Ron Eden's team was rated number one among the nation's high school soccer teams.

During his time with U.S. Soccer, Ralph has been able to teach-coach-mentor a host of U.S. players who have earned 100 or more caps.

He recalls a long car ride with one of those players, Tab Ramos: "He was still playing and I asked him if he ever had any thoughts about later going into coaching. Now I asked that knowing that within the soccer coaching community Tab as a player was not the easiest guy to handle. I recall him telling me, 'I don't think I ever want to coach. I know what players think of coaches and I don't want any part of that.'"

"I think that once his playing career ended, Tab reflected on things and changed his attitude. Of course he has had a good run with our U-20s and today is coach of the Houston Dynamos."

"I think seeing such stories take place is just one of the rewards we coaches receive during our careers."

Terry Fisher – A Varied Soccer Career

Stuck behind All-America striker Eddie Austin, his Hartwick playing career was spotty, but there were two other acquaintances he made in Oneonta that played roles in his subsequent soccer odyssey—namely, Francisco Marcos and Timo Liekoski.

Researching Terry Fisher's soccer travels, including those instances when he was loosely tied to the game, is a remarkable exercise.[184]

From his Yellow House (PA) upbringing, this soccer junky has followed his passion from one coast to the other and places in between, all while viewing events with a "glass half full" approach to life.

Al Miller's Impact

It was at a high school awards dinner that then-SUNY New Paltz coach Al Miller and Terry met. Fisher, a star at Oley Valley (PA) High School, had been named his league's most valuable player.

In retrospect, Fisher terms that event "the luckiest moment in my life. He's been like a father figure for me." Asked to list Miller's attributes, Terry cited his passion for the game, his soccer intellect, and his approach to team building. "On top of that he was a good communicator and a very good motivational speaker."

When Miller became coach at Hartwick College job, Fisher was one of his first recruits. Having taken a European soccer tour with Hubert Vogelsinger his senior year of high school, in 1966 it was Terry who planted the seed for the Warriors becoming the first U.S. college team to undertake a foreign tour.

Stuck behind All-America striker Eddie Austin, his Hartwick playing career was spotty, but there were two other acquaintances he made in Oneonta that played roles in his subsequent soccer odyssey—namely, Francisco Marcos and Timo Liekoski.

Right Places – Right Times

"I had the best job in America. Seriously, I'd have done the job for nothing." –Terry Fisher

In 1972, Fisher succeeded Timo as coach at Whittier (CA) College. It wouldn't be the last time their lives would be intertwined.

With his networking skills sharpened and with a USSFA License in hand, in 1973, Terry became assistant to UCLA's coach, Dennis Storer. Upon Storer's resignation in 1974, Fisher became, at age 23, one of intercollegiate soccer's youngest coaches. He led the Bruins to the 1974 NCAA final round, where a semifinal loss to home-standing St. Louis was followed by a 3-1 consolation match loss to Liekoski-coached Hartwick, 3-1.

Asked about his brief time at UCLA, Fisher reflected that it was his dream job. "I imagined myself going on to earning a doctorate and staying there for the rest of my life. I had the best job in America. Seriously, I'd have done the job for nothing."

However, a UCLA regular-season match changed his soccer trajectory. Having borrowed on the soccer marketing savvy of Hartwick teammate Francisco Marcos, during the 1974 regular season, Fisher was credited with utilizing the long tradition of UCLA-USC athletics to promote a soccer match between the two rivals. The game not only attracted 7,000 fans to South Torrance High School but also, and more importantly, motivated a group of San Jose investors (including Alan Rothenberg) to buy the Los Angeles Aztec franchise and move it to El Camino College from its then-East LA location.

The Second American NASL Coach

"If you never have tried to do something difficult, you'll never be fired." –Terry Fisher

In 1975, Terry became the second American NASL soccer coach (Miller the first with the Philadelphia Atoms in 1973) when he was hired as Aztec coach. Always marveling at soccer's progress, he recalls a conversation he had with UCLA AD J.D. Morgan at the time of his resignation: "He was paying me $3,000 at the time. He asked what the Aztecs were going to pay me and when I told him $17,500, he told me, 'I will never pay a soccer coach that type of money.' Wow – have we come a long ways!"

With 11 different nationalities on its roster, including the renowned George Best, Fisher lead the team to three postseason playoffs. As for the mercurial Best?

"He and I actually got along great. At any moment, he could have gone to ownership and said, 'Get rid of this guy.' But he didn't."

"I remember one game, against the Oakland Stompers at the Rose Bowl, where he missed two penalties in one game. I don't know if it had anything to do with what he did the night before; I think it had more to do with Shep Messing being in goal. But after that game, I told my wife, 'I'm out of there.'" Sure enough, he was fired in 1978.

Related to dismissals, he shrugs off such events: "If you never have tried to do something difficult, you'll never be fired." His second pink slip followed the 1979 season coaching the San Jose Earthquakes.

A 10-0 loss to the Detroit Express probably sealed his fate. With his usual sense of gallows humor he recalled the match. Behind 0-3 at halftime, he emptied his bench. "But those British guys on the Detroit team, they smelled blood ... "We were lucky they didn't have 25. We did quite well to hold them to 10.

Actually, the Detroit Lightning MISL franchise was his next coaching stop, followed by assisting German coach Eckhard Krautzin with the NASL Houston Hurricane in 1980. In 1981, he assisted Al Miller as coach (Marcos was the player personnel director) with the short-lived NASL Calgary Boomer franchise. Succinctly, Terry summarized it: "We had a five-year plan worked out; it lasted six months and cost the owner, Nelson Skalbania, millions."

Beginning in 1984, Fisher located to San Francisco and held a number of jobs, some of which involved Francisco Marcos.

On to WYSA and Youth Soccer

Two years later, in 2009, and with the endorsement of U.S. Soccer's CEO Dan Flynn, he began what has been his longest soccer-related tenure as CEO of the Washington State Youth Soccer Association (WYSA), the nation's sixth largest. Echoing his earlier UCLA statement, he refers to WYSA "as the best soccer job in America."

Haven't we heard that accolade earlier?

Update: In July 2021, Terry Fisher was appointed the chief executive officer of the California South Soccer Association. Cal-South oversees youth and adult soccer in the Greater Los Angeles region. It is the latest "best soccer job" for the well-traveled Fisher.

CHAPTER IX

CLIFF MCCRATH – SOCCER'S BEST AMBASSADOR

While his coaching travels have taken him from the Midwest to the East and West coasts, everywhere Cliff McCrath has trod, he has left a soccer imprint.[185]

With a larger-than-life persona, a keen intellect (one friend thinks he's a genius!), and boundless energy, perhaps no other American soccer coach has lent his expertise to so many different areas of the game.

Coaching expertise? Five NCAA men's soccer championships won ranks him second only to Indiana's Jerry Yeagley.

Rules oversight? For 40 years he served as secretary-rules editor of the NCAA Men's and Women's Rules Committee.

Soccer promotion? Here few can match his organization of leagues, camps, clinics, and other major events that have collectively marketed the game.

Relationships? His unique personality has endeared him to people throughout the country.

In 1978 and in celebration of Seattle Pacific's first NCAA Division II soccer title, coach Cliff McCrath crawled 2.7 miles up to the city's Space Needle. (Photo by Seattle Pacific Athletics)

385

Communication? His tongue-in-cheek humor and unique ability to bring audiences to both laughter and tears is legendary.

Legacy? The game will endure in part because an estimated 150 former players have given back to soccer as coaches, including his son Steve.

Upbringing and Bob Baptista

"I thought he had contracted a disease!" –Cliff McCrath

Raised in Detroit by an abusive father and a loving, supportive mother, Cliff credits his home life for helping him develop an underdog approach to every roadblock that stood in his way.

He credits his mother with offering him ways to approach the loss at age eight of three fingers of his left hand. "She continually propped me up, never let me feel ashamed. She also reminded me of how others coped with far greater handicaps than mine."

Soon McCrath was playing ice hockey and dreaming of starring for the hometown Detroit Red Wings while also playing a number of other sports.

His Christian upbringing matched the underlying philosophy found at Wheaton (IL) College, where he enrolled in 1952. He had never before played soccer, but that changed when his college roommate, All-American basketball player Mike Easterling, enticed him to join the college soccer team coached by the legendary Dr. Bob Baptista. By his senior year he earned All-America honors. Before coach Baptista left on sabbatical ("I thought he had contracted a disease!"), he appointed McCrath to fill in for him as coach of the 1958 team. Although the prospects of a law career died out as a result, a soccer coaching career that has spanned nearly a century was launched.

First Administrative/Coaching Positions

In 1960, the multi-faceted McCrath joined the faculty at Gordon (MA) College. There, he was involved in admissions and public relations work, and, in addition to his divinity studies, he was the school's soccer and ice hockey coach. He also organized a group of small New England schools into the Colonial Intercollegiate Soccer Conference (CISC).

By 1967, he moved to Spring Arbor (MI) College to serve in similar capacities. At an introductory bonfire seeking to drum up soccer enthusiasm, he promised Spring Arbor would make it to the nationals in three years. In 1969, Spring Arbor made it to the NAIA tournament and, in the opening-round game defeated previously unbeaten Eastern Connecticut, 1-0. Arguably spent, they lost a second-round match to defending champion Davis & Elkins (WV) College. While at Spring Arbor, McCrath served as president of both the ISAA (1966-69) and the NAIA soccer coaches (1968-69).

Spring Arbor was a sister school to Seattle Pacific University and was shifting from a two-year to a four-year school when President David McKenna enticed McCrath to become the first dean of students and soccer coach at SPU. He was "a man on a mission" when he moved to the West Coast in 1970.

Seattle Pacific and Professional Soccer

Seattle's response to its new soccer franchise is credited with convincing the NFL to award a franchise to the city.

... McCrath crawled an estimated 2.7 miles up and over the city's Queen Anne Hill and, upon arrival at the Space Needle, shaved his mustache.

Beginning in 1970 and through 2007, McCrath was the face and voice of Seattle Pacific University (SPU) soccer and an important force in bringing professional soccer to the Emerald City.

At SPU, he inherited an inexperienced team that initially played a group of unaffiliated small schools. SPU went 0-7-3 his first season, and it was later discovered that 30 percent of the opposing teams' players were ineligible. As he did in Massachusetts, Cliff, who was the only full-time coach among the teams, formed the Northwest College Soccer Conference (NCSC). The NCSC quickly expanded from six to 12 teams. By 1972, SPU soccer was playing at the NCAA Division II scholarship level.

By 1972, his "go to" personality quickly integrated itself into the Seattle community. He became a confidant of Walt Daggatt, head mover and shaker in the city, as Walt and others sought an NFL franchise for Seattle. NFL Commissioner Pete Rozelle along with Lamar Hunt met with the group in 1972, and, during the negotiations, Hunt mentioned that Seattle might also be a possible location for a NASL franchise.

With the group's money and a seven-page pro forma developed by McCrath driving events, by 1974, the new Sounder franchise was playing its first NASL season. The McCrath planning document forecast an average attendance of 6,000 fans. Led by coach John Best and a group of largely former English professionals— abetted by hometown star Jimmy McAllister—the team averaged 12,000 spectators in each of its first two seasons.

Seattle's response to its new soccer franchise is credited with convincing the NFL to award a franchise to the city. By 1976, the city had constructed the indoor King Dome to house the Seahawks and the Sounders. The Sounders opened the facility with a match versus the New York Cosmos. Fifty-eight thousand fans saw Pele notch two goals that day. Naturally, McCrath was the color analyst on Sounder telecasts for five seasons.

Meanwhile, SPU soccer was also riding the Seattle soccer boom, and its competitive teams finished as NCAA DII runners-up three times (1974-75 and 1977). In 1978, the Falcons won the first of their five NCAA DII championships. To celebrate, and to honor a bet with a local sportswriter, McCrath crawled an estimated 2.7 miles up and over the city's Queen Anne Hill and, upon arrival at the Space Needle, shaved his mustache.

Remembering "The Crawl"

The event was nationwide news and, as with many of McCrath's undertakings over the course of his career, garnered publicity for the sport of soccer. Sigi Schmid remembered "The Crawl": "People forget how difficult it was in those days, how we had to fight for things. Part of what kept soccer going in Seattle was Seattle Pacific, and he [McCrath] has got to be commended for that rebirth. His notoriety kept soccer in view. He created an interest in the sport from a sector that normally would not be interested in soccer. His personality drew them to it."[186]

Unfortunately, 1983 was a bittersweet year for Seattle, as the NASL folded and with it the Sounder franchise. The good news was that SPU won the second of its five NCAA DII titles, with later championships won in 1985, 1986, and 1993.

In 1987, as a measure of his contributions to the Seattle community and the fact that the Falcons had made NCAA Division II soccer history by capturing two consecutive (1985-1986) titles, McCrath was named Seattle Sports Star of the Year over contenders from the Seahawks, Sonics, Mariners, and Washington Huskies.

Following the 1994 World Cup, planning was underway for the founding of Major League Soccer. It was McCrath along with local business magnate Yogi Hutsen who headed a group seeking a charter MLS franchise. Then-U.S. Soccer President Alan Rothenberg dismissed the application as "unfeasible." Thirteen years later, the same twosome were again co-bid chairs who saw their dreams come true when the 2009 Seattle Sounders FC debuted at the then-Quest Field.

As noteworthy as his immersion in soccer at the college and professional levels was, it was McCrath's creation of the Northeast Soccer Camp that many youngsters recall as sparking their interest in the game.

Wearing Varied Soccer Hats

In the late 1970s, upon the resignation of Alan King as secretary-editor of the NCAA Men's Soccer Committee, chairman Bob Guelker appointed McCrath as his successor. He would serve in that position for 40 years.

He was also an NSCAA fixture, annually serving as the presenter (and entertainer) of the organization's Honor Award for 39 years. When MetLife was a major NSCAA sponsor, its liaison, Ivar Quigley, brought some of his salesforce to the Honor Award Banquet for some fun and soccer exposure. He frequently bemoaned that Cliff's time on the dais was not long enough!

Relative to that, his speaking presentations were numerous. They ranged from addressing 25 millionaires to motivating talks to corporate clients including Nike, Microsoft, and Charles Schwab. He is credited with campaigning that led to a successful vote for the construction of Seattle's Century Link Field.

The PAC 12 Conference called on Cliff's managerial expertise when it grappled with the startup of women's soccer as a conference sport. Adopted in 1991, the move helped generate interest in coach Lesle Gallimore's program at the University of Washington.

His SPU Termination

The details were vague ... [but] it has left its mark on the person who brought such notoriety to the institution.

Ideally, Cliff McCrath's career would have ended at age 99 (his prediction!), having built on his 597 soccer-coaching victories (10 short of the record at the time). However, in 2007 a new SPU administration shocked Seattle and the U.S. soccer communities by terminating him after 38 seasons.

The details were vague, and though his 2017 selection to the school's Falcon Legends Hall of Fame somewhat soothed matters, it has left its mark on the person who brought such notoriety to the institution. Of little consolation is the fact that his termination occurred in the midst of a "new broom sweeps clean" initiative, when 15 of 16 longtime SPU staffers departed or were released.

While from 2009-14 he served an unfulfilling five-year term as executive director of the National Intercollegiate Soccer Officials Organization, his legacy will survive through the fact that over 150 former players have gone on to play significant roles as coaches or in other capacities in the game. That includes son Steve, who led Barry University men to the 2018 NCAA Division II championship and was named United Soccer Coaches and national Division II Coach of the Year—exactly 40 years after his father's SPU team won its two consecutive NCAA Division II titles!

Obviously, while cutting a wide swath in U.S. soccer circles, coach McCrath has endeared himself to many who have, in turn, acknowledged his impact with presentation of numerous accolades.

Lesle Gallimore – Honored Player and Coach

Lesle Gallimore has had an expanded role in the development of women's soccer, beginning as an honored player at her alma mater and extending to a 34-year coaching career at the intercollegiate level of play, during which she assumed a number of leadership roles.[187]

Bill Merrell's Influence

"He had amazing people skills, including an ability to empower people. Those are basic abilities needed for effective coaching." – Lesle Gallimore

Raised in Redondo Beach (CA), Lesle was fortunate to be on the cutting edge as women's sports took a major leap forward following the passage of Title IX legislation in 1972. Following a less than inspired involvement in Girl Scouts, it was Lesle's single mother who encouraged her daughter's enrollment in AYSO soccer. "I loved the team aspect and exercise of soccer. It stuck and obviously, the older I got, the more 'into it' I got."

Following a stellar career at South Torrance High School and FRAM Soccer Club, Lesle enrolled at Cal-Berkeley in 1982 and, along with several FRAM teammates, played for coach Bill Merrell as he initiated the school's first women's team. She became a four-time All-America defender and led the team to three NCAA tournament appearances, including two seasons when the team reached the semifinal round. As a measure of her impact on PAC-12 sports she was named California's Athlete of the Decade for 1976-86. In 2015, the conference named her to its Women's Soccer All-Century Team.

The transition from player to coach was seamless, as coach Merrell hired her as the Bears assistant coach following her 1986 graduation. In addition to serving as a father figure and giving her a start to her coaching career, Merrell, an attorney by profession, offered other important examples to the fledgling coach. "He had amazing people skills, including an ability to empower people. Those are basic abilities needed for effective coaching." Coach Merrell later started the program at Wellsley (MA) College.

The South Bay's Impact

"He [Schmid] was a man who loved the game and found ways to share that with myself and other coaches." –Lesle Gallimore

Growing up in the South Bay area and being immersed in its rapidly expanding soccer culture had a lasting impact on Lesle's career. "For those of us who love the game there were plenty of fine players who we watched and emulated and coaches who encouraged us." She recalls watching talented Torrance products Dale and Glenn Irvine. The LA Aztecs' George Best's skillful play also had its influence on her and her impressionable soccer friends. The Irvine brothers, whose father sold quality soccer shoes out of the family home, later starred for West Coast coaching legend Sigi Schmid at UCLA.

In addition to Bill Merrell, Lesle has spoken effusively about the support she's received from coach Schmid. "He was so kind, respectful and supportive of us as younger players and later as coaches. I recall him attending one of our UW games at UCLA and hanging around afterwards to talk about the game. He was a man who loved the game and found ways to share that with myself and other coaches. Later, when he came to Seattle to coach the Sounders we continued our soccer relationship. In fact, we had front row seats behind the team bench so we could watch him in action."

She also credits the late Clive Charles with supporting her coaching career. She recalls attending a clinic being presented by a reputed foreign coach and asking the presenter a question. "Afterwards, Clive came up to me and complimented me on both having the confidence to ask the question and the depth of it. I, and others have to credit Clive, Sigi and others like Peter Reynaud and Jen Verheess, with offering their encouragement as we grew as coaches."

From Player to Coach

Ready to assume head coaching responsibilities, in 1990, Gallimore headed to San Diego State, where she not only upgraded the program's schedule but was able to take the Aztecs to a 32-25-9 record in her four seasons at the helm. She did continue her playing career, captaining the West team to a gold medal at the Olympic Soccer Festival in 1993 in San Antonio (TX), and remained in the USWNT player pool from 1990-92. In recounting her playing career, she noted, "It would've been cool to dress for the U.S. once, but I have zero regrets about my playing career ... I played well into my 40s and had a ton of fun doing it."

It was while at San Diego State that she upgraded her coaching methodology, achieving a U.S. Soccer A License in 1993. "I took the courses with USWNT friends (Michelle Akers, Amy Allman, Shannon Higgins, and others) and we learned as much as we could while earning the staff's respect because we all could play."

In 1995, Lesle became a U.S. Soccer and NSCAA National Staff Instructor. What were her takeaways after having been engaged in the two national coaching programs? "I think getting an NSCAA diploma was not as intimidating as was the U.S. Soccer license. I think also though the Academy staff were not always well-recognized 'name' coaches, I found them collectively to be outstanding teachers of the game."

Moving on to Washington

In 1994, the now-established young coach took the reins at the University of Washington. In her first season, the team played their way to the NCAA regional tournament final and set two new school records by scoring the most goals in a season and also allowing the fewest.

By the time of her 2019 retirement, Gallimore had led Husky teams to 15 NCAA appearances, including two at the Elite Eight level. In addition, she was named PAC-12 COY on two occasions (2000, 2019). In 2000, she was named NSCAA West regional COY, an honor replicated in 2019. Sixty-seven UW players have been accorded All-PAC 12 honors and two, Hope Solo (2001) and Tina Frimpong (2003-04), have earned NSCAA All-America honors. Solo is the most recognized UW product, having starred on the USWNTs from 2000-16, and is a World Cup champion and two-time Olympic gold medalist.

Well-respected in the coaching community, Gallimore elected to serve on the NCAA National Committee for Division I Women's Championships. She also found time to be active in the Washington SYSA. In 2001, she assisted April Heinrichs with the USWNT in 2001 when it competed in the Algarve Cup in Portugal. From

Lesle Gallimore has served soccer in a number of roles, including leading the University of Washington women's team for 25 years.

2014-17, she assisted with the USWNT U-23 team. She also served as the head coach of the USWNT U-19 team at the USYS/Adidas Cup tournament in 2000.

Women's Advocate

After long resisting overtures to become an NSCAA officer, Lesle served five years on its Board of Directors and, in 2018, rose to the presidency of the 30,000-member coaching organization. She had earlier helped start its Women's Committee.

In 2012, as part of the U.S. Embassy's Sports Envoy program, Lesle traveled to North Africa, where she and others conducted soccer clinics and leadership training sessions for women and girls in Morocco. Over 100 young female coaches from the host country and from Tunisia and Libya attended the sessions. In 2016, she returned to Africa, this time to Ethiopia on a solo envoy trip to run clinics and coach education in two different cities over a nine-day period.

In the fall of 2020, and just months following her retirement from coaching, Lesle took on another soccer challenge when she was named Commissioner of the Girls Academy (GA). The GA is a 69-club organization of seven conferences offering an estimated 7,000 female players a nationwide competitive playing environment.

'The GA is a completely new challenge for me. It's a start-up league borne out of the necessity as U.S. Soccer dropped the Development Academy. I wasn't really looking for the next thing, but was approached and felt that it was an environment in which I could have an impact. It's a real challenge because we're a huge country, soccer is a big business in the U.S., and youth soccer specifically has really become a convoluted and confusing environment for players and parents. I am still finding my way in my role. It's been a huge learning experience in a short period of time and we'll see when all is said and done if I've made the impact I've hoped for when I started. I want girls to see a broader version of what the game can be to them."

If past is prologue, the Girls Academy will have made a positive impact before Lesle Gallimore has completed her work.

Honors

Honors accorded Lesle include induction into the Cal-Berkeley Athletic Hall of Fame in 1995. In 2019 she was named to the Washington Youth Soccer Hall of Fame and presented with the "Key to Cal Women's Soccer" for lifetime achievement in the sport.

CHAPTER X

BRINGING SOCCER INTO THE 21ST CENTURY

Soccer coaching and the game itself today bare scant resemblance to the exacting oversight Douglas Stewart and his disciples had hoped to promote in the early 1900s.

From the development of player equipment to the application of technology to its teaching to the fact that the sport has established its place in our American sports culture, soccer has arrived! And in no small measure, that battle for public acknowledgement for the sport has been the untiring work of the U.S. soccer coaching community.

While there are any number of contemporary coaches to recognize, those chosen for their recent contributions have one characteristic in common: their careers can be linked to earlier U.S. coaching icons who took up soccer's cause with little idea of where their labors would lead.

Bob Bradley, current coach of the MLS Los Angeles FC, is a case in point. While at Princeton, his career path was influenced by coach Springfield graduate, Bill Muse. Muse, in turn, was mentored by Irv Schmid, and the Schmid introduction to the game came under one of the game's true pioneer coaches, John Brock. Further, Bradley's career has been influenced by U.S. coaching maestro, Bruce Arena.

And so, when examining the contributions of several of today's progressive coaches, or coach/administrator, their story lines will reflect the fact that, although they themselves might be hard-pressed to acknowledge the contributions of any particular soccer coach preceding them, one or more of those coaches before them—directly or indirectly—impacted their own careers.

And, to a large degree, this interconnectedness is a central theme in the story of soccer's ascendency in this country. As with any other successful endeavor or enterprise, soccer is an iterative process: Coaches today are building their own identities and legacies, and their accomplishments, in turn, build on the prior accomplishments and experiences of their mentors."

And so it has been for our subjects Bruce Arena, Bob Bradley, Sasho Cirovski, Ray Reid, and Hank Steinbrecher.

The careers of these six coaching legends—whether they themselves are aware or not—have been influenced by others whose own careers stretch back to soccer coaching pioneers.

Coaches Arena and Steinbrecher: Setting New Standards for American Soccer

When reflecting on the current status of soccer in the American sports scene, there comes a time when credit has to be bestowed on individuals who have, above others, have played historic roles in aiding that ascendency.

And while there are other individuals who can be cited for playing various roles in soccer's current elevated U.S. status, there is plenty of evidence that two soccer coaches, one retired and one now in his fourth decade, deserve accommodation as pacesetters as new frontiers were breached for the sport.

And in honoring Hank Steinbrecher and Bruce Arena as two individuals who demand recognition for their efforts to lift soccer, we discover that in addition to sharing similar personality traits (self-confidence, creativity, persistence, and passion among them), both their careers were impacted by fortuitous events that changed their lives and, in the long run, have enormously influenced the standard of American soccer.

Their stories follow.

Hank Steinbrecher – Changing the Face of U.S. Soccer

Hank Steinbrecher's contributions to the game first centered on his playing it, later on coaching it, and, most significantly, in his role marketing and administering it when serving as Secretary-General of U.S. Soccer.

One can capture the spirit of his work by sharing some portions of an address he gave at Davis & Elkins (WV) College in 2017. An accomplished public speaker, he titled his talk, "Lessons Learned from My Journey."

Perhaps, he offered, the ultimate objective of teaching success is "getting the kid right so the world will be right." Known for fashioning short axioms, he offered listeners, "Smart is just a start." And, "Hard work pays off, but it isn't the ticket to success." Finally, "Passion is essential in everything you do."

Also emphasized with the West Virginia audience by the former coach was the necessity for teamwork, the need to work in concert with others. Referencing his life in sport, he noted, "Teammates are more important than you can possibly imagine."

There is little question that such thoughts, when served with a dash of integrity, have led the New York native to one of the most productive careers in U.S. soccer.

Early Soccer Immersion

Born in Queens, Hank grew up in Levittown, one of those New York suburbs that were created when Americans left their urban environments following World War II. But whether it was by rail, subway, or bus, Hank's youthful passion for the game took form in the city. There he would hone his skill playing for the Kollsman Football Club and the First German-Brooklyn Sport Club. Among his contemporaries were Paul LaSeur, Werner Roth, and Sepp Messing.

Noting that he didn't "feel worthy" about pursuing a college degree following high school, Hank worked construction for two years. In 1967, he was still playing in the German-American League when Mitchell Junior College (CT) coach Warren Swanson offered the skilled defender a soccer scholarship. Following Mitchell, he moved on to Davis & Elkins (D & E) College in 1969. In 1970, coach Dr. Greg Myers' D & E squad captured the NAIA men's soccer title in a 2-0 victory over Quincy (IL) College. A friend, Wolfgang Woischke, had preceded him to Mitchell.

The Fatherly Influences

"Warren was a dedicated coach, a man of integrity who I wanted to grow up to be." ...
–Hank Steinbrecher

In coaches Swanson and Myers, Steinbrecher found two male models with whom he formed bonds that never had been shaped with his own father

At Mitchell, he changed diapers of the two Swanson children, Gregg and Gary. Later, both played for him when he coached Boston University. "The experience with Warren was more than about kicking a ball," Hank recalled. "He and his wife Karen showed me what a close family looked like. Warren was a dedicated coach, a man of integrity who I wanted to grow up to be.

A Brazilian teammate at Mitchell recommended Steinbrecher to Gregg Myers. A former Marine drill instructor, Myers ran a "tight ship" at D & E. Recollecting his initial start with Myers, Hank noted, "I was not his ideal player with long hair and a mustache. But it worked as he beat us up physically and he knew how to reach us psychologically." Such was the Myers influence that Hank shared that he never made a decision at U.S. Soccer without consulting him. Myers later spent 29 years coaching at the U.S. Naval Academy, where he compiled a career second only to Navy coaching legend Glenn Warner.

Appreciated for his fine-tuned vocabulary, Hank credits D & E's Dr. Lois Latham for influencing that aspect of his career. He was an older student at the time and was a "house boy" living at the Latham residence during his undergraduate years. "She frequently entertained other professors and I began to appreciate how well-spoken they were. Later she and I would spend time reading a dictionary. She would select a word and ask me to repeat it three times. Further, to then explain its meaning. She was a special person in my life."

Hank Steinbrecher is one of soccer's finest public speakers.

Establishing a Coaching Reputation

The sport and the University gained nationwide attention when Sports Illustrated ... *published an article featuring the coach's quote-worthy interactions ...*

After earning his master's degree in education from West Virginia University in 1973, Steinbrecher joined Warren Wilson (NC) College as soccer coach and AD. During his five-year stay, he sparked a soccer rejuvenation, as the team won a NAIA regional title and he was named NAIA COY in 1975. On one occasion, classes were cancelled so students could attend a NAIA regional playoff match. He was celebrated for his "larger than life" personality when inducted into the Warren Wilson HOF in 2017.

In 1978, Steinbrecher moved to Appalachian (NC) State University, where he inherited a talented group of players headed by Nigerian Thompson Usiyan. Over three seasons, the Mountaineers achieved a 33-10-2 record, including an unmatched record of 20-0-0 in Southern Conference play. Further, home crowds averaged 5,000 spectators attracted in large part by Usiyan, who scored a NCAA-record 109 goals in three seasons, including eight in one NCAA playoff match! As for "Tommy," Hank remarked, "The best part of coaching him was that he worked harder off the field than he did on." Following the 1978 season, Hank was named Southern Conference Coach of the Year and NSCAA Regional Coach of the Year.

The sport and the University gained nationwide attention when *Sports Illustrated* (11/10/1980) published an article featuring the coach's quote-worthy interactions with the varied nationalities on the team roster. Indicative of the effectiveness of his mentorship was the comment of Usiyan. While bemoaning the cold climate of Boone (NC), the star striker noted, "The coach makes us very warm though."

Building on his successes, in 1980 Steinbrecher moved back East to coach at Boston University. By 1984, he concluded his coaching career, having led the Terriers to an ECAC playoff appearance and producing a number of All-America players.

Soccer at the 1984 Olympic Games

When Boston was announced as one of the 1984 Olympic soccer sites, Steinbrecher knew he had to be involved, noting, "I would have picked up towels in the locker rooms."

Instead, following an unannounced visit to its headquarters, by the opening of the competition at Harvard University's Stadium, Hank had been appointed site coordinator by Olympic sites chairman Bill Schmidt.

He called the experience "like putting out a fire each day." One situation had international political implications and involved a group of Iraqi spectators who were going to display "Death to Saddam" signs during the Iraq versus France match. "I told the group you either watch the match without the signs but not both. The next day the Boston Globe crucified me for violating the fans' civil rights."

Attendance for the U.S. Olympic soccer competitions surpassed FIFA's expectations as 1,425,181 viewed the matches, including a record 101,199 at the Rose Bowl who watched France defeat Brazil for the gold medal. The U.S. reception for soccer was a deciding factor in FIFA's awarding the 1994 World Cup to the United States.

The Quaker Oats Experience

Following the Boston Olympic venture, Steinbrecher left his coaching position at Boston University and took his now-polished managerial and marketing skills to corporate America, joining a Fortune 100 company, the Quaker Oats Company.

He termed the experience as "Sounding and rounding" his professional career." The Quaker connection was in the person of Bill Schmidt, head of Quaker's beverage division. There, for the next five years, Hank focused on the strategic planning of the marketing of its Gatorade power drink. That included cementing marketing agreements with the major U.S. sports leagues, including Major League Baseball, the National Basketball League, the National Football League, and the National Hockey League.

Queried as to the revenue increase during his Gatorade tenure, Steinbrecher would only state, "A lot."

Joining and Jolting U.S. Soccer

"What people don't realize was that if Alan hadn't won there was a very good chance that FIFA would have pulled the World Cup from the United States."–Hank Steinbrecher

By 1990, and with preparations heightened for the 1994 World Cup, a somewhat disorganized U.S. Soccer Federation named Steinbrecher its secretary-general.

The timing of his hire was fortuitous in that it involved planning for the 1994 World Cup. "There was no way they [USSF] were going to fire me with so much at stake," Steinbrecher noted. "I could play hardball with our staff. Actually I think that one of my major accomplishments was changing the culture within the organization. I feel I made everyone accountable."

One of his first acts was to hire Frank Longo as his chief of staff. Frank had orchestrated programs for the Intercollegiate Soccer Association of America (ISAA), and their relationship had begun when Hank served as the ISAA rating board chairman.

In assuming the position, Steinbrecher renewed a relationship with its new president, Alan Rothenberg, as the two had worked together at the 1984 soccer Olympics. Rothenberg's last-minute addition to the 1990 USSF presidential election slate was, in part, orchestrated by FIFA. Hank shared a little known fact: "What people don't realize was that if Alan hadn't won there was a very good chance that FIFA would have pulled the World Cup from the United States."

Hank Steinbrecher changed the culture at U.S. Soccer. He is pictured in front of the organization's Chicago headquarters.

The Rebranding of U.S. Soccer

Upon assuming control in 1991, one of the most innovative things Steinbrecher coordinated was an organizational name change; USSF became U.S. Soccer.

He shared the reason behind the decision: "The Federation was represented by various acronyms. We created the name U.S. Soccer to appeal to all of the US. It is about the US. We focused on a young demographic and rebranded the Federation. Our research was that many people viewed the Federation in a negative way. The name change was one part of a needed cultural change within the organization."

This change within U.S. Soccer was part of plan that involved changing the group's brand. Steinbrecher explained: "Our aim was to end our roots with the ethnic brand of soccer. We wanted to enhance that we were the group that fostered soccer as the favored family weekend activity."

With his Quaker marketing experience in tow, Hank utilized that skill set in securing enhanced contractual agreements for U.S. Soccer. Case in point was Nike replacing an earlier adidas agreement. By comparison, Nike's cash infusion to U.S. Soccer was ten times that of adidas. Also, a new deal with Gatorade valued at $1.0 million far surpassed that previous contract struck with Coca-Cola.

Before resigning from U.S. Soccer in 2000, Hank did lose a battle about how the organization would conduct its marketing ventures. "I felt that we could handle our marketing in-house. Others were of the opinion that we should be client of SUM [Soccer Marketing United]." That's where U.S. Soccer finds itself today.

U.S. Soccer's Legacy

"Being in the Rose Bowl to see the USA defeat Colombia was a high point for me personally..."
–Hank Steinbrecher

There is little question that the success of managing three major international tournaments on U.S. soil solidified Steinbrecher's worldwide standing. Nearly 3.6 million spectators viewed the 1994 World Cup, and another 1,364,142 fans attended the combined men and women's Olympic soccer matches in 1996. The culminating event, the 1999 FIFA Women's World Cup, attracted 1,214,221 fans as the U.S. women capture the gold medal. The 1994 and 1999 tournaments are considered by many to be the most successful FIFA tournaments of all time.

A 2012 retrospective summarized Hank's role in moving soccer forward during his 10-year tenure at U.S. Soccer: "I look back on those days with warmth," he recalled. "The most significant achievements for the Federation were to create a men and women's team that our country could be proud of. We started off without a professional league and a few players stationed in Europe. Our men performed well and our women won World Cups. We made the country proud. Being in the Rose Bowl to see the USA defeat Colombia was a high point for me personally and to witness our women play in the Rose Bowl before 94,000 people and win was euphoric."

Following completion of the 1994 World Cup, Hank and Sunil Gulati were the architects of a planning document labeled Project 2010. Basically, it was a blueprint of what steps U.S. Soccer needed to undertake in order to not only qualify for but win the 2010 World Cup. Obviously, that goal was not achieved and, further, failure to qualify for the 2022 event is of even more concern to Steinbrecher: "I think our current crop of players are 'soft.' Players in other countries walk distances to train with their shoes hung around their shoulders, ours arrive in their Lexuses, in their training suits and $200 boots stored in fancy bags."

Acknowledging Steinbrecher's Contributions

As mentioned, during his collegiate coaching days, Steinbrecher was active with the Intercollegiate Soccer Association of America, serving as ISAA's chairman for its then weekly college rating committee. The group would compile regional and national team ratings as a means of keeping college soccer in the news. Eventually, of course, the rating system included women's teams, and another change was to have the process broken down by NCAA divisions (I, II, etc.). In the 1990s, team ratings were introduced for secondary school teams, both boys and girls.

Following his retirement from U.S. Soccer, the still-energetic and connected soccer enthusiastic Steinbrecher found himself in charge of hospitality for the 2014 World Cup in Germany. It was there that he reconnected with life-long friend Wolfgang Wishek. Seems the relocated German now was president of a hospitality company.

For his overall contributions to the game, the Steinbrecher name has been affixed to a wide range of soccer honors, including The Bill Jeffrey Award (1990); The Davis and Elkins Hall of Fame (1992); The NAIA Hall of Fame (1996); The North Carolina Hall of Fame (2000); Elected a 'Life Member' of U.S. Soccer (2004); The Boston University Hall of Fame (2005); The United Soccer Coaches Honor Award (2005); The United States Soccer Hall of Fame (2006); The Mitchell College Hall of Fame (2006); The New England Soccer Hall of Fame (2009); The U.S. Soccer Werner Fricker Award (2012); The Warren Wilson College Hall of Fame (2013); The West Virginia Soccer Association Soccer Hall of Fame (2015); The Eastern New York Senior and Youth Soccer Association Hall of Fame (2017); Named United Soccer Coaches Honorary All-America recipient (2019).

Additionally, in 2013, Steinbrecher was named chairman of the board of the U.S. Soccer Hall of Fame.

Bruce Arena – America's Most Honored Coach

If but for Dame Fortune, the ascension of Bruce Arena to the rank of arguably the most successful U.S. soccer coach might never have taken place.

For Arena's sports-related career prior to enrolling at Cornell in 1971 was principally focused on lacrosse. While he also played soccer at Long Island's Carey High School, it was his lacrosse play that attracted attention, specifically of opposing Elmont High School coach Richie Moran.

When Moran was hired to oversee Cornell lacrosse fortunes in 1969, he recruited Arena from Nassau Community College, where Bruce had earned junior college All-America honors. Of interest was that, under the guidance of Shep Messing, Bruce was also a JC All-America soccer goalkeeper.

By the fall of 1971, Arena was enrolled at Cornell with the full intention of focusing his energies on his studies—and Big Red lacrosse.

A Change in Plans

Central to the establishment of Arena's coaching reputation was his tenure as U.S. National Team coach from 1996-2006.

It was at this point in his life that a series of events occurred that eventually resulted in Arena's shelving lacrosse and led to his stellar soccer-coaching career.

Cornell soccer coach Dan Wood, knowing of Arena's goalkeeping background, had reached a "handshake agreement" with Moran that, should the soccer team goalkeeping position somehow open, Arena could fill in. By midseason, both of Wood's goalkeepers were injured, and Arena was "borrowed" to fill the breach.

By the end of the season, he helped lead Cornell to its first ever NCAA Division I Tournament appearance. The following season, with Arena in the nets, the 1972 team advanced to the semifinal round of the D1 tournament in Miami. For his overall tournament play, Arena was named the tournament defensive MVP.

While he dabbled at professional lacrosse, in 1976, Arena joined Wood at Tacoma where he was a backup goalkeeper for the Tides. More significantly, that fall he had his first soccer coaching opportunity when he was hired as the part-time coach at the University of Puget Sound.

In 1978, he was named the soccer coach (also to assist in lacrosse) at the University of Virginia. By the time he left in 1998, he had led the Cavaliers to five NCAA Division I men's soccer titles. Coaching success would later continue with Major League Soccer coaching stints in Washington, New York, and Los Angeles, yielding five MLS Cup titles.

Central to the establishment of Arena's coaching reputation was his tenure as U.S. National Team coach from 1996-2006. That stretch included a record 71 international coaching victories, including those at the 2002 World Cup, where the United States reached the quarterfinal round.

At the onset of his coaching career, what were some lessons that helped Bruce Arena form his coaching philosophy?

Early Coaching Lessons

"...the coach developed relationships with every team member, starter or not, noting "He saw you first as a person and secondly, as an athlete. ..." –Bruce Arena

Perhaps it was Mike Candel, his lacrosse coach at Nassau, who spoke for many when he was quoted in the Arena book, *What's Wrong with US?*, as saying, "He was one of those kids who would do what you told him. But in a million years, I would have never imagined him to be the national soccer coach."

What were some key events, other than the Cornell scenario, that helped form Arena's coaching philosophy?

At Nassau, he and his teammates looked forward to playing under soccer coach Bill Stevenson. The likeable coach laid down eight simple rules that began with "Play your best boys" and ended with "Be Sportsmanlike." Messing, Bill's goalkeeper coach, added another Stevenson unwritten rule: "Have fun!"

Cornell's diverse student body opened up Bruce to persons from different backgrounds and perspectives. Another takeaway resulted from his time with coach Moran. He admired Moran's enthusiasm and commitment, but he also liked how the coach developed relationships with every team member, starter or not, noting, "He saw you first as a person and secondly, as an athlete."

While coaching at Puget Sound, Arena still harbored dreams of playing professionally. He tried out for the English-dominated Seattle Sounder franchise and, following exposure to that team's culture, came away with an unshakeable belief that would underpin his coaching. Namely, "Americans could play the game with the best of them and coach this game with the best of them as well."

Bruce also credits a part-time job teaching troubled high school students at Ithaca High School with imbuing him with two facets of his personality that needed some fine-tuning—namely, patience and tolerance for others. That exposure led him to always question: How does that individual learn best?

Honing His Craft at UVA

"... we don't spend a lot of time in training on our opponents. Instead we spend it on ourselves, getting better at the things we do well. ..." –Bruce Arena

Coincidence again changed the trajectory of Arena's career when a Cornell grad alerted him to a dual lacrosse-soccer coaching opening at the University of Virginia.

Hired by AD Gene Corrigan, Arena's soccer coaching immersion soon supplanted his assistant lacrosse responsibilities.

His two-year relationship with a young assistant named Bob Bradley helped him recognize the value of forming a good coaching team, and that awareness would follow him through the rest of his career. Later, Dave Sarachan would be one of his assistants.

It was also at Charlottesville that Arena answered the question of who he wanted to be in terms of his coaching personality. Exposure to high-quality staff coaches such as then-women's assistant basketball coach Gino Auriemma helped firm up that query. Even his office location, next to the visiting team's locker room, paid dividends, as it allowed him to eavesdrop on the communication expertise of basketball coaching luminaries Dean Smith and Mike Krzyzewski.

One coaching tenant formed at UVA that Arena advocates for is "simpler is better." Asked in 1997 about his advice on corner-kick strategy, he was quoted as saying, ". . . you need someone who can put the ball in the box, someone who can get a head on it, and if it comes out, you need someone who can put it back on goal. We don't spend a lot of time on corner kicks, we spend time playing soccer." In part, he credits coach Manny Schellscheidt with helping form a practical approach to his coaching, noting that Manny is a "hidden gem."

That simplification of matters applies also to preparing a team to face the opposition. Noting that his teams might watch some video of an upcoming opponent, he returned to basic facts, stating ". . .we are who we are and we have a style of play. We make slight adjustment in accordance to our opponents, but we don't spend a lot of time in training on our opponents. Instead we spend it on ourselves, getting better at the things we do."

To this day he credits lessons imparted from basketball coaches, such as Virginia's Terry Holland and later Virginia player turned-NBA coach Rick Carlisle, with impacting his coaching methodology. "From a practical standpoint they [U.S. coaches] are more available to talk to than some European coach. Because basketball mirrors our sport in many ways I have been able to apply their ideas about tactics, offense and defense, how they press, etc."

Arena knew full well the important role relationships play in coaching. It aided in the recruitment of stellar soccer players from around the country to UVA.

Claudio Reyna, from New Jersey, and Jeff Agoos, from Texas, are but two examples. It was an Arena-nurtured friendship with Virginia supporter Harry van Beek that played an important role in the construction of UVA's Klockner Stadium.

At the end of his Virginia tenure (1978-95), Arena had built a program that won 95 percent of its matches, including five national intercollegiate titles.

Moving on to MLS and the USMNT

He credits Brian McBride, who scored two crucial goals in Korea, as one of his favorite players, not so much for play, but rather, for his "team first" attitude.

Key to coaching success is identification of talent, and there is little question that, in 1996, Arena's keen eye for that was crucial, as he accepted the initial challenge of coaching that year's U.S. Under23 Olympic team and stocking the roster of a new MLS team, DC United. "You have to learn how to spot players who can make the jump to international competition, which is faster and more intense," was how Bruce shared that key component of coaching.

At the Atlanta Olympics, Arena was assisted by Bradley and Glenn "Mooch" Myernick as the team failed to exit the first round.

Sarachan now emerged as his assistant at DC United, and, aided by several former UVA players on its roster, United captured the inaugural MLS Cup by overcoming a two goal LA Galaxy lead to win in overtime, 3-2.

Arena admitted in the book that he was on a steep learning curve, but the confident coach felt that by the 2002 World Cup in South Korea he had constructed a competitive U.S. team. Speaking of the Arena approach, De Marcus Beasley remarked, "He made sure that I was part of the team. It didn't matter how young you were; it didn't matter how inexperienced. If you were in camp, you were there for a reason."

One further refinement of Arena's coaching was a simplification of his team communication. Before taking on favored Portugal in the opening round, the coach informed the team that it needed to take an aggressive approach to take advantage of its athleticism and speed. "First tackle today, first foul, first shot, first goal" was his succinct message prior to the 3-2 upset over the Luis Figo-led team. A 2-0 win over Mexico advanced the United States to the quarterfinals for the first time since 1930. There, despite a dominant t effort by the Americans, the potent Germany team eliminated them, 1-0.

Arena credits Brian McBride, who scored two crucial goals in Korea, as one of his favorite players, not so much for his play, but rather, for his "team first" attitude.

By the 2006 World Cup, Arena had integrated Beasley, Landon Donovan, and Clint Dempsey into the U. S. team. Needing to win or tie with Ghana to advance from the first round, expectations died following a 2-1 defeat.

Los Angeles Galaxy

In 2007, the then-struggling Los Angeles Galaxy hired Arena, and many wondered how Arena would deal with the team's star import, David Beckham.

The experienced coach harked back to the basics. He met with Beckham and determined that his public persona hid the fact that once he stepped on the field he was committed to be "all business."

The coach was also able, through personal meetings, to smooth the on-field relationship between Beckham and Landon Donovan, and the later addition of Robbie Keane also went seamlessly.

By 2011, the three stars would combine on a Keane goal that secured LA's second MLS Cup, and, in 2014, the team won its third Cup and the fifth in Arena's MLS career.

Upon his Galaxy retirement in 2016, Arena noted in his book that MLS had expanded from 12 to 19 teams, 10 new soccer stadiums had been constructed, and overall attendance had doubled. Then in his 38th season in coaching, and having earned the reputation as a premier team builder, he was proud of the role he had played in getting more people excited about soccer.

The U.S. World Cup Failure

It is a well-known fact that Arena's attempt in 2016 to ride in on a white horse and spearhead the U.S. National Team's World Cup qualification effort ended with a 2-1 away defeat to Trinidad.

One of Arena's coaching tenants was to be prepared for the unexpected events that have always been part of soccer.

A flooded Trinidad field on October 9, 2017, resulted in a delusionary, short practice by the U.S. team that went viral on the country's social media and fired up the home team, who came into the match with nothing to lose. An own goal by the United States followed by a "Hail Mary" 40-plus yard shot by the home-standing team was enough to eliminate the United States on what the coach termed "my worst day."

His Coaching Legacy

... The Arena legacy continues through the coaches he has mentored, including the long careers of two of his former assistants, Bob Bradley and David Sarachan.

In the referenced book, Arena offered different pathways for future improvement of the U.S. game, principally focusing on placement of greater numbers of experienced soccer personnel in positions of influence at U.S. Soccer or within the ranks of MLS.

It was in that vein that, in the spring of 2019, he returned to MLS as coach and general manager of the New England Revolution. In the position, he retains total control of all elements of the club's soccer operations.

The Arena legacy continues through the coaches he has mentored, including the long careers of two of his former assistants, Bob Bradley and David Sarachan. Another assistant, Richie Williams, is head coach of DC United. One of his first Virginia recruits, George Gelnovatch, has won two NCAA Division I titles in his 24-year career as head coach at Virginia. Another, Jeff Agoos, is a senior VP at MLS. Also, Claudio Reyna is the sporting director for the new MLS franchise in Austin (TX), and John Harkes heads up the Greenville (NC) USL franchise. Meanwhile, son Kenny Arena is assisting Bob Bradley with the MLS Los Angeles FC franchise.

Arena's stellar role in the game has been acknowledged by induction into the U.S. Soccer (2010) and United Soccer Coaches halls of fame (2018). In 2015, U.S. Soccer presented him with the Werner Fricker Builder's Award in recognition of his work to elevate the sport in this country. Three MLS Coach of the Year awards are on his resume, and, moving back to his first love, in 2008, the National Junior College Athletic Association honored him with induction into its lacrosse hall of fame.

Optimistic about the future of the professional game, in 1998, he made a valid point when asked if MLS could ever attract NFL-like crowds of 65,000. "No," he replied, "but we will be playing at least twice as many games. Right now, in our own marketplace (D.C.), we sell about as many tickets a game as do the Wizards (NBA) and the Capitals (NHL)."

Based on their long association, Dave Sarachan's comments deserve mention. In summary, he has concluded that Arena is a ". . . master builder. He has a keen eye for talent and understands how teams are constructed. Further, he knows how to manage rosters. Bottom line, he is a competitive guy and is just a winner. Oh – I forgot to mention, it always helps when you have better players!"

Bradley, and Marsch – Elevating American Soccer Coaching to New Levels

While the accomplishments of soccer coach Bruce Arena have been well documented, his linkage to the subsequent coaching careers of Bob Bradley and Jesse Marsch is noteworthy for a study of those relationships offers a tutorial in the further refinement in U.S. soccer coaching that is not only influencing this country's soccer coaching domestic proficiency, but also is slowly achieving international notice.

The story of American soccer is in a sense a story of the interrelationship of these three coaches. Their careers allow the story of the American soccer coaching to come full circle in that their lives and coaching successes, like those of many of their predecessors, have been long intertwined. Further, to a large degree, their associations mirror what has also taken place historically within the U.S. soccer community. Namely, as they have had their collective impact on soccer coaching, they have, like many before them, unfailingly shared their expertise with others also bent on improving both the pedagogy and methodology of soccer coaching.

Bob Bradley.

While we have chronicled the accomplishments of coach Arena, a look at first Bob Bradley and then Jesse Marsch will put the nitty-gritties of their accomplishments in perspective.

A Soccer Lifer[200]

Introduced to soccer at West Essex (NJ) HS, Montclair native Bradley's soccer career continued at Princeton University, where he played for coach Bill Muse. Muse was part of the Springfield College coaching network and served his coaching apprenticeship under Al Miller at Hartwick College. "Bill's importance was that as a member of the USSF coaching staff, he brought the latest in coaching trends to our Princeton teams," reflected Bradley.

A forward at Princeton, Bradley knew his playing limitations and, in 1980 at age 22, entered graduate school at Ohio University, where he coached the school's foreign student-dominated team.

The Bradley–Arena relationship began in 1981 when Bob served as the latter's assistant at the University of Virginia. There he was given full coaching rein during the spring when his mentor was coaching Cavalier lacrosse. While conceding that the two saw the game and coaching through a different lens, the Charlottesville stop occurred at a good time in their coaching development, with Bradley noting, "We were both able to challenge each other, bounce coaching ideas off each other." And on one topic he is in agreement with Arena, namely that their exposure to the coaching knowhow of UVA coaches (Terry Holland, George Welch, etc.) was also valuable, citing, "we all can learn from expert coaches of other sports."

Exposure to the international game came in 1984 when Arena, Bradley, and Paul Milone (who, as a Virginia graduate student, had alerted Arena and Bradley to the Virginia coaching positions) traveled to view that year's European Cup. There watching the great title-winning French team formed by coach Michael Hidalgo and orchestrated by Michael Platini added to their appreciation of how great teams play.

Now prepared to manage his own teams but still open to examining other avenues to cement his coaching philosophy, Bradley returned to Princeton in 1984, where he succeeded Muse and began a 12-year stay as coach.

In addition to leading Princeton to two Ivy League titles and an appearance in the 1993 NCAA College Cup, Bradley began what he terms a "lucky" lifelong exposure to his most influential soccer mentor, Manfred Schellscheidt.

Lessons From Manny

With Manny on the USSF coaching school staff at the time, Bob's enrollment there exposed him to the Dettmar Cramer curricula and its more academic theory of coaching. It was Schellscheidt who revealed to him the more practical coaching model espoused by a fellow German coach, Hennes Weisweiler. Hennes had been among Manny's instructors when he earned his German coaching license in the late 1960s.

Schellscheidt encouraged Bradley to become involved in New Jersey ODP soccer (Bob recalls driving home a then 16-year-old and now USMNT coach Gregg Berhalter from an ODP camp). He also credits assisting coach Schellscheidt with the USYSA U-19 champion Union Lancer team as an important step in his growth as a coach, noting, in particular, the German's understanding of the game and how that knowledge can be imparted.

"He let the game be the teacher," shared Bradley when queried as to the "Manny methodology." "His lessons to players were subtle. He might, following a small-sided game, get a player aside and mention some aspect of the game, be it his need to expand his field vision or some other aspect of the player's game that needed improvement. Probably my appreciation of Manny comes from his 'soccer wisdom.' He 'sees' the game so clearly and can convey his lessons with clarity using clean, simple words to do so."

One Bradley anecdote epitomizes his mentor's never-ending absorption in teaching the game. It occurred when Bob, Manny, and then-five-year-old Michael Bradley were walking together to a training session, with Michael casually poking a soccer ball ahead. "Manny quietly snuck up behind Michael and poked his ball away, reminding him as he did so, 'You always have to look around you when playing soccer!'"

Saachi on Soccer

In addition to his ongoing relationship with Schellscheidt, Bradley names AC Milan coach Arrigo Saachi as being a huge, albeit distant, influence on his development as a coach. It was Saachi who, during the period of 1987-91, transformed Italian soccer and offered new ideas to worldwide soccer.

Among the concepts introduced as the "Milan Way" was a collective, unified approach to play on both sides of the ball. "While the coaching schools had introduced us coaches to the German philosophy that focused on winning individual duals all over the field, Saachi's teams moved together, played as a unit," explained Bradley. He noted that the basketball concept of pressurizing opponents in their defensive half of the field, comprising midfield play and building the attack from the back, were all featured in the "Saachi method."

"With that," said the coach, "when I went back to my Princeton team in 1992, I told them we were going to change how we played the game." By 1993, with Marsch earning All-America accolades, the Tiger team made its way to the College Cup, losing to Arena's eventual national champion Virginia team in the semifinals.

A Record of Success

Bradley took another step up the coaching ladder when, in 1996, he reconnected with Arena, this time as his assistant with the new MLS DC United team. The Arena–Bradley DC United team captured the inaugural MLS Cup and the U.S. Open Cup in 1996, won the Supporters' Shield the following season, and repeated as U.S. Open Cup winners in 1996. On that 1997 team was midfielder Jesse Marsch, whom Bradley convinced the team to select in the later round of the MLS draft.

Player Marsch followed Bradley when the latter was named coach of the new MLS Chicago Fire franchise in 1998. That year they paired to win the MLS Cup (defeating Arena's DC United in the process!) and the first of three U.S. Open Cups while also capturing the Supporters' Shield in 2003. In 1998, Bradley won the first of three MLS Coach of the Year accolades.

Of note is that several members of Fire teams have entered the professional coaching ranks, including Marsch with Leipzig (Germany) and Leeds (England); Chris Armas with both Red Bull New York and Toronto FC; C.J. Brown with New York Red Bull; Zach Thornton, assistant with DC United; Josh Wolff, head coach of Austin FC; Ante Razov, assistant with Bradley at Los Angeles FC; Peter Nowak, head coach of Lechia Gdansk (Poland); Frank Klopas, assistant coach of Chicago Fire; and Tom Soehn, head coach of USL Birmingham Legion.

One of the leaders on the Fire teams was the then well-traveled former FC Barcelona legend, Hristo Stoichkov. Stoichkov believes that Bradley's coaching impact in America, along with Arena's, shouldn't be underestimated. "I believe both of them have done important things for this country, like being managers of the U.S. national team ... I consider them both as the influencers, fathers, and friends of all these players-turned-coaches we are talking about."[201]

Coaching the U.S. Men's National Team

Following short coaching spells with the New York Metro Stars and Chivas USA, Bradley was appointed USMNT coach in 2006. In his first year, the team achieved a record of 12-1-5, including a win over Mexico in the 2007 Gold Cup Final. In 2009, Bradley led the U.S. men to a second-place finish in the FIFA Confederations Cup, beating Spain 2-0 in the semifinal and ending Spain's 35-game unbeaten streak before losing in the final to Brazil, 3-2. A successful CONCACAF qualifying campaign led the United States to the 2010 World Cup, where Bradley's team won its group before losing to Ghana in the knockout stage in extra time. Reportedly a second choice to Jurgen Klinsmann, Bradley lasted five seasons (43-25-12) before being fired in July of 2011 and replaced by the German.

Including at Princeton, Bob Bradley has performed his magic at every level of soccer in the United States, but much like earlier American coach Al Miller, who in the 1970s left the comfort of college coaching to coach professionally, the ambitious and "fully in" Bradley left the friendly confines of his home country and achieved recognition for his accomplishments in the Middle East and Europe.

Coaching at the International Level

In September of 2011, Bradley was hired to coach the Egyptian National Team. In addition to the pressures of being a foreign coach, Bradley had to deal with two events that worked against his being successful. Earlier that year, the country had revolted against the regime of President Hosni Mubarak. On February 1, 2011, a riot at a professional game in Port Said resulted in 74 deaths and over 500 spectator injuries. Following that, all professional soccer was suspended.

"(Egypt) was a crazy lifestyle for him," Marsch explained after recalling a visit he paid to Bradley in Cairo. "He and his wife, when I was there, it was like they were Egyptians. They ate like Egyptians, they obviously didn't speak Arabic, but the way they interacted with the Egyptian people led them to embrace the Bradleys as part of their family. I was overwhelmed by how much the people there loved him."[198]

A great advocate of open player communication, and because his every movement was under the microscope of the soccer-mad Egyptian community, Bradley had to secretly meet with the country's best player, Mohamed Aboutrika, following the Port Said disaster and convince him of his sincere interest in leading the country to the Brazilian World Cup.

Aboutrika's team, Al Ahly, was one of the teams involved in the Port Said riot and he had been traumatized by the experience. Following the meeting, Aboutrika presented the coach with a Brazilian soccer shirt, indicating his commitment to the cause. Emerging to later stardom on the Egyptian team was 19-year-old Mohammed Salah, later of Liverpool fame. While the team lost but eight matches of the 36 Bradley was in charge of, one was to Ghana in the decisive match that eliminated the country from play in Brazil.

Move to Coaching in Europe

In January 2014, Bradley signed on to manage Stabaek Football Club in Norway, making him the first American to manage a club in top-level European competition. He later coached at Le Havre AC (France) in Ligue 2 and missed promotion into Ligue 1 based on a goal scored tiebreaker.

In 2016, Bradley was appointed coach at Swansea City, becoming the first American to coach in the Premiership. While it was a historic moment, the appointment lasted only 80 days.

Returning to the United States, in 2017, Bradley was named head coach of Los Angeles FC for its inaugural MLS season, winning the Supporter's Shield in 2019 and again being named MLS Coach of the Year.

Bradley Accolades Abound

In early 2021, in a virtual visit with the Princeton University coaching staff, athletes, and alumni, Bob Bradley discussed leadership, communication in the team-building process, social justice, family, and education and spent time talking with them about ways to connect with people across different cultures. Accolades followed.[202]

Current head coach and former Bradley player Jim Barlow termed the group "... lucky to have Bob share his experiences and wisdom ... His lessons in pursuing excellence with others, honesty, leadership, dealing with adversity and standing up for justice were valuable for us to hear."

Princeton women's coach Sean Driscoll echoed Barlow and added that she valued the consistency of Bradley's message. "He has a real conviction in his values and beliefs that I admire and, most importantly, he is authentic. His suggestion that we need to engage people in a meaningful way through reflection, perspective and truth resonated with me."

Echoing those responses was the later perspective of coaching colleague Jesse Marsch: "I respect him perhaps more than anybody else because I've seen him up close, along the way. I've seen how much he puts into it. I've seen how hard he thinks about things and the attention to detail. I think everywhere he has been, among the inner circles, there is the highest amount of respect for who he is and what he does."[203]

The Emergence of Jesse Marsch as Coach

Racine, Wisconsin, native Jesse Marsch has been quoted as follows: "Where I'm from, kids don't go to Princeton." But he did enroll with the way eased by coach Bob Bradley, who was initially impressed by the then-16-year-old's heady play in a tournament he was scouting. Later, by personal letter and interaction (he picked up Jesse at the airport), the coach helped pave the way for Marsch to attend the Ivy League institution in 1991.

Once on the team, Marsch soon discovered Bradley's tough love. The coach never held back about what players needed to do to improve, which was difficult at first for Marsch, who was accustomed to being the best player on every team he joined. "I remember thinking back then, 'This guy is a jerk!'" says Marsch. "But over time I grew to love his feedback and yearn for him to critique me ... and I realized the more he challenged you, the more he believed in you."[204]

Longevity in the MLS

From an MLS playing career that included oversight by coach Bradley in Washington, Chicago, and Los Angeles, Marsch moved into coaching as his mentor's assistant with the 2010 U.S. national World Cup team. That experience led to a short-lived stint as head coach with the fledgling MLS Montreal Impact in 2011. Following an interim year spent as assistant at Princeton, in 2015, the ambitious Marsch became coach of the New York Red Bull franchise, leading it to the Supporter's Shield and earning the MLS COY award the first season.

Binghamton (NY) University coach Paul Marco first met Marsch when his team played at Princeton in 2014. They later met again when Paul conducted three NSCAA match analysis seminars in conjunction with Red Bull games. Marco recalled the meetings: "He's an outstanding individual, humble, intense with a whole lot of energy. He met with our seminar coaches following each match and his analysis was spot on. Of interest was the fact that his Red Bull teams played a fast and furious style, in many ways reflecting the energy product they were representing."[205]

Emulating the career of his mentor, in 2018, Marsch was off to carve a coaching legacy in Europe, first assisting at RB Leipzig in the German Bundesliga. He credits his time at Leipzig as instructive in terms of being exposed to the staff's degree of study of the game and the resultant detail involved in match preparation. He then applied those lessons when he landed the head job at Red Bull Salzburg in 2019. His management success at that club included capturing the Austrian double of league and cup championships in his first two seasons.

"In its simplest form, as much as the game has grown in the U.S., players and coaches earning respect in Europe is still not easy," Bradley has stated. So, as was with his crusading mentor, when Marsch was installed in 2021 as coach of RB Leipzig and became the first American to coach in the German Bundesliga, he sought to further enhance the reputation of U.S. coaching expertise in the international soccer community. While his sojourn with Leipzig was brief, he emerged as coach of Leeds United in the English Premier League in 2022.

What does the future hold for Jesse Marsch? Many have speculated that, at some point, he will be a strong candidate to direct the fortunes of the USMNT. If so, he'd be building on his 2010 team experience. "Having been on the inside with Bob and the national team, I have a really good picture of what that team requires," says Marsch.

Whatever the future holds, Marsch is not only grateful for the role Bradley has played in propelling his success in soccer but also for how their relationship has evolved. "He was a mentor, then he was almost like a father, then he became my boss, and then he became my friend," stated Marsch.[206]

Sasho Cirovski – Tackling Division I Issues

Standing tall among the modern crop of soccer coaches is University of Maryland's men's coach Sasho Cirovski.[207]

The Macedonian-born Cirovski has not only revived Terrapin soccer but has been a national leader in the coaching fraternity in terms of his advocacy for resolution to hurdles that have plagued Division I men's soccer since the staging of the first NCAA men's soccer tournament in 1959.

Namely, the fact that the traditional one-seasonal approach to the play of Division I soccer has led many to question its importance in terms of player development. Meanwhile, having to stage its culminating showcase event, the College Cup, in less-than-optimal late fall playing dates has long diminished the significance of the event. But more on that later.

Maryland coach Sasho Cirovski is seeking to pass NCAA legislation that will change the face of Division I soccer.

Playing Aspirations Linked to Ferguson

Having departed Macedonia, the Cirovski family settled in Windsor, Ontario, Canada. There, Scottish-born Tom Dearie influenced son Sasho's soccer immersion. Dearie was a fixture in Windsor soccer, coaching the W.D. Lowe HS and Teutonia SC teams where Cirovski honed his play.

With a boost from Dearie, who was acquainted with then-Aberdeen FC coach Alex Ferguson, in 1980, Cirvoski, age 17, departed for an intended two-week trial with the Scottish club. Recollecting his time with the coaching legend (two weeks turned into six weeks!), Sasho still treasures the experience with "the boss." "He had a huge presence even then, a man 'bigger than life,'" he recalled. "He was also 'thoughtful, polite and personable, but demanding.'" Offered an Aberdeen contract, Cirovski set aside his professional playing aspirations and took coach Dan Harris's scholarship offer to play at the University of Wisconsin-Milwaukee.

Coming Under the Gansler Influence

"If there were U.S. soccer coaching faces on Mount Rushmore, I'd say he should be one of them."

Cirovski was finishing his junior year in 1984 when UWM was seeking to replace its men's soccer coach. Named to the search committee, he supported candidate Bob Gansler as Harris's successor.

But sponsorship of someone and playing for that individual can be two different things. However, Sasho did thrive under the new coach, captaining the team his senior year and later being named recipient of the UWM Herman Kluge Award for Male Athlete of the Year. Later, in 1998, he was inducted into the UWM Athletic Hall of Fame. Following graduation, he spent parts of three seasons as a professional player and coach in the Canadian Soccer League. His first taste of coaching came in 1987 when he led York of the CSL.

Sasho, now in his 29th year at the University of Maryland and holder of three NCAA Division I men's titles, states that his relationship with coach Gansler has been a career-changing event. "He made a tremendous first impression on me. He had such a presence and was the consummate teacher-coach. Going into my senior year I had aspirations to play in the NASL, but unfortunately that was the year the league folded. But after playing for him I soon wanted to be like him."

While playing indoors for the Milwaukee Wave, he first volunteer-assisted coach Brian Tompkins with the UWM women and then Gansler with the men's team. Of the latter experience, he recalled, "I was like a sponge. I tried to extract everything I could from working with Bob."

Seeking to add to his coaching repertoire and encouraged by Gansler, Sasho completed the highest coaching courses offered by U.S. Soccer and the United Soccer Coaches. Those experiences introduced him to coaching personalities Jay Hoffman, Jay Miller, and the late Glenn Myernick.

It was through the Gansler network that doors were opened for Cirovski.

That included landing his first job at the University of Hartford in 1991. There he took the Hawks to two NCAA Division I tournament appearances.

As for his rating of coach Gansler? "I would say that looking at my hand that Bob Gansler is one of the top five coaches I've met. If there were U.S. soccer coaching faces on Mount Rushmore, I'd say he should be one of them."

Turning Up the Heat at College Park

Beginning in the 1950s, Maryland soccer had enjoyed national prominence under coaching legend Doyle Royal, dominating Atlantic Coast Conference play and co-winning the NCAA title in 1968. But since his retirement in 1973, only one of Royal's successors has taken the team to NCAA post-season play.

As part of his preparatory work when he assumed the Maryland position in 1993, Cirovski journeyed to England for a tutorial with Alec Ferguson, then at

Manchester United. "The purpose of the visit was to observe how he managed the huge United enterprise. It was an eye-opener for me and I have incorporated many of his ideas here." Most recently, that has included installation of a Terrapin staff that numbers two assistant coaches, a volunteer coach, a performance coach, an academic director, an equipment manager, a public relations and social director, and a marketing strategy and game experience director!

Well supported, beginning in 1993, Cirovski has transformed Maryland into a national soccer power, leading the Terps to the 2005, 2008, and 2018 NCAA titles, nine College Cup appearances, and 15 conference titles.

In addition to restoring Terrapin soccer to intercollegiate preeminence, Cirovski has turned Maryland into a prime intercollegiate incubator of U.S. professional soccer talent. Various Terps have participated in three consecutive FIFA World Cups and 12 have earned caps for the USMNT.

Some of the most prominent players in the last 20 years of American soccer, including Taylor Twellman, Maurice Edu, Robbie Rogers, Clarence Goodson, Omar Gonzalez, Zack Steffen, and Graham Zusi, have gone from Ludwig Field to professional stardom.

Under Cirovski's guidance, entertaining Terp teams have brought fans out to Ludwig Field in record numbers. Maryland was tops in attendance nationally in 2016, averaging over 4,000 fans per game and annually transforming Ludwig into one of the top Division I soccer venues in the country.

A Driving Force in the Game

"His enthusiasm for our sport is infectious and it will unite Division I college coaches to pursue our objectives and achieve them."

When the ISAA was folded into the NSCAA in 1996, it was Sasho Cirovski among others who was a driving force that convinced the NSCAA to hire a full-time person to advocate for intercollegiate soccer with the NCAA. He has also chaired the Division I Coaches Committee and cemented his legacy as one of the most influential persons in college soccer.

Among the committee's accomplishments has been to serve as a lobbying voice with the NCAA, including keeping tabs on any legislation impacting the game. The committee has also encouraged colleges to upgrade their playing facilities, to better market their programs, and to annually look for new ways to promote its championship event, the College Cup.

While it was short-lived, it was his leadership that was vital in brokering a television partnership between Fox Soccer Channel and the NSCAA, guaranteeing a weekly spot for college soccer on television. Subsequently, televising of intercollegiate soccer matches has exploded for both Divisions I men's and women's teams.

"Sasho has not only a vision and a passion to improve and promote college soccer but he has the knowledge and the dedication to pursue new ideas," current George Mason head coach Elmar Bolowich has stated. "His enthusiasm for our sport is infectious and it will unite Division I college coaches to pursue our objectives and achieve them."

Since 2013, a major goal of the tireless Cirovski has been a pursuit of the sanction of a two-season playing calendar for Division I men's soccer. Termed "the 21st Century Model for College Soccer," it advocates for fall and spring seasons that would overcome some long-standing issues that have impacted the DI game. Intended in its projected outcomes would be a spacing out of games on a more palatable once-a-week basis, allowing for a better balance between the sport and academics and enabling player development over a longer time span. Inherent in the proposition is the fact that the annual College Cup would be played in the more desirable spring weather.

The Covid epidemic postponed Division I soccer play to the spring of 2021, and it also delayed the highly anticipated vote on the proposal by the NCAA Division I Council until spring 2022.

The ever-optimistic Cirovski, when queried as to the status of the monumental legislation, noted that the proposal has generated increased support, including from the influential ACC and the Big 10 Conference. As an indirect consequence of Covid, the College Cup was recently held in the spring on a trial basis. "I just want it noted that for the first time since 1995, the College Cup was sold out for the Marshall-Indiana final. We have always felt that our showcase event would fare much better in the spring of the year and that was demonstrated in Raleigh. It can't but help our proposal," stated the untiring Cirovski.

[Unfortunately on April 13, 2022, and except for one minor proposal related to summer football activity, everything was put on hold while the work of the NCAA Division I Transformation Committee and Division I Legislative Committee

Modernization of the Rules Subcommittee continues. Not dead in the water, but paddling to stay afloat might be its status as this is written.]

The Cirovski Coaching Tree

Numerous former Terrapin players have followed their mentor's lead and entered the soccer coaching profession as assistants. Two, including Russ Payne (Northwestern) and Mark Marchiano (Drexel), are currently head coaches and one, Mike Dellorossa, served a spell as assistant with the MLS Houston Dynamo. Of note is the career of Taylor Twellman, the St. Louis-born product now playing a featured role as ESPN soccer television analyst.

The Cirovski family tree includes his wife, the former Shannon Higgins, who played collegiate soccer at North Carolina and was inducted into the National Soccer Hall of Fame in the fall of 2002. The couple has three daughters: Hailey, Karli, and Ellie.

Ray Reid – Successfully Replacing a Legend

His college coach credits him with being one of the most reliable players he ever had and, later, as his assistant coach, as someone willing to outwork everyone else to get the job done.[208]

In any case, whatever personal attributes he brings to the table, the recently-retired University of Connecticut coach Ray Reid has managed to parley them into an enviable coaching record. In his 33-year career, the Reid record (457-149-78, .742) is surpassed by few others.

Not the least of his many accomplishments has been successfully following in the footsteps of one of this country's soccer coaching legends.

Ray Reid.

Reid's legacy lives on in the form of his coaching tree, where an extensive number of former players have established their own soccer success stories. Lastly, not forgetting his roots, Reid's personal generosity speaks to his concern that soccer's advancement continues.

His Soccer Start

Two individuals, Ray Perez and Bob Schimpf, have helped establish Reid on his road to soccer success. Ray Perez (brother of soccer notable Ralph) was his Brentwood High School soccer coach and also served as guidance counselor at the multi-cultural Long Island school. He credits coach Perez with steering him to a post-graduate year at Suffolk (NY) Community College in order to "get his feet on the ground."

There he came under the influence of coach Bob Schimpf, who he terms a "tough, no nonsense guy who taught us to compete all the time, to 'play with an edge.'" Reid also played on three Schimpf-coached Empire State Games teams that represented Long Island.

At Brentwood and Suffolk, he was honored as a student-athlete, and he earned regional All-NJCAA playing honors at Suffolk.

Southern Connecticut and Dikranian

Upon entering Southern Connecticut State (New Haven) in 1980, Reid was a three-year starter and two-year captain for coach Bob Dikranian's Owl teams that made three NCAA Division II semifinal appearances. Dikranian's coaching methods were, in part, formed when played at Bridgeport under HOF coach John McKeon.

Dikranian valued Reid's steady play at the back, noting that he rarely made mistakes and always "played within his ability."[209]

Upon graduating from Southern with a degree in economics, Reid was hired as Dikranian's assistant in 1983 and assumed that role through 1989. "While I continued to play various roles needed in our soccer community, Ray focused on his coaching role with the team," recalled Dikranian. Reid, however, did get involved in coaching various Connecticut ODP age-group teams.

The coach also noted that, with little scholarship money, Southern needed to "discover players," and that his hard-working assistant was adept at identifying hidden talent. In 1987, Southern captured its first NCAA Division II national championship.

Named to succeed his mentor in 1990, Reid captured the first of three NCAA DII titles in his second season. Other titles followed in 1992 and 1995, as did NSCAA COY honors in 1990, 1992, and 1994. Put in perspective, over his six-year Southern coaching career, Reid lost but 17 matches of the 179 the team played.

Succeeding a UConn Legend

"Good players; good assistants; hard work – and a lot of discipline." –Ray Reid

By the time he succeeded New England coaching legend Joe Morrone at the University of Connecticut in 1997, Reid had absorbed some important coaching lessons. At Southern, he came to appreciate coach Dikranian's emphasis on perfection and his continued persistence to set and achieve short- and long-term goals and acknowledged his being "the best at tactical solutions."

He also credits the now-deceased Doug May as providing valued coaching insights when they staffed Victory Soccer Camps.

For many coaches, succeeding two Hall of Fame coaches has proven untenable. But for coach Reid, it seemingly has been no problem. By 2000, in his fourth season at the helm of UConn soccer, his Husky team replicated Morrone's lone NCAA Division I championship. Entering the 2020 season, UConn had entered NCAA Tournament play on 18 occasions, led by over three dozen Husky players who have played on Major Soccer League rosters.

Queried as reasons for his coaching successes, Reid succinctly summarizes matters:

"Good players; good assistants; hard work – and a lot of discipline." Of the latter attribute, he cautions that it is not easy to attain. "Kids are different today. They tend to 'know it all and you have to be ready to be challenged.'"

The Morrone Legacy

It should be noted that coach Reid inherited a solid soccer program constructed by the late Joe Morrone.

He has sought in his 23-year career to maintain certain some of Morrone's way of doing things, but circumstances have made it necessary to set aside others.

Perhaps most telling has been a change in the player recruiting process. Coming forward from the 1970s, there was an emphasis on attracting American-bred players, and that certainly was true under coach Morrone. But a look at the anticipated UConn roster of 2020 revealed players hailing from Canada (2), France (2), Germany, Ghana, Morocco and Senegal (2).

Also, with other college programs upgrading their infrastructures, UConn has constructed a new Joe Morrone Stadium (on the footprint of its predecessor) that, prior to COVID-19, was set to debut during the 2020 season.

In another program change, the team does not play its matches on "UConn Soccer Sundays," though the Friends of Connecticut Soccer still assume supportive roles under the new regime, and the Morrone Soccer Scholarships still help support the soccer program.

Prior to Morrone's passing in 2015, Reid held monthly meetings with the former coach, and when Connecticut traveled to Charlotte in 2000, the former coach accompanied the team when it captured the school's second NCAA Division I national title.

Reid followed the example set by his mentor Bob Dikranian in terms of "giving back and community service" by donating $100,000 to two soccer-related projects. The first was to UConn to aid in the construction of Morrone Field on the Storrs campus. The second was to the United Soccer Coaches Foundation to underwrite soccer scholarships for coaches from underrepresented communities.

The Reid Coaching Tree

As we have detailed in the lives of many U.S. soccer coaches, their legacy includes former players who have moved on to assume, in addition to coaching, important roles in soccer.

Ray Reid's contributions in that realm are outstanding and include the following individuals:

John Deeley, University of Connecticut (Associate Head Coach); Mike Miller, University of Connecticut (Associate Head Coach); Kevin Anderson, Columbia University (Head Men's Soccer Coach); Joe Barrosso, Sacred Heart University (Head Men's Soccer Coach); Dave Castellanos, Drexel University (Assistant Men's Coach); Chris Gbandi, Northeastern University (Head Men's Soccer Coach); George Kiefer, North Carolina State University (Head Men's Soccer Coach); Robert Muuss, Wake Forest University (Head Men's Soccer Coach); Tim O'Donohue, U.S. Naval Academy (Head Men's Soccer Coach); Tom Poitras, University of Hartford (Head Men's Soccer Coach); Bo Oshoniyi, Dartmouth College (Head Men's Soccer Coach); Dane Brenner, Wake Forest University (Men's Soccer Associate Head Coach);

Flo Liu, Drexel University (Men's Soccer Assistant Coach); Michael Mordocco, LIU Post (Head Men's Soccer Coach); Dan Scheck, Stony Brook University (Men's Soccer Assistant Coach); Ken Pollard, Columbia University (Men's Soccer Assistant Coach); Kris Bertch, St. Louis University (Men's Soccer Assistant Coach); Cruz Hernandez, (Cal Poly Pomona (Men's Soccer Assistant Coach); Bryheem Hancock, (Head Men's Soccer Coach – UT RGV).

[It should be noted that upon Coach Reid's retirement in 2021 it was announced that Northeastern coach Chris Gbandi was appointed his successor. Gbandi's UConn playing career included being named the recipient of the Hermann Trophy as the nation's top collegiate player in 2000 while leading the team to the NCAA title. He later played in the MLS for eight seasons.]

Professional Positions

Brian Bliss, Sporting KC (Director of Player Personnel); Christian DaSilva, U.S. Soccer (Technical Advisor); Paul McDonough, Inter Miami CF (Sporting Director); Juan Carlos Osorio, Colombia National Team (Head Coach); Brian Clarhaut, NyKoPing BIS – Swedish Division I (Head Coach); Kevin Mellon, New England Revolution (Director of Operations).

BIBLIOGRAPHY

Note: For brevity's sake, where an individual interviews are cited as having been conducted, any quotations in the text are attributable to those discussions.

Introduction

1. *Soccer Journal.* 1996. "Center Circle." The National Soccer Coaches Association of America, July-August. p. 6. https://www.UnitedSoccerCoaches.org/SJ.com
2. Bean, Joseph and Tim Schum. 1992. *The History of the National Soccer Coaches Association of America, 1941-1991.* National Soccer Coaches Association of America. p. 12.

Chapter I Early History

3. *Soccer Journal.* Jan/Feb, 1991.
4. *Ibid.*
5. Bean, *op. cit.,* p. 12
6. Cahill, T. Editor, 1921. *Official Soccer Football Guide.* A.G. Spaulding and Brothers. p. 129.
7. Bean, *op. cit.,* p. 58.
8. *Soccer Journal.* Jan/Feb, 1989.
9. Walter Bahr interview, January, 2009.
10. Interviews with Buss, Coder, and Shellenberger, fall, 2015.
11. Bean, *op. cit.,* pp. 28-29.
12. Bean, *ibid.,* p. 18.
13. *Soccer Journal.* Jan/Feb, 1991.
14. Peter Gooding interview, Spring, 2020.
15. *Soccer Journal.* Jan/Feb, 1991.

16. Bahr interview, *op. cit.*
17. Bean, *op. cit.*, p. 21.
18. Bean, *ibid.*, p.18.

Chapter II Building on the Past

19. Walter Bahr communication, 2010.
20. Walter Bahr interview, *op. cit.*
21. Barry Gorman email, 2018.
22. *Soccer Journal.* Mar/Apr, 1993.
23. Bean, *op. cit.*, pp. 28-29.
24. Peter Nevin article on John Eiler in the *Pocono Record*, April 19, 2006. https://www.poconorecord.com
25. Al Miller interview, March, 2020.
26. Jim Lennox interview, April, 2020.
27. Nevin, *op. cit.*
28. Bean, *op. cit.*, p. 46.
29. *Soccer Journal*, Mar/Apr, 1993.

Chapter III U.S. Coaching Education Takes Huge Steps Forward

30. Most probably at a US Soccer Coaching School in the 1970s.
31. Gansler interview, spring, 2020.
32. Woitalla, Mike. "Dettmar Cramer Reminds Us: It's All About the Ball," *Soccer America*, September 25, 2015. https://www.socceramerica.com
33. Gansler, *op. cit.*
34. Walter Bahr interview, *op. cit.*
35. Peter Gooding interview, spring, 2001.
36. William Gordon, "The Legacy of Walter Chyzowych," unpublished research, August, 2019.
37. William Gordon, *Ibid.*
38. *Soccer Journal*, Nov/Dec, 2015.

39. Bob Gansler interview, spring, 2020.
40. Nick Zlatar interview, spring, 2020.
41. Al Miller interview, spring, 2021.
42. Timo Liekoski interview, fall, 2020.
43. Jeff Tipping interview, spring, 2020.
44. Liekoski, *op. cit.*
45a. Gooding, op. cit.
45b. Jeff Tipping Interview, *op. cit.*
46. Tipping, *ibid.*
47. Tipping, *op cit.*
48. Tipping, *op. cit.*

Chapter IV Coaches' Roles in Soccer's Progress

49. Bean, *op. cit.*, p. 18.
50. Cliff McCrath interview, spring, 2020.
51. Joe Machnik interview, spring, 2020.
52. Machnik, *ibid.*
53. Bean, *op. cit.*, p. 19.
54. *Ibid.*, p. 112.
55. Al Miller, *op. cit.*
56. Bean, *op. cit.*, p. 112.
57. *Ibid.*, p. 211.
58. Joe Bean interview, spring, 2020.
59. Doug Williamson interview, spring, 2021.
60. Code as adopted by the NSCAA, 5/4/99.
61. Hank Steinbrecher interview, spring 2020.
62. Terry Fisher interview, spring, 2020.
63. Lehigh University athletic website, 1/19/2012. https://www.lehighsports.com
64. USYSA press release, 12/26/2012. https://www.usyouthsoccer.com
65. Bean, *op. cir.*, p. 177.
66. Karl Dewazien interview, spring, 2020.
67. *Ibid.*
68. *Soccer Journal*, Nov-Dec, 1998.

69. Johnson Bowie interview, spring, 2021.

70. Anson Dorrance interview, summer, 2020.

71. As reported to the author on many occasions.

Chapter V Building on the Past in New England, New York, and Middle Atlantic Regions

72. Jeff Tipping email, 1/31/2020.

73. Morrone, Joe, "Marketing and Promoting Your Program," unpublished manuscript, 2002.

74. *Soccer Journal*, Nov/Dec, 2015.

75. Walter D. Windle, "It's All in the State of Mind," (1900).

76. Stevenson Hall of Fame citation, Brown University athletics website, 1979. https://www.brownbears.com

77. Amherst College *Magazine*, "Peter Gooding Retires," Winter issue, 2007. https://amherst.edu.com

78. *Soccer Journal*, Jan/Feb, 2001.

79. Amherst, *op. cit.*

80. Peter Gooding interview, spring, 2021.

81. Bob Dikranian interview, spring, 2020.

82. "Former Staples Soccer Coach Dies," *The Hour*, 9/5/2009. https://www.thehour.com

83. James Brown as referenced in Wikipedia, 2022.

84. "New Coach Steps into Successful Soccer Tradition," *Hartford Courant*, 4/5/2002. https://www.courant.com

85. John Rennie interview, fall, 2020.

86. *Ibid.*

87. Manny Schellscheidt interview, spring, 2020.

88. *Ibid.*

89. Al Miller interview, spring, 2020.

90. Bruce Arena interview, summer, 2020.

91. Woitalla, Mike. "Thanks Manny Schellscheidt," *Soccer America*, 1/2/2012. https://www.socceramerica.com

92. Schellscheidt interview, *op. cit.*

93. Tim Schum, "Pennsylvania's Soccer Coaching Hotbed," *Soccer Journal,* November/December, 2020.

94. Bob Dikranian interview, *op. cit.*

95. Jim Lennox interview, spring, 2020.

96. Jay Miller interview, summer, 2020.

97. Jay Hoffman interview, spring, 2020.

98. "Campus Mourns Passing of Longtime Coach," *Allied (PA) News,* 8/16/2011. https://www.alliednews.com

99. Steve Erber email, 4/19/2020.

100. Francisco Marcos interview, fall, 2020.

101. Tim Schum, "Coach Joe Palone of West Point," *Soccer Journal,* March/April, 2018 issue.

102. Al Miller, *op. cit.*

103. Joe Casey interview, summer, 2017.

104. Bob Behncke interview, summer, 2017.

105. Al Miller, *op. cit.*

106. Tim Schum, "The Small School that Made Soccer King," *Soccer Journal,* September/October, 2018.

107. *Ibid.*

108. Terry Gurnett interview, fall, 2020.

109. Jeff Vennell email, 11/20/2020.

110. Aliceann Wilber interview, spring, 2020.

111. Graham Ramsey interview, spring, 2020.

112. David Sarachan interview, winter, 2021.

Chapter V Establishing the Game in Football Country

113. Bart Barnes, "Doyle Royal, U-Md. Coach and Decorated Combat Veteran, Dies at 101," *Washington Post,* 11/5/20. https://www.washingtonpost.com

114. Ray Alley interview, fall, 2021.

115. Mark Berson interview, fall, 2021.

116. Ray Alley, *op. cit.*

117. Tim Schum, "Howard University and Racial Injustice," *Soccer Journal*, September/October, 2020.

118. John Rennie interview, fall, 2020.

119. Bill Holleman interview, spring, 2021.

120. Kevin Sims both interviewed and shared materials informing of Robert Sims soccer involvement.

121. Holleman, *op. cit.*

122. University of North Carolina publication, *The Well*, 9/21/2021. https://www.thewell.unc.edu

123. Anson Dorrance interview, summer, 2020.

124. Dorrance, Anson (With Tim Nash), "Training Soccer Champions." JTC Sports, Inc., 1996. p. 28.

125. Mia Hamm Sports Illustrated, 1998.

126. Crothers, Tim. "The Man Watching: A Biography of Anson Dorrance, The Unlikely Architect of the Greatest Sports Dynasty Ever." Ann Arbor Media Group, September, 2006. https://amazon.com

127. Walter Bahr, *op. cit.*

128. April Heinrichs interview, summer, 2020.

129. Guy Greening interview, summer, 2020.

130. Schellas Hyndman interview, winter, 2021.

131. Becky Burleigh interview, fall, 2021.

132. Nancy Feldman interview, fall, 2021.

133. Bonnie May interview, fall, 2021.

134. Kim Wyant interview, spring, 2021.

135. Michael Lewis, "The Kim Wyant File," Front Row Soccer, 11/10/18. https://www.frontrowsoccer.com

Chapter VII Adding to a Midwestern Soccer Tradition

136. Fred Schmalz interview, spring, 2020.

137. Dan Flynn interview, spring, 2021.

138. Bean, *op. cit.*, p. 155.

139. Dan Flynn, *op. cit.*

140. *Ibid.*

141. Bean, *op. cit.*, p. 81.
142. Bean, *ibid.*, p. 164.
143. Bean, *ibid.*, p. 128.
144. Joe Bean interview, spring, 2020.
145. Jerry Yeagley, interview, winter, 2020.
146. Indiana University men's soccer website, 2019. https://www.iuhoosiers.com
147. Fred Schmalz, *op. cit.*
148. Tim Schum, "Stu Parry: He Put the Zip in Akron Men's Soccer," *Soccer Journal*, July/August, 2017.
149. Tim Schum, "Mickey Cochrane," *Soccer Journal*, July/August, 2020
150. Bean, *op. cit.*, p. 139
151. Bean, *ibid.*, pp. 144-146.
152. Evan Rothman, "Father of the Year: Bob Nye," *Golfweek*, 2/26/02. https://www.golfweek.usatoday.com
153. Gary Avedikian interview, spring, 2020.
154. Jay Martin interview, winter, 2020.
155. Branch Rickey, website *inspiringquotes.us*, 2022.
156. Walter Bahr, *op. cit.*

Chapter VIII The Emerging Face of Western U.S. Soccer

157. Bean *op. cit.*, p. 81.
158. Irv Moss, "Guennel's Guidance Put Colorado Soccer on the Map," *Denver Post*, 6/14/10. https://www.denverpost.com
159. G.K. "Joe" Guennel induction, Colorado Sports Hall of Fame, 1992, https://www.coloradosports.org
160. Horst Richardson interview, spring, 2020.
161. "Horst Richardson Elected to the United Soccer Coaches Hall of Fame," Colorado College website, 11/15/20. https://www.cctigers.com
162. *Ibid.*
163. Luis Sagastume interview, spring, 2020.
164. Theresa Echtermeyer interview, summer, 2020.

165. Woitalla, Mike. "Whether Boys or Girls: Be Consistent, Send Clear Message," *Soccer America*, Youth Soccer Insider, 4/15/11. https://www.socceramerica.com
166. Jeff Tipping email, 10/31/20.
167. Woitalla, *op. cit.*, 4/15/11.
168. Marcelo Curi interview, spring, 2021.
169. Steve Kroner, "Steve Negoesco who led USF to 4 National Titles Dies," *San Francisco Chronicle*. 2/4/19. https://www.sfchronicle.com
170. Sagastume, *op. cit.*
171. Joe Dugan interview, fall, 2020.
172. "The University of San Francisco Mourns the Loss of Steve Negoesco," 2/4/19. https://www.usfdons.edu
173. Sagastume, *op. cit.*
174. Bean, *op. cit.*, p. 173.
175. "Bob DiGrazia: 1927-2006/"An All-Time Great in Cal's Soccer Program," San Francisco Bay Gate, 12/13/06. https://www.sfgate.com
176. Bean, p.174.
177. Clarissa Aljentera, "Rolling with the Punches," *Spartan Daily*, 10/6/01. https://www.sjsunews.com
178. Bean, p. 174.
179. Lohthar Osiander interview, spring, 2020.
180. Press release, Walt Chyzowych Award, December, 2006. https://www.waltslegacy.com
181. Steve Sampson interview, spring, 2020.
182. Scott French, "Brian Schmelzer on Seattle Soccer Culture . . .his mentors . . . ," *Soccer America*, 2/19/21. https://www.socceramerica.com
183. Ralph Perez interview, fall, 2021.
184. Terry Fisher interview, spring, 2020.

Chapter IX Cliff McCrath – Soccer's Best Ambassador

185. Cliff McCrath interview, spring, 2020.
186. Frank MacDonald, "The Gifts of Cliff McCrath," Frank MacDonald Blog, 2/8/19. https://www.frankmacdonald.net.com
187. Lesle Gallimore interview, summer, 2021.

Chapter X Bringing Soccer Into the 21st Century

188. "Steinbrecher to Speak at Celebrate D&E Athletics,' *The Inter Mountain* newspaper, 3/23/17. https://www.theintermountain.com

189. Hank Steinbrecher interview, spring, 2020.

190. Jim Trecker aided the research for this segment.

191. Bruce Arena interview, fall, 2021.

192. Arena, Bruce (with Steve Kettmann), "What's Wrong With US?" HarperCollins Publishers, 195 Broadway, New York, NY 10007, 2018. https://www.harpercollins.com

193. "Soccer News" newsletter, spring, 1997. https://www.soccernews.com

194. *Soccer Journal*, July/August, 1998, p. 47.

195. Arena, *op. cit.*

196. *Ibid.*

197. *Ibid.*

198. *Soccer Journal,* May/June, 1998, p. 9.

199. Dave Sarachan interview, *op. cit.*

200. Bob Bradley interview, fall, 2021.

201. Greg Lalas, "Bob Bradley and Bruce Arena are the Fathers of the Next Generation of MLS Coaches," 9/7/14. https://www.mlssoccer.com

202. "Men's Soccer Chats With Bob Bradley '80." 1/29/21. https://www.goprincetontigers.com

203. Marsch, Jesse and Bob Bradley. "Between Two Coaches/A Conversation With Bob Bradley and Jesse Marsch," YouTube educational videos, June 12, (53:28) and June 22, 2020 (28:19). https://www.youtube.com

204. Sebatian Abbot, "Princeton Duo Blazing Trails for U.S. Soccer,' *Princeton Alumni Weekly,* 7/18/19. https://www.pawprinceton.edu

205. Paul Marco interview, fall, 2021.

206. Sebatian Abbot, *op. cit.*

207. Sasho Cirovski interview, summer 2021.

208. Ray Reid interview, winter, 2020.

209. Dikranian, *op. cit.*

ABOUT THE AUTHOR

Tim Schum has amassed a noteworthy career in soccer both on and off the field.

Athletic Career

The author was raised in an athletic environment, as his father, Harold "Chick" Schum, was the multi-sport (including soccer) coach and AD at Spencerport High School outside Rochester, NY. Tim, from age eight, would serve as ballboy and later earn All-Monroe County selection in the fall sport.

Tim Schum.

A 1960 graduate in history from the University of Rochester, he earned All-NYS soccer team selection (1957-59) and in 1957 was a member of the school's only undefeated soccer team. In baseball in 1960, he set what was believed to be a then-NCAA record by hitting four homes runs in a baseball game versus Hamilton College.

In his later years, his focus on golf has seen him earn Triple Cities Golf Association senior golfer of the year honors in both 2001 and 2003.

Coaching Career

After earning his master's at Columbia University in 1960-61, Schum's coaching career began at Rochester-area's West Irondequoit HS (1961-62). He would coach men's soccer at Binghamton University from 1963-92, accumulating a 259-116-43 record. Beginning in 1972, the team would appear in 16 post-season tournaments, including eight NCAA Division III Tournament appearances and eight ECAC Tournament selections (1972 and 1976 titles). Additionally, six Colonial teams would capture SUNY Athletic Conference titles, while in both 1982 and 1987 BU was named New York's top DIII team.

These team honors were the result of quality players being attracted to the BU campus. In all, seven BU players earned NSCAA All-America honors while 42 were named to the All-State team and 66 were accorded All-SUNYAC selection.

Individual honors included Schum being named both New York State and SUNYAC Coach of the Year in 1974. Holder of the USSF B coaching license from 1995-2012, he would later serve as a senior member of the national NSCAA Academy coaching staff.

He would coach BU baseball for five seasons (1973-78), with the team selected for post-season play the final three seasons.

BU graduates who have entered the soccer coaching field include Jake Diamond [Thayer (MA) Academy; 1980-2018]; Dr. Andew DiNitto (Fulton-Montgomery CC [NY; 1972-83]; Mike Doherty [Colgate University; 1985-2005]; Roy Gordon [Mary Washington College; 1977-2010]; Oystein Ostebo [Corning (NY) West HS; 1982-99]; David Schneider [Syosett (NY) SC; 2015-present]; Bill Stepanovsky [Vestal and Union-Endicott (NY) HSs; 1999-2018]).

Soccer Contributions

As with other of his colleagues in the soccer coaching community, Schum has made many contributions to the game.

In the Binghamton, NY, area he is credited with the formation of the Broome County Soccer Association and has staged coaching and officiating courses for its affiliated clubs. From 1979-81, BCSA administered the first USYSA Region I championships at Binghamton University.

He served as the rules interpreter for the local soccer referee organization and counts several NCAA tournament officiating assignments on his resume.

In the 1970s, he was active in the Intercollegiate Soccer Association of America (ISAA), serving as New York State's rating board chair. He also chaired both NCAA New York Division I and III Tournament selection committees during that time.

As a member of the National Soccer Coaches Association of America, he served as president in 1982-83 and, subsequent to that, was a member of its executive committee until 2002.

Writing/Publishing Career

The author has enjoyed a long career in writing and publishing.

His introduction began at the University of Rochester, where he served as sports editor of the campus newspaper as well as campus correspondent for the local newspapers.

In 1980, he was tabbed by Don Yonker as his successor as editor of the NSCAA publication, *Soccer Journal*. He thus began a 22-year career with the magazine that saw it transit from a three times a year publication to one that reached the membership eight times annually. Its 48-page content kept members abreast of both soccer coaching information as well as timely membership communication.

On May 29, 1983, his article, "The U.S. World Cup Bid Had Some Serious Failing," appeared in the *NY Times*, and in 1991 he co-authored with Joe Bean, "50 Years (1941-1991): A History of the National Soccer Coaches Association of America." Subsequently, he has edited or published four soccer-related books, with the most extensive research devoted to the book "From Colonials to Bearcats, A History of Binghamton University Athletics, 1956-2006," published in 2007.

Honors

In 1987, he received the National Intercollegiate Soccer Officials/NSCAA Merit Award for sportsmanship.

In 1995, he was recipient of the NSCAA Honor Award for lifetime contributions to the organization, and in the same year was presented with the Bill Jeffrey Award for service to intercollegiate soccer. In 2004, he was inducted into the NSCAA Hall of Fame.

He is also a member of the Spencerport High School (1977), the University of Rochester (1996), Binghamton University (1999), and the Monroe County Soccer (2004) Halls of Fame.

In 2017, the 1980 Binghamton men's soccer team was collectively honored by induction into the BU Hall of Fame.

Family

He and wife Ann Furlong oversee eight children, 18 grandchildren, and one great-grandchild and reside in Endwell, New York.

Credits
Cover and interior design: Anja Elsen
Layout: DiTech Publishing Services, www.ditechpubs.com
Cover image: © AdobeStock
Managing editor: Elizabeth Evans
Copy editor: Carly O'Connor